RESPONSES TO SEA MIGRATION AND THE RULE OF LAW

In the current debates on sea migration there is a dearth of works drawing on the rule of law. This important book addresses this failing.

Considering the question from that conceptual framework, it is able to broaden the sometimes fragmented and incomplete perspective of existing scholarship. The book takes as its central case study the experience of Italy, exploring the legal issues at play there and its institutional practices and policies. From here its focus broadens out to the wider EU experience, looking in particular at those problems common to southern EU states, such as failures and delays in assisting migrants in distress at sea and contested legal grounds and practices concerning interceptions at sea. It combines both legal and empirical data, charting both the black letter law and how it operates in practice.

In a field as complex as this, this clarity is key; it allows lawyers, political scientists and policymakers to truly engage with the challenges sea migration poses today.

Volume 94 in the series Studies in International Law

Studies in International Law

Recent titles in this series

The Law of Humanity Project: A Story of International Law Reform and State-making
Ukri Soirila

Extraterritoriality and Climate Change Jurisdiction: Exploring EU Climate Protection under International Law
Natalie L Dobson

International Law and the War with Islamic State: Challenges for Jus ad Bellum and Jus in Bello
Saeed Bagheri

Private Actors as Participants in International Law: A Critical Analysis of Membership under the Law of the Sea
Armando Rocha

Truth and Transitional Justice: Localising the International Legal Framework in Muslim Majority Legal Systems
Alice Panepinto

State Responsibility for Non-State Actors: Past, Present and Prospects for the Future
Richard Mackenzie-Gray Scott

International Agreements between Non-State Actors as a Source of International Law
Melissa Loja

Judicial Decisions in International Law Argumentation: Between Entrapment and Creativity
Letizia Lo Giacco

South-South Migrations and the Law from Below: Case Studies on China and Nigeria
Oreva Olakpe

Territorial Status in International Law
Jure Vidmar

Marine Bioprospecting, Biodiversity and Novel Uses of Ocean Resources: New Approaches in International Law
Edited by Niels Krabbe and David Langlet

The Standard of Review Before the International Court of Justice: Between Principle and Pragmatism
Felix Fouchard

Responses to Sea Migration and the Rule of Law
Katia Bianchini

For a complete list of titles in this series see www.bloomsbury.com/uk/series/studies-in-international-law/

Responses to Sea Migration and the Rule of Law

Katia Bianchini

•HART•
OXFORD • LONDON • NEW YORK • NEW DELHI • SYDNEY

HART PUBLISHING

Bloomsbury Publishing Plc

Kemp House, Chawley Park, Cumnor Hill, Oxford, OX2 9PH, UK

1385 Broadway, New York, NY 10018, USA

29 Earlsfort Terrace, Dublin 2, Ireland

HART PUBLISHING, the Hart/Stag logo, BLOOMSBURY and the Diana logo are trademarks of Bloomsbury Publishing Plc

First published in Great Britain 2024

A catalogue record for this book is available from the British Library.

A catalogue record for this book is available from the Library of Congress.

ISBN: HB: 978-1-50997-848-9
ePDF: 978-1-50997-850-2
ePub: 978-1-50997-849-6

Typeset by Compuscript Ltd, Shannon

For Camilla

Acknowledgements

I FEEL VERY privileged for having had the opportunity to spend so much time researching one of the most currently debated topics in the area of migration. This would not have been possible without the support of Professor Foblets and my colleagues at the Max Planck Institute for Social Anthropology. It would also not have been possible without the help of various research assistants, and especially Krista Bonello Rutter Giappone and Federica Toso.

I want to thank Charlie Zaharoff for revising and improving the manuscript, and all the research participants who agreed to be interviewed or spoke to me to share their knowledge and experiences.

I am also grateful to my husband Andrea and my daughter Camilla for their continuous encouragement and support.

Finally, I am grateful to the Max Planck Society for granting me a period of study leave in 2022/2023 to pursue this project, and the Law School of Fordham University, where I was a Visiting Researcher.

Contents

List of Abbreviations

ADIF	Associazione Diritti e Frontiere
AFM	Armed Forces of Malta
ANSA	Agenzia Nazionale Stampa Associata
App	Corte d' appello
Arts/arts	Article/s
ASGI	Associazione Studi Giuridici sull'Immigrazione
CEPS	Centre for European Policy Studies
CoE	Council of Europe
Cass civ	Corte di Cassazione sezione civile
Cass pen	Corte di Cassazione sezione penale
Corte Cost	Corte Costituzionale
CUP	Cambridge University Press
ECCHR	European Center for Constitutional and Human Rights
ECHR	European Convention on Human Rights
ECJ	European Court of Justice
ECRE	European Council on Refugees and Exiles
ECSA	European Community Shipowner's Association
ECtHR	European Court of Human Rights
EEAS	European Union External Action Service
EU	European Union
EUBAM	EU Border Assistance Mission to Libya
EUNAVFOR Med	European Union Naval Force Mediterranean
FIDH	International Federation for Human Rights
FRA	European Union Agency for Fundamental Rights
GLAN	Global Legal Action Network

IAMSAR	International Aeronautical and Maritime Search and Rescue
ICC	International Criminal Court
ICCPR	International Covenant on Civil and Political Rights
ILC	International Law Commission
IMO	International Maritime Organization
IMRCC	Italian Maritime Rescue Coordination Centre
IOM	International Organization for Migration
MoU	Memorandum of Understanding
MRCC	Maritime Rescue Coordination Centre
MRSC	Maritime Rescue Sub Centre
nd	no date
NGO	Non-Governmental Organisation
NRG	Numero di Ruolo Generale
OHCHR	Office of the United Nations High Commissioner for Human Rights
OUP	Oxford University Press
PACE	Parliamentary Assembly, Council of Europe
POS	Place of Safety
RCC	Rescue Coordination Centre
RGNR	Registro Generale Notizia di Reato
ROL	Rule of Law
SAR	Search and Rescue
SAR Convention	International Convention on Maritime Search and Rescue
SOLAS	International Convention for the Safety of Life at Sea
TAR	Tribunale Amministrativo Regionale (Regional Administrative Tribunal)
TEU	Treaty on the European Union
TFEU	Treaty on the Functioning of the European Union
Trib	Tribunale

TUI	Testo Unico sull' Immigrazione
UCG	Coast Guard Units
UN	United Nations
UNCLOS	UN Convention on the Law of the Sea
UNGA	United Nations General Assembly
UNHCR	United Nations High Commissioner for Refugees
UNHRC	United Nations Human Rights Committee
UNSMIL	United Nations Support Mission in Libya

List of Table and Figures

Tables of Cases

Regional Case Law

Court of Justice of the European Union

European Court of Human Rights

Italian Case Law

Corte d'Appello [Court of Appeals]

Tribunale Ordinario [Civil Court/Criminal Court]

Tribunale Militare [Military Tribunal]

Tribunale Amministrativo Regionale [Regional Administrative Court]

Corte Costituzionale [Constitutional Court]

Legal Documents Filed with International Courts, Quasi-Judicial Bodies and National Courts

Table of Legislation

International Instruments

United Nations' Treaties and Protocols

Other United Nations Instruments and Publications

International Maritime Organization's Conventions and Guidelines

Other International Treaties and International Instruments

Regional Instruments

Council of Europe

International Treaties

Other Instruments and Publications

European Union

Legislation

Other Instruments and Publications

Organization for Security and Co-operation in Europe (OSCE)

Italy's National Legislation, Decrees, Policies and other Instruments

Legislation, Decrees, and Ministerial Directives

Various Parliamentary Documents

Guidance and Communications

Agreements and International Instruments between Italy and Third Countries

US National Legislation

1

Introduction and Scope of the Book

I. INTRODUCTION

IN THE SUMMER months, when weather and sea conditions are more favourable, small boats overcrowded with migrants travel from North Africa to Europe on an almost daily basis. Mishaps on the journey are just as frequent. The images of these boats that are broadcast and the subsequent public discourse often reflects contrasting ideological positions on migration, ranging from those who see migrants as 'victims' to those who see them as 'invaders'.[1]

These 'mixed' migration flows, composed of both asylum seekers and economic migrants,[2] have gradually challenged the European Union (EU) asylum and reception systems. They have also tested solidarity among Member States due to disagreements on who should be responsible for rescuing migrant boats distressed at sea, for accepting disembarkation, and for processing applications for international protection.[3]

The question of how to manage the mass arrivals of sea migrants, mainly to Italy, Malta, Spain and Greece, has divided the EU for years. Southern Member States 'have accused wealthier countries of failing to do more, while a number of central and eastern nations are openly resistant to the idea of taking in a quota of migrants'.[4] It has been argued that the continuous occurrence of sea arrivals and related incidents, the involvement of criminal organisations, traffickers and smugglers in migrants' journeys, and the consequent emergence of security, economic and political concerns, have shifted Member States' focus away from the international obligations to protect refugees to the intensification of controls and prevention of access to the territories.[5] Furthermore, it has

[1] C Siccardi, *I Diritti Costituzionali dei Migranti in Viaggio: Sulle Rotte del Mediterraneo* (Napoli, Editoriale Scientifica, 2021) 26; A Geddes and P Scholten, *The Politics of Migration and Immigration in Europe* (London, Sage Publications Ltd, 2016) ch 1.

[2] For a definition of the terms 'asylum seeker' and 'migrant', see Glossary.

[3] E Fassi and S Lucarelli, 'The EU Migration System and Global Justice: An Assessment' in M Ceccorulli, E Fassi and S Lucarelli (eds), *The EU Migration System of Governance: Justice on the Move* (New York, Palgrave Macmillan, 2021); S Fine, 'All at Sea: Europe's Crisis of Solidarity on Sea Migration' (Policy Brief, European Council on Foreign Relations, October 2019) 2.

[4] BBC, 'Migrants Allowed Off Maersk Tanker After 30 Days at Sea' *BBC News* (13 September 2020), available at: www.bbc.com/news/world-europe-54136627.

[5] D Breen and United Nations High Commissioner for Refugees Regional Bureau for Europe, 'Desperate Journeys: Refugee and Migrant Children Arriving in Europe and How to Strengthen

been noted that some Member States point to the inapplicability of regional and international legal obligations outside their territorial waters in an attempt to shrug off their responsibilities.[6] When, in the absence of a coordinated search and rescue effort by the Member States, private vessels and non-governmental organisations (NGOs) intervene to assist migrants in distress in international waters, Member States often refuse to allow migrants to disembark at their ports.[7] Some authors describe this behaviour as promoting the creation of a 'protection-free zone' at sea where migrants' rights are not guaranteed, thereby creating tension both among and within the Member States as well as confusion as to which of them should be held responsible. The problem has intensified in recent years to the point that Tsourdi has spoken of 'refugee protection backsliding'.[8] As such, addressing irregular sea migration to the EU and its Member States has become one of the most pressing political, legal and humanitarian issues of our time.

Against this background, the book considers the gaps and clashes among the different legal provisions at stake, connected policies and practices, judicial responses, and their consequences for the rule of law (ROL). The book contributes to the debates on sea migration and the protection of sea migrants by providing a better understanding of the interrelated legal frameworks that apply – the law of the sea, refugee law, human rights, anti-smuggling and trafficking legislation, etc, at the international, regional and national levels – as well as relevant institutional practices, and offers a broader critical reflection on the issues at stake. The typical approach that scholars take when discussing sea migration is a fundamental rights or international law of the sea analysis. They have neither thoroughly explored the different layers of legislation concerned

their Protection. January to September 2019' (UNHCR, 13 October 2019) 6; T Spijkerboer, 'Moving Migrants, States and Rights: Human Rights and Border Deaths' (2013) 7 *Law & Ethics of Human Rights* 213; M Giuffré and V Moreno-Lax, 'The Rise of Consensual Containment: From "Contactless Control" to "Contactless Responsibility" for Migratory Flows' in S Singh Juss (ed), *Research Handbook on International Refugee Law* (Cheltenham, Edward Elgar Publishing, 2019) 85; B Frelick, IM Kysel and J Podkul, 'The Impact of Externalization of Migration Controls on the Rights of Asylum Seekers and Other Migrants' (2016) 4 *Journal on Migration and Human Security* 190, 197.

[6] E Papastavridis 'Is There a Right to be Rescued at Sea? A Skeptical View' (2014) 4 *Questions of International Law* 17, 19; C Salau, 'The Extra-Territorial Application of the Principle of Non-Refoulement in the Context of Sea Borders' (Bachelor's Thesis, University of Twente, 2014) 26. For a more detailed discussion on the meaning of 'jurisdiction', see S Kim, 'Non-Refoulement and Extraterritorial Jurisdiction: State Sovereignty and Migration Controls at Sea in the European Context' (2017) 30 *Leiden Journal of International Law* 49.

[7] There are no provisions as to what standards must be followed if Member States are unable to agree on the location of disembarkation. I Papanicolopulu, 'The Duty to Rescue at Sea, in Peacetime and in War: A General Overview' (2016) 98 *International Review of the Red Cross* 491, 501; S Carrera and R Cortinovis, 'Search and Rescue, Disembarkation and Relocation Arrangements in the Mediterranean. Sailing Away from Responsibility?' (CEPS Papers in Liberty and Security in Europe, No 2019–10, 28 June 2019) iii.

[8] E Tsourdi, 'Asylum in the EU: One of the Many Faces of Rule of Law Backsliding?' (2021) 17 *European Constitutional Law Review* 471.

nor the practices of the actors involved. The lack of focus on the ROL is surprising given that the issues involved are not mere human rights or law of the sea violations, but are connected with broader weaknesses of fundamental state principles and institutional and political dynamics. By contrast, I adopt an ROL lens because it allows one to appreciate a wider set of institutional and constitutional issues and thus to see how responses to sea migration affect the basic principles on which modern states are built. However, I use ROL principles only to elucidate legislation, policies and practices, and do not undertake a theoretical study of the ROL.

In the next sections, I briefly describe the situation in the Mediterranean (section II) and then introduce the research question, aim and scope of the book (section III). Furthermore, I explain the methodology adopted, including the choice to use legal and empirical data (section IV). I also identify and summarise the main existing debates in the areas of refugee law, human rights and the law of the sea, as far as sea migration to Europe is concerned (section V). Finally, I present the structure of the book (section VI).

II. AN OVERVIEW OF SEA MIGRATION IN THE MEDITERRANEAN

Sea migration flows to Europe began to be an issue in 2011 as a result of the Arab Spring.[9] However, they obtained public and media attention only after 2015, when the number of arrivals reached a peak. Additionally, in that year, four consecutive shipwrecks off the Sicilian coast, which together caused at least 1,200 deaths,[10] shook public opinion – despite similar incidents in the years before.[11] Since then, the term 'refugee crisis' has started being used to describe a unique circumstance that put extraordinary pressure on systems for handling the arrival of refugees.[12] The expression has since then become embedded in populist narratives that portray migrants and refugees as a threat to 'our' societies.[13]

[9] Al Jazeera Staff, 'What is the Arab Spring, and How Did It Start?' (*Al Jazeera Media Network*, 17 December 2020), available at: www.aljazeera.com/news/2020/12/17/what-is-the-arab-spring-and-how-did-it-start.

[10] C Cantat, 'Rethinking Mobilities: Solidarity and Migrant Struggles Beyond Narratives of Crisis' (2016) 2(4) *Intersections: East European Journal of Society and Politics* 11.

[11] eg, a shipwreck in October 2013 had claimed over 300 lives. BBC, 'Italy Boat Sinking: Hundreds Feared Dead off Lampedusa' *BBC News* (3 October 2013), available at: www.bbc.com/news/world-europe-24380247; Francesca Romana Partipilo, 'The Role of NGOs within Search and Rescue Activities at Sea' (*News*, Lebanese American University, 6 April 2022), available at: soas.lau.edu.lb/news/2022/04/the-role-of-ngos-within-search-and-rescue-activities-at-sea.php; Neske Baerwaldt, 'The European Refugee Crisis: Crisis for Whom?' (*Border Criminologies*, University of Oxford, 20 March 2018), available at: blogs.law.ox.ac.uk/research-subject-groups/centre-criminology/centreborder-criminologies/blog/2018/03/european-refugee.

[12] JS Lee and A Nerghes, 'Refugee or Migrant Crisis? Labels, Perceived Agency, and Sentiment Popularity in Online Discussions' (2018) 4(3) *Social Media + Society* 1.

[13] ibid; Baerwaldt (n 11) 3.

The number of migrant sea arrivals in the Mediterranean has significantly dropped since 2015, but the rate of mishaps has increased, as shown in the following list by the United Nations High Commissioner for Refugees (UNCHR):[14]

Table 1 Demography of Mediterranean Sea Arrivals from January 2022

Previous years	Arrivals[15]	Dead and missing
2022	159,410	2,439
2021	123,318	3,231
2020	95,774	1,881
2019	123,663	1,510
2018	141,472	2,277
2017	185,139	3,139
2016	373,652	5,096
2015	1,032,408	3,771

In the first four months of 2023, it is estimated that more than 98 per cent of irregular migrants reaching Europe came by sea[16] – almost double the rate of the same period in the previous year.

The three main sea routes through the Mediterranean are the Central Mediterranean route (from North Africa, mainly Libya and Tunisia, to Italy or Malta), the Western Mediterranean route (running from Morocco and Algeria to Spain), and the Eastern Mediterranean route (from Turkey to Cyprus or Greece).[17] The nationalities of those who travel through the Mediterranean vary according to route and period, but in 2023, most of them originated from the Ivory Coast, Guinea, Egypt and Pakistan.[18]

In many cases, sea journeys are very dangerous, as vessels are overcrowded and unseaworthy. According to the International Organization for Migration (IOM), in 2022, out of approximately 75,101 recorded maritime crossing attempts via the Mediterranean Sea to Europe, 43,101 people arrived while

[14] UNHCR, 'Demography of Mediterranean Sea Arrivals from January 2022' (Refugees Operational Data Portal, UNHCR), available at: data2.unhcr.org/en/situations/mediterranean.

[15] 'Include[s] sea arrivals to Italy, Cyprus, and Malta, and both sea and land arrivals to Greece and Spain (including the Canary Islands). Data are as of 31 December 2021 for all countries'. ibid.

[16] Sana Noor Haq, Caolán Magee an Barbie Latza Nadeau, 'Europe's Migration Policies in Chaos as Arrivals Surge' *CNN* (16 April 2023), available at: www.cnn.com/2023/04/16/europe/europe-migration-chaos-boat-arrivals-intl/index.html.

[17] European Border and Coast Guard Agency, 'Migratory Routes: Eastern Borders Routes' (Frontex, nd), available at: www.frontex.europa.eu/what-we-do/monitoring-and-risk-analysis/migratory-routes/eastern-borders-route/.

[18] European Council, Council of the European Union, 'Infographic – Migration Flows: Eastern, Central and Western Mediterranean Routes' (data up to April 2023), available at: www.consilium.europa.eu/en/infographics/migration-flows-to-europe/.

896 people went missing or died.[19] Nevertheless, the absence of alternative routes pushes migrants to attempt such journeys to reach the EU, often through networks of smugglers.[20]

In addition to those who die or go missing in the Mediterranean, there are those who are returned to unsafe countries, in particularly Libya, where human rights are not guaranteed and a general situation of lawlessness prevails.[21] Between 2017 and March 2023, the Libyan Coast Guard intercepted and returned more than 36,000 sea migrants,[22] partially with funding from the EU and its Member States in exchange for cooperation in stopping migratory flows.[23] This is because migrants heading to Europe mostly travel through Libya and, more recently, Tunisia.[24] Moreover, it is important to remember that the journey through the Mediterranean is often a small segment of the whole migratory journey, which may involve transiting through other countries, making detours, as well as facing several risks.[25]

It is argued that one of the causes of this problematic situation is Member States' failure to address the causes of departure from the countries of origin, which would require improving economic migration routes and protection pathways to Europe.[26] Another factor is the lack of state-led and coordinated search and rescue (SAR) missions in the Mediterranean.[27] In this regard, it is worth noting that the only effective state-led SAR response to the increased number of fatalities at sea was 'the short-lived Italian Mare Nostrum operation',[28] started in 2013 to rescue migrants in international

[19] Compared with 2020, the current numbers suggest an increase of 58% in maritime migration. International Organization for Migration (IOM) Global Migration Data Analysis Centre, 'Migrant Deaths on Maritime Routes to Europe in 2021' (IOM GMDAC, 14 July 2021) 4–5, available at: www.iom.int/news/deaths-maritime-migration-routes-europe-soar-first-half-2021-iom-brief.

[20] Frontex, 'Profiting from Misery – How Smugglers Bring People to Europe' (Frontex, 18 February 2016), available at: www.frontex.europa.eu/media-centre/news/focus/profiting-from-misery-how-smugglers-bring-people-to-europe-aUYY2f.

[21] UNHCR, 'UNHCR Position on the Designations of Libya as a Safe Third Country and as a Place of Safety for the Purpose of Disembarkation Following Rescue at Sea' (Policy Brief, UNHCR September 2020), available at: www.refworld.org/docid/5f1edee24.html.

[22] Al Jazeera Staff, '"Deadliest Quarter" for Migrants in the Central Med Since 2017' (*Al Jazeera Media Network*, 12 April 2023), available at: www.aljazeera.com/news/2023/4/12/deadliest-quarter-for-migrants-in-the-central-med-since-2017.

[23] ibid.

[24] Fine (n 3) 10; Roberto Forin and Bram Frouws, 'What's New? Analysing the Latest Trends on the Central Mediterranean Mixed Migration Route to Italy' (*Mixed Migration Centre*, 9 February 2022), available at: mixedmigration.org/articles/whats-new-analysing-the-latest-trends-on-the-central-mediterranean-mixed-migration-route-to-italy/; UNHCR, 'Italy Sea Arrivals Dashboard' (UNHCR, July 2022), available at: data.unhcr.org/en/documents/details/94797.

[25] Mark Rice-Oxley and Mona Mahmood, 'Migrants' Tales: "I Feel for Those Who Were with Me. They Got Asylum in the Sea"' *Guardian* (20 October 2014), available at: www.theguardian.com/world/2014/oct/20/-sp-migrants-tales-asylum-sea-mediterranean.

[26] Al Jazeera Staff, '"Deadliest Quarter" for Migrants in the Central Med Since 2017' (n 22).

[27] ibid.

[28] M Stierl, 'The Mediterranean as a *Carceral Seascape*' (2021) 88 *Political Geography*, available at: www.sciencedirect.com/science/article/abs/pii/S0962629821000779?via%3Dihub.

waters. The operation covered about 70,000 square kilometres, including areas near the Libyan coast, and rescued over 150,000 persons.[29] Moreover, it facilitated the arrest of over 350 smugglers.[30] Nevertheless, one year later, Mare Nostrum was discontinued because of its high cost and the EU's unwillingness to co-finance it. In addition, some Member States considered the operation as 'an unintended pull factor' of migration.[31] Triton, Themis, and EUNAVFOR Med, subsequent European law enforcement and military missions coordinated by the EU agency Frontex, have mostly avoided engaging in SAR operations.[32] Instead, they have focused on border monitoring and the fight against irregular immigration. As such, Member States remain individually responsible for providing SAR services.[33] Moreover, the Member State that has carried out the rescue operation, which is usually also the place of disembarkation, is automatically the first country of arrival and thus responsible for dealing with asylum applications under the Dublin Regulation.[34]

As a consequence of Member States' resistance to establishing and sharing responsibility for SAR services, numerous NGOs and civil society organisations have tried to fill the void with their own vessels. It is estimated that NGOs rescued around 115,000 migrants between 2014 and October 2019.[35]

However, NGOs have also been accused of being a pull factor of irregular migration, a claim often used by certain European governments, populist parties and the media in Italy, Malta, Spain and Greece to justify criminal proceedings, administrative acts and disinformation campaigns against these organisations.[36] As a result, their capacity to provide SAR services has been undercut. According to the most recent data, in June 2023, there were 18 NGO ships dedicated to SAR in the Mediterranean, but six of them were undergoing maintenance work.[37] The Annex lists the NGOs that have been active in the Mediterranean over the years, as well as their vessels and flag state. As can be seen, most of them

[29] Fine (n 3) 5.

[30] I Lloyd-Damnjanovic, 'Criminalization of Search-and-Rescue Operations in the Mediterranean Has Been Accompanied by Rising Migrant Death Rate' (Report, Migration Policy Institute, 9 October 2020) 2.

[31] E Cusumano and M Villa, 'Sea Rescue NGOs: A Pull Factor of Irregular Migration?' (Policy Brief, Robert Schuman Centre, November 2019) 2.

[32] Siccardi (n 1) 152; Cusumano and Villa, 'Sea Rescue NGOs' (n 31) 2.

[33] See ch 3, section III.

[34] Siccardi (n 1) 153. See Dublin Regulation III, Regulation (EU) no 604/2013 of the European Parliament and of the Council of 26 June 2013 establishing the criteria and mechanisms for determining the Member State responsible for examining an application for international protection lodged in one of the Member States by a third-country national or a stateless person (recast) [2013] OJ L180/31.

[35] Cusumano and Villa, 'Sea Rescue NGOs' (n 31) 2.

[36] Partipilo (n 11); Lloyd-Damnjanovic (n 30) 4; Fine (n 3) 6.

[37] FRA, 'June 2023 Update – Search and Rescue Operations in the Mediterranean and Fundamental Rights' (FRA, 11 October 2023) 4, available at: fra.europa.eu/en/publication/2023/2023-update-ngo-ships-sar-activities.

fly the German flag and only one (*Mare Jonio* of Mediterranea Saving Humans) flies the Italian flag.[38] As explained by Cusumano and Villa, these NGOs 'vary significantly in their ability to rescue migrants in distress' and use different rescue models according to the capacity of their vessels, financial resources and political views.[39] Most of them have had their activities seriously limited or even barred by different governments' measures.

Because the Dublin Regulation has been recognised as a major issue for coastal Member States, in October 2023, the EU Council reached a deal on a Crisis and Force Majeure Regulation in order to respond to mass arrivals of refugees. According to the new agreement, states at the forefront of irregular immigration could adopt exceptional measures involving expedited asylum procedures and ask for assistance from other EU states, either in the form of relocation or financial help. Despite the opposition of Poland and Hungary, it received a majority vote and now requires approval from the EU Parliament. The deal has been pushed by the right-wing Italian government of Meloni, who is playing an influential role in shifting Europe towards conservative and anti-migrant policies.[40] According to the EU Council, the proposal shows solidarity with coastal states and at the same time allows these states to adopt exceptional measures only as long as they are proportionate and necessary, comply with human rights, and have been approved by the Council.[41] As such, the EU Council takes the view that the proposal provides enough limits to states' power to derogate to ordinary EU and national law. On the other hand, some human rights organisations such as Amnesty International have raised concerns that the proposed regulation would normalise the use of emergency measures and jeopardise the coherence of the EU asylum system.[42] In conclusion, whereas the proposal represents an acknowledgement of the urgency to respond to mass

[38] NGOs also rely on five aircraft to search the Mediterranean area near Libya and communicate to their ships where vessels in distress are located. In 2019, Italy did not authorise these aircraft to fly from Italian ports, explaining that they did not meet the prerequisites for flights engaged in professional activities. Manuela di Perrone, 'Migranti, 16 Navi e 5 Aerei per Pattugliare il Mediterraneo: Ecco la Flotta delle ONG' *Il Sole 24 Ore* (14 November 2022), available at: www.ilsole24ore.com/art/migranti-16-navi-e-5-aerei-pattugliare-mediterraneo-ecco-flotta-ong-AE9sJxGC. 'An indirect role in SAR operations has also been played by Alarm Phone, an NGO operating a hotline for migrants in distress in the Mediterranean Sea'. E Cusumano and M Villa, 'From "Angels" to "Vice Smugglers": The Criminalization of Sea Rescue NGOs in Italy' (2021) 27 *European Journal on Criminal Policy and Research* 23, 25.

[39] See Cusumano and Villa, 'From "Angels" to "Vice Smugglers"' (n 38) 25–28.

[40] Lisa O'Carroll, 'Historic EU Deal Reached on How to Manage Sudden Rise in Asylum Seekers' *Guardian* (4 October 2023), available at: www.theguardian.com/world/2023/oct/04/historic-eu-deal-reached-how-to-manage-sudden-rise-asylum-seekers.

[41] European Council, Council of the European Union, 'Migration Policy: Council Agrees Mandate on EU Law Dealing with Crisis Situations' (4 October 2023), available at: www.consilium.europa.eu/en/press/pressreleases/2023/10/04/migration-policy-council-agrees-mandate-on-eu-law-dealing-with-crisis-situations.

[42] Amnesty International, 'EU: New Migration Agreement "Dangerous and Disproportionate"' (Amnesty International, 4 October 2023), available at: www.amnesty.org/en/latest/news/2023/10/eu-new-migration-agreement-dangerous-and-disproportionate.

arrivals, including by sea, there is a risk that derogations to the common EU asylum system may be instrumentalised by populist parties. It remains to be seen how it will be received by the EU Parliament, how it will be implemented, and how the emergency measures will be applied.

III. RESEARCH QUESTIONS, AIMS AND SCOPE OF THE BOOK

In light of the situation discussed above, this book investigates the challenges posed by the responses to sea migration in the Mediterranean through a particular lens – that of the ROL. As such, I ask what legislation, policies, practices and case law are relevant in the context of sea migration, and how they challenge the ROL in the case of Italy.

The aim is to contribute to the debate on these issues by providing a better understanding of the legal framework and its implementation. In so doing, I broaden the fragmented and incomplete perspective of existing scholarship. In particular, I employ the ROL as a theoretical lens because it analyses issues that lie beyond human rights and the law of the sea. In particular, the ROL approach helps us to understand how the responses to sea migration affect fundamental principles of the state, as well as to take into account the role and responsibilities of the actors involved. Much has already been written about sea migration in individual countries or at the international level. However, the question of the implications of the responses to sea migration for the ROL has not been systematically studied.

Considering that the ROL concept is most significant at the national level, the state dimension is crucial.[43] Therefore, I focus on the case of Italy, which is a salient example of an EU country impacted by sea migration given its geographical location. The Central Mediterranean route is one of the main migratory routes to the EU.[44] It is also the deadliest sea route, where more than 20,000 of the registered deaths in the Mediterranean have taken place since 2014.[45] It is estimated that one out of six people departing on small and unsafe boats dies on the journey.[46] Italy is the EU country most affected by sea migration. In 2022,

[43] See ch 2, sections II, V.

[44] Frontex, 'Migratory Routes: Central Mediterranean Route' (Frontex, nd), available at: www.frontex.europa.eu/what-we-do/monitoring-and-risk-analysis/migratory-routes/central-mediterranean-route/; United Nations, Office of the High Commissioner for Human Rights, 'Türk Sounds Alarm at Escalating Migrant Crisis in Central Mediterranean' (Press Release, Office of the High Commissioner for Human Rights, OHCHR, 13 April 2023), available at: www.ohchr.org/en/press-releases/2023/04/turk-sounds-alarm-escalating-migrant-crisis-centralmediterranean#:~:text=Since%202014%20over%2026%2C000%20people,migration%20routes%20in%20the%20world; UNHCR, 'Mediterranean Situation' (Refugee Operational Data Portal, UNHCR, 21 May 2023), available at: data2.unhcr.org/en/situations/mediterranean.

[45] IOM, 'Deadliest Quarter for Migrants in the Central Mediterranean' (IOM, 12 April 2023) 2, available at: www.iom.int/news/deadliest-quarter-migrants-central-mediterranean-2017.

[46] Al Jazeera Staff, '"Deadliest Quarter" for Migrants in the Central Med Since 2017' (n 22).

more than 105,000 migrants arrived in Italy by sea.[47] As of September 2023, 144,591 people have arrived in Italy from the beginning of the year, almost twice the number of arrivals in the same period in 2022.[48]

Thus, an analysis of Italy within the ROL framework can illuminate the legal issues at stake when EU coastal states respond to sea migration: the obligation to save migrants at sea but the absence of clear rules on disembarkation and the lack of cooperation between states; states' strategies of using commercial ships in rescue operations and the related issues of blurred accountability for disembarking migrants to unsafe places; the measures taken against NGOs performing SAR operations; the issues connected with the delegation of tasks that should be performed by the state to NGOs; conflicts among state powers; and accountability for violations of the legal obligations. Whereas I acknowledge that the analysis of a single case does not allow one to draw definitive arguments, it does shed light on abstract concepts or issues. It also ties in the EU dimension and addresses problems common to all southern EU states. With this in mind, I will now turn to the methodology used to answer the research question.

IV. METHODOLOGY

My analysis adopts a qualitative approach based on a variety of primary and secondary sources, including legislation, case law, policy and secondary literature. First, I carried out desk research on academic works, legislation, case law and policies, using the most important databases in the English[49] and Italian literature on the topic[50] as well as institutional websites. Most of the reviewed literature was composed of legal works in the areas of international law, the law of the sea, human rights, as well as Italian studies in constitutional law and criminal law. It also included a smaller amount of social science publications. Additionally, I employed newspaper articles and other civil society publications.[51] Concerning the case law, as I was unable to locate it in a central

[47] Ministero dell'Interno, 'Sbarchi e Accoglienza dei Migranti: Tutti i Dati. Cruscotto Statistico del 31 Dicembre 2022' (Ministero dell'Interno, 31 December 2022), available at: www.libertaciviliimmigrazione.dlci.interno.gov.it/sites/default/files/allegati/cruscotto_statistico_giornaliero_31-12-2022-rev.pdf.

[48] Ministero dell'Interno, 'Sbarchi e Accoglienza dei Migranti: Tutti i Dati. Cruscotto Statistico del 2 Novembre 2023' (Ministero dell'Interno, 9 November 2023), available at: www.interno.gov.it/sites/default/files/2023-11/cruscotto_statistico_giornaliero_02-11-2023.pdf.

[49] eg, Lexis, Westlaw, HeinOnline, Brill, Cambridge, Oxford.

[50] The sources I used were mostly online journals, including, eg, *Diritto e Questioni Pubbliche*; *Diritto, Immigrazione e Cittadinanza*; *Diritto Penale Contemporaneo*; *Giurisprudenza Penale; Questione Giustizia*; *Sistema Penale*.

[51] Civil society publications included reports, short articles and blogs. Whereas I acknowledge that some blogs and Twitter notes may be characterised by biased views or report imprecise facts, I was careful to verify the information with other sources. For a discussion on the use of blogs in legal research, see, eg, A Duval, 'Publish (Tweets or Blogs) or Perish? Legal Academia in Times of Social Media' (2018) 23(1) *Tilburg Law Review* 91.

database, I limited the analysis to the decisions and legal actions that have been reported in the media or the literature. Hence, it is plausible that there exist additional cases beyond the scope of this review – although other experts confirmed that those analysed in this book are the most relevant ones.

At a second stage, I used semi-structured interviews with experts, such as NGOs, public officials, representatives of the shipping industry, lawyers and academics, in order to clarify a number of issues, as well as integrate and update the data. I identified the interviewees through preliminary desk research and the snowball method (some interviewees suggested new potential research participants).[52]

I designed and carried out the semi-structured interviews[53] between 2020 and 2023 with the help of a research assistant. They were conducted via telephone or Zoom meetings or written questions via email, which allowed convenient communication with participants who were geographically located in different places.[54] I triangulated the data[55] by checking their validity with opinions and evidence from other interviewees and desk research, especially given some of the interviewees' agendas and 'narration strategies'.[56] Overall, the interviews proceeded as expected, and they helped enrich the data and analysis. Ethical issues tended not to be a particular problem, as there was a reciprocal relationship with the interviewees. However, the political sensitivity of the subject matter and the particular agendas of some interviewees, as well as the difficulties in accessing clear data on events at sea due to their remoteness and sometimes contrasting reports on social media, required additional efforts to establish the accuracy of the information. Furthermore, the number of public officials that I interviewed was limited due to the difficulties in accessing them and their reluctance to speak on the topic – however, I hope future studies will further explore their views.

After the data collection, I carried out the analysis using the ROL framework, which I explain in the next chapter. In the analysis, I focused on three key themes of sea migration that emerged as particularly problematic from a preliminary review of the literature and remain at the centre of academic and political debates: (1) the law of the sea and states' failure to carry out effective SAR operations for migrants in distress at sea; (2) pushbacks and pullbacks of migrants to third countries in violation of the non-refoulement principle and other fundamental human rights; and (3) the adoption of measures criminalising

[52] O de Sardan, *Epistemology Fieldwork and Anthropology* (New York, Palgrave Macmillan, 2015) 48.

[53] ibid 21–44; K O'Reilly, *Ethnographic Methods* (Abingdon, Routledge, 2005) 59–174.

[54] J Salmons, 'Designing and Conducting Research with Online Interviews' in J Salmons (ed), *Cases in Online Interview Research* (Thousand Oaks, CA, Sage Publications Ltd, 2015) 12.

[55] O'Reilly (n 53) 154; see also, de Sardan (n 52) 46–47.

[56] I van Liempt and V Bilger, 'Methodological and Ethical Dilemmas in Research among Smuggled Migrants' in R Zapata-Barrero and E Yalaz (eds), *Qualitative Research Methods in European Migration* (IMISCOE Research Series, Spring Open, 2018) 281.

and preventing NGOs from carrying out SAR activities in the Mediterranean.[57] As rules of the utmost importance are routinely violated in these areas, such as those concerning limitations of state powers and fundamental human rights, they deserve close scrutiny. The analysis will reveal that the ROL is systematically weakened in all three thematic areas, affecting not only migrants' rights but also the domestic and international legal systems themselves.

V. AN OVERVIEW OF ISSUES IN SEA MIGRATION RESEARCH

A growing body of scholarship over the past 15 years has examined migrants' and asylum seekers' sea routes to Europe and the relevant international treaties. Since the so-called 'refugee crisis' in 2015, sea migration across the Mediterranean Sea has become a hot topic for European states.[58] The previously unseen levels of migration and asylum seeking have put EU Member States' cooperation and solidarity to the test; prior to 2015, southern countries like Spain, Italy and Malta dealt with the increasing influx of individuals entering the country without significant external support. As further discussed in this section, the rise of sea migration has unearthed the problematic clashes and gaps in international, regional and national legislations and policies concerning the law of the sea, human rights, refugee law, and smuggling and trafficking provisions that regulate a number of state and non-state bodies and actors.[59] In addition, it poses questions concerning wider issues such as the ROL, the integrity and functioning of the EU Common Asylum System, and EU solidarity.[60]

[57] See, for instance, F Pusterla, 'Legal Perspectives on Solidarity Crime in Italy' (2021) 59(3) *International Migration* 79; C Costello and I Mann, 'Border Justice: Migration and Accountability for Human Rights Violations' (2020) 21 *German Law Journal* 311; J Klabbers, 'The Accountability of International Organizations in Refugee and Migration Law' in C Costello, M Foster and J McAdam (eds), *The Oxford Handbook of International Refugee Law* (Oxford, OUP, 2021); B Schotel, 'EU Operational Powers and Legal Protection: A Legal Theory Perspective on the Operational Powers of the European Border and Coast Guard' (2021) 22 *German Law Journal* 625; I Mann, 'Maritime Legal Black Holes: Migration and Rightlessness in International Law' (2018) 29 *European Journal of International Law* 347; V Türk and R Dowd, 'Protection Gaps' in E Fiddian-Qasmiyeh et al (eds), *The Oxford Handbook of Refugee and Forced Migration Studies* (Oxford, OUP, 2014).

[58] K Bianchini, 'En Route to Protection: A Literature Review of Key Issues in Refugee Law' (Working Paper No 203, Halle, Max Planck Institute for Social Anthropology, 2020) 3.

[59] In this regard, see for instance, G Bevilacqua (ed), *Sicurezza Umana negli Spazi Navigabili: Sfide Comuni e Nuove Tendenze – Human Security in Navigable Spaces: Common Challenges and New Trends* (Napoli, Editoriale Scientifica, 2021).

[60] C Costello and M Mouzourakis, 'The Common European Asylum System: Where Did It All Go Wrong?' in M Fletcher, E Herlin-Karnell and C Matera (eds), *The European Union as an Area of Freedom, Security and Justice* (London, Routledge, 2016); R Byrne, G Noll and J Vedsted-Hansen, 'Understanding the Crisis of Refugee Law: Legal Scholarship and the EU Asylum System' (2020) 33 Leiden *Journal of International Law* 871; P Bendel, 'Contemporary Politics of International Protection in Europe. From Protection to Prevention' in A Weinar, S Bonjour and L Zhyznomirska, *The Routledge Handbook of the Politics of Migration in Europe* (London, Routledge, 2018); Fassi and Lucarelli (n 3).

The current literature mainly focuses on the relevance of the law of the sea to sea migrants, or rather the application and feasibility of the UN Convention on the Law of the Sea (UNCLOS Convention)[61] and the two conventions of the International Maritime Organization (IMO) – the International Convention for the Safety of Life at Sea (SOLAS Convention)[62] and the International Convention on Maritime Search and Rescue (SAR Convention)[63] – 'which establish the competences and duties of states'[64] with regard to rescue at sea. Several works have discussed rescue operations in the light of these instruments, mainly focusing on international human rights, refugee law and issues of jurisdiction. In particular, they argue that major gaps remain in the legal framework regarding which state should bear responsibility for SAR operations as well as for receiving migrants. Studies have increasingly highlighted a number of implementation problems concerning the international framework,[65] such as the failure on the part of some states to incorporate maritime treaties into national legislation and/or to ratify their most recent amended versions (eg, Malta).[66] Scholars have further described the varying interpretation of international law[67] and its consequences on rescue operations: instead of acting as a guiding tool to support rescue at sea, maritime conventions have contributed to conflicts among states as well as between states and other non-state actors such as NGOs. The continuing battle between coastal states and NGOs (and their rescue vessels) is one of the consequences of existing gaps and/or vague formulations in international conventions. The absence of an absolute right of a ship in distress to enter foreign ports is one example of an ongoing dispute in the Mediterranean Sea. While NGOs argue for the opening of ports for both migrant boats and

[61] United Nations Convention on the Law of the Sea (Montego Bay, 10 December 1983) UN Doc A/CONF 1833 UNTS 397 (UNCLOS Convention).

[62] International Convention for the Safety of Life at Sea (London, 1 November 1974) 1184 UNTS 278 (SOLAS Convention).

[63] International Convention on Maritime Search and Rescue (Hamburg, 27 April 1979) 1405 UNTS 97 (SAR Convention).

[64] Bianchini, 'En Route to Protection' (n 58) 12.

[65] Papastavridis (n 6) 21; Carrera and Cortinovis (n 7).

[66] J Coppens, 'Migrants at Sea. A Legal Analysis of a Maritime Safety and Security Problem' (PhD Thesis, University of Ghent, 2013) 75; Papanicolopulu (n 7) 502; SF Martin, S Weerasinghe and A Taylor (eds), *Humanitarian Crises and Migration: Causes, Consequences and Responses* (London, Routledge, 2014) 6. One of the most crucial factors to consider when evaluating how international standards have been applied is to assess whether and to what extent they have been incorporated into the respective national legal systema. Other factors to consider include a state's enforcement of treaty commitments, its discretion in doing so, and its political will. B Conforti, *International Law and the Role of Domestic Legal Systems* (Dordrecht, Martinus Nijhoff, 1993) 25–26; GS Goodwin-Gill and J McAdam, *The Refugee in International Law*, 3rd edn (Oxford, OUP, 2007) 528–30; K Bianchini, *Protecting Stateless Persons: The Implementation of the Convention Relating to the Status of Stateless Persons across EU States* (Leiden, Brill/Nijhoff, 2018) 28–37, 301.

[67] D Guilfoyle and E Papastavridis, 'Mapping Disembarkation Options: Towards Strengthening Cooperation in Managing Irregular Movements by Sea' (paper commissioned in connection with a meeting organised by UNHCR under the auspices of the Bali Process Regional Support Office on 'Mapping Disembarkation Options: towards Strengthening Cooperation in Managing Irregular Movements by Sea' Bangkok, 3–4 March 2014) 15, 17.

rescue vessels, many states like Italy reject this interpretation.[68] The disputes over who holds responsibility for SAR operations and related disembarkation issues have caused several delays or complete failures to save individuals at sea.[69] At the heart of these controversies are the broader discussions on 'responsibility sharing' among EU Member States, which have to date not found effective agreements to develop legal avenues to Europe for refugees,[70] nor to distribute those who arrive irregularly in the coastal states across the EU.

One less discussed aspect relates to the practice of the actors involved, especially private vessels and NGOs which carry out sea rescue missions as well as state agents (ie, coast guards, prosecutors, judges, etc). The few studies exploring the practices of these actors usually focus solely on one set of actors (mostly NGOs),[71] do not develop a complete view of the ROL aspects involved,[72] do not deal with the issue of their accountability, and are mostly in the form of journal articles. Although some scholarship has addressed important policy considerations, how state actors are driven by populist logics,[73] and the trend among EU governments to control immigration through criminal law,[74] there is no comprehensive study on how different actors implement overlapping frameworks either to comply with the obligations or to circumvent the law as well as their shared responsibility.

Some articles examine how the increasing tensions between northern and southern Member States as well as between NGOs and coastal Member States have led to 'policing humanitarianism', which entails criminalising NGOs as

[68] See Coppens (n 66) 33; Carrera and Cortinovis (n 7).

[69] E Koka and D Veshi, 'Irregular Migration by Sea: Interception and Rescue Interventions in Light of International Law and the EU Sea Borders Regulation' (2019) 21 *European Journal of Migration and Law* 26, 43.

[70] MC Foblets and L Leboeuf, 'Introduction: Humanitarian Admission to Europe. From Policy Developments to Legal Controversies and Litigation' in MC Foblets and L Leboeuf (eds), *Humanitarian Admission to Europe* (Baden-Baden, Nomos/Hart, 2020).

[71] See, eg, F Patane et al, 'Asylum-Seekers Prosecuted for Human Smuggling: A Case Study of Scafisti in Italy' (2020) 39 *Refugee Survey Quarterly* 123; K Santer, 'Governing the Central Mediterranean through Indirect Rule: Tracing the Effects of the Recognition of the Joint Rescue Coordination Centre Tripoli' (2019) 21 *European Journal of Migration and Law* 141; L Masera, 'L'Incriminazione dei Soccorsi in Mare: Dobbiamo Rassegnarci al Disumano?' (2018) 2 *Questione Giustizia* 225; P Cuttitta, 'Repoliticization through Search and Rescue, Humanitarian NGOs and Migration Management in the Central Mediterranean' (2018) 23 *Geopolitics* 632.

[72] See, for instance, F Alagna, 'The Continuation of Criminalization by Other Means: The Role of the Judicial Agency in the Italian Policing of Humanitarian Assistance at Sea' (2022) *Mediterranean Politics* 1, 2, available at: www.tandfonline.com/doi/full/10.1080/13629395.2022.2135072; S Carrera, JS Vara and T Strik (eds), *Constitutionalising the External Dimensions of EU Migration Policies in Times of Crises: Legality, Rule of Law and Fundamental Rights Reconsidered* (Cheltenham, Edward Elgar Publishing, 2019); Bevilacqua (n 59).

[73] M Minetti, 'The Facilitators Package, Penal Populism and the Rule of Law: Lessons from Italy' (2020) 11 *New Journal of European Criminal Law* 335; Alagna (n 72); C Berti, 'Right-wing Populism and the Criminalization of Sea-rescue NGOs: The "Sea-Watch 3" Case in Italy, and Matteo Salvini's Communication on Facebook' (2000) 43 *Media, Culture & Society* 532.

[74] GL Gatta, V Mitsilegas and S Zirulia (eds), *Controlling Immigration Through Criminal Law: European and Comparative Perspectives on 'Crimmigration'* (Oxford, Hart Publishing, 2020).

well as adopting other strategies of 'suspicion, intimidation and harassment'.[75] NGOs and private vessels that enter Italian ports have been confronted with continuous investigations and proceedings[76] as well as 'increasing demands and pressures for registration, coordination and financial transparency, which have profound repercussions for their independence and impartiality from government interference'.[77] Nevertheless, most works focus on whether the challenges brought against NGOs are lawful and their consequences for NGOs or refugee protection, without comprehensively analysing them from an ROL point of view.[78]

The weak incorporation of international human rights law in the Law of the Sea, SOLAS, and SAR Conventions is another important debate among scholars. Surprisingly, while human rights apply to the rescue of people on the high seas, there remains a lack of clarity about the point when state parties have to enforce treaty-related rights.[79] In particular, the principle of non-refoulement in Article 33 of the Convention Relating to the Status of Refugees (Refugee Convention) states that contracting states are required not to return refugees to a place in which they have a well-founded fear of being persecuted.[80] This principle has become an essential element of other main international human rights treaties and part of customary international law.[81] In the context of irregular

[75] Alagna (n 72); S Carrera, J Allsopp and L Vosyliūtė, 'Policing the Mobility Society: The Effects of EU-Anti-Migrant Smuggling Policies on Humanitarianism' (2018) 4 *International Journal of Migration and Border Studies* 236, 239; J Allsopp, L Vosyliūtė and S Smilalowski, 'Picking "Low-Hanging Fruit" While the Orchard Burns: The Cost of Policing Humanitarian Actors in Italy and Greece as a Strategy to Prevent Migrant Smuggling' (2021) 27 *European Journal of Criminal Policy and Research* 65, 68.

[76] T Basaran 'Saving Lives at Sea: Security, Law and Adverse Effects' (2014) 16 *European Journal of Migration and Law* 365, 375; Minetti (n 73).

[77] S Carrera et al, *Policing Humanitarianism: EU Policies Against Human Smuggling and Their Impact on Civil Society* (Oxford, Hart Publishing, 2019) 3.

[78] See, for instance, FRA, 'Fundamental Rights Considerations: NGO Ships Involved in Search and Rescue in the Mediterranean and Criminal Investigations – 2018' (FRA, 1 October 2018), available at: fra.europa.eu/en/publication/2019/fundamental-rights-considerations-ngo-ships-involved-search-and-rescue; Malcolm Wu, 'The EC's Guidance on the Facilitation Directive: Ending the Criminalisation of NGO-led SAR Operations?' (*Opinio Juris*, 30 October 2020), available at: opiniojuris.org/2020/10/30/the-ecs-guidance-on-the-facilitation-directive-ending-the-criminalisation-of-ngo-led-sar-operations; Cusumano and Villa, 'From "Angels" to "Vice Smugglers"' (n 38); Masera (n 71) 227; Minetti (n 73); S Zirulia and G Martinico, 'Criminalising Migrants and Securitising Borders: The Italian "No Way" Model in the Age of Populism' in V Stoyanova and S Smet (eds), *Migrants' Rights, Populism and Legal Resilience in Europe* (Cambridge, CUP, 2022) 270.

[79] Papastavridis (n 6) 27; Bianchini, 'En Route to Protection' (n 58) 13; Salau (n 6) 25–27.

[80] Convention Relating to the Status of Refugees (Geneva, 28 July 1951) 189 UNTS 150 (Refugee Convention) Art 33.

[81] eg, the Convention against Torture and Other Cruel, Inhuman or Degrading Treatment or Punishment (New York, 10 December 1984) 1465 UNTS 85 (CAT) Art 3; International Covenant on Civil and Political Rights (New York, 16 December 1966) 999 UNTS 171 (ICCPR) Art 2(1), 7; Convention (IV) Relative to the Protection of Civilian Persons in Time of War (Geneva, 12 August 1949) 75 UNTS 287, Art 45; UN Human Rights Committee, 'General Comment No 31 [80]. The Nature of the General Legal Obligation Imposed on States Parties to the Covenant' (26 May 2004) UN Doc CCPR/C/21/Rev 1/Add 13, paras 10, 12.

sea migration, the non-refoulement obligation means that states are required to take steps to ensure that rescued persons are given the opportunity to demonstrate their protected status.[82] This involves the need to avoid disembarkation in territories 'where the lives and freedoms of those alleging a well-founded fear of persecution would be threatened',[83] such as Libya.[84] However, it should be noted that non-refoulement does not automatically permit access to a state's territory and its national refugee determination mechanism. Usually it involves quite complex considerations, particularly with regard to its scope and extraterritorial application.[85] The literature points out that in several areas, states use atypical and informal regulation in order to avoid accountability for violation of non-refoulement, as in the case of cooperation agreements on sea migration between Italy and some North African countries.[86]

Costello and Mann have pointed to the widespread human rights violations in the context of sea migration and 'the apparent lack of accountability for such violations'.[87] In particular, they have identified the following main characteristics of migration control practices that affect accountability: the exceptional treatment of migrants under international law (their right to enter a country 'is treated as an exception to states'' interest in regulating migration);[88] the limitations of refugee law, especially related to the narrowness of the refugee definition;[89] the externalisation and delegation of migration control (migration control from abroad can more easily evade checks and responsibility);[90] and the debated issue of courts' lack of jurisdiction for states' acts or omissions occurring outside their territories.[91] They have indicated the need for further lines of

[82] R Kilpatrick and A Smith, 'The International Legal Obligation to Rescue During Mass Migration at Sea: Navigating the Sovereign and Commercial Dimensions of a Mediterranean Crisis' (2015–16) 28(2) *University of San Francisco Maritime Law Journal* 141, 148.

[83] Maritime Safety Committee, Guidelines on the Treatment of Persons Rescued at Sea, UN Doc MSC78/26/Add.2, Resolution MSC167(78) (20 May 2004) (2004 IMO Guidelines) point 6.17; E Koka, 'Irregular Migration by Sea: A Critical Analysis of EU and EU Member State Extraterritorial Practice in Light of International Law' (PhD Thesis, University of Kent, 2018) 173, fn 879.

[84] UNHCR, 'UNHCR Position on the Designations of Libya as a Safe Third Country' (n 21).

[85] See Koka and Veshi (n 69) 40; K Wouters and M Den Heijer, 'The Marine I Case: A Comment' (2010) 22 *International Journal of Refugee Law* 1; S Trevisanut, 'The Principle of Non-refoulement at Sea and the Effectiveness of Asylum Protection' (2008) 12 *Max Planck Yearbook of United Nations Law* 205.

[86] FL Gatta, 'Migration and the Rule of (Human Rights) Law: Two "Crises" Looking in the Same Mirror' (2019) 15 *Croatian Yearbook of European Law & Policy* 99.

[87] Costello and Mann (n 57) 311.

[88] ibid 313.

[89] ibid.

[90] ibid 313–14.

[91] See, for instance, D Guilfoyle, 'Jurisdiction at Sea. Migrant Interdiction and the Transnational Security State' in T Gammeltoft-Hansen and J Vedsted-Hansen (eds), *Human Rights and the Dark Side of Globalisation. Transnational Law Enforcement and Migration Control* (London, Routledge, 2017); T Spijkerboer, 'Wasted Lives: Borders and the Right to Life of People Crossing Them' (2017) 86 *Nordic Journal of International Law* 1, 1; Mann (n 57); V Moreno-Lax, 'The Architecture of Functional Jurisdiction: Unpacking Contactless Control – On Public Powers, S.S. and Others v Italy, and the "Operational Model"' (2020) 21 *German Law Journal* 385.

enquiry to find out more about the role of the courts for criminal and tort law cases, and the role of new technologies in this scenario.

In conclusion, the literature reveals several problems pertaining to the regulation of sea migration and a number of challenges for Member States, asylum seekers' protection, private ships, NGOs, and the EU as a whole. Responsibility for SAR operations, the duty to investigate missing or dead migrants at sea, the measures adopted by Member States to prevent NGOs from rescuing migrants at sea, and reallocation of the rescued migrants to other Member States remain highly debated.[92] According to Moreno-Lax, one main cause of this situation is that the applicable provisions are not 'sufficiently precise and clear to enable the individuals concerned to know the extent of their rights and obligations'.[93] As such, they weaken the principle of legal certainty, which is central to the ROL. Despite the importance of these matters, very few scholars have discussed how laws, policies and practices adopted to address or prevent sea migrants' journeys challenge the ROL[94] – but even those tend to focus on the externalisation policy or the internal EU asylum dimension. In addition, most of the studies are not based on empirical data, are written in Italian, and focus on a few specific government initiatives that have affected some of the ROL principles.[95] These studies are usually in the form of journal articles and do not analyse the issue comprehensively. It is therefore appropriate for this work to focus on the several layers of legislation, policies and practices concerning sea migration in the Mediterranean and the main challenges for the ROL.

VI. STRUCTURE OF THE BOOK

This book is divided into seven chapters. Chapter one contains the introduction, explanation of the scope and aim of the book, methodology and literature

[92] Bianchini, 'En Route to Protection' (n 58) 15.

[93] V Moreno-Lax, *Accessing Asylum in Europe: Extraterritorial Border Controls and Refugee Rights Under EU Law* (Oxford, OUP, 2017) 477.

[94] The very few works include: Tsourdi (n 8) 471; P Rossi, 'The Role of National Courts for the International Rule of Law: Insights from the Field of Migration' (2019) 12 *European Journal of Legal Studies* 195; A Sánchez Legido, 'The Walls of Fortress Europe: Externalization of Migration Control and the Rule of Law' (2019) 23 *Spanish Yearbook of International Law* 345; V Mitsilegas, 'Extraterritorial Immigration Control in the 21st Century: The Individual and the State Transformed' in B Ryan and V Mitsilegas (eds), *Extraterritorial Immigration Control: Legal Challenges* (Leiden, Martinus Nijhoff Publishers, 2010) 63.

[95] See, for instance, S Zirulia and F Cancellaro, 'Caso Diciotti: il Tribunale dei Ministri Qualifica le Condotte del Ministro Salvini come Sequestro di Persona Aggravato e Trasmette al Senato la Domanda di Autorizzazione a Procedere' (*Diritto Penale Contemporaneo*, 28 January 2019), available at: archiviodpc.dirittopenaleuomo.org/d/6450-caso-diciotti-il-tribunale-dei-ministri-qualifica-le-condotte-del-ministro-salvini-come-sequestro-d; A Jr Golia, 'La Fortezza che Resiste. Potere Estero, Conflitto di Attribuzione e Prescrittività Costituzionale' 2019 3(1) *La Democrazia A-Costituzionale* 47; E Olivito, 'Il Cul-de-Sac Costituzionale degli Accordi in Forma Semplificata: Iniziativa Legislativa Parlamentare ed Esternalizzazione delle Politiche Migratorie' (2018) 2 *Diritto Pubblico* 435.

review. Chapter two includes an explanation of the ROL framework of analysis that I adopt for the book. After discussing the general concept of ROL, I elucidate the meaning of ROL and its constitutive elements with respect to the legal provisions and practices that are relevant in the context of sea migration. I draw from legal studies, political theory, as well as EU and Council of Europe legal and policy texts.

In chapter three, I introduce the relevant international and EU provisions concerning the obligation to rescue, Member States' SAR operations, disembarkations of rescued persons to a place of safety, as well as anti-trafficking and smuggling legislation and the international and EU framework on safety of navigation. I highlight the contradictions and shortcomings of the frameworks at the international and EU levels, which are then reflected at the national level, as revealed in the following chapters.

In chapters four to six, I investigate the three aforementioned themes of sea migration in terms of their implications for the ROL principles. In particular, in chapter four, I explore Italy's national framework on SAR operations, states' creation of SAR areas, the obligation to rescue, and related practices. I discuss the fact that, whereas legal implementation is in line with the international and EU provisions and even exceeds them, major problems remain in practice. For instance, disagreements among Member States about who is responsible for carrying out rescue operations, the contested Maltese and Libyan SAR zones, and the attempts of Member States to avoid their obligations, raise concerns about the certainty of the law, the legality of a number of actions, and lack of accountability for violations of the law.

In chapter five, I analyse the informal cooperation agreements between Italy on one side and Libya and Tunisia on the other, and the pushbacks and pullbacks carried out on the basis of these agreements. I show how such agreements weaken the ROL from a procedural point of view (they are not adopted with Parliament's approval and often are not published as required by the Italian Constitution) and a substantial point of view (they breach the principles of non-refoulement and other fundamental human rights). I also consider legal actions against the lawfulness of the cooperation agreements, pushbacks and pullbacks and their meaning in terms of accountability.

In chapter six, I analyse the legal framework and practices adopted by the Italian authorities to prevent NGOs' SAR operations. The strategies of the authorities have changed over the years, and shifted from a criminal approach to the adoption of administrative measures which continue to create obstacles to NGOs' activities in the Mediterranean. Such measures and policies have affected the principles of certainty of the law, equality of the law (a number of measures were specifically intended to target certain NGOs), as well as legality (due to abuse of power on the part of some authorities). I also study the case law and discuss how the courts have interpreted some debated provisions and adopted a human rights approach to interpret them. At the same time, however,

I acknowledge how the ongoing litigation affecting NGOs has had a negative impact on their activities.

Finally, chapter seven is devoted to final reflections on the responses to sea migration in light of the ROL and the data discussed in the previous chapters, both from the perspective of the case study of Italy and more generally. In particular, I highlight how ROL principles are weakened in the context of sea migration due to the fact that there are multiple overlapping and sometimes conflicting regulations, several actors with different aims interacting with each other, and a number of legal and practical difficulties for migrants in accessing justice, although in general the courts have attempted to uphold human rights and have sanctioned legal violations. Importantly, the choice of the ROL approach flips the common populist plea for 'law and order' on its head by showing how 'immigration control' and a security-oriented approach (ie, anti-immigrant practices and arrangements) can actually weaken 'law and order'. Finally, I expose the limits of the ROL concept, as it is closely connected to state sovereignty and jurisdiction, whereas some events affecting sea migrants occur in extraterritorial spaces. Nevertheless, I conclude that, in general, an ROL approach to sea migration offers a more in-depth understanding of national responses to the phenomenon and how they concern not only sea migrants' rights but also fundamental principles of the state. As such, I hope that future debates on sea migration will take this dimension into account.

2

The Rule of Law as a Critical Lens

I. INTRODUCTION

IN THIS CHAPTER, I present the analytical framework and theoretical positions that underpin this investigation. The principle of the rule of law (ROL), situated at the core of the entire book, is probably the most 'powerful and often repeated political ideal'[1] underlying government legitimacy and action.[2] It is also a concept that applies to everyone within a community, regardless of immigration status,[3] and has often been used to evaluate a large variety of legal instruments, institutional arrangements and dynamics. However, the ROL is an elusive concept, and therefore in this chapter I address the questions of its meanings, requirements and limitations.

By the ROL I mean the idea that 'all persons and authorities within the state, whether public or private, should be bound by and entitled to the benefit of laws publicly and prospectively promulgated and publicly administered by the courts'.[4] Moreover, 'any derogation must be closely assessed and justified'.[5] The permissible exceptions to the ROL are narrower than those applicable to human rights[6] and thus more difficult to excuse – they must be necessary and adopted

[1] BZ Tamanaha, 'The History and Elements of the Rule of Law' [2012] *Singapore Journal of Legal Studies* 232.

[2] ibid.

[3] BZ Tamanaha, 'The Rule of Law for Everyone?' (2002) 55 *Current Legal Problems* 97. The notion of 'community', as it pertains to the ROL, is debated. Some authors take the position that the ROL requires a specific political community. W Kymlicka, *Liberalism, Community, and Culture* (Oxford, OUP, 1986); J Foundez, 'Legal Pluralism and International Development Agencies: State Building or Legal Reform?' (2011) 3 *Hague Journal on the Rule of Law* 18. On the other hand, I agree with Sevel that, in the context of the sea, the community is wider and is composed of seafarers, the law-making community, and the traditional political community. M Sevel, 'Maritime Rule of Law: Some Preliminaries' (2023) 15 *Hague Journal on the Rule of Law* 385, 397–98.

[4] T Bingham, 'The Rule of Law' (2007) 66 *Cambridge Law Journal* 67, 69; T Bingham, *The Rule of Law* (London, Penguin Press, 2010) chs 3–10. See also, section IV of this chapter.

[5] Bingham, 'The Rule of Law' (n 4) 69; R McCorquodale, 'The Rule of Law and Migration: Some General Themes' (Conference, Asilah, Morocco, 21 July 2010) 2, available at: www.biicl.org/files/5066_rule_of_law_and_migration1.pdf.

[6] Whereas some fundamental human rights are 'absolute' – such as the right to life and the prohibition on torture – and cannot be limited, most rights are 'non-absolute' – for instance, the freedom of speech and freedom of movement – in the sense that the state can derogate to them if the measures adopted are justified by being proportionate, non-discriminatory, and towards a legitimate aim. G Gunatilleke, 'Justifying Limitations to Freedom of Expression' (2021) 22 *Human Rights Review*

only in emergency situations,[7] when 'the life and security of the whole nation is under threat'.[8] Moreover, the ROL is necessary to ensure the effectiveness of human rights.[9] As such, for the purposes of studying responses to sea migration, the ROL allows us to capture a broader variety of issues than a mere human rights approach – issues that concern the foundations of the state.

In the section II, I introduce the concept of the ROL. Then, in section III, I briefly summarise its importance at the European level. In section IV, I break down the ROL into its constituent parts and select the elements most pertinent to issues of sea migration. In section V, I discuss the limitation of the approach taken. The application of this framework in the next chapters will allow me to assess the weaknesses and gaps in the different legal instruments and in their implementation through the policies and practices of the different actors involved. It will also help me to identify accountability of state and non-state actors for violations of international and national legal obligations.

II. MAIN LEGAL DEBATES ON THE ROL

An evaluation of the available research suggests that the ROL is a multifaceted principle with a long history and tradition – one that is central to political, legal and philosophical thought and that is still being debated today.[10] In part, this is because the ROL is a working political idea as well as a contested normative matter.[11] In addition, the ROL is composed of many elements, and different views

91; D Little, 'The Justification of Human Rights' (2014) 3 *Brigham Young University Law Review* 585. For a more detailed discussion on the topic, see I Bantekas and L Oette, *International Human Rights Law and Practice* (Cambridge, CUP, 2020).

[7] F Tamburini, 'The State of Emergency and Exception in Algeria, Morocco and Tunisia: The "License to Kill" the Rule of Law' (2021) 56(6) *Journal of Asian and African Studies* 1286; for a critical view of 'the state of exception', see G Agamben, *Lo Stato di Eccezione* (Torino, Bollati Boringhieri, 2003).

[8] D Dedov, 'How State of Emergency Affects Democracy. Fair Trial for Political Activists' in M Elósegui, A Miron and I Motoc (eds), *The Rule of Law in Europe: Recent Challenges and Judicial Responses* (Cham, Springer International Publishing, 2021) 24.

[9] RP Peerenboom, 'Human Rights and the Rule of Law: What's the Relationship?' (University of California Los Angeles, Public Law & Legal Theory Series, 10 January 2005) 4.

[10] Given the rich literature on the topic, this chapter can only provide a brief overview. See, eg, BZ Tamanaha, *On the Rule of Law: History, Politics, Theory* (Cambridge, CUP, 2004); S Beaulac, 'The Rule of Law in International Law Today' in G Palombella and N Walker (eds), *Relocating the Rule of Law* (Oxford, Hart Publishing, 2009) 201; A Bedner, 'An Elementary Approach to the Rule of Law' (2010) 2 *Hague Journal on the Rule of Law* 48, 48; R McCorquodale, 'Defining the International Rule of Law: Defining Gravity?' (2016) 65 *International & Comparative Law Quarterly* 277, 279; see also, J Chevallier, *L'État de Droit*, 5th edn (Paris, Montchrestien, 2010); J Raz, *The Authority of Law: Essays on Law and Morality* (Hong Kong, OUP, 1979).

[11] R Fallon, '"The Rule of Law" as a Concept in Constitutional Discourse' (2007) 97 *Columbia Law Review* 6, quoted in J Waldron, 'Is the Rule of Law an Essentially Contested Concept (in Florida)?' (2001) 21 *Law and Philosophy* 137.

tend to focus on some of its aspects rather than others.[12] In general, however, the ROL has increasingly assumed the role of an overarching and foundational principle of modern constitutions, which refers to 'the ascendancy of the law as such and of the institutions of the legal system in a system of governance'.[13]

At the centre of contemporary debates is the distinction between formal (or thin) and substantive (or thick) understandings of the ROL concept. According to Tamanaha, 'formal theories focus on the proper sources and form of legality, while substantive theories also include requirements about the content of the law (usually that it must comport with justice or moral principle)'.[14] 'While the distinction is informative, it should not be taken as strict'[15] because 'formal versions have substantive implications'[16] and some human rights overlap with formal elements (eg, the right to a fair trial).[17] In this context, one of the main proponents of the formal theories, Raz, maintains that even an authoritarian state may in theory comply with the ROL.[18] So as long as formal requirements of the ROL are met (ie, the law must be public, clear, prospective and stable, and due process must be ensured), the nature of a state and the moral element of the law are not relevant.[19] On the other hand, substantive theories may overlap with wide social justice ideas, meaning that only good laws fit under the concept.[20] For example, according to Hayek, the ROL 'includes the recognition of the inalienable, individual right of man'.[21] Dworkin maintains that the ROL has substantive elements, which include equality and rights.[22] 'Many other theorists have similarly added various substantive'[23] rights for individuals to the definition of the ROL, raising even more debates 'over whether the ROL should include one or more substantive elements, and if so, which ones'.[24]

[12] See, for instance, Tamanaha, *On the Rule of Law: History, Politics, Theory* (n 10) 3–4; R Kleinfeld, 'Competing Definitions of the Rule of Law' in T Carothers (ed), *Promoting the Rule of Law Abroad: in Search of Knowledge* (Washington, DC, Carnegie Endowment for International Peace, 2006).

[13] G Napolitano, 'The Rule of Law' in P Cane et al (eds), *The Oxford Handbook of Comparative Administrative Law* (Oxford, OUP, 2020).

[14] Tamanaha, *On the Rule of Law: History, Politics, Theory* (n 10) 92. See also, L Fuller, *The Morality of Law* (New Haven, CT, Yale University Press, 1969).

[15] Tamanaha, *On the Rule of Law: History, Politics, Theory* (n 10) 92.

[16] Council of Europe (CoE), European Commission for Democracy through Law (Venice Commission), 'Rule of Law Checklist. Adopted by the Venice Commission at Its 106th Plenary Session (Venice, 11–12 March 2016)' [2016] CDL-AD 007rev, 9.

[17] ibid.

[18] Raz (n 10) 208–26.

[19] A Magen, 'Crack in the Foundations: Understanding the Great Rule of Law Debate in the EU' (2016) 54 *Journal of Common Market Studies* 1050, 1054.

[20] Raz (n 10) 211; Tamanaha, 'The History and Elements of the Rule of Law' (n 1) 235; McCorquodale, 'The Rule of Law and Migration (n 5) 2.

[21] FA Hayek, *The Road to Serfdom* (Chicago, IL, University of Chicago Press, 1944) 63.

[22] RM Dworkin, *A Matter of Principle* (Oxford, OUP, 1985).

[23] Napolitano (n 13) 2.

[24] ibid; see also, M Versteeg and T Ginsburg, 'Measuring the Rule of Law: A Comparison of Indicators' (2017) 42 *Law & Social Inquiry* 100.

In this study, I follow a substantive conception of the ROL. I base this choice upon the consideration that European Union (EU) instruments and policy documents adopt such an understanding,[25] and that the recent case law of the European Court of Justice (ECJ) as well as of the European Court of Human Rights (ECtHR) indicates a human rights approach to the ROL.[26] Furthermore, in light of the reviewed literature, it is clear that the responses to sea migration affect a number of fundamental rights. Therefore, the present analysis would miss important aspects of the issues at stake if it only adopted a formal understanding of the ROL.

While in this book I focus on the *national level*, as the state is primarily responsible for guaranteeing the ROL within its territory and this duty falls to its legislative, executive, and judicial institutions, it is worth mentioning that when there are weaknesses in this regard, 'the traditional recourse is to international law'.[27] While it is outside the scope of this study to engage with the rich scholarship on the ROL at the international level, I would like to draw attention to McCorquodale's argument that an international ROL 'would benefit all states, so that each of them have confidence in reaching binding legal agreements to secure their own interest and to assist in attaining international peace and security'.[28] This point pertains to cross-national matters such as search and rescue (SAR) operations in international waters, disembarkation of rescued migrants to a place of safety, and their redistribution across different EU states.

Moreover, according to Watts,

> The protection of the interests of all states and the creation of international stability requires that state-to-state relations be subject to a long-term framework [of an international rule of law], which ensures that international law is applied in conformity with principles of justice [... and enables states to have a] stable, safe and predictable world in which they can better pursue their political and economic goals.[29]

[25] L Pech, 'Rule of Law as a Guiding Principle of the European Union's External Action' (CLEER Working Papers 2012/3, Centre for the Law of EU External Relations, TMC Asser Institute, 2011) 26; European Commission, 'Communication from the Commission to the European Parliament and the Council. A New EU Framework to Strengthen the Rule of Law' (2014) COM 158 final, 4; Magen (n 19) 1054.

[26] L Pech, 'A Union Founded on the Rule of Law: Meaning and Reality of the Rule of Law as a Constitutional Principle of EU Law' (2010) 6 *European Constitutional Law Review* 359, 369 ff; see Joined Cases C-402/05 P and C-415/05 P *Kadi and Al Barakaat* P [2008] ECR I-6351, para 316, ECLI: EU:C:2008:461; Case C-5/88 *Wachauf v Bundesamt für Ernährung und Forstwirtschaft* [1989] ECR 2609, para 19, ECLI:EU:C:1989:321; Case C-260/89 [18 June 1991] *Elliniki Radiophonia Tileorassi (ERT) AE v Dimotiki Etairia Pliroforissis et al*, ECLI:EU: C:1991:254. See G Lautenbach, *The Concept of the Rule of Law and the European Court of Human Rights* (Oxford, OUP, 2013) ch 5.

[27] P Craig, 'The Rule of Law. National, International, and Regional Dimensions' in B Faedda (ed), *The Rule of Law: Cases, Strategies and Interpretations* (Vicenza, Ronzani Edizioni Scientifiche, 2021) 62.

[28] McCorquodale, 'The Rule of Law and Migration' (n 5) 2.

[29] A Watts, 'The International Rule of Law' (1993) 36 *German Yearbook of International Law* 15, 25, 41.

Furthermore, an international ROL would be beneficial to people who travel to other states or who are subject to certain aspects of international law,[30] such as asylum seekers and refugees,[31] as it would extend the substantive and procedural guarantees they can benefit from during their journeys or in the host country. However, it has been pointed out that some features of the international legal system are less developed than those of the national systems, as there is no 'permanent legislator, and for most cases no judiciary with obligatory jurisdiction'.[32] In addition, the international legal system must be loose enough to accommodate greater diversity. Very often, in cases of breaches of international law, international organisations and bodies can only admonish the non-complying state. Such admonitions are important but limited 'both formally and substantively'[33] given that a wide political consensus is required. Accordingly, in most cases, international organisations are unable to bring about real meaningful change.[34] On the other hand, as further explained in the next section, regional systems such as that of the EU have developed the ROL as a 'principle applicable to its own legal system'.[35]

III. THE ROL FROM THE EUROPEAN POINT OF VIEW

The ROL, as a set of principles and values[36] that regulate the public powers, is one of the most important and common normative principles of today's European constitutions, including the Italian Constitution.[37] It is also a foundational principle of the Council of Europe (CoE) and the EU.[38]

[30] McCorquodale, 'The Rule of Law and Migration' (n 5) 2.

[31] S Kneebone, *Refugees, Asylum Seekers and the Rule of Law: Comparative Perspectives* (Cambridge, CUP, 2009).

[32] Venice Commission (n 16) 10.

[33] Craig (n 27) 62.

[34] ibid 63.

[35] Venice Commission (n 16) 10.

[36] E Tsourdi, 'Asylum in the EU: One of the Many Faces of the Rule of Law Backsliding?' (2021) 17 *European Constitutional Law Review* 471.

[37] In the Italian Constitution there is no specific mention or definition of the ROL. However, some of its Articles refer to ROL principles: the government, Parliament and judiciary are bound by the Constitution (Part II); all public decisions must be based upon the law, and constitutional law limitations to the discretion of the legislature shall be respected (Arts 13, 14, 16(1), 23 and 97); criminal law, in particular, shall have no retroactive effect (Art 25(2)); laws must be of general character and apply to everyone without discrimination (Art 3); the making of legislation is subject to specific provisions preventing abuse of power (Arts 70–82); the inviolable rights of the person are recognised and protected (Art 2); the Italian legal system shall conform to the generally recognised principles of international law (Art 10); anyone may bring a case before a court of law to protect his/her rights, and legal aid is guaranteed for those who cannot otherwise afford legal representation (Art 24(1) and 24(3)); equality before the law (Arts 3, 8(1), 29(2), 111(2)); the right to seek asylum (Art 10(3)); the right to personal freedom (Art 13).

[38] Tsourdi (n 36) 475–77.

The CoE has worked to strengthen the ROL through different means, most particularly through the Venice Commission and the ECtHR. The Venice Commission – the consulting body of the CoE in constitutional matters – assists states that need to change their national systems in order to comply with the ROL.[39] Moreover, over the years, the ECtHR, established to interpret the European Convention on Human Rights (ECHR),[40] has developed case law reinforcing the principles of the ROL, especially in cases concerning the independence and impartiality of judicial systems in contracting states. In particular, the ECtHR has stated that the ROL envisaged in the ECHR requires laws to be clear, not excessively vague, not discriminatory, and not retroactive if concerning criminal matters.[41] The ROL demands that all authorities have limited powers and are bound by law.[42] Furthermore, laws must be overseen by the courts.[43]

[39] F Mauri, 'Un Nuovo Approccio Alla Rule of Law: La Checklist della Commissione di Venezia' (2020) 2 *Associazione Italiana del Constituzionalisti* 37, 38–40.

[40] European Convention for the Protection of Human Rights and Fundamental Freedoms, as amended by Protocols Nos 11 and 14 (Rome, 4 November 1950) ETS 5 (ECHR).

[41] Regarding the principle of legal certainty, see *Cantoni v France* App no 17862/91 (ECtHR, 29 March 1995) para 29; *Kafkaris v Cyprus* App no 21906/04 (ECtHR, 12 February 2008) para 140; Case *Del Rio Prada v Spain* App no 42750/09 (ECtHR, 21 October 2013) para 79; *Liivik v Estonia* App no 12157/05 (ECtHR, 25 June 2009) paras 96–104; *The Sunday Times v. the United Kingdom* App no 6538/74 (ECtHR, 26 April 1979) para 49; *Medvedyev and others v France* App no 3394/03 (ECtHR, 29 March 2010). Concerning the principle of equal treatment, see *Hämäläinen v Finland* App no 37359/09 (ECtHR, 26 July 2014) para 108; *Burden v the United Kingdom GC* App no 13378/05 (ECtHR, 29 April 2008) para 60; *Molla Sali v Greece* App no 20452/14 (ECtHR, 19 December 2018) para 135; *Fabris v France* App no 16574/08 (ECtHR, 7 February 2103) para 56; Case *Unal Tekeli v Turkey* App no 29865/96 (ECtHR, 16 November 2004) para 66; *Mazurek v France* App no 34406/97 (ECtHR, 1 February 2000) paras 46 and 48; *Larkos v Cyprus* App no 29515/95 (ECtHR, 18 February 1999) para 29.

[42] Concerning the principle of legality, see for instance, *Čonka v Belgium* App no 51564/99 (ECtHR, 5 February 2002); *Amann v Switzerland* App no 27798/95 (ECtHR, 16 February 2000) para 47 ff; *Slivenko v Latvia* App no 48321/99 (ECtHR, 9 October 2003) para 100; *X v Latvia* App no 27853/09 (ECtHR, 26 November 2013) para 58; *Kurić and others v Slovenia* App no 26828/06 (ECtHR, 12 March 2014) para 341; *A and others v the United Kingdom* App no 345/05 (ECtHR, 19 February 2009) 178, 182; *Lawless v Ireland* App no 332/57 (ECtHR, 1 July 1961).

[43] Robert Spano, 'Rule of Law: la Lodestar della Convenzione Europea dei Diritti dell'Uomo. La Corte di Strasburgo e l'indipendenza della Magistratura' (*Giustizia Insieme*, 10 March 2021), available at: www.giustiziainsieme.it/it/costituzione-e-carta-dei-diritti-fondamentali/29-europa-corti-internazionali/1607-rule-of-law-la-lodestar-della-convenzione-europea-dei-diritti-dell-uomo-la-corte-di-strasburgo-e-l-indipendenza-della-magistratura-di-robert-spano. For the principle of access to justice, see *Ramos Nunes de Carvalho e Sá v Portugal* App nos 55391/13, 57728/12, 74041/13 (ECtHR, 6 November 2018) paras 150 and 152; *Denisov v Ukraine* App no 76639/11 (ECtHR, 25 September 2018) paras 61–64; *Gudmundur Andri Astradsson v Iceland* App no 26374/18 (ECtHR, 1 December 2020) paras 218 ff, 231 ff and 295; *Golder v the United Kingdom* App no 4451/70 (ECtHR, 21 February 1975) 28–36; Case *Zubac v Croatia* App no 40160/12 (ECtHR, 5 April 2018) 49; *Naït-Liman v Switzerland* App no 51357/07 (ECtHR, 15 March 2018) 112–13; *D v Bulgaria* App no 2947/17 (ECtHR, 20 June 2021); *Shazhad v Hungary* App no 12625/17 (ECtHR, 8 June 2021); *MA v Belgium* App no 19656/18 (ECtHR, 27 November 2020). See, eg, *Micallef v Malta* App no 17056/06 (ECtHR, 15 October 2009) para 78 ff; *Neziraj v Germany* App no 30804/07 (ECtHR, 8 February 2013); *Murtazaliyeva v Russia* App no 36658/05 (ECtHR, 18 December 2018) para 91; *Zahirović v Croatia* App no 58590/11 (ECtHR, 25 April 2013) para 42; *Ibrahimov and others v Azerbaijan* App nos 69234/11, 69252/11, 69335/11 (ECtHR, 11 February 2016) para 95. See, eg, *Oferta Plus SRL v Moldova* App no 14385/04 (ECtHR, 19 December 2006) para 145.

At the EU level, the ROL has been adopted as a foundation within the EU institutions[44] and in relation to other states, and as an instrument to help achieve peace, democracy and the protection of human rights – including in relations with non-EU states.[45] Compliance with the ROL is also one of the membership criteria, as stated in Article 49 of the Treaty on European Union (TEU), meaning that the functioning of the regional system relies upon the assumption that all Member States are normally in compliance with the ROL. In this regard, in a 2014 Opinion on EU accession to the ECHR, the ECJ underlined how the EU is

> based on the fundamental premise that each Member State shares with all the other Member States, and recognises that they share with it, a set of common values on which the EU is founded, as stated in Article 2 TEU. That premise implies and justifies the existence of mutual trust between the Member States that those values will be recognised, and, therefore, that the law of the EU that implements them will be respected.[46]

Despite its relevance as one of the main principles of modern democracies and as a consensual concept of the international and national legal orders,[47] European instruments are imprecise as to what the ROL means and its scope *at the national level – in contrast, it is clearly spelled out in the founding treaties when applied to the EU's own institutions*.[48] In this regard, Magen states that EU law does not define what the ROL is or provide a set of ROL requirements.[49] However, some guidance can be found in a few EU documents and legal

[44] See European Commission, 'Upholding the Rule of Law', available at: commission.europa.eu/strategy-and-policy/policies/justice-and-fundamental-rights/upholding-rule-law_en (nd).

[45] Treaty on European Union [1992] OJ C 191/1 (TEU) Art 2. Moreover, the Preamble of Consolidated Version of the Treaty on the Functioning of the European Union (TFEU) recognises that the EU is attached to the ROL. Similarly, Art 21(1) TFEU sets forth that the Union's international activities shall be governed by democracy and ROL, similarly to the principles it has adopted for its own development. It has been widely recognised that the internal integrity of democracy and ROL within the EU is linked to the external capacity to promote the ROL in other countries. Magen (n 19) 1057; F Timmermans, 'The European Union and the Rule of Law – Keynote Speech at Conference on the Rule of Law' (Tilburg University, 31 August 2015); M Hertogh, 'Your Rule of Law is *Not* Mine: Rethinking Empirical Approaches to EU Rule of Law Promotion' (2016) 14 *Asia Europe Journal* 43, 44; I Manners, 'Normative Power Europe: A Contradiction in Terms?' (2002) 40 *Journal of Common Market Studies* 235; Pech, 'Rule of Law as a Guiding Principle of the European Union's External Action' (n 25).

[46] Opinion 2/13 of the Court of Justice of the EU, *Accession to the ECHR (II)* (18 December 2014) para 168, ECLI:EU:C:2014:2454; Magen (n 19) 1056.

[47] CoE, OCSE and UN, 'Multilateral Organizations Rule of Law Pledge' (Press Release, OSCE Secretariat, 18 February 2005), available at: www.osce.org/secretariat/57213; OECD, 'Equal Access to Justice and the Rule of Law Report' (Organisation for Economic Co-operation and Development, 2005); Council of EuropeE, 'The Principle of the Rule of Law' Resolution 1594 (Parliamentary Assembly of the Council of Europe, Council of Europe, 23 November 2007); Organization for Security and Co-operation in Europe (OSCE), Helsinki Ministerial Council Decision (Final Document of Sixteenth Meeting of the Ministerial Council, Helsinki, 4 and 5 December 2008); UNGA, 'Declaration of the High-level Meeting of the General Assembly on the Rule of Law at the National and International Levels' (24 September 2012) 67th Session UN Doc A/RES/66/102.

[48] Magen (n 19) 1052.

[49] ibid.

sources. For instance, in a 2014 Communication of the Commission to the EU Parliament and the Council – echoed in the recent Regulation 2020/2092 of 16 December 2020 on the general regime for the protection of the Union budget[50] – it is acknowledged that

> [t]he precise content of the principles and standards stemming from the rule of law may vary at national level, depending on each Member State's constitutional system. Nevertheless, case law of the Court of Justice of the European Union ('the Court of Justice') and of the European Court of Human Rights, as well as documents drawn up by the Council of Europe, building notably on the expertise of the Venice Commission, provide a non-exhaustive list of these principles and hence define the core meaning of the rule of law as a common value of the EU in accordance with Article 2 TEU. Those principles include **legality**, which implies a transparent, accountable, democratic and pluralistic process for enacting laws; **legal certainty; prohibition of arbitrariness of the executive powers; independent and impartial courts; effective judicial review including respect for fundamental rights; and equality before the law.**[51]

In addition, it specifies:

> Both the Court of Justice and the European Court of Human Rights confirmed that those principles are not purely formal and procedural requirements. They are the vehicle for ensuring compliance with and respect for democracy and human rights. The rule of law is therefore a constitutional principle with both formal and substantive components.[52]

With regard to enforcement, *each Member State has the main duty to ensure the ROL within its jurisdiction*. This duty respects its behaviour towards other states and – when ROL violations entail a breach of EU law – towards the Union as a whole. Only when 'the national rule of law safeguards do not seem capable of addressing threats to the rule of law in a Member State, [is it] a common responsibility of the EU institutions and the Member States to take action to remedy the situation'.[53] In particular, as the ROL is a general principle that permeates the whole EU system, *whenever Member States' activities fall under the shadow of EU law, they are subject to both national and EU-level checks*.[54] Primarily, national judges may adopt a number of measures including

[50] Regulation (EU) 2020/2092 of the European Parliament and of the Council of 16 December 2020 on the general regime for the protection of the Union budget [2020] OJ L433I/1, Art 2. See Vladimiro Zagrebelsky, 'L'Unione Europea e lo Stato di Diritto. Fondamento, Problemi, Crisi' (*Giustizia Insieme*, 28 May 2021), available at: www.giustiziainsieme.it/it/diritto-ue/1739–l-unione-europea-e-lo-stato-di-diritto-fondamento-problemi-crisi-di-vladimiro-zagrebelsky.

[51] European Commission, 'Communication from the Commission to the European Parliament and the Council. A New EU Framework to Strengthen the Rule of Law' (n 25) 4.

[52] ibid.

[53] UN Human Rights Regional Office for Europe, *The Case for a Human Rights Approach to the Rule of Law in Europe* (OHCHR, May 2020) 4.

[54] European Commission, 'Communication from the Commission to the European Parliament, the European Council, the Council, the European Economic and Social Committee and the Commit-

ordering the disapplication of national law that is incompatible with EU law[55] and, where needed, referring to the ECJ for preliminary rulings.[56] On the other hand, an ROL check can be exercised by the EU institutions either through the infringement procedure provided for within Articles 258–60 of the Treaty on the Functioning of the European Union (TFEU) or, as a last resort measure, through Article 7 of TEU procedure.[57] However, the ROL has never been invoked in formal proceedings or actions by the EU against non-compliant Member States in the context of sea migration issues. In part, this may be due to the fact that the EU itself is responsible, together with its Member States, for the adoption of several measures aiming to prevent or deter the arrivals of irregular sea migrants and fight against traffickers, as I will discuss in the next chapters.

IV. THE ROL FRAMEWORK APPLIED TO RESPONSES TO SEA MIGRATION

The definition of ROL that I use in this book is based on the leading work of Bingham, which is considered 'the modern foundation for thinking about the rule of law'.[58] As I mentioned in section I, according to Bingham 'all persons and authorities within the state, whether public or private, should be bound by and entitled to the benefit of laws publicly and prospectively promulgated and publicly administered by the courts'.[59] Moreover, 'any derogation must be closely assessed and justified'.[60]

Bingham's view has also been adopted by the Venice Commission. According to the Venice Commission, this definition 'covers most appropriately the essential elements of the rule of law'.[61] In addition, this concept of ROL encompasses

tee of the Regions, Strengthening the Rule of Law within the Union. A Blueprint for Action' (2019) COM 343 final, 13.

[55] ibid 4.

[56] ibid.

[57] 'The role of the EU institutions should be to facilitate cooperation and dialogue in order to prevent problems from reaching the point where a formal response is required under the Rule of Law Framework, by infringement procedures or by actions under Art 7 of the Treaty on European Union'; ibid 9. 'The Commission also continued to exercise its role as guardian of the EU Treaties by launching infringement procedures. In some specific cases, the Commission has requested the CJEU to order interim measures to prevent irremediable harm. Besides infringement proceedings, which aim to address specific breaches of EU law, Art 7 of the Treaty on European Union provides the more general procedure for upholding the common values of the Union, including the rule of law'. European Commission, 'Communication from the Commission to the European Parliament, the Council, the European Economic and Social Committee and the Committee of the Regions. 2021 Rule of Law Report. The Rule of Law Situation in the European Union' (2021) COM 700 final, 1.

[58] C Barnard and S Fraser Butlin, 'The Rule of Law and Access to the Courts for EU Migrants' (2020) 58 *Journal of Common Market Studies* 1621, 1622.

[59] Bingham, *The Rule of Law* (n 4); Bingham, 'The Rule of Law' (n 4) 67.

[60] ibid.

[61] Venice Commission (n 16) para 17. See also Bedner (n 10) 50; R Peerenboom, 'Varieties of Rule of Law' (Research Paper no 03–16, University of California Los Angeles School of Law, 2004) 3; Tamanaha, *On the Rule of Law: History, Politics, Theory* (n 10) 7–9, 18–19.

the equivalent notions that have been developed in the common law systems and in the continental traditions (the German *Rechtsstaat*, the French *état de droit*, the Italian *stato di diritto*)[62] since it refers to 'features that are generally attributed to all of them'.[63] As Bedner notes, this is possible because 'virtually everyone agrees on the two main functions that the ROL serves':[64] to protect anyone from both private individuals and arbitrary and unfair state authority.[65]

Bingham divides the ROL into eight core principles, which I group into five to simplify the analysis (while acknowledging that others have proposed more or fewer sub-rules).[66]

(1) **Legality**: Public authorities must be authorised by law and act according to the law (including procedural and substantive law, human rights, and international law).[67] Public authorities must 'exercise the powers conferred on them reasonably, in good faith, for the purpose for which the powers were conferred, and without exceeding the limits of such powers'.[68] This principle, considered 'as the core of the rule of law',[69] involves the separation of powers in modern democracies. Only in extraordinary circumstances

[62] The notion of ROL finds one of its origins in Roman jurisprudence, which conceives it as a universal value – this is closer to the ROL concept found in civil law countries. By contrast, '[t]he uncodified English common law offered an alternative notation of law, in some ways more flexible [in its availability to different interests] as a medium through which social conflict could find expression, especially where the sense of "natural justice" of the jury could make itself felt'. E Palmer Thompson, *Whigs and Hunters: The Origin of the Black Act* (Harmondsworth, Penguin, 1977) 209. As Palmer Thompson puts it, the common law tradition historically developed in a way that favoured not only those in power, but also placed 'inhibitions upon power' through law, which gave rise to 'the notion of the regulation and reconciliation of conflicts through the rule of law – and the elaboration of rules and procedures which, on occasion, made some approximate approach towards the ideal'; ibid 207.

[63] The notions of ROL in common law systems and continental countries are nowadays often used interchangeably. Bedner (n 10) 50. See also, P Costa and D Zolo, *Lo Stato di Diritto: Storia, Teoria, Critica* (Milano, Feltrinelli, 2002); Zagrebelsky (n 50); G Silvestri, 'Lo Stato di Diritto nel XXI Secolo' (2011) 2 *Associazione Italiana dei Costituzionalisti* 1. A detailed discussion on the historical meaning of ROL in the common law and civil law traditions is outside the scope of this study. For a historical distinction between the two concepts of ROL in common law and civil law jurisdictions, see, eg, N Barber, 'The Rechtsstaat and the Rule of Law' (2003) 53 *University of Toronto Law Journal* 443.

[64] Bedner (n 10) 50.

[65] The reason for including protection from fellow citizens is that human rights have become increasingly important in relations between private citizens, not only between states and individuals; ibid 50–51.

[66] In addition to those that I have adopted, Bingham adds that 'questions of legal right and liability should ordinarily be resolved by application of the law and not the exercise of discretion'. Bingham, 'The Rule of Law' (n 4) 72. However, I have decided to cluster this under the principle of legality for the sake of simplicity. Furthermore, Bingham also acknowledges the principle that 'means must be provided for resolving, without prohibitive cost or inordinate delay, bona fide civil disputes which the parties themselves are unable to resolve'; ibid 77. Nevertheless, I consider this a corollary of the legality as well as of the access to justice principles. See also, Bedner (n 10) 54; Tamanaha, *On the Rule of Law: History, Politics, Theory* (n 10) 91, 93; Peerenboom, 'Varieties of Rule of Law' (n 61) 1.

[67] Venice Commission (n 16) 11–12; Bingham, 'The Rule of Law' (n 4) 82.

[68] Bingham, 'The Rule of Law' (n 4) 72, 77–78.

[69] ibid 77–78.

can public authorities derogate from this principle.[70] It also involves that those public authorities' discretionary power be constrained in specific, predictable, and transparent ways – in part through the principle of legal certainty.[71]

(2) **Legal Certainty**: This means that '[t]he law must be accessible and, so far as possible, be intelligible, clear and predictable'.[72] The law must also be general rather than in the form of individual decrees (the latter is frequently referred to as 'rule by exception').[73] Any person must be easily able to understand (even if with the support of legal advice, which must be accessible) and foresee[74] the consequences of the law so as to be able to act accordingly.[75] To this end, legislation and executive action must be stable and consistent[76] – in other words, legislation, rules and decisions 'should be adopted by the bodies that are constitutionally competent to do so and must be accessible, clear, intelligible and predictable, as well as respectful of the hierarchy of norms recognised by the Constitution and/or precedent'.[77]

(3) **Equality and Non-Discrimination**: The law 'should apply equally to all', unless 'objective differences justify differentiation'.[78] Legislative exceptions can be made only in some objective circumstances for some categories of people (such as children, people with disabilities, and non-nationals)[79] based on their special situations or qualities and to pursue a legitimate aim. Furthermore, in case of exceptions, the principle of proportionality must be complied with.

(4) **Access to Justice**:[80] This means that adjudicative procedures must be fair and provide effective protection and remedies by ensuring adjudicators

[70] Venice Commission (n 16) 12; Bingham, 'The Rule of Law' (n 4) 78.

[71] Bedner (n 10) 59.

[72] Bingham, 'The Rule of Law' (n 4) 69; McCorquodale, 'The Rule of Law and Migration' (n 5) 2; *Nejdet Sahin and Perihan Sahin v Turkey* App no 13279/05 (ECtHR, 20 October 2011) para 56.

[73] Bedner (n 10) 57.

[74] HS Richardson, 'Administrative Policy-making: Rule of Law or Bureaucracy?' in D Dyzenhaus (ed), *Recrafting the Rule of Law: The Limits of the Legal Order* (Oxford, Hart Publishing, 1999) 310.

[75] This principle is relevant in cases involving complex and voluminous legislative instruments, as well as lengthy and inaccessible judicial decisions. Bingham, 'The Rule of Law' (n 4) 70. Bingham states that the ECtHR has stressed this principle in the case of *The Sunday Times v United Kingdom* App no 6538/74 (ECtHR, 6 April 1979) para 49.

[76] Venice Commission (n 16) 16.

[77] K Nicolaidis and R Kleinfeld, 'Rethinking Europe's "Rule of Law" and Enlargement Agenda: The Fundamental Dilemma' (SIGMA Papers no 49, OECD 2012) 37.

[78] Bingham, 'The Rule of Law' (n 4) 73–74; Venice Commission (n 16) 18–19; see also ECHR, Art 14; Protocol 12 ECHR; Charter of Fundamental Rights of the European Union, Arts 20, 21; ICCPR, Arts 12, 26.

[79] See International Convention on the Elimination of All Forms of Racial Discrimination (New York, 21 December 1965) 660 UNTS 185 (CERD) Arts 1.4, 2.2; Convention on the Elimination of All Forms of Discrimination against Women (New York, 18 December 1979) 1249 UNTS 49 (CEDAW) Art 4; Convention on the Rights of Persons with Disabilities (New York, 12 December 2006) 2515 UNTS 3 (CRPD) Art 5.4; Bingham, 'The Rule of Law' (n 4) 73–74.

[80] Venice Commission (n 16) 20–28; Bingham, 'The Rule of (n 4) 80.

who are independent (free from external influence and deciding only on the basis of the facts and the law) and impartial[81] ('unbiased by any personal interest or partisan allegiance').[82] Although I will focus only on this aspect of access to justice, it should be noted that the following widely recognised essential principles must also be guaranteed and are important factors to consider in future studies: the right to be heard; the right of a person to be informed of the liability or charges against them; the right to be informed of damaging evidence and to present evidence; legal aid where a party's interests could not be protected otherwise;[83] and in criminal proceedings, the presumption of innocence 'until guilt is proved'.[84]

(5) **Legal Protection of Fundamental Human Rights:**[85] Legal protection of fundamental human rights must be ensured.[86] Though there are different views on the standards of human rights that shall be universally protected,[87] Bingham points out that the ROL demands 'legal protection of such human rights as, within that society, are seen as fundamental',[88] including, for example, the right to life, the prohibition of inhuman and degrading treatment, and freedom from discrimination.[89] Furthermore, the ROL and some human rights overlap (eg, the right to a fair trial).[90] In the field of refugee law, there is agreement that the Refugee Convention and its 1967 Protocol are included.[91]

Whereas I acknowledge that the catalogue of rights included in most substantive approaches to the ROL is wider, I will pay particular attention to the following rights – those that from a review of the literature appear as the most debated and at risk in the context of sea migration: the right to life; the principle of non-refoulement;[92] the prohibition of torture, inhuman and degrading treatment; the right to seek asylum; and the prohibition of arbitrary detention.[93]

[81] ECHR, Art 6.1; ICCPR, Art 14.1.

[82] Bingham, 'The Rule of Law' (n 4) 80.

[83] ECHR, Art 6.3 b–c; ICCPR, Art 14.3; Bingham, 'The Rule of Law' (n 4) 80.

[84] Bingham, 'The Rule of Law' (n 4) 81; ECHR, Art 6.2; ICCPR, Art 15.

[85] Bingham, 'The Rule of Law' (n 4) 77.

[86] McCorquodale, 'The Rule of Law and Migration' (n 5) 2.

[87] For analysis of the differing approaches, see A Quintavalla and K Heine, 'Priorities and Human Rights' (2019) 23 *International Journal of Human Rights* 679.

[88] Bingham, 'The Rule of Law' (n 4) 77.

[89] McCorquodale argues that a number of human rights are included in the ROL, but including 'all human rights in the rule of law would blur the difference between the rule of law and human rights, when they are distinct ideas'. McCorquodale, 'Defining the International Rule of Law: Defying Gravity' (n 10) 283.

[90] Venice Commission (n 16) 9.

[91] Very few scholars have addressed the content of the international ROL as applied to refugees and asylum seekers. Among them, see for instance Kneebone's work discussing the relevant content of the ROL in national systems for refugees. Kneebone (n 31).

[92] See ch 1, section V.

[93] As the scholarship has already broadly discussed the Italian implementation of the Refugee Convention and the major human rights treaties, I will not analyse it further. See, eg, Centro di

Clearly, the ROL elements that I have selected, especially the substantive ones, can be subject to several qualifiers. However, such elements have received widespread acceptance, as confirmed by the academic literature,[94] EU institutions,[95] and the case law of the two European Courts.[96] Additionally, the focus of this study is not to critically analyse them, but rather to apply them to determine which legislation, policies, procedures and practices weaken the ROL as an instrument for fulfilling various tasks such as good governance, abiding by certain quality standards for legislation, and prevention of state and private actors' abuses and illegal practices. The conclusion in chapter seven will nevertheless reflect on the adequacy of the concept and elements of ROL as applied to the responses to sea migration, and on whether there is anything they fall short of doing or accounting for: in other words, how do the chosen data and analysis raise new challenges?

Ateneo per i Diritti Umani Antonio Papisca, Università di Padova, *Annuario Italiano dei Diritti Umani 2021* (Padova, Padova University Press, 2022); Centro di Ateneo per i Diritti Umani Antonio Papisca, Università di Padova, 'Il Diritto d'Asilo: i Sistemi di Protezione dei Richiedenti Asilo e dei Rifugiati' (Center for Human Rights 'Antonio Papisca' University, 24 November 2015), available at: unipd-centrodirittiumani.it/it/dossier/Il-diritto-dasilo-i-sistemi-di-protezione-dei-richiedenti-asilo-e-dei-rifugiati/26 (see further publications within the same website); M Odello, *Il Diritto dei Rifugiati: Elementi di Diritto Internazionale, Europeo e Italiano* (Milano, FrancoAngeli, 2021); A Marchesi, *La Protezione Internazionale dei Diritti Umani* (Torino, Giappichelli, 2021); R Pisillo Mazzeschi, *Diritto Internazionale dei Diritti Umani: Teoria e Prassi* (Torino, Giappichelli, 2020); S Tonolo and G Pascale, *La Dichiarazione Universale dei Diritti Umani nel Diritto Internazionale Contemporaneo* (Torino, Giappichelli, 2020); A di Blase, G Bartolini and M Sossai, *Diritto Internazionale e Valori Umanitari* (Roma, RomaTrE-Press, 2019).

[94] See, eg, Bedner (n 10); A Venn Dicey, *Introduction to the Study of the Law of the Constitution*, 9th edn (London, Macmillan, 1939); Fuller (n 14); Kneebone (n 31); FL Gatta, 'Migration and the Rule of (Human Rights) Law: Two "Crises" Looking in the Same Mirror' (2019) 15(1) *Croatian Yearbook of European Law & Policy* 99; A Magen and L Morlino, *International Actors, Democratization, and the Rule of Law: Anchoring Democracy?* (Abingdon, Routledge, 2008); UN Human Rights Regional Office for Europe (n 53); United Nations, *The United Nations Rule of Law Indicators. Implementation Guide and Project Tools* (United Nations, 2011), available at: www.un.org/ruleoflaw/blog/document/the-united-nations-rule-of-law-indicators-implementation-guide-and-project-tools/.

[95] See section III of this chapter.

[96] Although the two courts do not refer to the work of Bingham, they embrace the core principles of his definition. The ECJ referred for the first time to the European Community being based on the ROL in the landmark case Case 294/83 *Parti écologiste 'Les Verts' v European Parliament* [1986] ECR 1986-01339. In this case, the Court specified that ROL means that 'neither its Member States nor its institutions can avoid a review of the question whether the measures adopted by them are in conformity with the basic constitutional charter, the Treaty … [which] established a complete system of legal remedies and procedures designed to permit the Court of Justice to review the legality of measures adopted by the institutions', para 23. According to Spielmann, 'It is thus a Union based on the rule of law as a result of the primacy of EU law, which is binding on the Union's own institutions, but also on those of the Member States'. D Spielmann, 'The Rule of Law Principle in the Jurisprudence of the Court of Justice of the European Union' in M Elósegui, A Miron and I Motoc (eds), *The Rule of Law in Europe: Recent Challenges and Judicial Responses* (Berlin, Springer International Publishing, 2021) 7. See also Case 64/16 *Associação Sindical dos Juízes Portugueses* [2018], EU:C:2018:117, para 2; L Pech and D Kochenov, 'Respect for the Rule of Law in the Case Law of the European Court of Justice: A Casebook Overview of Key Judgements since the Portuguese Judges Cases' (Report no 3, Swedish Institute for European Policy Studies, September 2021).

V. LIMITATIONS OF THE ADOPTED ROL APPROACH

In this book, I focus on those aspects of the national ROL dimension that are most relevant to analysing responses to sea migration. As Kneebone has pointed out, the emphasis on the national ROL provides a clear picture of how the law operates, given that international law is subject to implementation at the national level.[97] Moreover, the choice of adopting a national ROL perspective has the advantage, as Bedner has argued, that some of the different views and convoluted debates on the ROL can be reconciled.[98]

This is not to say that the ROL at the EU level is irrelevant to the issue, but such a perspective could add more unnecessary complexity to the framework. I acknowledge that some have questioned the appropriateness of using the ROL concept, but I do not wish to engage in a more theoretical discussion on its limitations. While I recognise and concur with those scholars who have raised concerns about the ROL idea as being a Western world-view or a way of imposing a particular form of democracy or political order on all states,[99] this debate seems to be more suitable when researching conceptions of the ROL outside the European context. Furthermore, I start from the premise that the ROL should not be seen as universal, but based on the generally accepted principles[100] that I discussed above.[101]

Additionally, I recognise that some authors have criticised empirical studies of the ROL, including those of the Venice Commission, because most of them are based on the views of lawyers and experts.[102] As a result, empirical studies on the ROL fail to take into account the opinions of other actors and the general public.[103] To partially deal with this criticism, the empirical data of this book will include interviews of different actors, such as representatives of the shipping industry and NGOs, alongside legal experts. Interviews with diverse stakeholders have become a significant method in legal research and have been proven to facilitate a better comprehension of legal issues and social

[97] Kneebone (n 31) 1–2.

[98] However, it is acknowledged that national legal systems, even within the EU, also provide different ROL definitions. Bedner (n 10) 49.

[99] R Peerenboom, 'Let One Hundred Flowers Bloom, One Hundred Schools Contend: Debating Rule of Law in China' (2002) 23 *Michigan Journal of International Law* 471, 473; Peerenboom, 'Varieties of Rule of Law' (n 61); Waldron (n 11) 139; R Ehrenreich Brooks, 'The New Imperialism: Violence, Norms and the "Rule of Law"' (2003) 101 *Michigan Law Review* 2275, 2322.

[100] B Faedda, 'Introduction' in B Faedda (ed), *The Rule of Law: Cases, Strategies and Interpretations* (Vicenza, Ronzani Edizioni Scientifiche, 2021) 17.

[101] ibid.

[102] Hertogh (n 45) 55–56; S Golub, 'Beyond Rule of Law Orthodoxy: The Legal Empowerment Alternative' (Working Papers no 41, Carnegie Endowment for International Peace, 2003) 3; Versteeg and Ginsburg (n 24).

[103] Nicolaidis and Kleinfeld (n 77).

phenomena.[104] However, the interviewees were not asked to present their views on the ROL principles discussed in this book and how they are being implemented, but only to provide information or clarification on relevant pieces of legislation, judicial decisions, policies and practices.

VI. CONCLUSION

In this chapter, I have discussed the meaning and relevance of the ROL concept and provided an overview of the relevant debates. I have explained Bingham's definition of the ROL, which I adopt to study the responses to sea migration, and shown how, drawing on his view and the work of the Venice Commission, I have broken down the ROL concept into its elements.

In the next chapters, I apply this analytical and normative framework to the main thematic issues arising in sea migration. My hope is that this approach can contribute to locating and organising information on legislation, policies and practices, as well as demonstrating its relevance for ensuring guarantees and protection that are currently lacking. Given the scope of the book, I do not attempt to treat any of the ROL elements exhaustively, and only offer a general idea of how they operate in the context of the responses to sea migration. This will help to better understand the challenges and the way forward. Overall, the book will disclose how the protection of sea migrants, from an ROL perspective, places more demanding requirements on states than does the mere protection of human rights.

[104] See, eg, L Webley, 'Qualitative Approaches to Empirical Legal Research' in P Cane and H Kritzer (eds), *Oxford Handbook of Empirical Legal Research* (Oxford, OUP, 2010); U Jaremba and E Mak, 'Interviewing Judges in the Transnational Context' (May 2014) *Law and Method* 1, available at: www.lawandmethod.nl/tijdschrift/lawandmethod/2014/05/RENM-D-13-00002/full-screen; E Korkea-aho and P Leino, 'Interviewing Lawyers: A Critical Self-Reflection on Expert Interviews as a Method of EU Legal Research' (2019) 12 *European Journal of Legal Studies* 17.

3

International and EU Legal Frameworks Relevant to Sea Migration

I. INTRODUCTION

IN THIS CHAPTER I explain the international and European Union (EU) regulatory frameworks, which shape the national legal responses to sea migration. In particular, I highlight gaps, ambiguities and contradictions of the relevant legal provisions which affect the principle of legal certainty at the international, EU and national levels.

First, I give an explanation of the international provisions on the obligation of states and private actors to save lives in danger at sea (section II). I also discuss the related EU framework and its connection to Frontex's activities (section III). Second, I analyse the international and EU legislation on human trafficking and smuggling (sections IV and V), as it is often used as a justification for carrying out interceptions of sea migrants. Moreover, this legislation constitutes the basis for criminalising humanitarian help at the national level.[1] Third, I discuss the framework on port state control (which is focused on safety of navigation), as it has also been used to limit non-governmental organisation (NGO) activities in the Mediterranean (section VI). Finally, I conclude with some reflections on the strengths and weaknesses of the discussed framework (section VII). Whereas the book focuses on the case study of Italy, this chapter provides the background to understand the wider international and regional context and thus applies to all EU Member States.

II. THE INTERNATIONAL REGULATORY FRAMEWORK ON SEARCH AND RESCUE (SAR)

The custom of sailors helping those in need stems from a maritime history with humanitarian roots.[2] With time this practice became an obligation of

[1] See ch 6.

[2] SF Friedell, 'Compensation and Reward for Saving Life at Sea' (1979) 77 *Michigan Law Review* 1218.

international customary law.[3] In the twentieth century, the obligation to provide assistance to persons and ships in distress at sea was more precisely defined in international treaties. The most important of such treaties are the Convention for the Safety of Life at Sea of 1974 (SOLAS),[4] the UN Convention on the Law of the Sea of 1982 (UNCLOS),[5] the International Convention on Search and Rescue of 1979 (SAR),[6] and the International Convention on Salvage of 1989 (Salvage Convention).[7] In the next sections, I summarise their main provisions and focus on those creating legal uncertainty, especially with regard to the unforeseen phenomenon of overcrowded migrant vessels heading for European coasts from North Africa.

A. Obligations of Coastal States to Provide Assistance and Carry Out SAR

The international legal framework imposes *the obligation on coastal states to provide assistance to persons in distress at sea*. To this end, UNCLOS requires contracting coastal states to 'promote the establishment, operation and maintenance of an adequate and effective search and rescue service regarding safety on and over the sea and, where circumstances so require, by way of mutual arrangements cooperate with neighbouring States for this purpose'.[8]

In order to prevent issues regarding which state is responsible for search and rescue (SAR) services, the SAR Convention additionally mandates states to set up Rescue Coordination Centres (RCCs) to monitor distress signals and conduct rescue responses within their SAR zone[9] – primarily in their coastal waters, and where appropriate in the high seas.[10] Thus, state parties must establish SAR

[3] Customary international law derives from 'a general and consistent practice of states followed by them from a sense of legal obligation'. Restatement of the Law, Third, Foreign Relations Law of the United States (1987) s 102(2); JL Goldsmith and EA Posner, 'A Theory of Customary International Law' (1999) 66 *University of Chicago Law Review* 1113.

[4] International Convention for the Safety of Life at Sea (London, 1 November 1974) 1184 UNTS 278 (SOLAS Convention) ch V, reg 33.1.

[5] United Nations Convention on the Law of the Sea (Montego Bay, 10 December 1982) UN Doc A/CONF 1833 UNTS 397 (UNCLOS Convention) art 98.

[6] International Convention on Maritime Search and Rescue (Hamburg, 27 April 1979) 1405 UNTS 97 (SAR Convention).

[7] International Convention on Salvage (London, 28 April 1989) 1953 UNTS 165 (Salvage Convention).

[8] UNCLOS Convention (n 5) art 98(2).

[9] A SAR zone 'is an area of defined dimensions associated with a rescue coordination centre (RCC) within which SAR services are provided'. International Maritime Organization and International Civil Aviation Organization, 'IAMSAR Manual', Volume III, 1–3 (2016). See also, RL Kilpatrick, 'The "Refugee Clause": Why Contractual Allocation of Rescue Costs is Critical during Periods of Mass Migration at Sea' (NUS Centre for Maritime Law Working Paper no 17/09, National University of Singapore, October 2017) 5.

[10] SAR Convention (n 6) Annex, ch 2, para 2.1.3. It should be noted that state parties to the SAR Convention have a unilateral right to declare a SAR region and must notify the IMO of such a decision. SAR Convention, Annex, para 2.1.4. ÁJ García-Carriazo, 'Small Island, Big Issue: Malta and

zones in agreement with other states and notify the International Maritime Organization (IMO) of such decisions.[11] States may establish joint SAR zones in cooperation with other states,[12] but should avoid having overlapping SAR regions.[13]

The SAR Convention does not specify how extended SAR regions shall be, but it states that there must be a proportionate relationship between the area of the SAR and the capacity to guarantee continuous and effective operation of SAR services.[14] In particular, states undertaking to establish an RCC shall designate coastal rescue units and provide naval vessels, rescue telecommunication centres and trained personnel. Also, the SAR Convention recognises that a SAR service, to be effective, must be specifically implemented through legal provisions at the national level.[15] However, the obligation to provide assistance to vessels in distress within a state's SAR zone is not an obligation of result but of due diligence, meaning that the state must use its best efforts.

The SOLAS, SAR and UNCLOS Conventions stress the importance of establishing *cooperation duties among coastal states* in order to save human lives at sea. In particular, SOLAS requires states to organise communication and coordination mechanisms to rescue people in distress around their coasts.[16] UNCLOS adds that, whenever necessary, coastal states shall collaborate through regional agreements.[17] The SAR Convention repeats that states have to promote the coordination of their SAR activities, and where concrete circumstances so require, they shall organise joint rescue services with neighbouring states.[18] In case of emergency, the state responsible for the SAR area shall immediately authorise the entry of foreign rescue units into its territorial sea. In such situations, 'search and rescue operations shall, as far as practicable, be co-ordinated by the appropriate rescue co-ordination centre of the Party which has authorised entry, or such other authority as has been designated by that Party'.[19]

The SAR Convention distinguishes among different emergency phases to assist the RCCs in determining which response to adopt when intercepting a vessel in distress: uncertainty, alert and distress phases.[20] In particular, it defines

Its Search and Rescue Region' (2019) 7 *Paix et Securité Internationales* 299, 301; I Papanicolopulu, 'The Duty to Rescue at Sea, in Peacetime and in War: A General Overview' (2016) 98 *International Review of the Red Cross* 491, 499.

[11] SAR Convention (n 6) Annex, ch 2, paras 2.1.4, 2.1.5 and 2.1.12.

[12] SAR Convention (n 6) Annex, ch 2, paras 2.1.6; 3.1.1.

[13] SAR Convention (n 6) Annex, ch 2, para 2.1.3.

[14] SAR Convention (n 6) Annex, ch 2, para 2.1.3.

[15] SAR Convention (n 6) Annex, ch 3, para 3.1.2; U Leanza and F Caffio, 'Il SAR Mediterraneo. La Ricerca e Soccorso nel Diritto Marittimo: l'Applicazione della Convenzione di Amburgo del 1979' (2015) 12 *Rivista Marittima* 10.

[16] SOLAS Convention (n 4) ch 5, Art 7.

[17] UNCLOS Convention (n 5) art 98.

[18] SAR Convention (n 6) Annex, ch 3, para 3.1.1.

[19] SAR Convention (n 6) Annex, ch 3, para 3.1.2.

[20] SAR Convention (n 6) Annex, ch 4, para 4.4.

'distress phase' as a 'situation wherein there is reasonable certainty that a person, a vessel or other craft is threatened by grave and imminent danger and requires immediate assistance'.[21] The distress phase is the one which triggers states' and shipmasters' obligations to rescue. However, the SAR Convention does not provide any guidance on how to determine when the situation of distress starts and ends.

Finally, it is important to say a few words on the geographical extension of a coastal state jurisdiction, which in the context of sea migration is particularly relevant to establish the application of human rights treaties. The creation of a SAR zone geographically defines an area where coastal states have responsibilities but not corresponding rights, which are limited to internal waters, the territorial sea, the contiguous zone, the exclusive economic area, and the continental platform.[22] Therefore, a SAR zone is not entirely under the sovereignty or territorial jurisdiction of the coastal state of reference. It remains disputed whether a state can be found to exercise extraterritorial jurisdiction in its SAR area given that jurisdiction is linked to an assessment of the particular facts at stake.[23] In chapters four, five and seven, I will discuss how this issue has been addressed, in light of concrete cases, by judicial and UN bodies and how it may affect access to justice.

B. Rescue Obligations on Private Vessels

While subsidiary to state obligations, the SAR Convention as well as the Salvage[24] *and SOLAS Conventions*[25] *impose similar rescue obligations on any private ship that happens to navigate near an endangered vessel.*[26] In particular, SOLAS specifies that the master of any ship is under the duty to render assistance to persons in danger at sea and 'to proceed with all speed'[27] to the rescue

[21] SAR Convention (n 6) Annex, ch 3, para 1.3.13.

[22] For an explanation of these different sea areas, where states enjoy specific rights, see Glossary. See also T Gammeltoft-Hansen and T Aalberts, 'Sovereignty at Sea: The Law and Politics of Saving Lives in Mare Liberum' (2014) 17 *Journal of International Relations & Development* 439, 445; I Papanicolopulu, 'Le Operazioni di Search and Rescue: Problemi e Lacune del Diritto Internazionale' (2019) 2 *Rivista Trimestrale di Diritto Pubblico* 507, 513.

[23] See ch 7, section V.A. Moreover, Papanicolopulu points out that the concept of extraterritorial jurisdiction has always been very circumscribed because exceptions could weaken the sovereignty of another state. In the case of the extraterritorial sea, there is no exception to the concept of jurisdiction, as there is no sovereign state. Therefore, the debate should focus on trying to find some criteria to establish jurisdiction at sea even if there are no sovereign states. Interview with Irini Papanicolopulu, Professor of International Law, SOLAS University of London (online, 10 May 2023).

[24] Salvage Convention (n 7) art 10.

[25] SOLAS Convention (n 4) ch V, reg 10(a) 33.1.

[26] SAR Convention (n 6) Annex, ch 2, para 2.1.9; Kilpatrick (n 9) 6.

[27] SOLAS Convention (n 4) ch V, reg 10(a) 33.1. This shipmaster duty is similarly defined by international instruments governing marine salvage, including both the Convention for the Unification of Certain Rules with Respect to Assistance and Salvage at Sea (Brussels, 23 September 1910) (Brussels

of such persons. However, the ship master is only required to save someone else if doing so will not put his boat, his crew, or his passengers at risk,[28] for instance if the weather conditions do not allow it.

To make this obligation effective, UNCLOS *obliges contracting states* '*to enforce private shipmaster obligations*'[29] by 'requiring' the *master of ships flying their flag* 'to render assistance to any person found at sea in danger of being lost' and 'to proceed with all possible speed to the rescue of persons in distress, if informed of their need for assistance'.[30] The duty to assist persons in distress is commonly applied 'in all maritime zones',[31] although it is included in the part of UNCLOS on high seas. The Salvage Convention similarly requires state parties to 'adopt measures necessary to enforce' the shipmaster's duty to render assistance.[32]

Importantly, the duty to render assistance to those in peril at sea allows for no distinction between different types of people in distress, such as between irregular migrants and nationals, or between those purposefully or accidentally put into a distress situation.[33]

C. States' Duties of Coordination and Cooperation to Ensure Disembarkation of Rescued Vessels to a Place of Safety (POS)

According to the 2004 amendments to the SOLAS and SAR Conventions,[34] which became effective on 1 July 2006, *states' duty* to provide assistance not only requires carrying out rescue operations but also to disembark the rescued persons in a 'place of safety' within a reasonable time.[35] They add that *the primary responsibility to ensure coordination and cooperation among states in order to provide a place of safety to the survivors rests with the state responsible*

Convention) and the more recent Salvage Convention. Article 11 of the Brussels Convention reads, 'Every master is bound, so far as he can do so without serious danger to his vessel, her crew and her passengers, to render assistance to everybody, even though an enemy, found at sea in danger of being lost'.

[28] SOLAS Convention (n 4) ch V, reg 10.

[29] Kilpatrick (n 9) 5.

[30] UNCLOS (n 5) art 98(1).

[31] García-Carriazo (n 10) ft 3 at 300, also citing AT Gallagher and F David, *The International Law of Migrant Smuggling* (Cambridge, CUP, 2014) 447.

[32] Salvage Convention (n 7) art 10.

[33] SAR Convention (n 6) Annex, ch 2, para 2.1.10.

[34] IMO's Resolution MSC.153 (78) modified the SOLAS Convention; IMO's Resolution MSC.155 (78) modified the SAR Convention.

[35] Adoption of Amendments to the International Convention on Maritime Search and Rescue, 1979, as amended, MSC Res.155(78), 78th sess, Agenda Item 26, IMO Doc MSC 78/26/Add.1 annex 5 (4 June 2004, adopted 20 May 2004) (2004 Amendments to the SAR Convention) Annex, ch 3, para 3.1.9; Adoption of Amendments to the International Convention on Safety of Lives at Sea, 1974, as amended, MSC Res.153(78), 78th sess, Agenda Item 26, IMO Doc MSC 78/26/Add.1 (4 June 2004, adopted 20 May 2004) (2004 Amendments to the SOLAS Convention) Annex, ch V, reg 33.4 (1–1).

for the SAR region where the persons were rescued, in light of the circumstances of the case and the guidelines of the IMO.[36]

However, *the absence of a predetermined rule designating which state shall receive the rescued persons* is a serious gap which creates tensions among coastal states when the rescued persons are irregular migrants. For instance, it is debated whether it is the 'state of nationality or departure, the flag state or the state'[37] from which the ship departed – especially if SAR areas overlap, as in the case of Italy and Malta,[38] or if a rescue has been carried out by private actors in international waters. In particular, there is no provision clarifying that, in case of failure to reach an agreement, 'people saved should be disembarked in the State responsible for the SAR zone'.[39] This is regrettable, as

> disembarkation of rescued people is often a matter of urgency, because the vessel that has saved them may be overcrowded, may not have the necessary food and facilities to host them, and may also not have an interest in not delaying its voyage any further.[40]

The Conventions also do not specify what 'place of safety' (POS) means, and only indicate that the obligation must be carried out in light of the 'particular circumstances of the case'.[41] The IMO's International Aeronautical and Maritime Search and Rescue Manual (IAMSAR Manual) adopted in 1999[42] and the IMO Guidelines on the Treatment of Persons Rescued at Sea (2004 IMO Guidelines) provide some guidance in this regard, although they are not binding.[43]

In particular, according to both the IAMSAR Manual and the 2004 IMO Guidelines, it is expected that the first RCC to receive information of a possible SAR emergency situation is responsible for taking the first immediate actions and coordination efforts to manage the situation, even if the event is outside its specific area of responsibility. Until an RCC capable of handling the situation in the region or otherwise able to offer more sufficient assistance takes official responsibility, the first RCC to arrive close to the scene of the SAR event shall undertake coordinating responsibilities.[44]

[36] 2004 Amendments to SAR Convention (n 35) Annex, ch 3, para 3.1.9. The IMO is the UN Agency responsible for regulating shipping. See IMO, 'About IMO' (IMO, 2019), available at: www.imo.org/en/About/Pages/Default.aspx.

[37] A Radjenovic, 'Search and Rescue in the Mediterranean' (Briefing, European Parliament Research Service, January 2021).

[38] Interview with Italian Coast Guard Official (email, 28 June 2023); see ch 4, section III.A.

[39] Papanicolopulu, 'The Duty to Rescue at Sea, in Peacetime and in War: A General Overview' (n 10) 501.

[40] ibid 503.

[41] 2004 Amendments to SAR Convention (n 35) Annex, ch 3, para 3.1.9.

[42] The IAMSAR Manual, published by the IMO and the International Civil Aviation Organization in 1999, provides guidance for setting up and providing SAR services. See IMO, 'IAMSAR Manual' (n 9).

[43] García-Carriazo (n 10) 318.

[44] IAMSAR Manual (n 9) s 3.1; Maritime Safety Committee, Guidelines on the Treatment of Persons Rescued at Sea, UN Doc MSC78/26/Add.2, Resolution MSC167(78) (20 May 2004) (2004

Regarding the meaning of 'place of safety', the 2004 IMO Guidelines refer to

> a location where rescue operations are considered to terminate. It is also a place where the survivors' safety of life is no longer threatened and where their basic human needs (such as food, shelter, and medical needs) can be met. Further, it is a place from which transportation arrangements can be made for the survivors' next or final destination.[45]

This is particularly important if the rescued persons are refugees, as the principle of non-refoulement prohibits the rescue boat from disembarking them to a place where they could face a serious threat to life or freedom. Moreover, the 2004 IMO Guidelines recommend that 'the situation on board the assisting ship, on scene conditions, medical needs, and availability of transportation or other rescue units'[46] shall also be taken into account.

However, there is no implied right of entry into the territory or of access to the ports of the state. 'A vessel that wants to disembark people rescued at sea into the ports of a State must have the consent of that State for entering into the port'.[47] The discussed provisions only require the coastal state to complete the rescue operation,[48] as confirmed by the IMO's Principles Relating to Administrative Procedures for Disembarking Persons Rescued at Sea, which state that:

> If disembarkation from the rescuing ship cannot be arranged swiftly elsewhere, the Government responsible for the SAR area should accept the disembarkation of the persons rescued in accordance with immigration laws and regulations of each Member State into a place of safety under its control in which the persons rescued can have timely access to post rescue support.[49]

The IMO Guidelines further suggest that 'even though a vessel may serve as a temporary "place of safety" the rescuer may also be obliged to facilitate disembarkation to the next land of destination'.[50] The rescuer may need to consider

IMO Guidelines) s 6.7. The IMO Maritime Safety Committee established these guidelines in response to IMO Assembly Resolution A.920(22), which required a review of safety measures and protocols for the care of those rescued at sea with the goal of identifying 'any gaps, inconsistencies, ambiguities, vagueness or other inadequacies associate with the treatment of person rescued at sea'; ibid s 6.15.

[45] 2004 IMO Guidelines (n 44) s 6.12.

[46] ibid s 6.10.

[47] Papanicolopulu, 'The Duty to Rescue at Sea, in Peacetime and in War: a General Overview' (n 10) 500.

[48] S Trevisanut, 'Search and Rescue Operations in the Mediterranean: Factor of Cooperation or Conflict?' (2010) 25 *International Journal of Marine and Coastal Law* 523, 530.

[49] International Maritime Organization (IMO), Principles Relating to Administrative Procedures for Disembarking Persons Rescued at Sea, FAL.3/Circ. 194 (22 January 2009) Principle 2.3.

[50] RL Kilpatrick and A Smith, 'The International Legal Obligation to Rescue During Mass Migration at Sea: Navigating the Sovereign and Commercial Dimensions of a Mediterranean Crisis' (2015) 28(2) *University of San Francisco School of Law Maritime Law Journal* 141, 147; 2004 IMO Guidelines (n 44) s 6.12–6.14.

factors other than the immediate local situation in order to determine whether the destination country is a secure one,[51] having regard to the characteristics of the place of disembarkation and the rescued persons.[52]

One additional important point to highlight is that the discussed provisions do not impose the obligation to disembark in a place of safety on private actors, although 'an RCC may request that they coordinate in facilitating such enquiries'.[53] Nevertheless, according to Kilpatrick and Smith, when private actors engage in rescues,

> there is at least an implied expectation that they are bound by the same legal principles underpinning the global SAR regime … In the case of NGOs in particular … through the lens of international law they are bound to coordinate under the authority of the RCCs at issue, especially in determining a safe place of disembarkation which would require consent by some coastal state authority.[54]

In practice, as shown in the next chapters, major controversies remain regarding the interpretation of which state is responsible for carrying out rescue operations, which duties exist in terms of disembarkation, and where disembarkation shall take place.[55] Accordingly, implementation of this framework 'remain[s] relatively fragmented'.[56]

III. SAR OPERATIONS UNDER THE EU FRAMEWORK

Search and rescue operations remain mostly within the competence of each Member State, except for those related to Frontex's border surveillance programme, which are set out in Regulation 2019/1896,[57] the Schengen Borders Code (SBC),[58] and

[51] Kilpatrick and Smith, 'The International Legal Obligation to Rescue During Mass Migration at Sea' (n 50) 147; 2004 IMO Guidelines (n 44) s 6.15–6.18.

[52] Kilpatrick and Smith, 'The International Legal Obligation to Rescue During Mass Migration at Sea' (n 50) 148; 2004 IMO Guidelines (n 44) s 6.15–6.18.

[53] RL Kilpatrick and A Smith, 'Balancing the SAR Responsibilities of States and Shipmasters' in V Mitsilegas, V Moreno-Lax and N Vavoula (eds), *Securitising Asylum Flows: Deflection, Criminalisation and Challenges for Human Rights* (Leiden, Brill/Nijhoff, 2020) 86.

[54] The 2004 Amendments to the SAR Convention point out that state parties 'shall co-ordinate and co-operate to ensure that masters of ships providing assistance by embarking persons in distress at sea are released from their obligations with minimum further deviation from the ships' intended voyage'; ibid 86–87.

[55] García-Carriazo (n 10) 318.

[56] Kilpatrick and Smith, 'Balancing the SAR Responsibilities of States and Shipmasters' (n 53) 85.

[57] Regulation (EU) 2019/1896 of the European Parliament and of the Council of 13 November 2019 on the European Border and Coast Guard and repealing Regulations (EU) 1052/2013 and (EU) 2016/1624 [2019] OJ L295/1.

[58] EU Member States' border surveillance at sea falls within the SBC, which applies 'without prejudice to … (b) the rights of refugees and persons requesting international protection, in particular as regards non-refoulement'. Regulation (EU) 2016/399 of the European Parliament and of the Council of 9 March 2016 on a Union Code on the rules governing the movement of persons across borders [2016] OJ L77/1 (Schengen Borders Code) Art 3(b).

Regulation 656/2014.[59] Accordingly, I only briefly refer to these provisions in the next subsection, and to the related EU activities in subsection III.B.

A. EU Legislation

Regulation 2019/1896 replaced Regulations 1052/2013 and 2016/1624 and expanded the role of Frontex (officially named the 'European Border and Coast Guard Agency') in SAR operations. Specifically, it provides that Frontex is in charge of managing the external borders in light of fundamental rights and the goal of combating transnational crime.[60] It specifies that Frontex is composed by national authorities of Member States 'responsible for border management'.[61] Its tasks include providing technical and operational assistance, as well as enhancing the exchange of information and surveillance services with Member States and non-EU countries to aid their SAR efforts.[62] However, the *national RCCs coordinate all SAR operations.*

Regulation 656/2014 on the surveillance of the external sea borders applies to all border surveillance operations coordinated by Frontex. It states that Member States' law enforcement vessels engaged in border surveillance operations at sea 'should respect their respective obligations under international law' and human rights law.[63] Member States have an obligation to require the master of a vessel flying their flag to render assistance without delay to any vessel or person in distress at sea 'regardless of the nationality or status' of such a person or the circumstances in which that person is found.[64] The Regulation adds that no one shall be 'disembarked in, forced to enter, conducted to or otherwise handed over to the authorities of a country'[65] where he or she would face a serious risk of death, torture, or other human rights violations.

When interception of vessels takes place in a Member State's territorial waters or contiguous zone, disembarkation shall normally occur in its territory.[66] Where interception occurs on the high seas, the preferred disembarkation point is 'in the third country from which the vessel is assumed to have departed'.[67] Should this not be possible, then disembarkation 'shall take place in the host

[59] Regulation (EU) 656/2014 of the European Parliament and of the Council of 15 May 2014 establishing rules for the surveillance of the external sea borders in the context of operational cooperation coordinated by the European Agency for the Management of Operational Cooperation at the External Borders of the Member States of the European Union [2014] OJ L189/93 (Sea Borders Regulation).

[60] Regulation (EU) 2019/1896 (n 57) Art 1.

[61] ibid Art 4.

[62] Regulation (EU) 2019/1896 (n 57) Arts 8, 10, 69, 71–74.

[63] Regulation (EU) 656/2014 (n 59) Preamble (8).

[64] ibid Preamble (14) Arts 4, 9.

[65] ibid Art 4.

[66] ibid Arts 6, 8, 10(1)(a).

[67] ibid Arts 7, 10(1)(b).

Member State'.[68] In the event of a SAR situation, the responsible RCC shall identify an appropriate 'place of safety' and arrange for a swift disembarkation. If that is not possible, then disembarkation shall take place in the 'host Member State'[69] – meaning the 'Member State in which a sea operation takes place or from which it is launched'.[70]

Regulation 656/2014 mandates that Member States taking part in coordinated joint operations with Frontex cooperate with the relevant RCC to locate a place of safety and ensure the quick disembarkation of the rescued individuals.[71] It clarifies that 'place of safety' means a 'location where rescue operations are considered to terminate and where the survivors' safety'[72] and fundamental human rights and the principle of non-refoulement are guaranteed.

Before any rescued person is disembarked in, 'forced to enter, conducted to or otherwise handed over to the authorities of a third country',[73] the Frontex unit is required to evaluate each individual situation and inform them of the final destination. Moreover, it must give the rescued persons the chance 'to express any reasons for believing that disembarkation in the proposed place would be in violation of the principle of *non-refoulement*'.[74]

As such, the obligations under Regulation 656/2014 regarding disembarkation after a SAR operation are clearer than those under the international law of the sea. Regulation 656/2014 is a first step towards the refinement of some international SAR provisions, especially those on disembarkation, which should be protection-driven.[75] Yet some scholars highlight the dichotomy between the stated human rights approach and Frontex's focus on securitisation.[76] Regulation 2019/1896 equips Frontex to fulfil its mandate to protect state security and prevent crime and irregular immigration, and expands its decisional, financial and staff capacity[77] without setting up an external and 'independent system of monitoring and reporting'[78] during its operations,[79] including when operating extraterritorially. In this regard, Hartig notes how Frontex

[68] ibid Art 10(1)(b).
[69] ibid Arts 9, 10(1)(c).
[70] ibid Art 2(3).
[71] ibid Art 10(1)(c).
[72] ibid Art 2(12).
[73] ibid Art 4(3).
[74] ibid Art 4(3).
[75] ibid Art 2(12).
[76] F Aas and HOI Gundhus, 'Policing Humanitarian Borderlands: Frontex, Human Rights and the Precariousness of Life' (2015) 55 *British Journal of Criminology* 1, 1–2.
[77] S Hartig, 'Frontex: From Coordinating Controls to Combating Crime' (2020) 2 *European Criminal Law Associations' Forum* 134.
[78] V Moreno-Lax et al (eds), 'The EU Approach on Migration in the Mediterranean' (Study, Policy Department for Citizens' Rights and Constitutional Affairs, European Parliament, June 2021) 79.
[79] See, for instance, Hartig (n 77) 137; E Koka and D Veshi, 'Irregular Migration by Sea: Interception and Rescue Interventions in Light of International Law and the EU Sea Borders Regulation' (2019) 21 *European Journal of Migration Law* 26, 43; SF Martin, S Weerasinghe and A Taylor (eds), *Humanitarian Crises and Migration: Causes, Consequences and Responses* (London, Routledge, 2014) 21.

> has moved far beyond a merely coordinating and supportive role and now engages in activities ranging from return operations to combating crime. This repressive turn is in itself highly problematic, given the fact that the vast majority of the persons directly confronted by the Agency are not criminals but people in dire need of protection.[80]

Overall, besides concerns regarding Frontex's activities and accountability, scholars, NGOs and international agencies have repeatedly stressed the problem of the absence of a *common dedicated EU legal framework* that provides principles of search, rescue and disembarkation activities for its Member States. As a consequence, this contributes to the uncertainty on the application of the general international duty to rescue persons in distress at sea.[81]

B. EU Operations on SAR and against Migrant Smuggling

Following the end of Operation Mare Nostrum at the end of 2014, Frontex deployed Operation Themis (formerly Triton) in the Central Mediterranean Sea to support Italy with border surveillance.[82] Although Frontex's webpage states that SAR is a key component of the operation, it specifies that the national coordination of such activities remains with the Italian RCC.[83]

There are no clear statistics available concerning the actual involvement of Operation Themis in SAR operations, but it is reported that Frontex rescued 267,223 persons between 2015 and 2021 – only 8 per cent of total rescues in the Central Mediterranean.[84] This can be explained by its focus on security and law enforcement, besides Themis's operational area being limited to 24 miles from the Italian coast (corresponding to the Italian SAR area) and not extending to

[80] Hartig (n 77) 137.

[81] Mungianu argues that Frontex should increase the transparency of its planning and actions regarding joint operations. R Mungianu, *Frontex and Non-Refoulement: The International Responsibility of the EU* (Cambridge, CUP, 2017) 230; see also, V Moreno-Lax, *Accessing Asylum in Europe: Extraterritorial Border Controls and Refugee Rights Under EU Law* (Oxford, OUP, 2017) 469.

[82] It should be noted that Operation Poseidon was established in the Eastern Mediterranean and Operation Indalo in the Western Mediterranean. European Council and Council of the European Union (Consilium), 'Saving Lives at Sea and Fighting Migrant Smuggling' (19 October 2021), available at: www.consilium.europa.eu/en/policies/eu-migration-policy/saving-lives-at-sea/.

[83] ibid; see Frontex, 'Types of Operations', available at: frontex.europa.eu/what-we-do/operations/search-and-rescue/: it is important to underline that SAR operations are always coordinated by the national Maritime Rescue Coordination Centre (MRCC). The MRCC orders vessels that are either the closest to the incident or the most capable ones (due to the specialised training of the crew, or the vessels' specifications, etc) to assist in the rescue. These may include national commercial or military vessels, vessels deployed by Frontex, private boats and others. During a standard border control operation, Frontex-deployed vessels operate under the command of the International Coordination Centre (ICC), but when contacted by the Maritime Rescue Coordination Centre and redirected to a SAR operation, it is the MRCC that takes command.

[84] Moreno-Lax et al (n 78) 77.

Maltese or Libyan waters, where most of the incidents occur.[85] Therefore, the SAR obligations under Regulation 656/2014 find limited application.[86]

On the other hand, Frontex's aerial surveillance in intercepting sea migrants leaving from the North African coasts and alerting the national authorities, including the Libyan Coast Guard, is more relevant. This practice occurs even in cases where NGOs' 'vessels or commercial ships were closer'[87] to distressed vessels. Although it is beyond the scope of this work to discuss the accountability of Frontex in interceptions, pushbacks and pullbacks, it is worth mentioning that the issue remains controversial.[88] Some scholars argue that Frontex is involved in unlawful practices and human rights violations, but its responsibility is difficult to establish, in part due to lack of transparency, and there has never been a judicial assessment.[89]

Aas and Gundhus have described the EU approach to Frontex as creating a 'humanitarian borderland':

> [A] uncertain, intermediate space or a region which is neither lawless nor marked by a well-functioning rule of law. In such a context, policing is conducted in a shifting terrain between conditions which are at the same time regulated and unregulated, humane and inhumane. This type of policing is, paradoxically, often conducted simultaneously *with*, *against* and *through* humanity. The mission is framed and legitimized through the language of humanitarianism and human rights, officers are partly required to perform their tasks as humanitarian agents, at the same time as they find themselves complicit and practically involved in deeply inhumane conditions.
>
> Moreover, policing in humanitarian borderlands is marked by the challenges of working in multi-jurisdictional spaces with unclear lines of responsibility and frequent blame shifting between EU bodies, national authorities of member states and third countries.[90]

[85] Interview with former ship captain of a unit participating in Mare Nostrum (email, 15 February 2023); M Laux, 'The Evolution of the EU's Naval Operations in the Central Mediterranean: a Gradual Shift Away from Search and Rescue' (Heinrich Böll Foundation, 16 April 2021), available at: us.boell.org/en/2021/04/16/evolution-eus-naval-operations-central-mediterranean-gradual-shift-away-search-and.

[86] Laux (n 85).

[87] Border Violence Monitoring Network, 'Black Book of Pushbacks' vol 2, updated edn (*Border Violence Monitoring Network*, 2022) 92, available at: acrobat.adobe.com/link/track?uri=urn%3Aaid%3Ascds%3AUS%3Acb5a9aaa-ee62-3286-a505-0d9122b69b8f.

[88] Moreno-Lax et al (n 78) 77.

[89] A Orav, 'Search and Rescue Efforts for Mediterranean Migrants' (Briefing, European Parliamentary Research Service 2022) 9. In 2021, two migrants brought a case against Frontex before the ECJ, requesting that all the agency's activities in the Aegean Sea be terminated due to their lack of compliance with fundamental rights. However, in 2022, the ECJ held that the case was inadmissible, as the complaint was not sufficiently detailed and substantiated. *SS and ST v Frontex* Case T-282/21 [2022] C 266/26. See also Aas and Gundhus (n 76) 1. In addition, the outcome of *Naass and Sea-Watch v Frontex* is pending. The General Court of the European Union scheduled a hearing on the case for 11 October 2023. The case pertains to Frontex's denial of disclosing documents related to its surveillance operations in the central Mediterranean on 30 July 2021, when the Libyan Coast Guard intercepted around 20 individuals in the Maltese SAR region and sent them back to Libya. Amnesty International, 'EU: Frontex's Lack of Transparency on Libyan Cooperation to Be Heard in Court' (Amnesty International, 10 October 2023), available at: www.amnesty.org/en/latest/news/2023/10/eu-frontexs-lack-of-transparency-on-libyan-cooperation-to-be-heard-in-court/.

[90] Aas and Gundhus (n 76) 14–15.

It should also be noted that Frontex works closely with the EU Border Assistance Mission to Libya (EUBAM)[91] and the EU Naval Force Operation Irini[92] (as also with its predecessor Operation Sophia).[93] Both EUBAM and Operation Irini contribute to capacity building, training and assistance of Libyan bodies such as the Border Guard and Coast Guard which carry out interceptions at sea.[94] The EU's use of these missions as well as 'technology and surveillance tools developed for military purposes to deter migration reflect[s] the framing of the issue as a security threat, with a focus on deterrence rather than protection'.[95]

Having briefly outlined the international and European regulatory framework for requiring state and private vessels to assist distressed migrants at sea and transferring them to a POS, as well as the EU operations concerning SAR activities in the Central Mediterranean, the next section explores the anti-trafficking and smuggling provisions which are commonly used to justify interceptions of vessels and strengthen the focus on security and transnational crime-fighting rather than the protection of human life.

IV. INTERNATIONAL FRAMEWORK AGAINST TRAFFICKING AND SMUGGLING

The Protocols to the UN Convention against Transnational Organized Crime (2000),[96] also known as the 'Palermo Protocols', which include the Protocol to

[91] This was approved on 22 May 2013 by the EU Council and is a civil mission aimed at supporting the Libyan authorities in the development and improvement of border management and control activities (by land, sea and air). In carrying out its mandate, EUBAM Libya carries out capacity building functions, consisting mainly of strategic and operational assistance to the Libyan authorities of 18 June 2021, amending Decision 2013/233/CFSP on the European Union Integrated Border Management Assistance Mission in Libya (EUBAM Libya) ST/8939/2021/INIT [2021] OJ L222/18.

[92] This is the military operation of the EU Naval Force in the Mediterranean. Its main task is to enforce the UN arms embargos against Libya. However, it also contributes to the fight against human trafficking and smuggling. European Union External Action Service (EEAS), 'EUNAVFOR MED IRINI: European Union Naval Force Irini – Military Operation' (EEAS, 30 November 2020), available at: www.eeas.europa.eu/eunavfor-med-operation-irini/eunavfor-med-irini-european-union-naval-force-irini-military-operation_en.

[93] According to an MoU between the Operation Irini Commander and the Libyan Navy Coast Guard and Port Security Commander, Operation Sophia directly delivered the first training to the Libyan Coast Guard in 2016. A second training package was agreed upon in 2017. EEAS, 'Operation SOPHIA: Package 2 of the Libyan Navy Coast Guard and Libyan Navy Training Launched Today' (EEAS, 3 January 2017), available at: www.eeas.europa.eu/node/19518_en.

[94] EEAS, 'Working Document of the European External Action Service: EUBAM Libya Strategic Review 2021' (Integrated Approach for Security and Peace Directorate, EEAS, 19 February 2021) 174, available at: www.statewatch.org/media/1964/eu-eeas-eubam-libya-strategic-review-eeas-2021–174.pdf.

[95] S Ardalan, 'EU and US Border Policy: Externalisation of Migration Control and Violation of the Right to Asylum' in V Mitsilegas, V Moreno-Lax and N Vavoula (eds), *Securitising Asylum Flows. Deflection, Criminalisation and Challenges for Human Rights* (Leiden, Brill/Nijhoff 2020) 297.

[96] United Nations Convention against Transnational Organized Crime (New York, 15 November 2000) 2225 UNTS 209.

Prevent, Suppress, and Punish Trafficking in Persons, Especially Women and Children (2000)[97] and the Protocol against the Smuggling of Migrants by Land, Sea and Air (2000),[98] aim to foster international cooperation against cross-border crime and the smuggling and trafficking of migrants, as well as strengthen the protection of victims of human trafficking and smuggling.[99] They provide the international provisions criminalising activities linked to irregular immigration, and the basis for interceptions at sea. Although the Palermo Protocols are not explicitly mentioned in the international cooperation agreements and measures of externalisation of immigration control discussed in chapter five, they constituted the rationale for the adoption of such agreements by Italy, Libya and Tunisia.[100]

The UN Smuggling of Migrants Protocol describes migrant smuggling as 'the procurement, in order to obtain, directly or indirectly, a financial or other material benefit, of illegal entry of a person into a State Party of which the person is not a national or permanent resident'.[101] It demands that states adopt measures to criminalise those who enable migrants' illegal entry or residence 'to obtain, directly or indirectly, a financial or other material benefit'.[102] It adds that aggravating circumstances to the offence should be set forth where there

[97] Protocol to Prevent, Suppress, and Punish Trafficking in Persons, Especially Women and Children 2000, Supplementing the United Nations Convention against Transnational Crime (New York, 15 November 2000) 2237 UNTS 319.

[98] Protocol against the Smuggling of Migrants by Land, Sea and Air 2000, Supplementing the United Nations Convention against Transnational Crime, United Nations (New York, 15 November 2000) 2241 UNTS 507. The Palermo Protocols also include the Protocol against the Illicit Manufacturing and Trafficking in Firearms, Their Parts and Components and Ammunition 2001, Supplementing the United Nations Convention against Transnational Crime, United Nations (New York, 31 May 2000) 2326 UNTS 208.

[99] E Koka, 'Irregular Migration by Sea: A Critical Analysis of EU and EU Member State Extraterritorial Practice in the Light of International Law' (PhD Thesis, University of Kent, 2018) 59. See the Protocol against the Smuggling of Migrants by Land, Sea and Air 2000 (n 98) arts 17 and 8. It should be noted according to art 8(7), a state party may board and search a vessel without nationality and take appropriate measures in light of the relevant national and international provisions.

[100] Italy signed the UN Convention against Transnational Organized Crime 2000 and the Trafficking and Smuggling Protocols on 12 December 2000 and ratified them with law no 146/2006. Legge 16 marzo 2006 n 146. As it is relevant for the discussion in ch 5, it should be noted that Tunisia signed the UN Convention against Transnational Organized Crime 2000 and the Palermo Protocols on 13 December 2000 and ratified them in June 2003. For a list of signatories see: United Nations Treaty Collection, 'Penal Matters Chapter XVIII: United Nations Convention against Organized Crime' (Status of Treaties, UN Treaty Collection, 2023). Libya signed the UN Convention against Transnational Organized Crime 2000 on 13 November 2001 and ratified it on 18 June 2004; ibid. It also signed the Palermo Protocols on 13 November 2011 and ratified the Smuggling and Trafficking Protocols on 24 September 2004. United Nations Treaty Collection, 'Penal Matters Chapter XVIII: Protocol to Prevent, Suppress and Punish Trafficking in Persons, Especially Women and Children, supplementing the United Nations Convention against Transnational Organized Crime (Status of Treaties, UN Treaty Collection, 2023); United Nations Treaty Collection, 'Penal Matters Chapter XVIII: Protocol against the Smuggling of Migrants by Land, Sea and Air, supplementing the United Nations Convention against Transnational Organized Crime' (Status of Treaties, UN Treaty Collection, 2023).

[101] Protocol against the Smuggling of Migrants (n 98) art 3(a).

[102] ibid art 6(1).

is a threat to 'the lives or safety of migrants', or a situation involving inhuman or degrading treatment of migrants.[103] The Interpretive Notes to the UN Convention against Transnational Organized Crime and its Protocols clarify that the words 'financial or other material benefit' were meant to target organised criminal groups and not migrants' close family members or support groups such as 'religious or non-governmental organisations'.[104]

The UN Trafficking Protocol defines 'trafficking' as

> the recruitment, transportation, transfer, harbouring or receipt of persons, by means of the threat or use of force or other forms of coercion, of abduction, of fraud, of deception, of the abuse of power or of a position of vulnerability or of the giving or receiving of payments or benefits to achieve the consent of a person having control over another person, for the purpose of exploitation.[105]

It specifies that 'the consent of the victim of trafficking' is 'irrelevant where any of the means' mentioned in the former sentence have been used.[106] The Protocol requires state parties to adopt legislation and other implementing measures to criminalise intentional conduct amounting to trafficking.[107]

The Palermo Protocols establish that states shall adopt specific national measures to reach their aims. In particular, the UN Smuggling of Migrants Protocol supports the creation of bilateral agreements among states in order to authorise 'a State other than the flag State to intercept vessels involved in criminal operations',[108] thus creating an exception to the rule that the flag state has sole jurisdiction over its vessels.[109]

The Protocols make clear that, although states can use several measures in border management to prevent the arrival of smuggling vessels, they shall comply with the international obligations and national law.[110] The international obligations include those arising from the Refugee Convention, especially the non-refoulement principle, requiring that no refugee may be returned to a place in which they have a well-founded fear of persecution. Therefore, states must have in place legal and administrative measures to prevent any person from

[103] ibid art 6(3)(a) and (b).

[104] UN General Assembly, 'Interpretative Notes for the Official Records (Travaux Préparatoires) of the Negotiation of the United Nations Convention against Transnational Organized Crime and the Protocols Thereto' (3 November 2000) A/55/383/Add.1, para 92; FRA, 'Fundamental Rights Considerations: NGO Ships Involved in Search and Rescue in the Mediterranean and Criminal Investigations – 2018' (Report, FRA, 1 October 2018), available at: fra.europa.eu/en/publication/2019/fundamental-rights-considerations-ngo-ships-involved-search-and-rescue. L Carballo Piñeiro, 'Occupational Hazards in the Light of the Maritime Migration Challenge' in PK Mukherjee et al (eds), *Maritime Law in Motion* (Cham, Springer, 2020) 86.

[105] Protocol to Prevent, Suppress, and Punish Trafficking (n 97) art 3(a).

[106] ibid art 3(b).

[107] ibid art 5(1).

[108] Koka (n 99) 59; Protocol against the Smuggling of Migrants (n 98) arts 17 and 8. It should be noted that according to art 8(7), a state party may board and search a vessel without nationality and take appropriate measures in light of the relevant national and international provisions.

[109] UNCLOS Convention (n 5) art 92.

[110] Koka (n 99) 61.

being returned to a place where they would be at risk of persecution, death, torture, or other cruel and inhuman treatment or punishment. To this end, states must make sure that rescued migrants who may be eligible for refugee status can submit an asylum application.[111] However, in practice, these provisions are not always read together, and states favour the security aspects of the Protocols over human rights considerations, as shown in chapters five and six.

V. EU FRAMEWORK AGAINST TRAFFICKING AND SMUGGLING

The Facilitation Directive,[112] Framework Decision 2002/946/JHA[113] (the EU Facilitators Package), and the Trafficking Directives[114] incorporate the provisions of the Palermo Protocols. The EU Facilitators Package is particularly relevant, as it was adopted with the goal of fighting against irregular immigration 'both in connection with unauthorised crossing of the border in the strict sense and for the purpose of sustaining networks which exploit human beings'.[115] As Minetti explains, one of the main features of the EU Facilitators Package is that it focuses 'on the prevention of irregular arrivals and on the crime of facilitation of illegal entry'[116] and has particular impact on NGOs' SAR activities in the Mediterranean discussed in chapter six.

The Facilitation Directive provides that EU Member States shall adopt 'appropriate sanctions' for anyone who intentionally helps a migrant to illegally enter or transit the territory of a Member State (Art 1(a)). They shall also adopt sanctions for anyone who intentionally facilitates irregular entry or transit for a financial benefit (Art 1(b)). The Facilitation Directive adds that Member States have the discretion to introduce an exception to such rules and not criminalise persons who provide humanitarian assistance to migrants (Art 1(2) of the Council Directive – the so-called 'optional humanitarian clause').[117] In turn, the Framework Decision sets forth that the unlawful conduct introduced by the Directive shall be sanctioned with criminal measures.[118]

[111] Kilpatrick and Smith, 'The International Legal Obligation to Rescue During Mass Migration at Sea' (n 50) 148; 2004 IMO Guidelines (n 44) s 6.17.

[112] Council Directive 2002/90/EC of 28 November 2002 defining the facilitation of unauthorised entry, transit and residence [2002] OJ L328/17.

[113] Council Framework Decision 2002/946/JHA of 28 November 2002 on the strengthening of the penal framework to prevent the facilitation of unauthorised entry, transit and residence [2002] OJ L328/1.

[114] Directive 2011/36/EU of the European Parliament and of the Council of 5 April 2011 on preventing and combating trafficking in human beings and protecting its victims, and replacing Council Framework Decision 2002/629/JHA OJ L101/1.

[115] Council Directive 2002/90/EC (n 112); M Minetti, 'The Facilitation Package, Penal Populism and the Rule of Law: Lessons from Italy' (2020) 1 *New Journal of European Criminal Law* 335, 336.

[116] Council Directive 2002/90/EC (n 112); Minetti (n 115) 336.

[117] Council Directive 2002/90/EC (n 112); UN Independent Expert on Human Rights and International Solidarity, 'Human Rights and International Solidarity' (UNHCR, 6 April 2019) para 2.

[118] Council Framework Decision 2002/946/JHA (n 113) Art 1, para 1.

Article 6 of the Framework Decision points out that it 'shall apply without prejudice to the protection afforded to refugees and asylum seekers in accordance with international law on refugees', in particular Article 31 (non-penalisation of unlawful entry or presence) and Article 33 (non-refoulement principle) of the Refugee Convention.

Despite the aforementioned safeguards, some scholars consider the European framework problematic because, compared with the UN Smuggling of Migrants Protocol, it broadens the definition of human smuggling by not requiring profit to be an element of the crime. Furthermore, it leaves individual Member States with the choice of whether or not to adopt the humanitarian clause. Therefore, 'Member States' domestic legislation on the facilitation of entry and stay of irregular migrants can lead to the punishment of those who provide humanitarian assistance'[119] – an issue that has become widely debated both in political discourse and in scholarly works.[120] As such, the European approach weakens the principle of legal certainty, which requires rules on prohibited behaviour to be clear and penalties to be foreseeable.[121] In this regard, it has been commented that the 'excessive breadth is nevertheless questionable and entails a considerable risk of over-prosecution, in particular with respect to Member States adhering to principle of mandatory prosecution'.[122]

In July 2018, in response to the criticisms of the Facilitators Package, the European Parliament issued guidelines urging Member States to implement the optional humanitarian clause in order to prevent needless criminalisation.[123]

[119] FRA (n 104). According to Zirulia, '[c]ontrary to what some reports state, no Member State includes profit-making among the elements making up facilitation of illegal entry'. Exceptions are Ireland and the UK – neither one bound by the Facilitators Package. S Zirulia, 'Is That a Smuggler? The Blurring Line between Facilitating Illegal Immigration and Providing Humanitarian Assistance at the European Borders' in GL Gatta, V Mitsilegas and S Zirulia (eds), *Controlling Immigration through Criminal Law: European and Comparative Perspectives on 'Crimmigration'* (Oxford, Hart Publishing, 2020), 235, 240. For examples of charges against NGOs and fishermen for saving sea migrants – a trend which, despite the fact that most cases are dismissed, has the power to deter private vessels from attempts at rescue – see Carballo Piñeiro (n 104) 86–87.

[120] S Carrera et al, *Policing Humanitarianism: EU Policies against Human Smuggling and Their Impact on Civil Society* (Oxford, Hart Publishing, 2019) 1, 3; International Commission of Jurists, 'Criminalization of Humanitarian and Other Support and Assistance to Migrants and the Defence of Their Human Rights in the EU' (Briefing Paper, 22 April 2022); S Carrera et al, 'Fit for Purpose? The Facilitation Directive and the Criminalisation of Humanitarian Assistance to Irregular Migrants: 2018 Update' (Technical Report, European University Institute, 2018); FRA (n 104); S Zirulia and G Martinico, 'Criminalising Migrants and Securitising Borders: The Italian "No Way" Model in the Age of Populism' in V Stoyanova and S Smet (eds), *Migrants' Rights, Populism and Legal Resilience in Europe* (Cambridge, CUP, 2022) 275.

[121] CM Ricci, 'Criminalising Solidarity? Smugglers, Migrants and Rescuers in the Reform of the "Facilitators' Package"' in V Mitsilegas, V Moreno-Lax and N Vavoula (eds), *Securitising Asylum Flows: Deflection, Criminalisation and Challenges for Human Rights* (Leiden, Brill/Nijhoff, 2020) 47.

[122] ibid 49.

[123] European Parliament, 'Resolution of 5 July 2018 on Guidelines for Member States to Prevent Humanitarian Assistance from Being Criminalised' [2018] RSP 2769.

Furthermore, in 2020, the Commission issued a Guidance on the Implementation of Facilitation Directive.[124] The Guidance

> invites Member States that have not yet done so to use the possibility provided for in Article 1(2) of the Facilitation Directive, which allows them to distinguish between activities carried out for the purpose of humanitarian assistance and activities to facilitate irregular entry or transit, and allows for the exclusion of the former from criminalisation.[125]

It adds that, in light of its 'general spirit and objective', the Facilitation Directive cannot be interpreted as allowing the criminalisation of activities that amount to obligations under international law (SOLAS, SAR, Convention on the Law of the Sea, customary international law).[126]

However, some scholars as well as civil society actors argue that the Guidance[127] is not sufficient to prevent prosecution or administrative penalties for assisting migrants.[128] In particular, the Guidance does not deal with criminal investigations of SAR NGOs – even after its adoption, a number of prosecutors opened investigations against NGOs. NGOs' SAR efforts would not be included in the criminal definition of the crime if the Facilitation Directive's text were changed to require that aiding an illegal entry be done for monetary or other material gain.

On the other hand, the Commission took the view that introducing the profit element as necessary to pursue the crime of facilitating irregular immigration would make the investigations against smugglers more difficult.[129]

Overall, EU legislation and policies mirror attitudes of most EU states that are unwilling to help people in distress in the Mediterranean. In the view of many politicians, these rescue operations – combined with non-refoulement – are most likely fostering sea migration.[130] The opposing view, however, argues

[124] European Commission, 'Commission Guidance on the Implementation of EU Rules on Definition and Prevention of the Facilitation of Unauthorised Entry, Transit and Residence' (Guidance) COM 2020 323/1; European Commission. 'New Pact on Migration and Asylum', available at: ec.europa.eu/info/strategy/priorities-2019–2024/promoting-our-european-way-life/new-pact-migration-and-asylum_en.

[125] European Commission, 'Commission Guidance on the Implementation of EU Rules on Definition and Prevention of the Facilitation of Unauthorised Entry, Transit and Residence' (n 124) 8.

[126] ibid 7.

[127] For more discussion on this, see JD Janer Torrens, 'Migrant Search and Rescue Operations in the Mediterranean by Humanitarian Organizations: Migrant Smuggling or Humanitarian Assistance?' (2020) 8 *Paix et Sécurité Internationales* 381.

[128] K Arrouche, A Fallone and L Vosyliūtė, 'Between Politics and Inconvenient Evidence. Assessing the Renewed EU Action Plan against Migrant Smuggling' (Policy Brief no 2021/01, CEPS, December 2021) 5, 8; Malcolm Wu, 'The EC's Guidance on the Facilitation Directive: Ending the Criminalisation of NGO-led SAR Operations?' (*Opinio Juris*, 30 October 2020), available at: opiniojuris.org/2020/10/30/the-ecs-guidance-on-the-facilitation-directive-ending-the-criminalisation-of-ngo-led-sar-operations.

[129] Zirulia (n 119) 252.

[130] Italian Coast Guard Official (n 38); G Clayton and G Firth, *Immigration and Asylum Law*, 8th edn (Oxford, OUP, 2018) 437.

that whether or not SAR operations are a 'pull factor' should not weigh in decisions to render assistance.[131]

VI. THE PARIS MEMORANDUM AND DIRECTIVE 2009/16/EC

Other international and EU instruments relevant in the context of state measures taken against NGOs engaged in SAR operations are the Paris Memorandum on Port State Control (Paris MoU)[132] and its implementing Directive 2009/16/EC.[133] Their goal is to harmonise the check system that port states carry out with regard to some categories of vessels in the areas of safety of navigation, labour and employment law of the crew, and protection of the environment.[134] Their aim is also to address inadequate controls on the part of some states, which can cause accidents at sea.[135]

In particular, Directive 2009/16/EC introduces the obligation for the flag states to guarantee a certain number of annual checks and criteria regarding the types of vessels that have to be inspected, the characteristics of the checks, the professional training of the inspectors, and the measures that may be adopted in cases of non-compliance.[136] Checks must be carried out taking into consideration the risks involved, which range from low to high depending on factors such as the vessel's age and performance, the reliability of the certifying entity and the owner, as well as outcomes of past inspections.[137] Member States are then classified, according to the outcomes of the inspections, in a list that is periodically updated and accessible online.[138]

Besides certificates of safety, the Paris MoU and Directive 2009/16/EC also require flag states to issue ships sailing in international waters a 'class certificate' ensuring that they are suitable to navigate in light of their activities. However, one problem, which I will discuss in chapter six, is that NGO vessels systematically engaged in SAR in the Mediterranean do not clearly fit under any of the

[131] Moreno-Lax et al (n 78) 74.

[132] The Paris MoU is 'an administrative agreement between 27 Maritime-Authorities' signed in 1982. Paris MoU, 'History: A short history of the Paris MoU on PSC' (Paris MoU, February 2023), available at: www.parismou.org/about-us/history.

[133] Council Directive 2009/16/EC of the European Parliament and of the Council of 23 April 2009 on Port State Control [2009] OJ L131/57.

[134] F De Vittor, 'Il Port State Control sulle Navi delle ONG che Prestano Soccorso in Mare: Tutela della Sicurezza della Navigazione o Ostacolo alle Attività di Soccorso?' (2021) 15 *Diritti Umani e Diritto Internazionale* 103.

[135] L Gennari, 'Navi in Porto, Naufragi nel Mediterraneo: la Dimensione Amministrativa del Contrasto alle Operazioni di Soccorso' (2021) XXI *Diritto e Questioni Pubbliche*, Special Issue 83, 91.

[136] Directive 2009/16/EC (n 133) Arts 1, 4, 5, 11, 13, 15; De Vittor (n 134) 94.

[137] Gennari (n 135) 93.

[138] ibid 91.

existing categories and are therefore classified in different ways.[139] This gap has given rise to disputes between NGOs and states with which criteria NGO vessels should comply.

The Paris MoU and Directive 2009/16/EC impose on flag states the primary role regarding safety checks and the issuing of related certificates. Port states have a secondary role in checking the safety of vessels and preventing the sailing of substandard vessels.[140] These provisions are thus in line with article 94 of UNCLOS, which sets forth the principle that the flag state exercises jurisdiction and administrative and technical control over its vessels and that the flag state is responsible for issuing certificates of safety.[141] They are also to be read together with the SOLAS Convention, which establishes the principle of mutual recognition of certificates,[142] so that the 'certificates issued by one state party are to be recognised by other states'.[143]

The Paris MoU and Directive 2009/16/EC give the Coast Guard the power to administratively detain vessels when they need to carry out an inspection for verifying compliance with the prerequisites.[144] The Coast Guard's detention order can be imposed until all risks are removed or they believe that the ship does not pose any more hazards.[145] The owner of the vessel can lodge an appeal against a detention order – in Italy this is possible before the Regional Administrative Tribunal (Tribunale Amministrativo Regionale – TAR).[146]

In summary, flag states are in charge of issuing certificates for the safety and classification of the boats, whereas port states can carry out checks limited to cases of concrete risks.[147] However, some port states such as Italy have strategically invoked the Paris MoU and Directive 2009/16/EC against NGOs to prevent their activities, including for non-Italian vessels. Other countries, such as Germany and the Netherlands, have implemented the Paris MoU and Directive 2009/16/EC through stricter implementing legislation, imposing 'stringent safety and maintenance requirements'[148] in order to prevent NGO vessels from operating.

[139] For instance, *Aita Mari* is classified as a fishing vessel, whereas the *Mare Jonio* is classified as a tug vessel; ibid 91.

[140] De Vittor (n 134) 94.

[141] ibid.

[142] SOLAS Convention (n 4), ch I, regs 17 and 5; De Vittor (n 134) 92.

[143] T Spijkerboer, 'Wasted Lives: Borders and the Right to Life of People Crossing Them' (2017) 86 *Nordic Journal of International Law* 1, 14.

[144] Directive 2009/16/EC (n 133) Art 20.

[145] ibid Art 20.

[146] ibid Art 20; Gennari (n 135) 93.

[147] Gennari (n 135) 92.

[148] P Müller and P Slominski, 'Shrinking the Space for Civil Society: (De)Politicizing the Obstruction of Humanitarian NGOs in EU Border Management' (2022) 48 *Journal of Ethnic and Migration Studies* 4474, 4783.

VII. CONCLUSION

The discussed provisions are affected by a number of gaps, ambiguities and contradictions which impact on the principle of legal certainty. Concerning the legal gaps,[149] for instance, there are no provisions supporting the duty to rescue imposed upon shipmasters; there are no standards to establish when the obligation of cooperation among states involved in SAR operations has been violated,[150] or provisions on safety of navigation for vessels operated by NGOs and engaged in SAR operations. There is also no common EU framework for dedicated SAR operations.

As far as the ambiguities are concerned, some of them were intentionally created due to disagreements between states during the drafting process of the international treaties. For example, this was the case for the 2004 SAR Regulation and its obligation that states involved in rescue operations cooperate in order to identify a POS. The drafters did not specify the content of the obligation for the state in charge of the SAR zone where the rescue operation takes place. The provision according to which such state 'shall exercise primary responsibility for ensuring such co-ordination and co-operation occurs' is the result of a compromise among states during the preparatory works of the drafting process.[151] Furthermore, the Regulation does not explain what a 'safe place' is. Only the 2004 IMO Guidelines – a non-binding instrument – specify that it is a place where human rights are guaranteed.[152]

Contradictions arise from the tension between the different aims of fighting against irregular immigration: the prevention of human smuggling and trafficking on one side and the protection of human life on the other.[153] In particular, the international law of the sea imposes an obligation to assist people and ships in distress, irrespective of their nationality, immigration status, or situation. However, the anti-trafficking and smuggling frameworks require states to criminalise activities connected to allowing or facilitating the illegal entry of foreigners. The EU Facilitators Package criminalises even those who do so without intent to profit.[154] As a consequence, these provisions have been used to the criminalise humanitarian organisations involved in SAR operations. Additionally, the EU rules on Frontex missions and related SAR operations show the discrepancy between the stated goals of defending human rights and safeguarding borders from criminal activity.

[149] M Starita, 'Conclusioni: I Lati Oscuri del Diritto Internazionale sul Soccorso in Mare' (2021) XXI *Diritto e Questioni Pubbliche*, Special Issue 133, 135.
[150] ibid 136.
[151] ibid 134.
[152] ibid.
[153] ibid 134–35.
[154] Interview with Marta Minetti, PhD Candidate, Queen Mary University of London (online, 9 February 2023).

Thus, the international and European frameworks are imperfect. One could argue that they only set out minimum standards and that much depends on states to implement them. However, given that sea migration is a very controversial topic which affects several states and the EU as a whole, the weaknesses at the international and EU levels impact on the ROL at the national level, as shown in the next chapters with respect to the Italian experience.[155]

[155] International Maritime Organization, UN High Commissioner for Refugees, and International Chamber of Shipping, *Rescue at Sea: A Guide to Principles and Practice as Applied to Refugee and Migrants* (UNHCR, 2015); Kilpatrick and Smith, 'The International Legal Obligation to Rescue During Mass Migration at Sea' (n 50) 149.

4

Failures and Delays in Assisting Migrants in Distress at Sea

I. INTRODUCTION

IN THIS CHAPTER I discuss Italy's implementation of the international provisions on search and rescue (SAR) and explore the related practices. In particular, I focus on failures to coordinate the SAR of migrants in distress in the Central Mediterranean Sea and delays in disembarking them to a place of safety (POS), and how these failures and delays affect the rule of law (ROL).

As mentioned in chapter one, these problems have become more frequent since 2014, when the Italian SAR operation Mare Nostrum came to an end.[1] Besides noting the reduction in SAR operations by Italy and other coastal states,[2] I explain how the other main roots of the problem are: (1) disagreements on the coordination of SAR operations among different states, especially when Italy and Malta are involved; (2) the increasing role of the Libyan Coast Guard in SAR operations since 2019[3] – despite Libya not generally being considered a POS, given the serious human rights violations occurring in the country;[4] and (3) the reliance on commercial vessels to save those in distress.[5] Another relevant factor is the drop in SAR initiatives by non-governmental organisations (NGOs) due to states' use of criminal and administrative measures to deter and prevent their operations, which I will discuss in chapter six.

In the next section, I start with an analysis of the national regulatory framework for implementing the international conventions on the law of the sea,

[1] U Leanza and F Caffio, 'Il SAR Mediterraneo. La Ricerca e Soccorso nel Diritto Marittimo: l'Applicazione della Convenzione di Amburgo del 1979' (2015) 12 *Rivista Marittima* 10, 13; interview with Martin Dorsman, Secretary General of European Community Shipowners' Associations, Brussels (online, 6 November 2020).

[2] Leanza and Caffio (n 1) 13; interview with Dorsman (n 1).

[3] OHCHR, 'Lethal Disregard: Search and Rescue and the Protection of Migrants in the Central Mediterranean Sea' (OHCHR, May 2021) 3, available at: www.ohchr.org/en/stories/2021/05/report-call-safeguard-migrants-central-mediterranean-sea; P Cuttitta, 'Repoliticization through Search and Rescue, Humanitarian NGOs and Migration Management in the Central Mediterranean' (2018) 23 *Geopolitics* 632.

[4] Commissioner for Human Rights, 'A Distress Call for Human Rights. The Widening Gap in Migrant Protection in the Mediterranean: Follow-up Report to the 2019 Recommendation' (Commissioner for Human Rights, Council of Europe, March 2021) 13.

[5] See ch 1, section V.

limiting the discussion to the provisions most relevant to SAR operations and disembarkations. In section III, I focus on the related practices as far as rescue operations by Italian authorities are concerned, and explain the main issues that arise when Malta and Libya are also involved. In section IV, I examine the provisions requiring private vessels to provide assistance and to rescue persons in distress at sea as well as the related practices. In section V, I address the issue of accountability for breaches of SAR obligations, focusing on omission of assistance and delays in disembarkations. In section VI, I conclude that the ROL elements particularly challenged in this area are those of legality, legal clarity and access to justice.

II. NATIONAL REGULATORY FRAMEWORK FOR IMPLEMENTING THE INTERNATIONAL CONVENTIONS ON THE LAW OF THE SEA

Italy ratified all the relevant international conventions on the law of the sea discussed in chapter three,[6] and put the Ministry of Transport and Navigation in charge of implementing the SAR Convention.[7]

In 1996, the Ministry of Transport and Navigation issued a regulatory act called the 'Piano Nazionale per la Ricerca e il Salvataggio in Mare' (National Plan for Search and Rescue at Sea), and later amended it in 2007 and in 2020.[8] The latter changes were adopted to reflect the 2004 amendments of the SAR Convention and the related IMO Guidelines,[9] as well as other national provisions on SAR in case of arrivals of high numbers of migrants.[10]

The 2020 National Search and Rescue Plan is particularly important as it aims to provide technical and operational guidance for SAR operations. In particular, its chapter 2 ('Coordination Authorities and Operational Situations') acknowledges that the Ministry for Transport and Navigation delegated the implementation of the SAR Convention to the Headquarters of the Coast

[6] Legge 23 maggio 1980 n 313 ratified the SOLAS Convention; Legge 2 dicembre 1994 n 689 ratified the UNCLOS Convention and its Annexes; Legge 12 aprile 1995 n 129 ratified the Salvage Convention; Legge 3 aprile 1989 n 147 ratified the SAR Convention and its Annex.

[7] See art 2, Decreto del Presidente della Repubblica 28 settembre 1994 n 662. Regolamento di attuazione della Legge 3 aprile 1989 n 147, come modificato da Decreto del Presidente della Repubblica 13 febbraio 2007 n 29. It should be noted that the Ministry of Transport and Navigation is currently named 'Ministry for Infrastructure and Transport'.

[8] The 1996 National Plan for Search and Rescue at Sea was adopted by Decreto Ministeriale 25 November 1996, available at: www.guardiacostiera.gov.it/normativa-e-documentazione/Pages/ricerca-e-soccorso.aspx. The 2000 National Plan for Search and Rescue at Sea was adopted by Decreto Ministeriale 4 Febbraio 2021 n 45, available at: mit.gov.it/normativa/decreto-ministeriale-numero-45-del-04022021.

[9] See ch 3, section II.C.

[10] See Decreto Legislativo 25 luglio 1998 n 286, Testo Unico delle disposizioni concernenti la disciplina dell' immigrazione e norme sulla condizione dello straniero (come modificato) (Testo Unico sull' Immigrazione – TUI) Art 10; Fulvio Vassallo Paleologo, 'Un Nuovo Decreto Ministeriale Disciplina il Salvataggio: Mai Più Abbandoni in Mare' (ADIF, 8 February 2021), available at: www.a-dif.org/2021/02/08/un-nuovo-decreto-ministeriale-disciplina-il-salvataggio-mai-piu-abbandoni-in-mare/.

Guard (Comando Generale del Corpo delle Capitanerie di Porto – a specialised body of the Maritime Armed Forces but only engaged in support and control of civil uses of the sea). The headquarters of the Coast Guard organises and coordinates national SAR services, including with the Rescue Coordination Centres (RCCs) of neighbouring states, through its peripheral structures: the Italian Maritime Rescue Coordination Centre (IMRCC), its central operational unit (Unit III) and territorial units (Maritime Rescue Sub Centres (MRSC), the Coast Guard Units (UCG), and the SAR Units (naval and aircraft units of the Coast Guard specially set up for SAR services). In case of necessity, Article 5 of the Decree of the President of the Republic no 662/1994 states that the IMRCC and MRSC can request assistance from the Air Force as well as the Navy.

The approximately 500,000 km^2 extension of the Italian SAR zone is set out in Annex 3 of the Decree of the President of the Republic no 662/1994. The Italian SAR zone is divided into 15 sub-areas, corresponding to 15 MRSCs on which the UCGs (whether ship or aircraft units) depend. According to Leanza and Caffio, the limits of national responsibility for the SAR zone are located reasonably close to the coast, with distances ranging between a few tens of miles from Lampedusa and about a hundred miles from the Sicilian coast.[11]

Paragraph 230 of the 2020 National Search and Rescue Plan states that emergency services shall be provided by the lowest level of the SAR structure – that is, the UCGs. Therefore, in case a vessel is reported to be in distress, the relevant UCG must set up the first emergency operations. At the same time, the UCG must inform the competent MRSC, which will be responsible for coordinating the event. If necessary, another UCG or MRSC could be required to handle the incident.

Paragraph 240 of the 2020 National Search and Rescue Plan, concerning *actions outside the Italian SAR zone*, specifies that the IMRCC shall communicate and maintain contact with foreign maritime Rescue Coordination Centres (RCCs), which are called upon to conduct SAR operations in the areas of their respective competence. In addition, *the IMRCC shall coordinate the rescue operations when acting as the first RCC informed of the event, even outside its SAR area, until such time as the competent coordination centre or another RCC can better assist and assume the coordination of SAR operations. If no other RCC assumes coordination of the event, the IMRCC retains responsibility – jointly with the concerned RCC. Accordingly, SAR obligations extend beyond a state's full maritime jurisdiction.*

Finally, in chapter 3 ('Emergency Stages') of the 2020 National Search and Rescue Plan, paragraph 370 describes the procedures to be adopted by the Italian authorities (ie, IMRCC, MRSC, UCG) in the different SAR phases. In particular, it distinguishes between a phase of *uncertainty* (when the safety of a vessel or person at sea is in doubt);[12] *alert* (when the maritime authorities have received

[11] Leanza and Caffio (n 1).
[12] See also para 320.

information that the vessel's efficiency is impaired but does not present a situation of danger);[13] and *distress* (when all the attempts to contact the vessel have failed or 'the person or the boat is in serious or imminent danger or in need of immediate assistance, or even when news has been received that the operational efficiency of the vehicle is impaired to such an extent as to make probable the occurrence of a situation of danger').[14]

According to the phase, the 2020 National Search and Rescue Plan sets out related obligations for the state and maritime authorities involved. In particular, in phases of uncertainty or alert, the maritime authorities must gather information on the event and warn the rescue services in advance of any imminent danger, whereas distress triggers the rescue operations.[15] The meaning of '*distress*' is widely interpreted and encompasses situations where a person is in danger of getting lost[16] as well as objective situations of difficulty that the vessel may find itself in, deriving from a multiplicity of factors – for example, the precarious state of buoyancy of the vehicle, its overcrowding, the absence on board of a professional crew, the lack or insufficiency of safety equipment, or the presence of persons needing medical care. It is up to the IMRCC to decide, on the basis of the information gathered, if and when to declare the existence of an SAR event. However, it shall declare the SAR event even in a situation of uncertainty.[17]

Concerning the identification of a POS to disembark the rescued persons, the 2020 National Search and Rescue Plan adopts the same approach of the 2004 IMO Guidelines and defines POS as a

> place where the rescue operations are considered to be concluded. It is also a place where the safety of survivors is no longer threatened and where their basic human needs (such as food, shelter and sanitary necessities) can be satisfied. Moreover, it is a place from where transport can be organised towards the survivors' next destination or the final destination.[18]

The 2020 National Search and Rescue Plan adds that the POS 'must be determined in light of the applicable laws and directives and guidelines issued by the Ministry of Transport and/or the Headquarters of the Coast Guard'.[19] In this regard, in September 2015, the General Command of the Port Authority approved

[13] See also para 330.
[14] Fulvio Vassallo Paleologo, 'Il Nuovo Piano Nazionale SAR 2020 ed i Soccorsi in Alto Mare, tra Prassi Operative e Diritto Internazionale' (2021) 3 *Diritto, Immigrazione e Cittadinanza* 316, 339. See also the 2020 National Plan for Search and Rescue at Sea (n 8) para 360.
[15] Vassallo Paleologo, 'Il Nuovo Piano Nazionale SAR 2020 ed i Soccorsi in Alto Mare, tra Prassi Operative e Diritto Internazionale' (n 14) 339.
[16] 2020 National Plan for Search and Rescue at Sea (n 8) Part I, para 140; LM Brigida, 'Ricerca e Soccorso in Mare: Questioni Giuridiche sulla Determinazione del Place of Safety' (Master's Thesis, University of Rome, 2020) 86.
[17] Para 310.
[18] Para 111(r).
[19] Para 370.

the Standard Operating Procedures SOP 009/15, which establish core operational procedures for identifying the POS when the IMRCC in Rome is responsible for the rescue.[20] The Operating Procedures recognise how, in light of the international provisions, *rescue operations may not be considered concluded until the disembarkation of the survivors at a POS*.[21]

In case of arrivals of irregular migrants and in the interest of maintaining public order, the Operating Procedures set out that *the identification of the POS shall be established in agreement with the Department of Civil Liberties and Immigration of the Ministry of the Interior*.[22] However, this administrative provision is subordinated to primary and secondary legislation and therefore cannot change the competence of the Coast Guard in SAR activities and identification of a POS. Moreover, the meaning of 'POS' should be understood consistently with international human rights and refugee law. In this regard, the UNHCR points to the need to respect the prohibition of non-refoulement and thus avoid disembarkation of rescued migrants in territories where their lives and freedoms would be threatened.[23]

Overall, with the adoption of the discussed provisions, Italy formally complies with the international conventions on the law of the sea as well as with the IMO Guidelines and IAMSAR Manual.[24] In particular, it incorporates into the framework the definition of POS and the obligations to cooperate with other states in SAR operations, making them binding.

However, the national legal framework is very complex and fragmented, and similarly to the international provisions, it does not predetermine which state

[20] Ministero delle Infrastrutture e dei Trasporti, Comando Generale del Corpo delle Capitanerie di porto – Guardia Costiera, Standard Operating Procedures SOP 009/15, settembre 2015.

[21] ibid 2.

[22] ibid 2–3. It should be noted that a Technical Roundtable for Coordination of Illegal Immigration by Sea, which took place upon the initiative of the former Minister of the Interior Salvini, 'revised' the Operating Procedures on 12 February 2019. Although the changes were not formalised, the authorities involved applied them in practice – in violation of the principles of legality and certainty of the law – until the start of the Covid-19 pandemic. According to the changes, the Ministry of the Interior would be competent, as the authority for security, to assign a POS (without the involvement of the Department for Civil Liberties and Immigration) after reaching an agreement with the European Commission and EU states on migrants' relocation to other EU countries. Fulvio Vassallo Paleologo, 'Salvini-Open Arms: un Processo Capovolto' (ADIF, 14 May 2022), available at: www.a-dif.org/2022/05/14/salvini-open-arms-un-processo-capovolto/. Since 2020, with the pandemic, the situation has changed, as finding an agreement with other EU states on migrants' relocation became unfeasible.

[23] UNHCR, 'General Legal Considerations: Search-and-rescue Operations Involving Refugees and Migrants at Sea' (UNHCR, November 2017), available at: www.refworld.org/pdfid/5a2e9efd4.pdf; see also, Maritime Safety Committee, Guidelines on the Treatment of Persons Rescued at Sea, UN Doc MSC78/26/Add.2, Resolution MSC167(78) (20 May 2004) (2004 IMO Guidelines) para 6.17, and ch 3, section II.C; Commissioner for Human Rights, 'Lives Saved. Rights Protected. Bridging the Protection Gaps for Refugees and Migrants in the Mediterranean' (Commissioner for Human Rights, Council of Europe, June 2019) 27, available at: rm.coe.int/lives-saved-rights-protected-bridging-the-protection-gap-for-refugees-/168094eb87; UNSMIL and OHCHR, 'Desperate and Dangerous: Report on the Human Rights Situation of Migrants and Refugees in Libya' (UNSMIL and OHCHR, 18 December 2018) 17.

[24] See ch 3, section II.C.

shall receive the rescued persons. Also, it does not provide special rules in cases of overlapping SAR zones. As a consequence, many problems arise in practice, especially concerning the interpretation of POS as well as the identification of which state is responsible for coordinating an SAR event when the latter occurs in international waters, as I explain in the next section.

III. ISSUES CONCERNING COORDINATION OF SAR OPERATIONS AND DISEMBARKATION TO A POS

The legal gaps, compounded by a lack of political will on the side of the states concerned due to migration concerns, give rise to failures to coordinate SAR events, sometimes ending with the loss of lives at sea and/or delays in disembarking the rescued migrants to a POS. Problems arise especially when Malta and Libya are the other states involved, due to: (1) the wide extension of the Maltese SAR zone and its overlapping with the Italian SAR zone; (2) the refusal of the Maltese government to sign the amendments to the 2004 SAR and SOLAS Conventions and different views on the concepts of POS and distress; and (3) the creation of a Libyan SAR zone and attribution of SAR operations to the Libyan Coast Guard. Although the focus of this work is on Italy, the Maltese and Libyan approaches to SAR must be explained to understand the ambiguous responses to migrant vessels.

A. Malta's Approach to SAR Operations

The Maltese SAR area extends over approximately 250,000 km^2 and *includes the Italian island of Lampedusa*.[25] As such, the Maltese SAR zone is extremely large compared with the islands' size. When a distress call comes from within the joint Maltese–Italian SAR area, the two countries often disagree on who should intervene. However, practice shows how, after an initial stalemate, Italy tends to assume coordination and assign a safe disembarkation place on its territory.[26] The NGO *Ocean Viking* vessel, which saved 118 migrants in the Italian–Maltese SAR zone on 25 June 2020, is an example of this scenario. Despite the repeated requests submitted to both the Italian and Maltese authorities for the identification of a safe disembarkation place, migrants remained stranded for over a week

[25] S Trevisanut, 'Search and Rescue Operations in the Mediterranean: Factor of Cooperation or Conflict?' (2010) 25 *International Journal of Marine and Coastal Law* 523; J Coppens, 'The Essential Role of Malta in Drafting the New Regional Agreement on Migrants at Sea in the Mediterranean Basin' (2013) 44 *Journal of Maritime Law and Commerce* 89, 98; The Malta Independent, 'Malta Stands Firm as Italy Insists on SAR Zone Reduction' *Malta Independent* (26 August 2009), available at: www.independent.com.mt/articles/2009–08–26/news/malta-stands-firm-as-italy-insists-on-sar-zone-reduction-262427/.

[26] ÁJ García Carriazo, 'Small Island, Big Issue: Malta and its Search and Rescue Region' (2019) 7 *Paix et Securité Internationales* 299, 311; Leanza and Caffio (n 1).

on the NGO boat that had rescued them. It was not until 7 July that the Italian authorities finally intervened to transfer the migrants onto a quarantine boat.[27]

Ronzitti explains that a plausible reason for Malta having declared such a large SAR area, despite not having the resources to ensure efficient operations, is that it aims to pursue other interests[28] – Malta derives around €8.23 million every year from air traffic over its Flight Information Region, which overlaps with the SAR zone. Other authors support this view and note how Malta has access to the related benefits of the large SAR zone, which include funding for the Coast Guard, fishing zones and oil exploration.[29]

Figure 4.1 Overlapping SAR Regions[30]

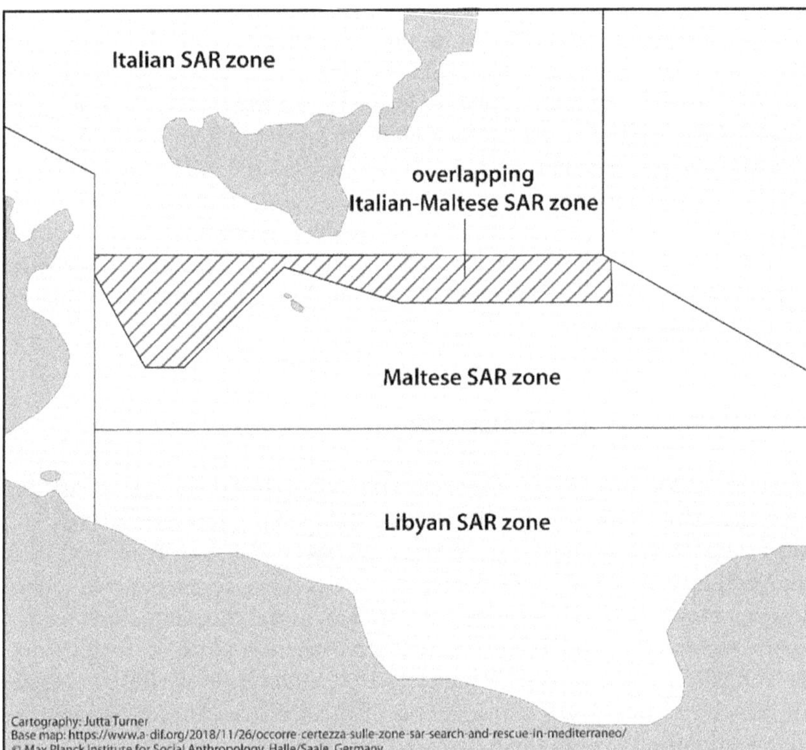

[27] InfoMigrants, 'Ocean Viking: Italy to Transfer Migrants to Quarantine Ship after Suicide Attempts' (*InfoMigrants*, 6 July 2020), available at: www.infomigrants.net/en/post/25803/ocean-viking-italy-to-transfer-migrants-to-quarantine-ship-after-suicide-attempts.

[28] N Ronzitti, *Diritto Internazionale*, 6th edn (Torino, Giappichelli, 2019) 136.

[29] Matthew Vella, 'Malta "Not for Sale", Borg Replies to Frattini' *Malta Today* (23 August 2009), available at: archive.maltatoday.com.mt/2009/08/23/t3.html; García-Carriazo (n 26) 302; Kurt Sansone, 'Malta Should Give Up its Large Search and Rescue Area, Italian Minister Says' *Malta Today* (13 June 2018), available at: www.maltatoday.com.mt/news/national/87550/malta_should_give_up_its_large_search_and_rescue_area_italian_minister_says#.YZeUsC1Q10s.

[30] García-Carriazo (n 26) 304.

Trevisanut criticises this approach for obfuscating the main function of the SAR zone, which is to provide SAR services.[31] However, the Maltese authorities deny avoiding their SAR responsibilities for such reasons.[32]

The lack of SAR collaboration between the Italian and Maltese authorities can also be ascribed to Malta's refusal to accept the 2004 amendments to the SAR and SOLAS Conventions as well as the IASMAR Manual and 2004 IMO Guidelines, which establish states' obligations to cooperate in and coordinate SAR activities to ensure a POS within a reasonable time, and which mandate that the first state to receive information of a possible SAR event is responsible for taking the first urgent actions.[33]

Malta also interprets the term 'distress' restrictively, taking the view that states shall rescue a migrant vessel only when it is sinking, but not when it faces other problems, such as the engines stopping.[34] In such cases, providing assistance is seen as a 'duty of care', while rescue is reserved for cases of 'immediate danger'.[35] This means that the Armed Forces of Malta (AFM), which are in charge of SAR services in their SAR zone, would not automatically intervene when they identify a migrant vessel. The AFM would instead check whether the migrant vessel has enough fuel to reach Italy[36] and provide it with 'directions,

[31] Trevisanut, 'Search and Rescue Operations in the Mediterranean' (n 25) 532, 538–39.

[32] *Times of Malta*, 'Updated: Malta's SAR Zone Too Huge for Country to Manage – Frattini' *Times of Malta* (22 August 2009), available at: timesofmalta.com/articles/view/malta-sar-zone-too-huge-for-country-to-manage-frattini.270320. 'The SAR zone is not a jurisdictional zone and the state's obligation is only to coordinate. The seas were split up into SAR zones in the International Convention on Maritime Search and Rescue 1979, in Hamburg'. Krista Bonello Rutter Giappone, Interview with Officer of Armed Forces of Malta (online, 28 January 2022).

[33] International Convention for the Safety of Life at Sea (London, 1 November 1974) 1184 UNTS 278 (SOLAS Convention) Chapter V, reg 33, para 1-1; International Convention on Maritime Search and Rescue (Hamburg, 27 April 1979) 1405 UNTS 97 (SAR Convention) Annex, ch 3, para 3.1.9. Additionally, para 6.5 of the 2004 IMO Guidelines, states that '[e]ach RCC shall have effective plans of operation … in place for responding to all types of SAR situations'. Such plans shall also consider situations occurring in an associated SAR region or outside their SAR region, until the RCC responsible for the region or better suited in the particular case can intervene. See ch 3, section III.C, and also Monique Agius, 'Malta is in Breach of its Obligations under International Law – Amnesty International' *Newsbook* (12 August 2018), available at: newsbook.com.mt/en/malta-is-in-breach-of-its-obligations-under-international-law-amnesty-international/.

[34] S Galani, 'Port Closures and Persons at Sea in International Law' (2021) 70 *International & Comparative Law Quarterly* 605.

[35] Officer of Armed Forces of Malta (n 32).

[36] D Zammit, 'The "Hermeneutics" of Suspicion: Linking Maltese Border Management and Migrant (Dis)integration Practices' ('Migration and Border Management. Challenges and Perspectives for Reform' Conference, University of Malta, 25 March 2022); Manuel Delia, 'Photos Show AFM Illegally Forced Migrants out of Maltese Waters and Sent Them to Sicily' (*Truth Be Told*, 20 May 2020), available at: manueldelia.com/2020/05/photos-show-afm-illegally-forced-migrants-out-of-maltese-waters-and-sent-them-to-sicily/; Lorenzo Tondo, '"We Give You 30 Minutes": Malta Turns Migrant Boat Away with Directions to Italy' *Guardian* (20 May 2020), available at: www.theguardian.com/global-development/2020/may/20/we-give-you-30-minutes-malta-turns-migrant-boat-away-with-directions-to-italy; Lorenzo Tondo, 'Italy Considers Charges over Malta's "Shocking" Refusal to Rescue Migrants' *Guardian* (29 May 2020), available at: www.theguardian.com/global-development/2020/may/29/italy-considers-charges-over-maltas-shocking-refusal-to-rescue-migrants.

water, and possibly food to people in distress, but without taking them on board, hence avoiding complications associated with rescue'.[37] However, this practice can be very dangerous for migrants, and according to several accounts, there have been cases where the AFM received calls to rescue and even approached the migrant boats, but did not intervene.[38] For instance, this occurred in August 2009, when five Eritreans rescued near Lampedusa reported that the other 75 migrants on board 'died of dehydration and starvation, notwithstanding that at least ten ships had passed them by, and further alleged that they had been supplied with water and food by Maltese authorities, who had not taken steps to rescue them'. The Maltese authorities confirmed the accounts of the event, but they stated that the vessel was not considered to be in a situation of distress.[39]

A similar event is the 'left to die' episode in March 2011, which involved 72 migrants sailing from the Libyan coast and heading towards Sicily.[40] Shortly after its departure, the boat ran out of fuel, food and water, and the migrants were left to drift for two weeks until they landed back in Libya. Only nine of them survived. Although emergency calls were made and the boat was located by the Italian and Maltese Coast Guards, no rescue was made.[41] The Italian and Maltese SAR centres argued that, as long as the boat is in motion, a situation of 'distress' does not arise to justify a sudden intervention.[42] A subsequent investigation carried out by the Council of Europe (CoE) strongly criticised the failures of Italy, Malta, Libya and NATO (at the time in control of the Libyan SAR zone) for not responding to the vessel in distress.[43] Some of the survivors, supported by a few associations, filed complaints in Italy, France, Spain, Canada and Belgium, but none of them has so far been successful.[44]

Moreover, according to Malta, POS means 'safe' in the maritime law sense rather than human rights sense. Malta takes the view that its international obligations are only to take the rescued migrants to the nearest safe port to the

[37] T Basaran, 'The Saved and the Drowned: Governing Indifference in the Name of Security' (2015) 46 *Security Dialogue* 205, 213.

[38] Zammit (n 36); Krista Bonello Rutter Giappone, Interview with Lawyer, Malta (online, 18 March 2022).

[39] Komp notes that Malta seems to take a narrow view of 'distress'. LM Komp, 'The Duty to Assist Persons in Distress: An Alternative Source of Protection against the Return of Migrants and Asylum Seekers to the High Seas?' in V Moreno-Lax and E Papastavridis (eds), *'Boat Refugees' and Migrants at Sea: A Comprehensive Approach* (Leiden, Brill, 2017); IOM, 'Protection of Migrants at Sea' (IOM, 17 September 2018) 89, available at: publications.iom.int/system/files/pdf/protection_of_migrants_at_sea.pdf; A Gallagher and F David, *The International Law of Migrant Smuggling* (Cambridge, CUP, 2014) 459, fn 269.

[40] C Heller, L Pezzani and S Studio, 'Report on the "Left-To-Die Boat"' (Centre for Research Architecture, Goldsmiths, University of London, 2012), available at: www.fidh.org/IMG/pdf/fo-report.pdf.

[41] ibid.

[42] Brigida (n 16) 118.

[43] PACE, Committee on Migration, Refugees and Displaced Persons, 'Lives Lost in the Mediterranean Sea: Who is Responsible?' (Strasbourg, PACE, 2012), available at: assembly.coe.int/CommitteeDocs/2012/20120329_mig_RPT.EN.pdf.

[44] Email from Lawyer no 2 to author (29 September 2023). For more information, see section V.B in this chapter.

rescue location,[45] as this can avoid 'unnecessary deviations by the rescue unit and rescued persons can be disembarked faster'[46] – while seeming to acknowledge that the non-refoulement principle shall be respected.[47]

In practice, according to several reports, Malta regularly evades SAR requests and the related appeals to identify a POS – according to the European Council on Refugees and Exiles, in 2022, Malta failed to rescue 7,459 sea migrants.[48] This occurs not only when rescue operations take place in the joint Maltese–Italian SAR area, but occasionally also when rescue calls come from within the Maltese SAR area. There are accounts that, when a distressed vessel is in the Maltese SAR zone, migrants are sometimes brought to another SAR region. For instance, this occurred on 16 July 2018, when migrants saved by a Maltese vessel in the Maltese SAR zone were transferred to the vessel *SAROST 5* and then diverted to Tunisia.[49] Another case took place in 2020 in Maltese territorial waters and concerned an AFM boat which gave a migrants' dinghy a new motor, fuel, life vests and water and redirected them towards Italy.[50]

Therefore, Malta's approach has an impact on Italian practice, especially when distress calls come from international waters. Malta's rejection of the latest amendments to the SAR and SOLAS Conventions and the lack of clear provisions and agreements between the two countries on where disembarkation shall take place create uncertainty around the legal obligations. It also raises issues of unclear accountability of the state actors involved in delayed or failed responses.

B. Delegation of SAR Services to Libya

The situation has become even more unclear and complex since 28 June 2018, when the government of Tripoli notified the International Maritime

[45] S Trevisanaut, 'Search and Rescue Operations in the Mediterranean: Factor of Cooperation or Conflict?' (2010) 25 *International Journal of Marine and Coastal Law* 523.

[46] ibid 532.

[47] 'In this regard, successive Maltese governments have always held that such migrants should be taken to the nearest safe port. Since the Convention on Safety of Life at Sea (SOLAS) is an international maritime convention, it is evident that the word "safe" refers to maritime law, not to human rights'. Tonio Borg, 'Where Does One Draw the Line?' *Times of Malta* (19 July 2018), available at: timesofmalta.com/articles/view/where-does-one-draw-the-line-tonio-borg.684756.

[48] The information and estimate are based on accounts of NGOs and journalists. Aditus Foundation, 'Country Report: Malta' (European Council on Refugees and Exiles, 2022) 23; García-Carriazo (n 26) 307;.

[49] Fulvio Vassallo Paleologo, 'Respingimenti Collettivi Vietati, Tunisia e Libia non Sono "Paesi Terzi Sicuri"' (ADIF, 31 July 2018), available at: www.a-dif.org/2018/07/31/respingimenti-collettivi-vietati-tunisia-e-libia-non-sono-paesi-terzi-sicuri/.

[50] Tondo, '"We Give You 30 Minutes": Malta Turns Migrant Boat away with Directions to Italy' (n 36); Delia, 'Photos Show AFM Illegally Forced Migrants out of Maltese Waters and Sent Them to Sicily' (n 36).

Organization (IMO) of its SAR zone, which extended about 174,000 km off its coast.[51] Until then, the IMRCC had regularly assumed the coordination of SAR for distressed vessels in international waters. However, the expansion of the Libyan SAR zone enabled Malta and Italy to 'legally' shift the responsibility to the Libyan authorities when a vessel requiring rescue is in Libya's SAR zone.[52] Consequently, there have been delays in SAR responses and fatal consequences, such as the drowning of 130 persons on 21 April 2021 in the Libyan SAR zone.[53] In this case, 'Alarm Phone'[54] – a hotline for boats in distress – communicated the position of the migrants to the Libyan and Italian authorities, as well as to a nearby merchant vessel flying the Italian flag. A Frontex aircraft was also flying over the area. However, despite the worsening sea conditions, no one intervened. The IMRCC told Alarm Phone to contact the Libyan Coast Guard and did not instruct the merchant vessel to intervene. According to the Libyan Coast Guard, they searched for three vessels, but had to stop because of the worsening weather conditions. On the night between 21 and 22 April 2021, three merchant ships in the area found the wreck of the boat and dead bodies.[55] Following the event, a number of civil society associations and lawyers addressed a complaint to the Rome Public Prosecutor's Office asking to establish the criminal responsibility of the actors involved. At the time of writing this book, the investigation is still pending.[56]

In such a scenario, a major problem is that, as Mann points out,

> the fundamental tenet of law according to which the responsibility for security is ultimately allocated to public authority doesn't hold on the high seas or in the SAR zone of a collapsed state such as Libya (…). In the SAR zone of a collapsed state there is a lacuna in responsibility.[57]

[51] Alice Cuddy, 'La Libia Crea la sua Zona SAR e Notifica l'IMO (con il Sostegno UE)' *Euronews* (9 July 2018), available at: it.euronews.com/2018/07/09/la-libia-crea-la-sua-zona-sar-e-notifica-l-imo-con-il-sostegno-ue-; Benjamin Bathke, 'Migrants in Distress Returned to Libya – On Malta's Request' (*InfoMigrants*, 29 June 2021), available at: www.infomigrants.net/en/post/33257/migrants-in-distress-returned-to-libya--on-maltas-request; Emma Wallis, 'Can the Law of the Sea Regulate the Stormy Standoffs between Private Rescue Ships and EU Governments?' (*InfoMigrants*, 9 July 2019), available at: www.infomigrants.net/en/post/18037/can-the-law-of-the-sea-regulate-the-stormy-standoffs-between-private-rescue-ships-and-eu-governments.

[52] Bathke (n 51); Wallis (n 51).

[53] Alessandra Ziniti, 'Migranti, le Foto Shock dell'Ultima Strage: "Noi Soccorritori in Mezzo ad un mare di Cadaveri". L'Italia Sapeva della Richiesta di Aiuto' *La Repubblica* (23 April 2021), available at: www.repubblica.it/cronaca/2021/04/23/news/migranti_la_foto_choc_dell_ultima_strage_noi_soccorritori_in_mezzo_a_un_mare_di_cadaveri_-297709835/; Vita, 'Ecco Come 130 Persone Sono State Lasciate Annegare al Largo della Libia' (*VITA*, 23 April 2021), available at: www.vita.it/it/article/2021/04/23/ecco-come-130-persone-sono-state-lasciate-annegare-al-largo-della-libi/159116/; ASGI, 'Naufragio del 22 Aprile 2021: Presentato l'Esposto per Accertarne la Responsibilita' (ASGI, 29 July 2021), available at: www.asgi.it/notizie/naufragio-aprile-2021-esposto-per-accertare-responsabilita/.

[54] Alarm Phone, 'FAQ' (*AlarmPhone*, May 2022), available at: alarmphone.org/en/faq_en/.

[55] Border Forensics, 'Chain of Events' (*AlarmPhone*, July 2021), available at: alarmphone.org/wp-content/uploads/2021/07/20210716_AP182_BF-COE.pdf.

[56] ASGI, 'Naufragio del 22 Aprile 2021' (n 23).

[57] I Mann, 'Maritime Legal Black Holes: Migration and Rightlessness in International Law' (2018) 29 *European Journal of International Law* 347, 366–67.

According to Smith, despite the poor human rights situation in Libya and its ineffective SAR services, neither the European Union (EU), its Member States, nor the international community have taken any action to limit Libya's control over its SAR zone.[58] This is because Libya's involvement in SAR operations in the Central Mediterranean is part of border control policies of the EU and some of its Member States[59] and reflects the difficulties that migrants face in accessing Europe and its system of protection. Indeed, a number of agreements between EU states and Libya support the Libyan approach to SAR operations. While I will discuss the agreements between Libya and Italy in the next chapter, I should mention the 2020 Maltese–Libyan deal for 'mutual collaboration' here. This agreement intends to divert migrant boats 'back to Libya before they come into'[60] Maltese waters, and has allowed more migrants to be transferred back to Libya. The Maltese authorities have also sometimes permitted Libyan patrol boats to enter the Maltese SAR area to intercept boats of migrants heading towards the Maltese or Italian coasts, even in areas where the Maltese and Italian SAR zones overlap. According to one report,

> in one incident recounted by a Somali woman, a boat of migrants was rescued by a Philippine tanker approximately 44 nautical miles from Malta. She reported that the ship captain radioed the Italian Maritime Rescue Coordination Centre (MRCC) to seek directions on disembarkation and reassured the migrants that they would be disembarked in a place of safety. Several hours later she realized they were being returned to al-Khoms, Libya. The migrants on board the tanker began crying and begging the crew not to return them to Libya. When they finally disembarked in Libya, the woman recounted that the LCG officials were laughing and mocked them, saying: 'Welcome to Malta!' After being disembarked, the woman recounted that many women and girls disappeared, and she later heard that they were sold to traffickers.[61]

In conclusion, what emerges is that, notwithstanding the incorporation of the international provisions into national legislation, questions persist concerning fundamental aspects of the SAR system and the coordination and collaboration

[58] A Smith, 'Uncertainty, Alert and Distress: The Precarious Position of NGO Search and Rescue Operations in the Central Mediterranean' (2017) 5 *Paix et Sécurité Internationales* 29, 39.

[59] ibid 51.

[60] Senior government source in Ivan Martin, 'Exposed: Malta's Secret Migrant Deal with Libya' *Times of Malta* (November 2019), available at: timesofmalta.com/articles/view/exposed-maltas-secret-migrant-deal-with-libya.748800; Government of National Accord of the State of Libya and The Government of The Republic of Malta, 'Memorandum of Understanding Between the Government of National Accord of the State of Libya and The Government of The Republic of Malta in the Field of Combatting Illegal Immigration' (28 May 2020).

[61] OHCHR, 'Lethal Disregard' (n 3) 21. See Fulvio Vassallo Paleologo, 'Soccorsi Clandestini e Respingimenti in Libia. Italia e Malta Violano gli Obblighi di Coordinamento SAR' (ADIF, 17 October 2018), available at: www.a-dif.org/2018/10/17/soccorsi-clandestini-e-respingimenti-in-libia-italia-e-malta-violano-gli-obblighi-di-coordinamento-sar/; Fulvio Vassallo Paleologo, 'Obblighi di Ricerca e Soccorso in Mare Imposti dal Diritto Internazionale e Accordi con gli Stati di Transito' (ADIF, 8 November 2019), available at: www.a-dif.org/2019/11/08/obblighi-di-ricerca-e-soccorso-in-mare-imposti-dal-diritto-internazionale-e-accordi-con-gli-stati-di-transito/.

between Italy and its neighbouring states. In particular, responsibilities are uncertain when SAR events occur on the high seas or in overlapping SAR zones. States intentionally exploit the overlapping SAR areas and legal gaps to dodge their obligations. As such, the ambiguities result in people being 'left to die'.

IV. NATIONAL RESCUE OBLIGATIONS ON PRIVATE VESSELS

Under the existing legislation, primary responsibility for SAR operations rests with states. Complementarily, the legal framework relies on private actors to assist in rescue efforts at the direction of the competent RCC. However, in the last few years, to substitute for the inadequacy of state SAR services, commercial vessels have been increasingly called on to rescue sea migrants. This substitution raises a number of issues concerning migrants' rights as well as the burden placed on the industry.

A. National Legal Framework

Articles 489–500 of the Navigation Code implement the international obligations on all private vessels to provide assistance to people in distress or in danger of getting lost at sea, and apply to all boats flying the Italian flag, even where the event takes place outside the territorial sea, and to captains of foreign ships in Italian waters. Moreover, they require all private vessels to rescue such persons if the boat is completely incapable of sailing.

Compared with the international conventions on the law of the sea,[62] Articles 489–90 of the Navigation Code identify a larger group of cases in which rescue is considered mandatory, going beyond situations in which there is danger to life. Brigida explains that the Italian jurisprudence has extended the scope of these Articles to apply in any situation of danger, even merely potential danger.[63] Such a wide-ranging position is particularly relevant since it may also apply to atypical dangerous situations, such as the presence of floating logs or the progressive worsening of meteorological and marine conditions.[64]

[62] Brigida (n 16) 86; Art 10 of the Brussels Convention states: 'Every master is bound, so far as he can do so without serious danger to his vessel and persons thereon, to render assistance to any person in danger of being lost at sea'. Convention for the Unification of Certain Rules with Respect to Assistance and Salvage at Sea (Brussels, 23 September 1910) (Brussels Convention). See ch 3, section II.B.

[63] Brigida (n 16) 85, 86; UNCLOS Convention art 98 also sets forth the duty to render assistance in situations where there is danger of getting lost at sea. The duty to render assistance encompasses a number of actions, such as providing food, towing the unseaworthy vessel, and contacting the maritime authorities. The duty to rescue implies retrieving the persons in distress, providing for their medical or other needs, and then delivering them to a POS. O Osamudiamen Eruaga, 'Irregular Migration in the Mediterranean and the Challenges of Observing the Duty to Render Assistance at Sea' (2018) 17 *Loyola Maritime Law Journal* 33, 39–42.

[64] Brigida (n 16) 86.

Furthermore, the omission of assistance provided for in Article 489 or the failure to attempt a rescue in cases where it is mandatory according to Article 490 is criminally punished under Article 1158 of the Navigation Code. Depending on the consequences of the omission, the penalty can involve reclusion for up to eight years.[65]

In practice, private vessels' obligation to rescue may arise either because they have identified an incident nearby or because they have received a mandatory rescue order from the Coast Guard authority, as per Articles 69 and 70 of the Navigation Code.[66] In light of the international and national legal provisions and the 2020 National Search and Rescue Plan,[67] when the captain of a vessel acts spontaneously, he or she shall communicate all the possible information to the competent RCC before providing such assistance or immediately afterwards.[68] The captain shall then follow the RCC's instructions concerning the transportation of migrants to the port of the responsible state or trans-ship them to ships of the Navy or the Coast Guard.[69]

Thus, the Italian framework provides greater protection than the international treaties of the law of the sea. The main problems concern its practical implementation, as explained in the next subsection.

B. Issues Linked to the Delegation of Rescues to Private Vessels

As a consequence of the duty to render assistance to persons in danger at sea and the incidence of shipping vessels in the Central Mediterranean, in 2018, commercial ships saved 1,438 migrants out of the total 19,778 rescued,

[65] According to Art 1158 of the Navigation Code:

> The commander of a national or foreign ship, float or aircraft, who fails to provide assistance or to attempt rescue in cases where he is obliged to do so under this code, is punished with imprisonment for up to two years.
>
> The penalty is imprisonment from one to six years, if a personal injury results from the fact; from three to eight years, if death ensues.
>
> If the offense is committed through negligence, the penalty is imprisonment for up to six months; in the cases indicated in the previous paragraph, the penalties provided for therein are reduced by half.

[66] According to part of the doctrine, the hypothesis of aid on the order of the Authority pursuant to Art 70 of the Navigation Code is to be included in the context of the requirement of services, ie, the case in which the private person is called upon to render a service to the Public Administration, even if this is to the advantage of another private individual, which in our case study is the ship in distress. Brigida (n 16) 89.

[67] See para 310: 'Segnalazione Emergenze e Valutazione delle Notizie'.

[68] SAR Convention, Annex, ch 4, Art 4.2.3; Codice della Navigazione, 30 marzo 1942, n 327 (Edizione 2020) Arts 69, 70.

[69] Codice della Navigazione (n 68) Arts 489–500, 1158.

and in 2017, 11,355 migrants out of the 114,286 rescued.[70] In light of this, critical voices have arisen from various sides – the European Community Shipowners' Association, the International Transport Workers Federation, as well as the Italian Union Confitarma – pointing out both economic losses and the inability of certain types of merchant vessels to host large numbers of migrants, which can put the crews (who are not trained for such operations) at risk.[71]

In particular, commercial vessels often encounter delays when having to transfer the saved migrants to a POS, due to disagreements between the concerned states over who should accept them.[72] One of these events involved the *Maersk Etienne*, a Danish-flagged chemical tanker which, on 4 August 2020, was asked by the Maltese RCC to rescue a boat of 27 migrants in distress about 70 nautical miles north of the Libyan coast.[73] Although the *Maersk Etienne* was en route to La Skhira, Tunisia, it changed its course to save the migrants and anchored 16 nautical miles southeast of Malta.[74] However, Malta did not allow disembarkation in its ports and denied having made the request, saying that the rescue occurred outside its territorial waters.[75] Other states refused to intervene and provide assistance, including Denmark as the flag state, which instead requested that Tunisia (the country closest to the

[70] Italian Coast Guard, 'Search and Rescue (S.A.R.), Activity in the Central Mediterranean Sea From January 1st to December 31st 2018' (December 2018), available at: www.guardiacostiera.gov.it/attivita/Documents/attivita-sar-immigrazione-2018/Annuale%202018%20ENG.pdf; Italian Coast Guard, 'Search and Rescue (S.A.R.), Activity in the Central Mediterranean Sea from January 1st to December 31st 2017' (December 2017), available at: www.guardiacostiera.gov.it/attivita/Documents/attivita-sar-immigrazione-2017/annuale%202017%20ing.pdf; Osamudiamen Eruaga (n 63) 49.

[71] European Community Shipowner's Association (ECSA), 'Merchant Ships' Involvement in Migrants' Search and Rescue Operations Growing Again' (ECSA, 24 May 2017), available at: www.ecsa.eu/news/merchant-ships-involvement-migrants-search-and-rescue-operations-growing-again; International Transport Workers' Federation (ITF), 'Boat Crisis "a Result of Inequality and Lack of Regulation"' (ITF, 26 May 2015), available at: www.itfglobal.org/es/node/988; Leanza and Caffio (n 1) 13; RL Kilpatrick, 'Why Evolving European SAR Policies Threaten Merchant Shipping' (2019–20) 7 *Maritime Safety and Security Law Journal*, Special Issue on the EU and Maritime Security 31.

[72] See also David Giancristofaro Alberti, 'Alexander Maersk a Pozzallo/Migranti, Salvini "Apre" il Porto: Guardia Costiera, "Risponderemo Sempre a Sos"' (*ilsussidiario.net*, 2 June 2018), available at: www.ilsussidiario.net/news/cronaca/2018/6/25/migranti-la-nave-cargo-alexander-maersk-sbarca-a-pozzallo-e-arrivato-l-ok-da-parte-del-viminale/827505/; Il Giornale di Sicilia, 'Migranti, in 40 Soccorsi da un Mercantile al Largo di Malta. Salvini: "Rimanga Dov'è"' *Il Giornale di Sicilia* (16 October 2018), available at: gds.it/articoli/cronaca/2018/10/16/migranti-in-40-soccorsi-da-un-mercantile-al-largo-di-malta-salvini-rimanga-dove-ca90c7fb-5366-4011-ae14-1c0366b638df/.

[73] Daniel Trilling, 'A commercial ship saved 27 Migrants, but now the EU has abandoned them at sea' *Guardian* (4 September 2020), available at: www.theguardian.com/commentisfree/2020/sep/04/ship-rescued-migrants-eu-sea-tanker-malta-european.

[74] Qandeel Shaam, 'I Enjoyed Being Commander of Such an Heroic Crew during the Rescue Operation' (*Maersk Tankers*, 7 December 2020), available at: maersktankers.com/newsroom/captain-yeroshkin-on-his-crews-rescue-and-care-of-27-persons-caught-at-sea-for–38-days.

[75] Julian Delia, 'Maersk Tankers Warns Supplies Running out for Migrants, Crew on Board' *Times of Malta* (2 September 2020), available at: timesofmalta.com/articles/view/maersk-tankers-warns-supplies-running-out-for-migrants-crew-on-board.815700.

rescue location)[76] accept responsibility for the migrants, but this request was also denied. The *Maersk Etienne* remained stranded in international waters for almost 40 days – one of the longest stand-offs in recent years. After conditions on board deteriorated due to lack of food, supplies and medical problems, the migrants were allowed to be trans-shipped to the *Mare Jonio*, an NGO vessel, which disembarked in Sicily the following day.[77]

From a strict legal point of view, Attard and Kilpatrick remark that Malta, in alerting the *Maersk Etienne* shipmaster to assist, was fulfilling its obligations under the 1979 SAR Convention. As Malta did not adopt the 2004 SAR Convention Amendments, it did not have a responsibility to 'arrange for such disembarkation to be effected as soon as reasonably practicable'.[78] 'Furthermore, Malta was not the closest place of safety at the time of the rescue, and therefore was not be compelled to accept disembarkation in line with the closest safe port doctrine'.[79] On the other hand, Attard and Kilpatrick note that other factors may compel a state to accept disembarkation, including humanitarian, security, or safety considerations concerning the ship, the crew, or passengers.[80]

Given the obstacles and delays faced by the shipping industry after rescuing sea migrants, Kilpatrick and Smith point out how the 'strong commercial disincentives to comply suggest at least some operators of commercial vessels may seek to avoid the obligation to render assistance'.[81] They state that private 'vessels may be turning off electronic tracking equipment when they are in the vicinity of migrant vessels so that they can evade the obligation to render assistance'.[82] Similarly, Aarstad notes trends amongst commercial vessels of avoiding 'migrant-heavy areas', 'refusing to reveal their position', or 'bypassing migrant vessels in distress' in order to prevent losses and risks connected with rescues of migrants.[83] Cusumano also explains how commercial ships 'have

[76] 'An interesting dimension of the *Maersk Etienne* incident is the status of the flag State in this case. Denmark is a European Union (EU) Member State. Consequently, it is bound by policies, in light of EU solidarity, to collectively manage irregular migratory flows.' Felicity G Attard and Richard L Kilpatrick, 'Reflections on the Maersk Etienne Standoff and its Ramifications for the Duty to Render Assistance at Sea' (*European Journal of International Law: TALK!*, 12 October 2020), available at: www.ejiltalk.org/reflections-on-the-maersk-etienne-standoff-and-its-ramifications-for-the-duty-to-render-assistance-at-sea/.

[77] BBC, 'Migrants Allowed off Maersk Tanker after 40 Days at Sea' *BBC News* (13 September 2020), available at: www.bbc.com/news/world-europe-54136627; Per Fredrik Jensen and Bjørg Eikeland, 'The Maersk Etienne Rescue Highlights the Difficulties in Disembarking Migrants Rescued at Sea' (*Gard Insight*, 8 October 2020), available at: www.gard.no/web/updates/content/30502985/the-maersk-etienne-rescue-highlights-the-difficulties-in-disembarking-migrants-rescued-at-sea.

[78] Attard and Kilpatrick (n 76).

[79] ibid.

[80] ibid.

[81] RL Kilpatrick and A Smith, 'The International Legal Obligation to Rescue during Mass Migration at Sea: Navigating the Sovereign and Commercial Dimensions of a Mediterranean Crisis' (2015) 28(2) *University of San Francisco School of Law Maritime Law Journal* 141, 160.

[82] ibid 161.

[83] Å Kalland Aarstad, 'The Duty to Assist and Its Disincentives: The Shipping Industry and the Mediterranean Migration Crisis' (2015) 20 *Mediterranean Politics* 413, 414.

financial disincentives to conduct SAR, and are even reported to deliberately avoid migrants' transit areas in order not to be obliged to conduct a rescue'.[84] Along the same lines, the Office of the United Nations High Commissioner for Human Rights (OHCHR) notes a significant reduction in rescue operations conducted by merchant ships starting from 2018, mainly due to the concern expressed by the merchant industry that they may suffer criminal charges[85] under the EU anti-smuggling and trafficking legislation for aiding and abetting illegal immigration.[86] However, complete and accurate data on commercial vessels' failure to respond to boats with migrants in distress are not available due to the 'invisibility' of private vessels in the international discourse, since they are not often mentioned in EU and national policy responses to sea migration.[87]

Consequently, as Klepp points out, states' inadequate responses to rescues of sea migrants by private ships cause unpredictability in the consequences of rescue operations and weaken the international SAR system.[88] Clear and effective legal and political measures are lacking to aid private ships in the context of sea migration and to establish accountability for their failures.

V. ACCOUNTABILITY FOR SAR VIOLATIONS

Generally, enforcing SAR obligations is complicated and it is difficult to establish accountability for breaches of these obligations. To simplify the analysis of the issue, in the next subsections I distinguish between violations of the duty to render assistance at sea by private and state actors and delays in disembarkation. Cases concerning NGO vessels, meanwhile, will be discussed separately in chapter six.

[84] E Cusumano, 'Emptying the Sea with a Spoon? Non-governmental Providers of Migrants Search and Rescue in the Mediterranean' (2017) 75 *Marine Policy* 91, 97. This is also confirmed by Luca Misculin, 'La Nave. Giorno 5 – Osservare l' Orizzonte' (Podcast, *Il Post*, 20 March 2023), available at: www.spreaker.com/user/ilpost/la-nave-5.

[85] OHCHR explains:

> 'Several migrants interviewed by OHCHR reported being sighted by private merchant or commercial vessels within international waters who failed to render assistance. On several occasions, migrants reported that the vessels came close enough to verify their coordinates, direction of travel, and the general situation on board the boat, but did not initiate actions to rescue them or render immediate assistance. Following the failure of these commercial vessels to render assistance, some of the migrants interviewed by OHCHR reported later being intercepted by the LCG [Libyan Coast Guard] and returned to Libya, where they claimed to have suffered arbitrary detention, torture and other human rights violations' OHCHR, 'Lethal Discharge' (n 3) 21–22.

[86] See ch 3, section V.

[87] Kalland Aarstad (n 83) abstract. See also, Alarm Phone, 'Central Mediterranean Regional Analysis' (*AlarmPhone*, 5 January 2020), available at: alarmphone.org/en/2020/01/05/central-mediterranean-regional-analysis/.

[88] S Klepp, 'A Double Bind: Malta and the Rescue of Unwanted Migrants at Sea, a Legal Anthropological Perspective on the Humanitarian Law of the Sea' (2011) 23 *International Journal of Refugee Law* 538, 548.

A. Accountability for Private Vessels' Omissions of Assistance

There are no judicial decisions against private vessels for failing to respond to calls of migrant vessels in the Mediterranean Sea.[89] Flag states' enforcement of a shipmaster's duty to render assistance at sea is lacking, which has serious consequences for the ROL. Papanicolopulu explains that this is partly due to the fact that, on the high seas, ships flying the flag of convenience are under the exclusive jurisdiction of their flag state, which is often 'unable or unwilling to enforce existing standards'.[90] Moreover, establishing a breach of duty entails proving that the migrant vessel was in need of assistance and that the shipmaster failed to properly exercise discretion in not intervening.[91] According to Basaran, information and evidence on private vessels not answering migrants' calls for assistance 'is difficult to obtain and mostly based upon testimonies of survivors and crewmembers'.[92] Even if a case has been lodged, migrant witnesses are often difficult to locate and may be in a different jurisdiction from that of the court. As such, facts cannot be easily proved.

Generally, a state's responsibility for private vessels' breaches of the obligation to provide assistance must be verified on a case-by-case basis. As Attard explains, it must be established that the conduct of the vessel (1) can be attributed to the state; and (2) entails a breach of a legal obligation.[93] More precisely, the conduct of the vessel can be attributed to the state when the shipmaster acted on the instructions of or under the direction or control of a state in breach of the duty to provide assistance.[94]

Furthermore, Attard adds, 'acts of the shipmaster can engage State responsibility if the flag, coastal, or SAR State fails to exercise due diligence to ensure that the shipmaster renders assistance to persons in distress'.[95] Due diligence entails the state 'to take reasonable steps to comply with its international obligation to provide assistance'. For the flag state, such steps include taking 'reasonable measures to prevent shipmasters of its registered vessels from failing to assist persons in distress'.[96] Reasonable measures require the state to adopt sanctions and to monitor cases of violations. Nonetheless, assessing whether or not the flag state has exercised due diligence is challenging, as it may depend on several factors, including considering the professional judgement of the shipmaster,

[89] Osamudiamen Eruaga (n 63) 43.
[90] I Papanicolopulu, 'The Duty to Rescue at Sea, in Peacetime and in War: A General Overview' (2016) 98 *International Review of the Red Cross* 491, 503.
[91] Osamudiamen Eruaga (n 63) 44.
[92] Basaran (n 37) 213. See also Klepp (n 88) 557.
[93] FG Attard, *The Duty of the Shipmaster to Render Assistance at Sea under International Law* (Leiden, Brill/Nijhoff, 2020) 280.
[94] ibid 280. See, in this regard, International Law Commission, *Draft Articles on Responsibility of States for Internationally Wrongful Acts, with Commentaries* (2001) Art 8.
[95] Attard (n 93) 280.
[96] ibid 264.

for example in situations where assistance was not provided because it would expose the crew or vessel to danger.[97]

Moreover, it should be noted that, where the RCC of a coastal state that is not competent for the SAR area affected by the event (eg, the Italian RCC in the Maltese or Libyan SAR area) contacts a private or public vessel flagged to another state near the distressed vessel and coordinates the operations, it 'is not necessarily responsible, under international law, for the conduct of assisting vessels involved in that response'.[98] According to the UNHCR,

> the mere fact that a coastal State's MRCC coordinates a SAR response outside its own SRR, or transfers coordination as appropriate to the authorities of another coastal State, would generally speaking be unlikely, by itself, to amount to an exercise of effective control or jurisdiction over persons receiving assistance.[99]

This is because, generally, the state of the RCC not competent for the SAR area does not exercise effective control or jurisdiction over persons receiving assistance.[100] The flag state is presumed responsible for the actions of its vessel.

B. Accountability for State Vessels' Omissions of Assistance

There are very few judicial decisions against state authorities for failing to respond to calls of migrant vessels in the Mediterranean Sea. Notable judicial decisions against state authorities include that of the Court of Rome of 16 December 2022. This is one of the rare instances where the Italian maritime authorities have been held liable for failing to rescue a vessel in distress *outside the Italian SAR zone*, in this case on 11 October 2013. The episode involved a vessel carrying over 400 migrants who departed from Libya. The migrants sent distress calls for five hours to the Italian and Maltese RCCs. The Maltese RCC assumed coordination of the event, as it occurred in the international waters of its SAR zone, but asked an Italian naval vessel only 17 nautical miles from the distressed migrants to intervene. However, the Italian RCC deliberately ordered this vessel to not approach the scene, as it did not take place in the Italian SAR zone. As a consequence, over 268 migrants, including several children, died by drowning.

The Court of Rome ruled that the captain of the Italian Coast Guard in charge of the RCC and the captain of the section of the Navy responsible for providing the resources for the rescue operation were jointly guilty, under Article 113 of the Criminal Code, of manslaughter and negligence due to the omission to rescue *by*

[97] ibid 265.
[98] UNHCR, 'General Legal Considerations: Search-and-rescue Operations Involving Refugees and Migrants at Sea' (n 23) 6–7.
[99] ibid.
[100] ibid.

failing to give immediate orders to the Navy unit which was the closest vessel to the incident, despite both of them being aware of the imminent danger.

Although the two captains accused 'were not convicted because the case was time-barred, as the trial was brought beyond the limitations period',[101] this is a landmark decision because it condemns the failure to coordinate the rescue of sea migrants. In particular, referring to the SOLAS, SAR and UNCLOS Conventions, as well as Article 69 (rescue of vessels and persons in distress), Article 489 (omission of assistance to vessels or persons in danger), and Article 490 (obligation to rescue) of the Navigation Code, the decision clarifies that the RCC's obligation to rescue is not limited to situations taking place within its SAR zone. On the contrary, these obligations apply also when another state takes on the coordination of the operations, and they include maintaining contacts with other states' RCCs and intervening using the means indicated by the responsible RCC.[102]

Moreover, although the court could have adopted a short judgment as the case was time-barred, it opted for a detailed and well-reasoned decision. According to Rolfi, this was probably due to the fact that the incident had attracted international attention, as it was also the object of *AS and others v Italy and Malta* of 27 January 2021,[103] a decision of the Human Rights Committee where both Italy and Malta were found accountable for violating the right to life, as protected under Articles 2(3) and 6 of the International Covenant on Civil and Political Rights. In this case, the Human Rights Committee had accepted the communication concerning Italy because of the unreasonably long investigations and proceedings, which took six years before the first hearing on the merits.[104]

Another relevant case concerns the 'left to die' episode mentioned in section III.A. The facts of the incident are particularly interesting because it saw the involvement of several actors belonging to different states, none of which took on responsibility to assist the vessel in distress. The IMRCC was the first to be informed of the vessel in distress, and it made a number of calls to other vessels within the vicinity, urging them to be vigilant and assist the distressed boat, but it did not undertake coordination of the event, in breach of the obligations set out

[101] Trib Roma, Sentenza 15.12.2022, n 14998; Pro Asyl and Alarmphone, 'Landmark Court Ruling on 2013 Shipwreck: Italian Coast Guard and Navy Responsible for Deaths of 268 Refugees' (*Alarmphone*, 19 January 2023), available at: alarmphone.org/en/2023/01/19/landmark-court-ruling-on-2013-shipwreck/.

[102] ASGI, 'Strage di Bambini dell'11 Ottobre 2013: le Responsabilità e la Cronaca della Tragedia nella Sentenza sul Naufragio' (ASGI, 5 January 2023), available at: www.asgi.it/asilo-e-protezione-internazionale/strage-bambini-2013-sentenza-responsabilita/.

[103] HRC, 'Communication no 3042/2017, Decision (Malta, CCPR/C/130/D/3042/2017) and (Italy, CCPR/C/128/D/3043/2017) of 27 January 2021, Views adopted by the Committee under article 5(4) of the Optional Protocol, concerning communication no 3042/2017'.

[104] Emma Rolfi, 'Il Tribunale di Roma, Nove Anni Dopo, sul "Naufragio dei Bambini": un Problematico Caso di Prescrizione dei Reati e di "Responsabilita'"delle Autorita' Italiane' (*Sistema Penale*, 21 April 2023), available at: www.sistemapenale.it/it/scheda/rolfi-la-sentenza-di-primo-grado-sul-cd-naufragio-dei-bambini-il-tribunale-di-roma-dichiara-i-reati-estinti-per-prescrizione-ma-non-tralascia-di-indicare-le-gravi-responsabilita-delle-autorita-italiane#_ftn16.

in the international convention and the implementing legislation.[105] Shortly after the IMRCC sent the initial distress signal, a military helicopter, whose nationality remains unknown, arrived at the scene, providing the passengers with water and food and assuring them that it would return to help further – but it did not. The migrants also encountered two fishing vessels during their journey, but neither provided any assistance. Approximately 10 days into the voyage, when half of the passengers had perished, an aircraft carrier or helicopter-carrying vessel approached the boat, close enough for the survivors to observe sailors on board. Despite the evident distress signals, the naval vessel chose to depart. Eventually, after 15 days at sea, the boat washed ashore on the Libyan coast. The 10 remaining survivors were subsequently detained, and due to inadequate medical care, one of them died. Eventually, nine survivors were released.[106]

Even though the IMRCC had verified the position of the vessel and issued a general distress call, it failed to coordinate the event and request the nearby vessels' assistance in rescuing the distressed individuals. NATO, which had officially designated the region as a military zone falling under its jurisdiction, neglected to respond to requests for assistance transmitted by the IMRCC. Information collected during the investigation of the facts by the CoE reveals that at least two military vessels engaged in NATO operations were in close proximity to the distressed boat at the time of the distress signal. These vessels included the Spanish Navy frigate *Méndez Núñez* and an Italian Navy vessel known as the *ITS Borsini*.[107]

In 2011, shortly after the shipwreck, some survivors (with the help of a few associations) filed a complaint with the prosecutors of the criminal courts in Agrigento, Naples and Rome, asking them to investigate the facts. In 2014, they also filed a case with the Military Court in Rome against the captain of the *ITS Borsini* in order to ascertain his criminal responsibility for omission of assistance.

All the criminal court prosecutors dismissed the complaints almost immediately, finding that the facts did not involve the commission of any crime. On the other hand, the Military Court in Rome opened and carried out formal investigations. However, in 2016, the proceedings had to stop due to the refusal of the Navy to release key evidence.[108] In 2016, one more attempt was made to ascertain the facts by filing a civil action with the Court of Rome against the Italian government, the Minister of Defence and the Minister of Infrastructure, relying on the investigations of the Military Court. In 2022, the Court of Rome held that the Italian administration had no responsibility for the shipwreck, as the migrants' own actions, which involved the destruction of the satellite phone and compass, interrupted the causality nexus between the authorities' action and the damage.[109] At the time of writing, the case is still pending before the

[105] See section II in this chapter and ch 3, sections II.A and II.C.

[106] PACE (n 43).

[107] ibid.

[108] Trib Militare Roma, Procura Militare della Repubblica, 'Avviso alla Persona Offesa di Richiesta di Archiviazione', 21.12.2015.

[109] Trib Roma, Sentenza 04.10.2022, n 14448.

Court of Appeals in Rome and a preliminary hearing is expected in December 2025. On appeal, it is argued that the authorities breached their obligations to coordinate the rescue and to follow up with other vessels in the Mediterranean about the fate of the distressed migrants. In addition, it is argued out that such violations were the primary cause of the shipwreck, and the destruction of the satellite phone and compass alone did not cause the death of the migrants – as the IAMSAR Manual explains, there are alternative methods to search for vessels in distress.[110]

Concerning failure to provide assistance *inside the Italian SAR zone*, there has never been a conviction, as generally the Italian authorities comply with their obligations.[111] One recent event, however, that triggered the opening of criminal investigations for omission of assistance concerns the 'Cutro Shipwreck', which occurred between 25 and 26 February 2023 off the Italian coast, where 96 migrants lost their lives. The facts are unclear and must be assessed, but it appears that the Italian Coast Guard had been informed about the vessel by a Frontex surveillance aircraft. However, the Coast Guard delayed the rescue operation and waited for the vessel to enter the territorial waters – according to them, Frontex informed them that the vessel did not appear to be in distress. The proceedings aim to establish the circumstances, and whether there were unjustified delays, omissions, or acts on the part of the authorities involved, that is the Italian Coast Guard, the Guardia di Finanza (Finance Police), and Frontex.

In the context of 'non-performance of SAR services', Trevisanut explains that:

> The main question to be answered here is whether … the non-rescued persons do fall within the jurisdiction of any state while they are in distress at sea. It can be argued that the distress call creates a 'relation' between the state, which receives it, and the persons who send it. The life of the persons in distress depends on the behaviour of the recipient state. The argument could go further and support the existence of an exclusive long distance *de facto* control that the state, which received the call, exercises on the lives of those people … This de facto control becomes also de jure when the distress situation is located within the SAR zone of the recipient state, which has an obligation to 'promote the establishment, operation and maintenance of an adequate and effective search and rescue service' (UNCLOS Article 98(2)). There is then an **assumption of authority … the coastal state exercises in its SAR zone**. The coastal state is then bound by an obligation of due diligence. The loss of lives or the risk of losses in its SAR zone may entail a violation of the right to life of the concerned persons, of their 'right to survival', and a violation of its obligations under law of the sea instruments (emphasis added).[112]

[110] App Roma, Atto di Citazione in Appello, 28.12.2022.
[111] Leanza and Caffio (n 1).
[112] Seline Trevisanut, 'Law of the Sea Symposium: Search and Rescue Operations at Sea – Who is in Charge? Who is Responsible?' (*Opinio Juris*, 28 May 2013), available at: opiniojuris.org/2013/05/28/law-of-the-sea-symposium-search-and-rescue-operations-at-sea-who-is-in-charge-who-is-responsible/.

A similar view was adopted by the Human Rights Committee in *AS and others v Italy and Malta* mentioned above. The main issue in the case was whether Italy and Malta exercised power or effective control over the victims and thus whether the Human Rights Committee could establish jurisdiction. The Committee confirmed the jurisdiction of both states. In particular, it reasoned that Malta's jurisdiction was created by the fact that the event occurred within its SAR zone, and that at some point it assumed coordination of the rescue – 'potentially resulting in a direct and reasonably foreseeable causal relationship between the State parties' acts and omissions and the outcome of the operation'.[113]

According to the Committee, Italy's jurisdiction was underpinned by the facts at stake and applicable legal obligations: Italy was the first-alerted state and had one vessel close to the sinking vessel, and as such 'a special relationship of dependency had been established between the individuals on the vessel in distress and Italy'.[114] Moreover, Italy had the obligation to respond reasonably to distress calls and cooperate with other states to carry out SAR operations. The victims 'were therefore directly affected by the decisions taken by the Italian authorities in a manner that was reasonably foreseeable'.[115]

Whereas some scholars, such as Papanicolopulu, consider this a landmark case and welcome the Human Rights Committee's expansion of jurisdiction at sea, some critical views raise the concern that such an approach may have a negative impact on future policies, as it goes beyond the power or effective control requirement for establishing jurisdiction and thus creates uncertainty. Some dissenting members of the Human Rights Committee, as well as other scholars, argue that one of the effects of an expanded approach to the concept of jurisdiction is that states may become unwilling to undertake international obligations. In addition, states may attempt new strategies to avoid accountability, for example by not sending their ships close to vessels in distress.[116] Some also note how the Committee erred in not differentiating 'situations in which States have the potential to place individuals under their effective control from situations of the actual placement of individuals under effective state control'.[117]

[113] HRC (n 103) para 6.7.

[114] ibid para 7.8. While the case against Malta was declared inadmissible for non-exhaustion of domestic remedies, the Committee found that Italy violated the victims' right to life under Art 6(1) ICCPR for failing to act with due diligence to protect their lives; ibid, paras 8.5 and 6.9. Cesare Pitea, 'The Applicability of Human Rights Treaties to Search and Rescue Operations in the High Seas: A Landmark Decision of the Human Rights Committee' (*Criminal Justice Network*, 4 March 2021), available at: www.criminaljusticenetwork.eu/en/post/the-applicability-of-human-rights-treaties-to-search-and-rescue-operations-in-the-high-seas-a-landmark-decision-of-the-un-human-rights-committee.

[115] Gabriella Citroni, 'No More Elusion of Responsibility for Rescue Operations at Sea: The Human Rights Committee's Views on the Case of A.S., D.I., O.I., and G.D. v Italy and Malta' (*Opinio Juris*, 9 March 2021), available at: opiniojuris.org/2021/03/09/no-more-elusion-of-responsibility-for-rescue-operations-at-sea-the-human-rights-committees-views-on-the-case-a-s-d-i-o-i-and-g-d-v-italy-and-malta/.

[116] See, for instance, the dissenting views of A Zimmermann and D Moore. HRC (n 103) 18–19.

[117] S Dimitrova, 'Rethinking "Jurisdiction" in International Human Rights Law in Rescue Operations at Sea in the Light of *AS and others v Italy* and *AS and others v Malta*: A New Right to be Rescued at Sea?' (2023) 56 *Israel Law Review* 120, 136.

Moreover, in the case of Malta, it has been noted that a state does not necessarily have jurisdiction in all of its SAR region. SAR regions are areas where the state in charge must ensure SAR services and cooperation and coordination with other coastal states, regardless of whether or not it has jurisdiction. Therefore, although the Committee's efforts to establish states' responsibility can be seen as a positive initiative, they risk going beyond what international law sets forth and negatively impacting the international ROL.[118] As such, Dimitrova comments that it remains to be seen whether these decisions 'will weaken or strengthen the duty of Coastal States to render assistance'.[119]

The Human Rights Committee's approach may see different and contrasting decisions in the future. At the time of writing, it is too early to assess its impact on future cases or state practice, although its non-binding nature certainly represents a limit.

C. Delays in Disembarkation

Two notable cases concerning delays of state vessels in disembarking migrants in distress involved the Coast Guard ships *Diciotti* and *Gregoretti*.

On 16 August 2018, the *Diciotti* rescued about 200 migrants in the Maltese SAR zone. On 20 August 2018, the ship docked in the port of Catania, where it obtained permission to disembark five days later. The *Diciotti* had contacted the IMRCC about the distressed vessel, and thus Italy became the first state informed of the event and as such – until Malta assumed the lead – responsible for launching the first necessary actions and coordinating the event. Following the Maltese authorities' unwillingness to intervene, Italy remained under the obligation to coordinate the rescue operation and conclude it by disembarking the migrants to a POS. However, the former Minister of the Interior, Salvini, without any legal basis, prohibited disembarkation until an agreement on migrants' relocation could be reached at the EU level, although the operation had been authorised by the IMRCC.[120]

As a consequence, the competent prosecutors started proceedings to ascertain whether the Ministry of the Interior committed any criminal act during the rescue operations.[121] After the investigations, the section for ministerial crimes of the Court of Catania[122] asked the Italian Senate[123] for authorisation

[118] Interview with Constitutional Law Professor (online, 25 May 2023).

[119] Dimitrova (n 117) 138.

[120] C Casiello and ME Venditti, 'Il Caso Diciotti: tra Obblighi di Soccorso in Mare e Garanzia dei Diritti Fondamentali' (2019) 39(2) *Diritto Pubblico Comparato ed Europeo Online* 947, 954.

[121] Senato della Repubblica, Atti parlamentari, XVIII Legislatura, Domanda di autorizzazione a procedere in giudizio ai sensi dell'articolo 96 della Costituzione, Doc IV-bis, n 1 (23 gennaio 2019) 2.

[122] Legge Costituzionale 16 gennaio 1989, n 1, art 9, para III.

[123] Pursuant to Art 96 of the Constitution, 'The Prime Minister and the Ministers, even if they have ceased from office, are subject, for crimes committed in the exercise of their functions, to ordinary

to proceed against Salvini for kidnapping,[124] aggravated by his position as a public official, for abuse of power, and also for having committed these acts against minors.[125] However, the Senate refused to authorise the proceeding,[126] as it found that Salvini acted solely on the basis of a 'political decision'[127] in the interest of the state, which entails the inability of a criminal judge to review his acts – a protection given to guarantee the independence of the executive power from judicial intrusion. However, this did not conclude the episode of the *Diciotti*: a civil case was started before the Civil Court in Rome on behalf of 41 migrants who were on the *Diciotti* with the aim to obtain recognition of the illegitimate conduct of the Ministry of the Interior and related damages. The Court of Rome rejected the case on the grounds that it did not have jurisdiction to decide on the merits because Salvini's conduct was a political act. An appeal has been lodged and a hearing is expected in 2024.[128] At the same time, a case has also been lodged with the European Court of Human Rights ECtHR on behalf of two migrants who were detained on board the *Diciotti* in violation of Article 3 (prohibition of inhuman and degrading treatment) and Article 5 (right to liberty) of the European Convention on Human Rights (ECHR).[129] The ECtHR case is pending.

Similar circumstances occurred at the end of July 2019, when the Coast Guard ship *Gregoretti* saved more than one hundred migrants and Salvini prohibited their disembarkation for five days, pending relocation agreements.[130] As a consequence, the Court of Catania's section for ministerial crimes filed criminal charges against Salvini alleging that he had abused his powers to kidnap

jurisdiction, subject to prior authorisation of the Senate of the Republic or of the Chamber of Deputies, according to the rules established by constitutional law'. See also Legge Costituzionale 16 gennaio 1989, n 1.

[124] See Art 605, Codice Penale 19 ottobre 1930 n 1398 (come modificato).

[125] Senato della Repubblica (n 121).

[126] The Senate Committee for Immunity refused to authorise the prosecution of Salvini on 19 February 2010. This decision was reaffirmed by the Senate on 20 March 2019. La Repubblica, 'Diciotti, il Senato Vota No all'Autorizzazione a Procedere Contro Salvini. Che in Aula Ringrazia il M5s: "Le Cose Si Fanno in Due"' *La Repubblica* (20 March 2019), available at: www.repubblica.it/politica/2019/03/20/news/salvini_voto_diciotti_senato-222049852/.

[127] Senato della Repubblica (n 121) 36.

[128] G Panattoni, 'La Controversa Figura dell'Atto Politico, alla Luce dei Casi "Diciotti" e "Gregoretti"' (2020) 8 *Federalismi* 212, available at: www.federalismi.it/nv14/articolo-documento.cfm?Artid=41618; Casiello and Venditti (n 120) 980–81. The judicial complaints can be found at Tribunale Civile di Roma, 'Ricorso ex art 702 bis cpc', available at: www.studiocataldi.it/allegati/news/allegato_33694_1.pdf; Redattore Sociale, 'Migranti, Rete legale: "Così Abbiamo Aiutato le Persone della Diciotti"' *Redattore Sociale* (Roma, 22 February 2019), available at: www.redattoresociale.it/article/notiziario/migranti_rete_legale_cosi_abbiamo_aiutato_le_persone_della_diciotti; Email from Lawyer n 1 to author (28 September 2023).

[129] La Repubblica, 'Il Caso Diciotti alla Corte Europea dei Diritti dell'Uomo' *La Repubblica* (13 February 2019), available at: www.repubblica.it/cronaca/2019/02/13/news/il_caso_diciotti_alla_corte_europea_dei_diritti_dell_uomo-219028551/.

[130] Brigida (n 16) 236. Although the events of the *Gregoretti* case occurred after the entry into force of the Security-bis Decree analysed in ch 6, I shall discuss them in this chapter: the case involved a Navy ship and as such was not subject to its general provisions, which give the Minister of Interior the power to prohibit its transit, entry, or docking into territorial waters. C Siccardi *I Diritti*

the migrants.[131] On this occasion, the Senate gave its authorisation to continue the investigations – such authorisation was given by the new majority formed by the Democratic Party and Five Star Movement, whereas Lega Nord, Salvini's party, became part of the opposition.[132] However, the Judge for Preliminary Investigations of the Court of Catania dismissed the proceedings, as it found that the former Ministry of the Interior did not violate any national or international law and that his decision was a political one shared with the government in charge at the time of the events.[133]

The *Diciotti* and *Gregoretti* cases are very similar from a factual and legal point of view, but they had different outcomes at the end of the parliamentary phase. Scholars explain that this was due to a change in the political majority of the Parliament which took place between the two proceedings, whereby Salvini's party lost its power to the Democratic Party.[134]

Therefore, as the proceeding in question involves a parliamentary phase, fundamental rights are not guaranteed independently of political considerations. According to Cancellaro, the procedures do not seem to satisfy the requisites of effectiveness required by Article 5 of the ECHR, which states that 'Everyone who is deprived of his liberty by arrest or detention shall be entitled to take proceedings by which the lawfulness of his detention shall be decided speedily by a court and his release ordered if the detention is not lawful'.[135] The matter is complex, as it concerns not only migrants' rights but also the balance of state powers, and I will further discuss it in chapter seven, section V.B.

In conclusion, no one in Italy has yet been convicted and sentenced for failures to rescue or delays in disembarkation, though a few cases have been brought against different state authorities. As discussed in chapter seven, section V, the lack of judicial response is largely due to severe limitations on access to justice. Some cases are still pending, however, which may result in greater accountability for the legal violations in question.

Costituzionali dei Migranti in Viaggio: Sulle Rotte del Mediterraneo (Napoli, Editoriale Scientifica, 2021) 185; see ch 6, section V.

[131] See Art 605 of the Criminal Code.

[132] FQ, 'Matteo Salvini, il Giorno della Prima Udienza a Catania: Perché il Caso Gregoretti è Diverso da Quello della Nave Diciotti e Della Open Arms' *Il Fatto Quotidiano* (3 October 2020), available at: www.ilfattoquotidiano.it/2020/10/03/matteo-salvini-il-giorno-della-prima-udienza-a-catania-perche-il-caso-gregoretti-e-diverso-da-quello-della-nave-diciotti-e-della-open-arms/5951954/.

[133] Il sole24ore, 'Caso Gregoretti, Salvini prosciolto "Non Luogo a Procedere, il Fatto Non Sussiste"' *Il sole24ore* (14 May 2021), available at: www.ilsole24ore.com/art/caso-gregoretti-salvini-prosciolto-non-luogo-procedere-fatto-non-sussiste-AEJSR5I. See also Alessandra Ziniti, 'Caso Gregoretti, Perché è Diverso da Quello Open Arms' *La Repubblica* (14 May 2021), available at: www.repubblica.it/politica/2021/05/14/news/gregoretti_e_open_arms_differenze-300962362/.

[134] Siccardi (n 130) 189; S Zirulia and G Martinico, 'Criminalising Migrants and Securitising Borders. The Italian "No Way" Model in the Age of Populism' in V Stoyanova and S Smet (eds), *Migrants' Rights, Populism and Legal Resilience in Europe* (Cambridge, CUP, 2022) 271.

[135] ECHR, Art 5(4); F Cancellaro, 'Dagli Hot-Spots ai "Porti Chiusi": Quali Rimedi per la Liberta "Sequestrata" alla Frontiera?' (2020) 3 *Diritto Penale Contemporaneo* 428, 440–41 (translation by the author).

VI. CONCLUSION

The Italian legislator has formally complied with the provisions on the international law of the sea, adopting implementing legislation as well as an updated version of the National Plan for Search and Rescue at Sea in 2020. Generally, the national provisions even exceed, in terms of obligations towards ships in distress, those set out under the international law of the sea. There remain grey areas, however, due to the lack of an agreement with Malta on the overlapping SAR area and the lack of provisions predetermining a POS.

Most problems concern implementation gaps, deriving from the lack of coordination between competent SAR authorities, the adoption of specific political measures aimed at hindering the disembarkation in a POS, and the encouragement of the intervention of the authorities of third countries – in particular Libya – which cannot identify a POS within their own borders. In this way, regular violations of international obligations (drawn from the SOLAS, UNCLOS and SAR Conventions), together with very serious breaches of the fundamental rights of individuals, are carried out with the assistance of the Italian authorities.

The current situation raises important questions with regard to the ROL. First, there appears to be an increasing tendency to try to circumvent the legal obligations through informal strategies and blurred practices 'rather than to implement them fully',[136] weakening the principle of legal certainty. For example, 'States are now actively trying to avoid' accepting 'rescued migrants on board' their vessels, especially if in international waters, and 'are leaving this to others, including' states not covered by the ECHR as well as commercial ships.[137]

Second, some practices breach the principle of legality, as they have no legal basis and constitute an abuse of power on the part of the Italian authorities. For instance, this occurred in the *Diciotti* and *Gregoretti* cases,[138] where rescued migrants were detained on vessels for an unreasonable number of days without any legal grounds.

Third, there are a number of factors that complicate the establishment of accountability for decisions on whether and how to render assistance. These include the extraterritoriality of the events at issue, the complex overlapping obligations of the actors involved, as well as the number of actors who may be required to render prompt assistance to persons in distress at sea – including coastal states, states responsible for coordinating their SAR zone, flag states and private vessels. Furthermore, on some occasions, the protection of fundamental rights outside the national borders depends on political considerations which are not subject to full judicial review.[139] This creates 'an area outside the law where individuals are covered by no legal system capable of affording them enjoyment of the rights and guarantees',[140] and therefore access to justice remains severely challenged.

[136] Commissioner for Human Rights, 'Lives Saved. Rights Protected' (n 23) 46.
[137] ibid.
[138] See ch 6, section V, and ch 7, section V.B.
[139] Siccardi (n 130) 191–92.
[140] Commissioner for Human Rights, 'Lives Saved. Rights Protected' (n 23) 49–50.

5

Contested Legal Grounds and Practices Concerning Interceptions at Sea

I. INTRODUCTION

IN THIS CHAPTER I discuss the national provisions and practices which result in pushbacks and pullbacks of intercepted sea migrants to unsafe countries, and how they challenge the rule of law (ROL).

The distinction between pushbacks and pullbacks reflects the development of the European Union (EU) and its Member States' responses to the arrivals of sea migrants and refugees: whereas pushbacks refer to EU coastal states' practice of sending back migrants/refugees to third countries, pullbacks occur when the authorities of a coastal third country 'take charge' of migrants upon the implicit demand of – and/or with support from – the EU or one of its Member States. Pullbacks are also frequently defined as 'pushbacks by proxy'.[1]

In particular, I focus on how Italy directly and systematically engaged in the use of pushbacks to avoid its obligations under the Refugee Convention and other human rights instruments through a number of agreements with Libya. This went on until the *Hirsi* judgment of 2012,[2] in which the European Court of Human Rights (ECtHR) declared pushbacks illegal. However, on the basis of a deal signed with Libya in 2017, Italy adopted a new strategy to circumvent the obligations to protect refugees. Since then, the interception and return of migrants attempting to leave from Libyan shores has been delegated to the Libyan Coast Guard, and it is estimated that, as of October 2022, the practice

[1] Alice Riccardi, 'Esternalizzazione delle Frontiere Italiane in Libia e Niger: una Prospettiva di Diritto Internazionale' (*Questione Giustizia*, 2020), available at: www.questionegiustizia.it/rivista/articolo/esternalizzazione-delle-frontiere-italiane-in-libia-e-niger-una-prospettiva-di-diritto-internazionale.

[2] See *Hirsi Jamaa and others v Italy* App no 27765/09 (ECtHR, 23 February 2012); M Martin, 'Prioritising Border Control over Human Lives: Violations of the Rights of Migrants and Refugees at Sea' (Policy Brief, *Euro-Mediterranean Human Rights Network*, June 2014) 15.

has affected about 100,000 people.[3] In line with this approach, Italy signed a number of similar bilateral agreements with Tunisia.[4]

Several scholars, non-governmental organisations (NGOs) and UN institutions have condemned these agreements between Italy and North African countries, not only because they return migrants to places where their fundamental rights may be violated and their claims for international protection left unconsidered,[5] but also because the executive has often adopted them without following the legal procedures. Moreover, these agreements push migrants towards more dangerous routes.[6]

Thus, in sections II and III, I focus on the agreements between Italy and Libya as well as Italy and Tunisia – the North African countries on the Central Mediterranean route with the highest numbers of migrant departures to Italy[7] – which form the basis for interceptions, pushbacks and pullbacks.[8] Specifically,

[3] InfoMigrants, 'Italy: 40 NGOs, Unions Ask Government to Revoke Libya Memorandum' (*InfoMigrants*, 26 October 2022), available at: www.infomigrants.net/en/post/44268/italy-40-ngos-unions-ask-government-to-revoke-libya-memorandum#:~:text=The%20organizations%20said%20that%20%22between,which%20cannot%20be%20considered%20safe.%22; UNHCR, 'Arrivals in Europe from Libya – 2021 in Review' (Regional Bureau for Europe, 21 April 2022) 1, available at: data2.unhcr.org/en/documents/details/92165.

[4] M Hendow, 'Tunisian Migrant Journeys: Human Rights Concerns for Tunisians Arriving by Sea' (2013) 2 *Laws* 187.

[5] It should be noted that the UNHCR has even been evacuating asylum seekers, including some from detention centres, from Libya since 2017. Libya Observer, '177 Asylum-Seekers Evacuated from Libya to Niger' *Libya Observer* (1 January 2022), available at: libyaobserver.ly/inbrief/177-asylum-seekers-evacuated-libya-niger; UNHCR, 'Libya: Last Evacuation Flight of the Year Brings 177 Vulnerable Asylum-seekers to Safety in Niger' (Press Release, 30 December 2021), available at: reliefweb.int/report/niger/libya-last-evacuation-flight-year-brings-177-vulnerable-asylum-seekers-safety-niger; Krista Bonello Rutter Giappone, Interview with UNHCR Malta (email, 21 February 2022); see also, European Council on Refugees and Exiles, 'Central Med: Civil Fleet Continue to Save Lives as Italian Authorities Drop Charges, Italy Urged to End MoU with Libya Where List of Crimes against Migrants Grows' (ECRE, 4 February 2022), available at: ecre.org/central-med-civil-fleet-continue-to-save-lives-as-italian-authorities-drop-charges-italy-urged-in-end-mou-with-libya-where-the-list-of-crimes-against-migrants-grows/; E Vari, 'Italy–Libya Memorandum of Understanding: Italy's International Obligations' (2020) 43 *Hastings International and Comparative Law Review* 105, 117.

[6] Hendow (n 4) 189. Sadegh explains that 'As there are no legal means to reach Europe, the system pushes migrants to engage in unsafe trips and break the law. Women may be exposed to additional gender-violence during the journeys. These may be unwanted consequences of the legal system, in some cases. In other cases, the danger faced my migrants may be used as a deterrent'. Krista Bonello Rutter Giappone, Interview with Ibtisam Sadegh, Lecturer and Lawyer, University of Malta (online,18 February 2022).

[7] Roberto Forin and Bram Frouws, 'What's New? Analysing the Latest Trends on the Central Mediterranean Mixed Migration Route to Italy' (*Mixed Migration Centre*, 9 February 2022), available at: mixedmigration.org/articles/whats-new-analysing-the-latest-trends-on-the-central-mediterranean-mixed-migration-route-to-italy/; UNHCR, 'Italy. Sea Arrivals Dashboard' (UNHCR, August 2023), available at: reliefweb.int/report/italy/italy-sea-arrivals-dashboard-june-2023.

[8] It should be noted that most of the literature focuses only on the agreements between Italy and Libya, overlooking that Tunisia is also an important actor as far as pushbacks and pullbacks are concerned.

I consider the legal nature of these agreements and the practices connected with their provisions, identifying where they breach or fall outside the law.[9] In section IV, I turn to Italy's use of privatised pushbacks and pullbacks to return migrants to third countries and how this practice allows it to circumvent its international obligations. In section V, I discuss some of the most notable cases before judicial and quasi-judicial bodies that deal with the issue of accountability for pullbacks, and in the last section I conclude that the ROL principles most affected in this context are those of legality, legal certainty, violation of fundamental human rights and access to justice.

II. AGREEMENTS AND INITIATIVES ON EXTERNALISATION OF IMMIGRATION CONTROL BETWEEN ITALY AND LIBYA

A. Provisions of Libyan–Italian Agreements

There are several agreements between Italy and Libya aimed at fighting irregular immigration to Italy and preventing unauthorised departures from the Libyan coast.[10] The first such agreement was signed on 13 December 2000 and started to be applied in 2007 with the adoption of two implementing protocols[11] which set forth the coordination of maritime patrols, temporarily providing the assistance of Italian naval units and Italian police in the maintenance of machinery and equipment as well as training Libyan personnel.

Since the 2008 Treaty on Friendship, Partnership and Cooperation,[12] the collaboration has intensified through a system that entrusts Libyan land border control to Italian companies[13] and additional measures aimed at preventing illegal immigration.[14] Despite the fall of the Libyan dictator Gaddafi on 17 February 2011, the relationship between the two countries has continued, as announced in the Tripoli Declaration of 2012.[15]

[9] OHCHR, 'Lethal Disregard: Search and Rescue and the Protection of Migrants in the Central Mediterranean Sea' (OHCHR, May 2021) 19, available at: www.ohchr.org/en/stories/2021/05/report-call-safeguard-migrants-central-mediterranean-sea.

[10] F Pacella, 'Cooperazione Italia–Libia: Profili di Responsabilità per Crimini di Diritto Internazionale' (2018) 4 *Diritto Penale Contemporaneo* 5, 7.

[11] Repubblica Italiana e la Gran Giamahiria Araba Libica Popolare Socialista, 'Protocollo tra la Repubblica Italiana e la Gran Giamahiria Araba Libica Popolare Socialista' and 'Protocollo Aggiuntivo Tecnico-operativo al Protocollo di Cooperazione per Fronteggiare il Fenomeno dell'Immigrazione Clandestina', both signed in Tripoli on 29 December 2007.

[12] Signed in Benghazi on 30 August 2008 and ratified by Italy with Legge 6 febbraio 2009, n 7.

[13] art 19(2).

[14] art 1(3).

[15] Pacella (n 10) 7–8.

On 2 February 2017, former Italian Prime Minister Gentiloni and President of the Libyan Presidential Council Fayez Mustafa Sarraj signed a Memorandum of Understanding (MoU),[16] according to which Italy undertakes to

> (i) support Libyan military and security institutions; (ii) provide technical and technological support to Libyan bodies in charge of combating illegal immigration, namely the Border Guard, the Coast Guard, the Coast Guard of the Ministry of Defence, and the competent bodies and departments within the Ministry of Interior; (iii) complete the land border control system South of Libya, implementing Art 19 of the Treaty of 2008; (iv) finance reception centers, provide medicines and medical equipment for reception health centers and train Libyan staff of these centers.[17]

Besides a reference to the duty to collaborate on the management of migration flows,[18] the text of the MoU is silent on search and rescue (SAR) areas or operations. Similar to the previous agreements, Vari notes how

> the language of the MoU is broad and sometimes legally imprecise. Certain issues, such as what projects exactly the agreement is meant to support and how much funds Italy is supposed to provide and where they would come from, are really unclear.[19]

Furthermore, while the MoU

> does not specify whether Libyan authorities should intercept migrants already en route to Italy and at sea, this goal can be inferred from the fact that Italy will be providing Libya with boats and border control systems 'in order to stem the illegal migrants' fluxes' (Art 1).[20]

As such, Giuffré points out that the power to intercept migrant vessels and divert their journeys back to Libya or a third country is not a power expressly set out in the 2017 MoU or in other agreements, and the question of whether 'enforcement jurisdiction' exists concerning the 'restriction of unauthorised arrivals of migrants in Europe … remains open'.[21]

[16] In the Preamble, the MoU between Italy and the Government of Tripoli refers to the Italy–Libya friendship Treaty signed by Gaddafi and Berlusconi in 2008. See Governo di Riconciliazione Nazionale dello Stato di Libia e il Governo della Repubblica Italiana, 'Memorandum d'Intesa sulla Cooperazione nel Campo dello Sviluppo, del Contrasto all'Immigrazione Illegale, al Traffico di Esseri Umani, al Contrabbando e sul Rafforzamento della Sicurezza delle Frontiere tra lo Stato della Libia e la Repubblica Italiana' (2 February 2017), available at: www.governo.it/sites/governo.it/files/Libia.pdf.

[17] Pacella (n 10) 7–8.

[18] The Preamble of the Memorandum states:

> Reaffirming the strong determination to cooperate to identify urgent solutions to the issue of illegal migrants who cross Libya to travel to Europe by sea, through the provision of temporary reception camps in Libya, under the exclusive control of the Libyan Ministry of the Interior, while waiting for repatriation or voluntary return to the countries of origin, and working at the same time in order for the countries of origin to accept their citizens or signing agreements with these countries.

[19] Vari (n 5) 114.

[20] ibid.

[21] M Giuffré, *The Readmission of Asylum Seekers under International Law* (eBook, Hart Publishing, 2020) 245.

In addition, the MoU mentions the provision of financial support for Libyan organisations that are involved in the return of migrants to their country of origin.[22] The agreement does not specify the treatment that Libya shall afford to these migrants, and therefore no protection is guaranteed against non-refoulement to other countries or inhuman and degrading treatment in Libya. Despite the MoU's strategic vagueness, Vari argues that it is clear that the parties' goal is to 'return migrants to their countries of origin'.[23]

The MoU between Italy and the Tripoli government was automatically extended for three years in 2020 and then in 2023, as it states 'to be valid for three years and will be tacitly renewed upon expiry for an equivalent period, unless notified in writing by one of the two Contracting Parties, at least three months before the expiry of the validity period'.[24] Additionally, Italy has provided support to the Libyan Coast Guard since 2017, when the Italian Parliament approved the government's request for participation in an international mission 'providing support to the Libyan security forces for the activities of controlling and countering illegal immigration and trafficking in human beings',[25] including through naval assets, economic support and surveillance cooperation. In the following years, the Parliament extended this support up to 2024, although it recently stopped training the Libyan Coast Guard.[26] However, no official information is available concerning the amount of funding that Italy has been providing to Libya.[27]

[22] art 2.

[23] Vari (n 5) 114.

[24] art 8; Lorenzo Bagnoli and Nello Scavo, 'Libyagate. Il Giallo della Nave "Italiana" che ha Respinto Migranti agli Ordini di Bija' *Avvenire* (1 February 2022), available at: www.avvenire.it/attualita/pagine/cinque-anni-accordo-libia-italia; Amnesty International, 'Memorandum d'Intesa Italia-Libia: Quattro Anni di Complicità in Crimini di Diritto Internazionale' (Amnesty International, 1 February 2021), available at: www.amnesty.it/memorandum-intesa-italia-libia-quarto-anniversario/.

[25] Pacella (n 10) 9; Camera dei Deputati, 'Le Missioni Internazionali Autorizzate e Prorogate nel 2017' (XVII Legislatura) (Camera dei Deputati, 18 February 2019); Camera dei Deputati, 'Le Missioni Autorizzate e Prorogate nel 2018' (Camera dei Deputati, 5 September 2019); Senato della Repubblica e Camera dei Deputati (XVIII Legislatura), 'La Partecipazione Italiana alle Missioni in Libia' Dossier, n 67 (19 April 2019); Senato della Repubblica e Camera dei Deputati (XVIII Legislatura), 'Autorizzazione e Proroga Missioni Internazionli e Interventi di Cooperazione e Sviluppo per l'Anno 2022 – DOC XXV, n 5 e DOC. XXVI n 5' (15 June 2022).

[26] Fulvio Vassallo Paleologo, 'Il Parlamento Ratifica le Missioni Military in Libia e Conferisce Pieni Poteri al Ministro dell'Interno' (ADIF, 28 July 2022), available at: www.a-dif.org/2022/07/28/il-parlamento-ratifica-le-missioni-militari-in-libia-e-conferisce-pieni-poteri-al-ministro-dellinterno/. It should be noted that 'Legislative Decree n. 84/2018, converted into Law n. 98/2018, provided for the sale of naval units to Libya (Art 1) and the maintenance of naval units, as well as the training of the Coast Guard personnel of the Ministry of Defence and the Coastal Security Bodies of the Libyan Ministry of the Interior (Art 2), with financing (€2,520,000) obtained from reductions and provisions of various funds (Article 3)'. M Magri, 'Obbligo di Soccorso in Mare, Funzioni della Guardia Costiera e Respingimenti "Delegati": sui Poteri del Ministro dell'Interno' (2019) 1 *Istituzioni del Federalismo* 149, 162, fn 27.

[27] M Ghebreigziabiher Ogbazghi, 'The Italy–Libya Agreements: Controversial Cooperation. Assessing the Human Rights Violations on Matters of Refugees and Migrants' Protection' (Master's Thesis, University of Macedonia, 2022) 39.

Therefore, the Libyan–Italian collaboration works both to the detriment of human rights and certainty of the law. Although the agreements involve financial obligations for Italy, they reveal the successive Italian governments' unwillingness to adopt a clear approach concerning interceptions and their consequences in order to dodge accountability. In this regard, the scholarship has shown why the collaboration rests on informal agreements: because their non-legally binding nature and imprecise language make it difficult to hold Italy responsible for pullbacks, which entail human rights violations.[28] In the next subsection, I explore the practices adopted on the grounds of these agreements.

B. Practices on the Basis of Libyan–Italian Agreements that Breach the ROL

The 2008 Treaty of Friendship, Partnership and Cooperation provided the basis for Italy to carry out several interceptions of sea migrants and push them back to Libya.[29] One of these cases occurred in May 2009, when ships of the Italian Financial Police and Coast Guard intercepted a boat holding about 200 migrants on the high seas (within the Maltese SAR zone) and sent them back to Libya. On 24 May 2009, 24 of those migrants filed a complaint before the ECtHR. In 2012, the ECtHR condemned Italy in the case of *Hirsi Jamaa and others v Italy*.[30] The ECtHR found that the applicants were under Italian jurisdiction according to Article 1 of the European Convention on Human Rights (ECHR): according to international law and its implementing provisions in the Italian Navigation Code,[31] when intercepted on the high seas, migrants are under the jurisdiction of the flag state. Consequently, they shall be entitled to the same rights as any individual within the jurisdiction of the respective state.

Thus, the Court found violations of the prohibition of inhuman and degrading treatment according to Article 3 of the ECHR because the applicants had been exposed to the risk of ill treatment in Libya as well as to the risk of repatriation to Somalia or Eritrea. In addition, the applicants' transfer to Libya was in breach of article 4 of Protocol no 4 on the prohibition of collective expulsions, as the migrants had been sent back without any examination of their individual situations and their need to submit claims for international protection. The Court reiterated that 'the special nature of the maritime environment could not justify an area outside the law where individuals were covered by no legal system

[28] P Müller and P Slominski, 'Breaking the Legal Link but Not the Law? The Externalization of EU Migration Control through Orchestration in the Central Mediterranean' (2021) 28 *Journal of European Public Policy* 801, 809.

[29] Global Legal Action Network, 'Privatised Migrant Abuse by Italy and Libya' (GLAN, 18 December 2019), available at: www.glanlaw.org/nivincase.

[30] *Hirsi* (n 2).

[31] Codice della Navigazione del 30 marzo 1942, n 327 (Edizione 2020) Art 4, states: 'Italian ships on the high seas and Italian aircraft in a place or space not subject to the sovereignty of any State are considered as Italian territory'.

capable of affording them enjoyment of the rights and guarantees protected by the Convention'.[32]

After *Hirsi*, Italy suspended the use of direct pushbacks, as it became clear that its direct involvement in extraterritorial operations would violate fundamental human rights. However, relying on the 2017 MoU, the Italian government began adopting

> strategies that increasingly involved 'contactless' measures, yet exercising strategic control over the Libyan Coast Guard, which has operated as its proxy to intercept migrants and bring them back to a country in which they would be subjected to extreme forms of violence and exploitation.[33]

The 2017 MoU was followed by the creation of a large Libyan SAR area in June 2018,[34] which has been used ever since by Italy as well as the EU and other Member States to accentuate the role of Libya as a 'controller' of the Central Mediterranean. Such a role has been conferred on Libya through a number of other international agreements, declarations and cooperation arrangements, including the Khartoum Process (November 2014),[35] the Valletta Declaration (November 2015),[36] and the Malta Declaration (September 2019).[37] Specifically, the latter declaration, signed by Italy, Malta, Germany and France, relies on the existence of a Libyan SAR zone to reiterate the responsibilities entrusted to the Libyan Coast Guard. It adds that private actors – implicitly referring to NGOs involved in SAR operations – shall not interfere with the orders given by the

[32] *Hirsi* (n 2) para 178.

[33] Global Legal Action Network, 'Privatised Migrant Abuse by Italy and Libya' (n 29); see also M Giuffré and V Moreno-Lax, 'The Rise of Consensual Containment: From "Contactless Control" to "Contactless Responsibility" for Migratory Flows' in S Singh Juss (ed), *Research Handbook on International Refugee Law* (Northampton, Edward Elgar Publishing, 2019).

[34] Since the creation of the Libyan SAR zone, Italy and Malta have taken the view that Libya has a working SAR system. Krista Bonello Rutter Giappone, Interview with Jean-Pierre Gauci, Senior Research Fellow, British Institute of International and Comparative Law, London (online, 8 July 2023). See ch 4, section III.B.

[35] 'The Karthoum Process is a platform for political cooperation amongst the countries along the migration route between the Horn of Africa and Europe', including Libya. Its aims encompass combating migrant trafficking and establishing cooperation among the affected countries. EU/Horn of Africa Migration Route Initiative, 'The Karthoum Process', available at: www.khartoumprocess.net/about/the-khartoum-process.

[36] At the Valletta Summit, the EU supported the externalisation of border controls through the collaboration with and financial support to Libya. See Valletta Summit on Migration, 'Political Declaration' (Valletta Summit, 11–12 November 2015), available at: www.consilium.europa.eu/media/21841/political_decl_en.pdf; Amnesty International, 'EU–Africa Summit in Valletta Must Not Dress Up Border Control as "Co-Operation"' (Amnesty International, 10 November 2015), available at: www.amnesty.org/en/latest/press-release/2015/11/eu-africa-summit-in-valetta/; CONCORD, 'CONCORD Position Towards the Valletta Summit on Migration' (CONCORD, 5 November 2015), available at: concordeurope.org/2015/11/05/concord-position-towards-the-valletta-summit-on-migration/.

[37] See S Carrera and R Cortinovis, 'The Malta Declaration on SAR and Relocation: A Predictable EU Solidarity Mechanism?' (Paper no 2019-14, Brussels, CEPS, October 2019) 5–6.

competent SAR centre.[38] From a human rights point of view, it is problematic that such instruments do not provide sufficient guarantees for the protection of people rescued at sea and, in particular, against refoulement to Libya.[39] In line with this approach, in 2020, Malta entered into an MoU with Libya similar to the one between Italy and Libya, agreeing to set up two 'co-ordination centres, one in Valletta and another in Tripoli'[40] (fully funded by the Maltese government,[41] with Malta requesting further financial support from the EU)[42] and to maintain communication for the stated purpose of 'combatting illegal immigration in Libya and the Mediterranean region'.[43] Simultaneously, Italy and the EU decreased their SAR operations in the Central Mediterranean Sea.[44]

In practice, even after the formalisation of the Libyan SAR area,[45] the operations initiated by the Coast Guard of the latter country have in substance been coordinated and/or managed by the Italian, European and Turkish authorities. In particular, scholars on the subject recognise a direct coordination role played until 2020 by the ships of the Italian Navy mission NAURAS (part of the operation Mare Sicuro), based in Abu Sittah, the military port of Tripoli.[46] However, after 2020, with the agreement between Turkey and the provisional government of Tripoli, 'the Turkish authorities have taken control of most of the coast near Tripoli'[47] and engage with 'the militias that previously controlled the various Libyan Coast Guards'.[48]

[38] Joined Declaration of Intent on a Controlled Emergency Procedure – Voluntary Commitments by Member States For a Predictable Temporary Solidarity Mechanism (Malta Declaration) (23 September 2019). The Malta Declaration aims to relocate rescued asylum seekers among participating states before disembarkation. It does not specify which procedures shall dictate the relocation process and therefore does not provide a predictable mechanism to deal with the issue. Carrera and Cortinovis (n 37) 4, 6; Elonora Frasca and Francesco Luigi Gatta, 'The Malta Declaration on Search & Rescue, Disembarkation and Relocation: Much Ado about Nothing' (EU Immigration and Asylum Law and Policy, 3 March 2020), available at: eumigrationlawblog.eu/the-malta-declaration-on-search-rescue-disembarkation-and-relocation-much-ado-about-nothing/.

[39] OHCHR, 'Lethal Disregard' (n 9) 23.

[40] Government of National Accord of the State of Libya and the Government of the Republic of Malta, 'Memorandum of Understanding Between the Government of National Accord of the State of Libya and The Government of The Republic of Malta in the Field of Combatting Illegal Immigration' (28 May 2020) art 1, available at: www.statewatch.org/media/documents/news/2020/jun/malta-libya-mou-immigration.pdf.

[41] ibid art 3.

[42] ibid art 5.

[43] ibid art 1. See ch 4, section III.B.

[44] Müller and Slominski (n 28) 808.

[45] Euronews, 'La Libia Crea la sua Zona SAR e Notifica l'IMO (con il Sostegno UE)' *Euronews* (9 July 2018), available at: it.euronews.com/2018/07/09/la-libia-crea-la-sua-zona-sar-e-notifica-l-imo-con-il-sostegno-ue-.

[46] Fulvio Vassallo Paleologo, 'Il Tribunale di Napoli Condanna i Respingimenti in Libia. Ma Occorre Ancora Fare Giustizia' (ADIF, 14 October 2021), available at: www.a-dif.org/2021/10/14/il-tribunale-di-napoli-condanna-i-respingimenti-in-libia-ma-occorre-ancora-fare-giustizia/.

[47] ibid.

[48] ibid.

To complicate the scenario, the Office of the United Nations High Commissioner for Human Rights (OHCHR) has denounced how the strengthened surveillance capabilities of Frontex – in the context of the Multipurpose Aerial Surveillance framework[49] – allow this EU agency to spot the departure of migrant ships from Libya in real time. From the interviews of migrants conducted by the OHCHR, it is clear that the ships on which they were travelling were intercepted by the Libyan authorities in international waters – even in the Maltese SAR area – and subsequently brought back to Libya thanks to the use of European aerial surveillance equipment,[50] raising issues about the involvement of Frontex and its accountability in 'delegated' pushback operations.

In light of all the above, the Libyan–Italian agreements raise concerns, first, because they allow Italy to provide assistance to the Libyan Coast Guard as well as to other Libyan institutions which are involved in abuses of migrants.[51] Second, the agreements finance Libyan institutions that in turn fund traffickers and armed groups to block departures for Italy and thereby ensure the implementation of the agreements.[52] Finally, interceptions and pullbacks are carried out in a non-transparent manner, without monitoring mechanisms for international organisations, NGOs[53] and the media. This leaves space for informal and unclear practices, where certainty of the law and accountability for human rights violations are challenged. As scholars have noted, the system set up after *Hirsi* does not breach the law directly, but it circumvents it by blurring the link between the orchestrator (Italy, the EU and its Member States) and the agents (Libya).[54] In the next section, I turn to the compliance of the current 2017 MoU with the principle of legality.

C. Legality of the 2017 Agreement between Libya and Italy

The compliance of the 2017 MoU with ROL principles is debated not only because of human rights violations against migrants and the evasion of accountability for such violations, but also because of its lack of conformity with Article 80 of the Italian Constitution. While the immigration literature on the matter tends to be highly critical of the government for adopting the 2017 MoU without

[49] Frontex, 'Multipurpose Aerial Surveillance' (Publications Office of the European Union, 2018). See ch 3, section II.C.

[50] OHCHR, 'Lethal Disregard' (n 9) 21.

[51] Alessandro Pizzuti and Clare Frances Moran, 'The Memorandum of Understanding between Italy and Libya: Does it Create Human Rights Obligations on the Part of Italy?' (*OpinioJuris*, 5 August 2021), available at: opiniojuris.org/2021/08/05/the-memorandum-of-understanding-between-italy-and-libya-does-it-create-human-rights-obligations-on-the-part-of-italy/.

[52] Pacella (n 10) 9–10.

[53] B Miltner, 'Human Security and Protection from *Refoulement* in the Maritime Context' in E and C Ferstman (eds), *Human Security and Non-Citizens: Law, Policy and International Affairs* (Cambridge, CUP, 2010) 215.

[54] Müller and Slominski (n 28) 801.

submitting it to parliamentary approval, a review of the broader constitutional law literature reveals a more complex debate on the government's power to adopt international agreements.

First, the Italian Constitution does not provide for 'an "exhaustive" procedure on the subject of negotiation and adoption of international treaties'.[55] Specifically, Article 87 and Article 80 of the Constitution *give the President of the Republic the power to ratify treaties, and to the Parliament that of authorising them through the adoption of ratifying legislation when the object of the agreement affects foreign policy, the legislative framework, or the state finances.* The Constitution does not formally recognise any government's power in the process of formation of treaties, but according to some scholars such power exists in matters of international relations because they concern a political function of the executive.[56] In practice, the executive has adopted several agreements without following the constitutional procedure. Constitutional scholars point out that the practice of adopting agreements in simplified form has become so frequent that they now represent the majority of those adopted, even when concerning areas prohibited by Article 80.[57] In part, they explain that this has occurred because the constitutional provisions are vague, but also because this approach satisfies the need for the government to take quick decisions and actions in particular situations.[58]

The scholarship has taken different views on the legality of these agreements. A minority of scholars argue that agreements adopted in simplified form can have a constitutional basis when limited to technical matters of individual ministers inasmuch as they can be considered administrative rather than political acts for which parliamentary approval is required.[59] Others are of the opinion that the executive's power to adopt agreements in simplified form derives from a constitutional custom interpreting Article 87 which recognises the prerogative to do so in areas not falling under Article 80 of the Constitution.[60]

[55] E Raffiotta, 'Potere Estero del Governo e Accordi Internazionali in Forma Semplificata: una Ricerca sulla Prassi' (2009) *Forum di Quaderni Costitutionali* 1, 1, available at: www.forumcostituzionale.it/wordpress/images/stories/pdf/documenti_forum/paper/0149_raffiotta.pdf.

[56] ibid 1–2; M Franchini, 'I Poteri del Governo nella Conclusione di Accordi Internazionali' (1980) 1 *Rivista Trimestrale di Diritto Pubblico* 36.

[57] A Jr Golia, 'La Fortezza che Resiste. Potere Estero, Conflitto di Attribuzione e Prescrittività Costituzionale' (2019) 3 *La Democrazia A-Costituzionale* 47, 56–57, 66; Raffiotta (n 55) 3.

[58] Raffiotta (n 55) 2–3.

[59] V Pupo, 'Le Istanze di Accesso Civico come Strumento di Trasparenza Democratica in Tema di Accordi Internazionli in Forma Semplificata' (2019) 2 *Diritto, Immigrazione e Cittadinanza* 211, 219. This would also find a legal basis in Decreto Legislativo 30 luglio 1999, n 300, which attributes decisional powers in international matters to individual ministers as long as they lie within their area of competence (see, for instance, arts 20 and 28). Raffiotta (n 55) 17–18.

[60] For a discussion on the different views, see Pupo (n 59) 219–20; A Spagnolo, 'The Conclusion of Bilateral Agreements and Technical Arrangements for the Management of Migration Flows: An Overview of the Italian Practice' (2019) 28(1) *Italian Yearbook of International Law Online* 209, 218; Raffiotta (n 55) 1, 3; M Buquicchio, *Il Procedimento Costituzionale di Formazione dei Trattati* (Napoli, Jovene, 1980) 66.

There is even one scholar who argues that such a power is allowed in areas mentioned in Article 80.[61] Some maintain that agreements in simplified form have a legal basis whenever there is tacit consent, or at least no disagreement, among the different branches of state power.[62] In support of this view, Pupo points out that the practice of adopting agreements in simplified form in international affairs has been confirmed by Law no 839/1984, which requires their communication to the Parliament as well as publication regardless of their denomination (ie, MoU, technical police agreements, etc) or adoption procedure.[63]

However, the majority of scholars take the position that the executive does not have the power to adopt agreements in simplified form regarding any of the subject matters prohibited by Article 80, as the guarantees of the provision, aimed at balancing the state powers, would be weakened.[64] According to this view, agreements in simplified form cannot be justified on the basis of constitutional custom or tacit approval. This is confirmed by the debates that took place during the preparatory works for the adoption of the Constitution. From these debates, the ratio of Article 80 becomes clear: to guarantee democratic control over the executive's foreign policy decisions.[65]

In 2018, one attempt was made by four parliamentarians, members of the opposition parties, to challenge the legality of the MoU before the Constitutional Court. The claim was that there was a conflict of competence among state powers because of the government's failure to obtain Parliament's authorisation for the agreement, which was political in nature, as it regulates border controls and foreign policy and prevents access to asylum.[66] Moreover, it was argued, the MoU was in breach of the obligations to publish and communicate agreements to Parliament as required by Law no 839/1984.[67] Therefore, the group sought a declaration of abuse of power due to failure to comply with Article 80 of the Constitution; a declaration to order the government to present draft legislation to obtain Parliament's ratification of the MoU; and finally a declaration voiding all the administrative acts and obligations undertaken by the executive until the Court's decision.[68] In reply, the Italian government stated that the 2017 MoU

[61] Pupo (n 59) 220; E Olivito, 'Il Cul-de-sac Costituzionale degli Accordi in Forma Semplificata: Iniziativa Legislativa Parlamentare ed Esternalizzazione delle Politiche Migratorie' (2018) 2 *Diritto Penale Contemporaneo* 435; Golia (n 57) 45–100; FM Palombino, 'Sui Pretesi Limiti Costituzionali al Potere del Governo di Stipulare Accordi in Forma Semplificata' (2018) 3 *Rivista di Diritto Internazionale* 870, 874; V Lippolis, *La Costituzione Italiana e la Formazione dei Trattati Internazionali* (Rimini, Maggioli Editore, 1989) 203.

[62] F Ghera, 'Commento all' Articolo 80' in R Bifulco, A Celotto and M Olivetti (eds), *Commentario alla Costituzione* (Torino, Utet Giuridica, 2006) 1569.

[63] Pupo (n 59) 221; Legge 11 dicembre 1984, n 839, arts 1(1)(f) and 4.

[64] See, eg, Pupo (n 59) 220; Spagnolo (n 60) 4; Ghera (n 62) 1570; T Treves, *Diritto Internazionale: Problemi Fondamentali* (Milano, Giuffrè, 2005) 678.

[65] Pupo (n 59) 220; Golia (n 57) 56–57, 61; C di Bologna, 'Accordi e Missioni Internazionali: la Prassi Governativa' in A Barbera and TF Giupponi (eds), *La Prassi degli Organi Costituzionali* (Bologna, Bononia University Press, 2004) 296.

[66] Corte Costituzionale, Ordinanza 25.07.2018, n 163; Golia (n 57) 80–89; Spagnolo (n 60) 211.

[67] Golia (n 57) 81.

[68] ibid 45–100, 84.

was nothing more than an act of implementing programmes and objectives contemplated in the 2008 Treaty of Friendship, Partnership and Cooperation, which had been legalised in Italy with Law no 7/2009[69] – thus the MoU had a legal basis and there was no conflict of power between state bodies. However, the Italian government's view was criticised by Golia, who noted that the 2017 MoU stands in contrast to the treaty adopted in 2008, as it sets forth new obligations concerning the transit, reception and detention of migrants.[70]

In the end, the Constitutional Court did not address the issue in the case and held it inadmissible for lack of standing.[71] According to the Constitutional Court, the matter of the government's abuse of competence had to be brought by the majority of Parliament rather than a few individual members.[72] No further attempts have been made in this regard because, as Golia points out, there is no political will for such action. At the same time, he adds, the Constitutional Court used procedural justifications to avoid addressing the sensitive political themes at stake.[73] Consequently, the issue of justiciability on this matter remains serious.[74]

Given the difficulties of seeking a general declaration of the MoU's unconstitutionality, an alternative way to challenge it would be to seek its disapplication in individual court cases on the grounds of formal defects.[75] For instance, this occurred in the *Vos Thalassa* case.[76] The events involved two migrants among 67 people rescued by the Italian tugboat *Vos Thalassa* in Libyan SAR waters in July 2018. The Italian Maritime Rescue Coordination Centre (IMRCC) was informed of the operation and contacted the Libyan Coast Guard, which ordered the *Vos Thalassa* to head towards the North African coast in order to transfer the people onto its patrol boats. Upon learning that the *Vos Thalassa* was en route to Libya, two of the rescued migrants proceeded to issue threats to the crew, demanding a change in course towards Italy. The migrants were eventually transferred to the *Diciotti*, an Italian Coast Guard ship that took them to Trapani. The two migrants were apprehended upon their arrival in Italy and charged with aggravated violence for inciting a mutiny against the crew in order to prevent their return to Libya, as well as for facilitating illegal immigration.

[69] Legge 6 febbraio 2009, n 9.

[70] Golia (n 57) 82.

[71] Redattore Sociale, '"Il Memorandum Italia-Libia ha Calpestato la Costituzione": Ricorso di Leu e Asgi' *Redattore Sociale* (Roma, 27 February 2018), available at: www.redattoresociale.it/article/notiziario/_il_memorandum_italia-libia_ha_calpestato_la_costituzione_ricorso_di_leu_e_asgi; ASGI, 'Mancata Ratifica Parlamentare del Memorandum Italia-Libia: al Via il Ricorso alla Corte Costituzionale' (ASGI, 28 February 2018), available at: www.asgi.it/asilo-e-protezione-internazionale/mancata-ratifica-parlamento-memorandum-italia-libia-ricorso-corte-costituzionale/.

[72] Corte Cost, Ordinanza 04.07.2018, n 163; Golia (n 57).

[73] Golia (n 57) 85.

[74] ibid 45–100.

[75] Duccio Facchini, 'Accordo Italia-Libia per Fermare i Migranti: se la Revisione è una Farsa' (*Altreconomia*, 13 November 2019), available at: altreconomia.it/accordo-italia-libia-revisione-farsa/.

[76] Trib Trapani, Giudice per le Indagini Preliminari, Sentenza 23.05.2019.

The Judge for Preliminary Investigations of the Court of Trapani ruled that the actions of the accused amounted to legitimate self-defence and therefore dismissed the case.[77] In its reasoning, the judge stated that the MoU could not be used to justify taking the 67 migrants rescued by the *Von Thalassa* in the Libyan SAR zone back to Libya: formally, the MoU is an international agreement adopted by the government and never approved by Parliament according to the procedures required by Article 80 of the Constitution. Henceforth, the MoU cannot be deemed to possess legal effects and cannot create any binding obligations.[78] Moreover, from a substantive perspective, the MoU breaches Article 10 of the Constitution, which provides that the Italian legal system shall comply with the generally accepted norms of international law, among them the right not to be returned to a place where life or liberty would be at risk (the principle of non-refoulement).[79] Libya cannot be considered a safe place, as migrants there risk being exposed to grave violations of their fundamental rights.

However, the Court of Appeals of Palermo overturned the decision in June 2020.[80] The Court of Appeals did not engage in an analysis of the MoU, and focused on the fact that the migrants put themselves voluntarily in a situation of danger. Accordingly, their violent and threatening behaviour towards the crew of the rescuing ship to prevent their return to Libya was not justified by the need to protect themselves from concrete and real danger.[81] The Court of Appeals commented that the Judge for Preliminary Investigations 'showed an ideological approach to the legal assessment of the issue at stake', indicating that 'these

[77] *Cf El Hiblu* case in Malta. The ongoing *El Hiblu* case has seen similar questions being raised. In this case, three teenagers mounted a protest against being returned to Libya and managed to negotiate the change of the boat's course to Malta, where they are being charged with hijacking and terrorism. NGOs have argued that the accused were acting in legitimate self-defence. Gauci (n 34); Matthew Vella, 'Not Piracy, but Self-defence against EU's Deadly Abdication – NGOs on El Hiblu Rescue' *Malta Today* (28 March 2019), available at: www.maltatoday.com.mt/news/national/93935/not_piracy_self_defence_against_eu_deadly_abdication_ngo_el_hiblu_rescue#. Y0kH0EzP02w.> Matthew Agius, 'All Possible Witnesses in El Hiblu 1 Case Have Testified, Court Told' *Malta Today* (12 April 2022), available at: www.maltatoday.com.mt/news/court_and_police/116247/all_possible_witnesses_in_el_hiblu_1_case_have_testified_court_told#.Yzs6Uy0Ro_U.

[78] Trib Trapani, Giudice per le Indagini Preliminari, Sentenza 23.05.2019; L Masera, 'La Legittima Difesa dei Migranti e l'Illegittimità dei Respingimenti verso la Libia (Caso Vos-Thalassa)' (*Diritto Penale Contemporaneo*, 24 June 2019), available at: archiviodpc.dirittopenaleuomo.org/d/6754-la-legittima-difesa-dei-migranti-e-lillegittimita-dei-respingimenti-verso-la-libia-caso-vos-thalassa; see Fulvio Vassallo Paleologo, 'Obblighi di Ricerca e Soccorso in Mare Imposti dal Diritto Internazionale e Accordi con gli Stati di Transito' (ADIF, 8 November 2019), available at: www.questionegiustizia.it/rivista/articolo/gli-obblighi-disoccorso-inmare-neldiritto-sovranazionale-enell-ordinamento-interno_548.php.

[79] Trib Trapani, Giudice per le Indagini Preliminari, Sentenza 23.05.2019.

[80] Jessica Noviello, 'Accordi Italia–Libia: tra Istituzionalità e Legalità. Il Doppio Volto del Fenomeno Migratorio nel Mediterraneo: Oggetto di Accordi Istituzionali e Fonte di Reddito per il Crimine Organizzato Transazionale' (Filodiritto.com, 19 July 2021), available at: www.filodiritto.com/accordi-italia-libia-tra-istituzionalita-e-illegalita-il-doppio-volto-del-fenomeno-migratorio-nel-mediterraneo-oggetto-di-accordi-istituzionali-e-fonte-di-reddito-il-crimine-organizzato-transazionale.

[81] The Court of Appeals of Palermo condemned the two migrants to three years and six months in jail. App Palermo, Sentenza 03.06.2020, n 1525.

problems must be adequately resolved in the only context designated for such matters, namely that of the interstate political debate'.[82]

Departing from this view, on 16 December 2021, the Supreme Court of Cassation (Corte Suprema di Cassazione)[83] overturned the Court of Appeals' decision, holding that migrants who are rescued at sea and oppose being returned to Libya by resisting a public official are justified in doing so because they are asserting their right not to be refouled. The Court did not address the legality of the MoU, but it referred to the decision of the Judge for Preliminary Investigations of the Court of Trapani, who strongly questioned it. Therefore, the Court concluded that the SAR authorities' order to return the migrants to Libya should neither have been issued nor executed: a situation of insecurity in Libya was well known, documented and based on concrete facts.[84]

Although the case finally ended with the Court of Cassation upholding migrants' rights, it is significant that it avoided directly addressing the issue of the legality of the MoU. Certainly, it is not only a legally complex but also a politically charged matter. It remains unclear how future cases will deal with the issue, but I would like to point out how individual court actions remain more limited in terms of impact than a declaration of unconstitutionality by the Constitutional Court, especially given the limited resources available to sea migrants to access judicial remedies.

III. AGREEMENTS AND INITIATIVES ON READMISSION AND COOPERATION BETWEEN ITALY AND TUNISIA

A. Provisions of Tunisian–Italian Agreements

An approach similar to that taken by Italy and Libya is reflected in the agreements and relations between Italy and Tunisia. As discussed in section II.C, whereas cooperation agreements and externalisation agreements are generally to undergo parliamentary checks and ratification, memoranda of understanding, readmission agreements and technical police agreements between Tunisia and Italy have usually been adopted in a simplified form and often evade any check – some even remaining secret.[85]

The two readmission agreements currently in force were adopted in 1998 and 2011, and they are key components of the broader international cooperation between the two countries. The first bilateral readmission and police cooperation agreement between the two countries was concluded on 6 August 1998, by which

[82] ibid 8.
[83] Cass pen, sez VI, Sentenza 16.12.2021, n 15869.
[84] ibid 23.
[85] Open Migration, 'Rimpatri Forzati a Tutti i Costi' (Open Migration, 16 June 2017), available at: openmigration.org/analisi/rimpatri-forzati-a-tutti-i-costi/.

Tunisia pledged to implement effective coastal control measures in exchange for annual entry quotas to Italy for Tunisian citizens.[86] In addition, both parties undertook to readmit, without formalities, their own citizens when found to be in a situation of irregular immigration status,[87] as well as citizens of third countries without permission to stay in the requesting party's territory and who resided or transited through the territory of the requested party.[88] This agreement was not a formal readmission agreement, but merely a diplomatic note between the Italian Ministry of Foreign Relations and the Tunisian embassy in Rome.[89]

Over the subsequent years, a number of additional agreements reinforced the collaboration between the two countries.[90] For example, in 2009, another agreement, 'never made public, was then signed by the Ministers of the Interior of the two countries with the aim of implementing an accelerated'[91] readmission procedure for Tunisian citizens without permission to stay in Italy and with no personal identity documents.

Later, in 2011, with the Spring Revolution and the surge of Tunisians arriving on Italian shores,[92] the Interior Ministers of the two countries entered into a new agreement to reinforce the one signed in 1998.[93] The document set forth a commitment by the 'Tunisian side to strengthen control of the coasts and to accept Italy's immediate rejection of Tunisian migrants who landed irregularly on Italian coasts after 5 April 2011'.[94] However, the Tunisian government did not allow Italy's 'interference with its domestic affairs'[95] and rejected the suggestion to 'deploy Italian warships in the Territorial sea of Tunisia to help in pushing

[86] P Cuttitta, 'The Case of the Italian Southern Sea Borders: Cooperation across the Mediterranean?' in P Cuttitta et al (eds), *Immigration Flows and the Management of the EU's Southern Maritime Borders* (Barcelona, CIDOB Editions, 2008); Ambasciata di Tunisia a Roma e Ministero degli Affari Esteri della Repubblica Italiana, 'Scambio di Note tra l'Italia e la Tunisia Concernente l'ingresso e la Riammissione delle Persone in Posizione Irregolare' (6 August 1998), available at: sciabacaoruka.asgi.it/wp-content/uploads/2020/12/Accordo-Italia-Tunisia-1998.pdf.

[87] Ambasciata di Tunisia a Roma e Ministro degli Affari Esteri della Repubblica Italiana (n 86) ss 2 and 3.

[88] ibid s 3.

[89] ibid.

[90] E Paoletti, 'Migration Agreements Between Italy and North Africa: Domestic Imperatives Versus International Norms' (Middle East Institute, 20 December 2012), available at: www.mei.edu/publications/migration-agreements-between-italy-and-north-africa-domestic-imperatives-versus#_ftnref16.

[91] M Cociglio, L Figoni and M Mattirolo, 'Le Conseguenze Concrete degli Accordi Fantasma: Italia e Tunisia fra Rimpatri e Opacità' (ASGI, 20 December 2020), available at: sciabacaoruka.asgi.it/accordi-italia-tunisia-migrazione/#smooth-scroll-top.

[92] K Natter, 'Tunisia's Migration Politics throughout the 2011 Revolution: Revisiting the Democratisation–Migrant Rights Nexus' (2022) 43 *Third World Quarterly* 1551, 1556.

[93] Minister of the Interior of the Tunisian Republic and Minister of the Interior of the Italian Republic, 'Procès Verbal de la Réunion Entre le Ministre de l'Interieur de la Republique Tunisienne et le Ministre de l'Interieur de la Republique Italienne (Tunis, 4–5 Avril 2011)' (Tunis, 4–5 April 2011), available at: inkyfada.com/wp-content/uploads/2023/05/note-entente-italie-tunisie-2011.pdf.

[94] Cociglio, Figoni and Mattirolo (n 91).

[95] A Boubakri, 'A Law for the Incorporation of the International Convention on Maritime Search and Rescue, 1979, as Amended into the Laws of Tunisia and to Provide for the Effective Implementation Thereof' (Master's Thesis, International Maritime Law Institute, University of Malta, 2021) 14.

back illegal migrants'.[96] Furthermore, in 2017, the Foreign Ministers of Italy and Tunisia signed an additional joint declaration whose aims include managing immigration and fighting irregular departures, especially by sea.[97] Finally, it has been noted that

> [s]tarting from the summer of 2020, numerous Italo–Tunisian meetings and diplomatic exchanges have strengthened the collaboration between these two countries with the aim of preventing the departures of migrants, implementing an activity of interception of boats in Tunisian territorial waters and increasing the repatriation of Tunisian citizens from Italy to Tunisia.[98]

More recently, Italy's approach has been strengthened by controversial agreements between Tunisia and the EU Commission – without the required involvement of the EU Parliament.[99] One such agreement was signed in 2014, another in 2020, and yet another on 16 July 2023 in order to 'strengthen border control'.[100] According to the most recent MoU, the EU Commission agrees to financially support Tunisia and allocate €100 million towards reinforcing border management, SAR operations and anti-trafficking measures in order to reduce the number of sea migrant arrivals in Southern Europe.[101] The MoU makes clear that, while the parties will repatriate undocumented immigrants to their places of birth, Tunisia will not accept non-Tunisian irregular migrants back into its territory. Like the other MoUs in this context, the language of this informal agreement is vague; it only mentions the necessity to respect human rights and does not designate an entrusted monitoring body to oversee its implementation.

[96] ibid.

[97] Minister of Foreign Affairs and International Cooperation of the Italian Republic and Minister of Foreign Affairs of the Tunisian Republic, 'Declaration Conjointe a L'Occasion de la Visite de S.E.M. Béji Caïd Essebsi à Rome le 9 février 2017' (9 February 2017) points 8 and 9, available at: sciabacaoruka.asgi.it/wp-content/uploads/2020/12/Tunisia-Dichiarazione-congiunta-09-02-2017.pdf; Cociglio, Figoni and Mattirolo (n 91).

[98] C Martine and D Arnaud, 'Studio sulle Condizioni di Soggiorno e Sui Percorsi dei Migranti Tunisini Rimpatriati dall'Italia' (ASGI, March 2022) 7, available at: www.asgi.it/wp-content/uploads/2022/03/Ita-version.pdf.

[99] The EU Council is in charge of negotiating and concluding agreements with third countries, which shall then be approved by the EU Parliament. See Treaty on the Functioning of the European Union [2008] OJ C 115/47, Art 218(6)(a)(v). However, in this case, the EU Commission appears to ignore the Parliament and Council. Moreover, Art 12 of the Treaty on the European Union [1992] OJ C 191/1 establishes that EU ties with third countries are to be governed by democracy, human rights and the ROL. Annick Pijnenburg, 'What's Wrong with the EU–Tunisia Migration Agreement?' (*Verfassungsblog on Matters of Constitutional Affairs*, 21 August 2023), available at: verfassungsblog.de/team-europes-deal/.

[100] Cociglio, Figoni and Mattirolo (n 91); Lisa O'Carroll, 'What is the Controversy over the EU Migration Deal with Tunisia?' *Guardian* (18 September 2023), available at: www.theguardian.com/world/2023/sep/18/what-is-the-controversy-over-the-eu-migration-deal-with-tunisia?CMP=Share_iOSApp_Other.

[101] European Commission, 'Memorandum of Understanding on a Strategic and Global Partnership between the European Union and Tunisia', available at: ec.europa.eu/commission/presscorner/detail/en/ip_23_3887; ASGI, 'Memorandum Ue-Tunisia: L' Ue Sottoscrive Rastrellamenti, Deportazioni Illegali e Violenze Contro i Migranti' (ASGI, 20 July 2023), available at: www.asgi.it/notizie/memorandum-tunisia-ue-sottoscrive-rastrellamenti-deportazioni-illegali-e-violenze-contro-migranti/.

Therefore, issues of accountability remain unaddressed.[102] On its side, the EU argues that this agreement is a strategic tool to address the common challenge of irregular migration, the fight against traffickers and smugglers, and respect for the law.[103] However, by not creating alternative pathways to enter the EU territory, this author is of the view that the MoU is not an effective tool to decrease the demand for smuggling. At the same time, given the success of the populist rhetoric behind these agreements,[104] it does not seem realistic to achieve political support for establishing lawful entries of refugees in Europe.

B. Practices on the Basis of Tunisian–Italian Agreements that Breach the ROL

On paper, the agreements between Italy and Tunisia focus on the technical support to be provided by Italy for the control of Tunisian borders, and on the facilitation of returns on the part of the Tunisian authorities. However, in practice, these agreements – similarly to those with Libya – have turned into an informal assignment of authority for interceptions and pullbacks at sea to the Tunisian authorities[105] through financial and operational support, including through Frontex's surveillance system.[106]

This is corroborated by the fact that the overall number of interceptions has experienced a significant surge in comparison to previous years. It is estimated that between January and August 2023 alone, the Tunisian Coast Guard has prevented more than 35,000 sea migrants from reaching the southern coast of Europe.[107] In 2022, the Tunisian Coast Guard intercepted over 23,500 migrants of different nationalities,[108] 24,116 in 2021, 11,900 in 2020, 3,588 in 2019 and 3,974 in 2018.[109] Alarm Phone also confirms an increase in the Tunisian Coast

[102] Pijnenburg, 'What's Wrong with the EU–Tunisia Migration Agreement?' (n 99).

[103] European Commission, 'The European Union and Tunisia: Political Agreement on a Comprehensive Partnership Package' (16 July 2023), available at: ec.europa.eu/commission/presscorner/detail/en/statement_23_3881.

[104] O'Carroll, 'What is the Controversy over the EU Migration Deal with Tunisia?' (n 100).

[105] Alarm Phone, 'Chain of Pushbacks from Tunisian Ports to the Libyan Desert!' (*Alarm Phone*, 3 October 2021), available at: alarmphone.org/en/2021/10/03/chain-of-pushbacks-from-tunisian-ports-to-the-libyan-desert/.

[106] According to Alarm Phone: 'For several months now, the European agency Frontex has been monitoring the Tunisian coastline using satellite images, radar and drones, with the aim of detecting boats as early as possible and alerting the Tunisian authorities so that they can take charge of maritime interceptions themselves. The EU and its Member States are thus directly supporting authorities involved in serious human rights violations. In recent months, several attacks on boats by the Tunisian Coast Guard, resulting in numerous casualties, have been reported to Alarm Phone'; ibid.

[107] N Zribi, 'Externalizing Borders or Externalizing Repression? Tunisia at the Center of a Failed Asylum Architecture' (The Thahir Institute for Middle East Policy, 21 August 2023), available at: timep.org/2023/08/21/externalizing-borders-or-externalizing-repression-tunisia-at-the-center-of-a-failed-asylum-architecture/.

[108] Infomigrants, 'Five Migrants Drown in Shipwreck Off Tunisia' (*Info Migrants*, 9 January 2023), available at: www.infomigrants.net/en/post/45957/five-migrants-drown-in-shipwreck-off-tunisia.

[109] Martine and Arnaud (n 98).

Guard's interceptions of boats leaving from Libya, and reports that several of these boats have experienced engine problems or fuel shortages in the Maltese SAR zone. However, as the Maltese authorities do not rescue these migrant vessels, they remain floating until the Tunisian authorities intervene.[110]

Several NGOs and the Council of Europe[111] have criticised this situation, arguing that Italy and the EU are violating a number of human rights. First, even though there is no international recognition on the condition of Tunisia as an 'unsafe official port', some authors argue that it does not have the typical characteristics of a safe port. This is due in particular to the fact that Tunisia lacks legislation allowing refugees to apply for international protection; thus, those who mix with Tunisian migrants on their journey to Italy[112] are exposed to the risk of being deported to neighbouring unsafe countries, including Libya.[113] For example, this occurred on 27 September 2021, when a few vessels carrying four sub-Saharan migrants and three Tunisians left the Tunisian coast and were subsequently intercepted by the Tunisian Coast Guard. The migrants were all taken back to Tunisia, but whereas the Tunisian citizens were released, the others were taken to the Libyan frontier, where they were forced to join a larger group of foreigners and cross the border. Once in Libya, some of them were arrested by the Libyan authorities and others kidnapped and detained in a private house by unknown kidnappers.[114] As such, the agreements between Italy and Tunisia have mostly been criticised for breaching the prohibition of collective expulsion, in violation of article 4 of Protocol IV of the ECHR and the non-refoulement principle.[115] Second, it is reported that on a number of occasions, the Tunisian Coast Guard has carried out violent attacks on migrant boats which have resulted in deaths.[116]

[110] Alarm Phone, 'Migrant Resistance against Yet Another New Level of Brutality' (*Alarm Phone*, 2 March 2022), available at: alarmphone.org/en/2022/03/02/migrant-resistance-against-yet-another-new-level-of-brutality/.

[111] Council of Europe, Commissioner for Human Rights, 'European States Migration Co-operation with Tunisia Should Be Subject to Clear Human Rights Safeguards' (Statement, 17 July 2023), available at: www.coe.int/sr-RS/web/commissioner/-/european-states-migration-co-operation-with-tunisia-should-be-subject-to-clear-human-rights-safeguards.

[112] Al Jazeera, 'Five Dead after Boat Carrying Refugees Sinks off Tunisia's Coast' *Al Jazeera Media Network* (7 January 2023), available at: www.aljazeera.com/news/2023/1/7/five-die-10-missing-after-boat-sinks-off-tunisia.

[113] Fulvio Vassallo Paleologo, 'Respingimenti Collettivi Vietati, Tunisia e Libia Non Sono "Paesi Terzi Sicuri"' (ADIF, 31 July 2018), available at: www.a-dif.org/2018/07/31/respingimenti-collettivi-vietati-tunisia-e-libia-non-sono-paesi-terzi-sicuri/; Fabio Tumminello, 'Il Soccorso in Mare: i Concetti di "Porto Sicuro" e "Porto Vicino" nel Diritto Internazionale' (*Ius In Itinere*, 9 August 2020), available at: www.iusinitinere.it/il-soccorso-in-mare-i-concetti-di-porto-sicuro-e-porto-vicino-nel-diritto-internazionale-22358.

[114] ASGI, 'Rimpatrio di Migranti Sub-Sahariani all Frontiera Libica della Tunisia' (ASGI, 2 October 2021), available at: sciabacaoruka.asgi.it/rimpatrio-di-migranti-sub-sahariani-alla-frontiera-libica-dalla-tunisia.

[115] Fulvio Vassallo Paleologo 'Accordi di Riammissione – Maroni in Tunisia' (*Melting Pot*, 26 January 2009) www.meltingpot.org/2009/01/accordi-di-riammissione-maroni-in-tunisia/.

[116] Alarm Phone, 'Chain of Pushbacks from Tunisian Ports to the Libyan Desert!' (n 105).

Third, since President Kais Saied orchestrated a 'constitutional coup', Tunisia has become an autocratic state.[117]

From the SAR point of view, it should be noted that Tunisia has ratified the SAR Convention and its subsequent amendments, but practice in this area remains unclear, as Tunisia presented the coordinates of its SAR region to the International Maritime Organization (IMO) only in 2020, and these are not yet officially recognised.[118] This SAR area includes 'the remaining area' from the SAR zones of its 'neighbouring States', but extends beyond Tunisia's flight information region.[119] Consequently, there would be two new overlapping SAR areas – one between Tunisia and Libya and one between Tunisia and Malta – and thus ambiguity on who is responsible for SAR operations in those areas. This scenario further raises the need for regional or bilateral agreements between the relevant states.[120] However, as at the time of writing, no such agreements exist.

Figure 5.1 SAR zones in the Central Mediterranean Sea[121]

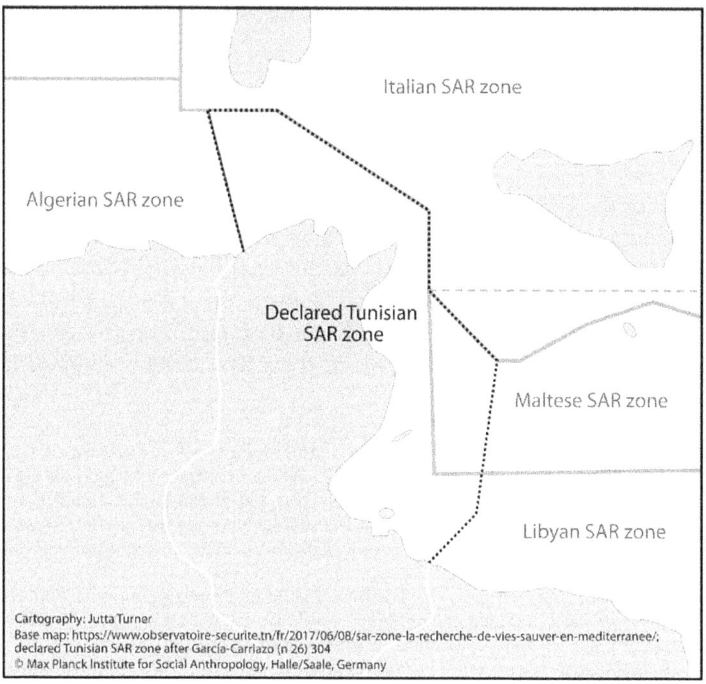

[117] Kersten Knipp and Tarak Guizani, 'EU–Tunisia Migration Deal: Encouraging the People Smugglers?' *Deutsche Welle* (Tunisia, 21 July 2023), available at: www.dw.com/en/eu-tunisia-migration-deal-encouraging-the-people-smugglers/a-66286821.

[118] Boubakri (n 95) 21, 23.

[119] This is the airspace where flight information and alerting services are provided; ibid 23.

[120] ibid 21, 23.

[121] ibid 24.

The ambiguity of the situation contributes to the increasing number of shipwrecks on the Central Mediterranean route. It also poses difficulties for NGOs performing SAR activities in international waters, 70–80 miles from the coast, where in the past coordination was always entrusted to the IMRCC in Rome, but now involves the engagement of the Libyan or Tunisian maritime authorities.[122] Additionally, there have been episodes where the Libyan Coast Guard intercepted migrants in the Tunisian SAR area in order to take them back to Libya. On a few occasions, the Libyan Coast Guard has also kidnapped and ransomed Tunisian fishermen who rescued migrants. As a consequence, fishermen have become reluctant to communicate their positions when coming across a migrant vessel in difficulty.[123]

Therefore, the practices carried out on the basis of the Tunisian–Italian agreements compromise the principle of non-refoulement and access to asylum. They also raise the same issues concerning accountability of the actors involved as the Libyan–Italian agreements. Finally, similar issues are reproduced at the EU level with the recent MoU between the EU Commission and Tunisia. As a consequence, the ROL is weakened not only at the national level but also at the EU and international levels.

C. Legality of the Tunisian–Italian Agreements

The content of the 1998 readmission agreement between Tunisia and Italy is typical of such agreements, which are enforced by Article 9.4 of Law no 40/1998,[124] but it fails to acknowledge this law as its the legal basis.[125] Most of the other successive agreements between Italy and Tunisia also take the form of diplomatic notes or informal documents and thus maintain a private character, far from transparent.[126] Furthermore, some of them have never been published: the

[122] Alarmphone, 'Migrant Resistance against Yet Another New Level of Brutality' (n 110); ECRE, 'Central Med: Despite Civilian Rescues Death Toll Continues to Rise, Interceptions and Returns to Libya, Cyprus' Only Registration Centre Overcrowded and in Deplorable Conditions' (ECRE, 29 April 2022), available at: ecre.org/central-med-despite-civilian-rescues-death-toll-continues-to-rise-interceptions-and-returns-to-libya-cyprus-only-registration-centre-overcrowded-and-in-deplorable-conditions/; Boubakri (n 95) 14–15.

[123] GlobalProject, 'Tunisia – Blocco del Porto di Zarzis in Protesta contro la Guardia Costiera Libica' (*GlobalProject*, 13 September 2021), available at: www.globalproject.info/it/mondi/tunisia-blocco-del-porto-di-zarzis-in-protesta-contro-la-guardia-costiera-libica/23667.

[124] This is also stipulated in art 11(4) of Decreto Legislativo 25 luglio 1998, n 286 and later expanded (by means of a paragraph introduced by art 10 of Legge 30 luglio 2002, n 189) to include the provision of collaboration agreements that 'may provide for the free transfer of movable property and equipment specifically identified to the authorities of the countries concerned, within the limits of functional and financial compatibility defined by the Minister of the Interior, in agreement with the Minister of the Treasury, Budget and Economic Planning'. Migreurop, 'Politique de Signature des Accords de Réadmission Italiens' (*Migreurop*, 2009), available at: migreurop.org/article1418.html.

[125] See Ministero degli Affari Esteri e della Cooperazione, 'Archivio dei Trattati Internazionali Online', available at: itra.esteri.it/Home/Search?chart=99&arg=1.

[126] EuroMed Rights, 'The Policy of Forced Returns between Italy and Tunisia' in *Return Mania: Mapping Policies and Practices in the EuroMed Region* (*EuroMed Rights*, April 2021) 1–23, 7, available at: euromedrights.org/wp-content/uploads/2021/04/EN_Chapter-4-Italy-Tunisia-1.pdf.

text of the 2009 agreement remains unknown, whereas the 2017 agreement was made public upon a public access request.[127] The 2011 agreement was released upon order of the ECtHR in the course of the *Khlaifia* case.[128] Moreover, on the basis of the agreements, Italy undertook to transfer financial support to Tunisia in order support the common immigration policies, although it never officially declared the precise amount.[129]

On the one hand, Cafaro argues that the 1998 agreement is in fact a political agreement, which therefore would have required scrutiny by both the Italian and Tunisian parliaments.[130] The absence of the necessary constitutional formalities as well as of the publication of the agreement, as required by law,[131] raises serious concerns about respect for the ROL in both countries.[132] On the other hand, as discussed above in section II.C, some constitutional law scholars try to find a legal basis for such agreements.

On 6 March 2022, Lamorgese, the Interior Minister at that time, adopted Ministerial Decree no 42/2022 with the aim of limiting public access to international treaties involving agreements with third countries on SAR and combating illegal immigration, as they are held to be covered by military secrecy. Its Article 2 states that cooperation and technical agreements for military development and for the support and cooperation of the police (also encompassing the forces mobilised for the management of borders and immigration) are to be included.[133] Thus, matters such as SARs and disembarkation, as well as MoUs may further evade Parliament and the scrutiny of public opinion. However, Vassallo-Paleologo points out that public access cannot be excluded without a justification – as set forth in Article 5 bis of Legislative Decree no 33/2013 – and therefore Decree no 42/2022 can be challenged through administrative review.

Finally, according to EU law, fast-track readmission agreements such as those between Italy and Tunisia are allowed only when the third country involved is

[127] Adelaide Massini and Diletta Agresta, 'Italia–Tunisia e Accordo Fantasma' (*Nigrizia*, 7 December 2020), available at: www.nigrizia.it/notizia/italia-tunisia-e-quellaccordo-fantasma.

[128] *Khlaifia and others v Italy* App no 16483/12 (ECtHR, 16 December 2016). This case concerned the use of hotspots and illegal detention in Italy.

[129] ibid.

[130] S Cafaro, 'La Ratifica dei Trattati Internazionali, Una Prospettiva di Diritto Comparato – Italia' (EPRS, Direzione Generale dei Servizi di Ricerca Parlamentare, 2018) 34.

[131] Prior to 1984, there was no obligation to publish the text of treaties which were not ratified. Law no 839/1984 filled this gap, providing that all agreements that bind the state shall be included in the Official Book and published in the Official Gazette, including those in simplified form. The same law provides for the quarterly publication in a specific supplement to the Official Gazette, as well as the transmission to the presidents of the two chambers of 'all the international acts to which the Republic is bound in foreign relations, treaties, conventions, exchanges of notes, agreements and other acts however named'. ASGI, 'Trasparenza e Accordi di Riammissione, il Consiglio di Stato al Governo: Va Chiarita la Natura dell'Accordo Italia-Gambia' (ASGI, 4 July 2022), available at: www.asgi.it/notizie/trasparenza-accordi-di-riammissione-gambia/; Cafaro (n 130) 34.

[132] See also Ambasciata di Tunisia a Roma e Ministro degli Affari Esteri della Repubblica Italiana (n 86).

[133] Fulvio Vassallo Paleologo, 'Al Viminale Stato di Guerra all' Informazione' (ADIF, 25 July 2022), available at: www.a-dif.org/2022/07/25/al-viminale-stato-di-guerra-allinformazione/.

presumed 'safe' – but the Procedure Directive leaves wide discretion to each EU Member State to identify which countries are 'safe'.[134] Italy, along with the majority of EU Member States, have designated Tunisia as a safe country of origin.[135] However, as mentioned above, Tunisia does not guarantee effective protection to refugees. Although Tunisia signed the Refugee Convention, it did not adopt implementing legislation, and the UNHCR conducts asylum proceedings on behalf of the Tunisian government. From the reviewed material, it seems that most of the criticism concerns the failure of Tunisia to provide social and economic rights to refugees, especially in the long term.[136] In October 2023, the Court of Florence confirmed this view by finding the expulsion of a Tunisian citizen to Tunisia to be unlawful. The applicant had not claimed to be specifically targeted by persecutory acts, but the Court accepted the argument that there is a serious socio-economic, health, water and food safety crisis in Tunisia. Moreover, the recent authoritarian turn in the country has rendered the Italian government's previous assessment of Tunisia as a safe country obsolete. The Court of Florence added that the government's policies must be updated in light of the current country conditions, as required by law.[137]

In light of all the above, from an ROL perspective, the readmission agreements discussed here raise legality issues as well as problems of compliance with fundamental human rights and refugee protection.

IV. PRIVATISED PUSHBACKS AND PULLBACKS TO UNSAFE COUNTRIES

The previous sections show how, on the basis of legally questionable international agreements, Italy has delegated its immigration control to North African countries. After its defeat in *Hirsi*, the government adopted new strategies to continue repelling sea migrants while avoiding legal accountability for these migrants' fate in third countries. In this section I explain how, in addition to pullbacks, Italy and other EU states rely on commercial ships to carry out sea rescues when they are near migrants in distress and coastguard vessels would not be able to intervene in a timely manner. It appears that states have a preference

[134] Open Migration (n 85).

[135] EASO, '"Safe Country of Origin" Concept in EU+ Countries. Situational Update' (Situational Update, Issue no 3, 9 June 2021) 5, available at: euaa.europa.eu/sites/default/files/publications/EASO-situational_update-safe_country_of_origin-2021.pdf.

[136] UNHCR, 'Tunisia – Operational Update' (Operational Update, 2018), available at: reporting.unhcr.org/sites/default/files/UNHCR%20Tunisia%20Operational%20Update%20-%20October-December%202017.pdf; Melting Pot Europa, 'Tunisia Is Not a Safe Country for Us' (*Melting Pot Europa*, 21 June 2022), available at: www.meltingpot.org/en/2022/06/tunisia-is-not-a-safe-country-for-us/.

[137] Alessandra Ziniti, 'Un' Altra Sentenza "Contro" il Decreto Cutro: la Tunisia non E' un Paese Sicuro, la Farnesina Riveda la Lista del Luoghi Che Non Rispettano I Diritti Umani' *La Repubblica* (5 October 2023), available at: www.repubblica.it/cronaca/2023/10/04/news/sentenza_tribunale_firenze_tunisia_non_e_paese_sicuro-416835126/.

for commercial vessels over NGO vessels when ordering migrant rescues, even when the latter are in the vicinity of the incident, because commercial ships comply with the maritime authorities' official orders even if this means disembarking the migrants in an unsafe location.[138] By contrast, NGOs involved in SAR operations would only take the rescued migrants to Italy or other European countries.

According to research, 'between 2011 and 2018, only one commercial ship returned migrants to Libya'.[139] 'Since 2018 [as of 20 March 2020] there have been about 30 such returns, involving roughly 1,800 migrants, in which merchant ships have either returned migrants to Libyan ports or transferred them to Libyan Coast Guard vessels'.[140] However, it is believed that 'the real number is likely to be higher'. These situations are referred to as 'privatised pushbacks' and have become a strategy used by states to avoid their protection obligations.[141]

One such case occurred on 11 January 2020, when the Libyan Coast Guard engaged the *Panther*, a German merchant ship, instead of the nearby *Open Arms* vessel to rescue 68 migrants[142] because the owner had agreed to follow the regulations and orders of the Libyan Coast Guard. It is reported that '[a]fter the Panther arrived in Tripoli, Libyan soldiers boarded, forced the migrants ashore at gunpoint, and drove them to a detention camp in the besieged Libyan capital'.[143] Kingsley argues that the tactics employed to avoid humanitarian rescuers expose more migrants to danger. Also, whereas the SAR Convention mandates that merchant vessels must adhere to directives issued by the competent Coast Guard, the treaty does not allow the authorities to selectively determine who provides assistance in times of emergencies.[144] Moreover, the SOLAS Convention allows shipmasters to refuse to follow disembarkation directions by the competent MRCC if these directions would put the ship, crew, or passengers in an unsafe situation.[145]

States, NGOs and scholars have debated whether privatised pushbacks comply with ROL principles. As migrants are often rescued by merchant ships in international waters, the Italian, Maltese and EU authorities take the view that

[138] Patrick Kingsley, 'Privatized Pushbacks: How the EU and Libya Use Merchant Ships to Block Migrant Boats' (*Migrants at Sea*, 23 March 2020), available at: migrantsatsea.org/2020/03/23/privatized-pushbacks-how-the-eu-and-libya-use-merchant-ships-to-block-migrant-boats/. According to Brentall, there have been no cases where a shipmaster has refused to follow the maritime authorities' directions. Interview with Estelle Brentall, Head of Maritime, European Transport Workers' Federation, Brussels (online, 12 November 2020).

[139] Forensic Oceanography, 'Privatised Push-Back of the Nivin', available at: forensic-architecture.org/investigation/nivin (nd).

[140] Kingsley (n 138); Forensic Oceanography (n 139).

[141] Kingsley (n 138).

[142] ibid.

[143] ibid.

[144] ibid.

[145] Interview with John Stawpert, Manager of Environment and Trade, International Chamber of Shipping, London (online, 10 November 2020). See International Convention for the Safety of Life at Sea (1 November 1974) 1184 UNTS 278 (SOLAS Convention) ch V, reg 10; ch 3, section II.B.

'migrants should therefore be returned to Libya, since Libya coordinates [SAR] operations'[146] in that area, and EU countries are not responsible for migrants' ill treatment there. On the other hand, several scholars and NGOs argue that the responsibility for SAR missions still lies with Italy and other EU Member States, owing to their pivotal role in establishing these operations through financing, training and equipping the Libyan Coast Guard.[147]

In this context, the pending case of *SDG v Italy*, communicated to the UN Human Rights Committee (UNHRC) in 2019, should be mentioned. The case is the first to be submitted to an international human rights body aimed at tackling 'privatised pushbacks'. The events under scrutiny took place in November 2019, when the claimant, a Sudanese migrant, was rescued together with other migrants in international waters by the *Nivin*, a Panamanian commercial vessel, under coordination of the IMRCC. Thereafter, the IMRCC ordered the *Nivin* to liaise with the Libyan Cost Guard, which directed the vessel to bring the migrants to Libya, where they were forced to disembark. The claimant was subsequently subjected to torture and forced labour in violation of the Convention against Torture and the International Covenant on Civil and Political Rights.[148] The claimant argues that Italy and the EU are responsible for the event because they exercise 'strategic overall control over'[149] the Libyan Coast Guard, and that this is not an isolated event.

Regarding the issue of jurisdiction, which prevented the claimant from pursuing national remedies as Italy considered the events to have taken place out of its control,[150] the claimant argues that the Italian government's strategy has changed since the *Hirsi* judgment. In particular, Italy increasingly resorts to 'contactless' measures rather than direct actions. These measures may amount to factual control 'given Italy's role in Libya's migration and SAR systems' as well as Italy's influence and support 'in migration-related operations conducted by Libyan forces, and for which it must be deemed to retain its own independent responsibility'.[151] In light of all this, the applicant's requests include asking the UNHRC: (1) to find violations of the International Covenant on Civil and

[146] ibid.

[147] Vari (n 5) 106–07; A Pijnenburg, 'From Italian Pushbacks to Libyan Pullbacks: Is *Hirsi 2.0* in the Making in Strasbourg?' (2018) 20 *European Journal of Migration and Law* 396; M Giuffré, 'State Responsibility Beyond Borders: What Legal Basis for Italy's Pushbacks to Libya?' (2012) 24 *International Journal of Refugee Law* 692; EuroMed Rights, 'Input for the Special Rapporteur's Report on Human Rights Violations at International Borders: Trends, Prevention and Accountability' (February 2022); Medecins Sans Frontière, 'Italy–Libya Agreement: Five Years of EU-Sponsored Abuse in Libya and the Central Mediterranean' (*Medecins Sans Frontière*, 2 February 2002), available at: www.msf.org/italy-libya-agreement-five-years-eu-sponsored-abuse-libya-and-central-mediterranean; Global Legal Action Network, 'Legal Action against Italy over its Coordination of Libyan Coast Guard Pullbacks Resulting in Migrant Deaths and Abuse' (GLAN, 8 May 2018), available at: www.glanlaw.org/single-post/2018/05/08/legal-action-against-italy-over-its-coordination-of-libyan-coast-guard-pullbacks-resulti.

[148] Communication to the United Nations Human Rights Committee in the case of SDG against Italy: submitted for consideration under the Optional Protocol to the International Covenant on Civil and Political Rights (2020) 1.

[149] ibid 23.

[150] ibid 6.

[151] ibid 23.

Political Rights;[152] (2) to recommend Italy to issue him a humanitarian visa in order to travel to Italy and apply for protection; (3) to urge Italy to recognise its role in the event; and (4) to adopt safeguards to avoid similar events in the future.[153]

In conclusion, privatised pushbacks are just one of several tactics used by Italy and other EU states to prevent migrants from reaching the European territory. So far, privatised pushbacks have not been subject to many judicial or quasi-judicial reviews, but the outcome of *SDG* may become an important precedent. Although the issue of jurisdiction is not straightforward, Pinjnenburg and van der Pas note how human rights bodies tend to embrace a wider interpretation of the concept than judicial bodies, and therefore recourse to these mechanisms has become a litigation strategy adopted by civil society organisations.[154]

V. ACCOUNTABILITY FOR PUSHBACKS AND PULLBACKS AND RELATED HUMAN RIGHTS VIOLATIONS

Besides the cases already discussed in this chapter, the research that I conducted reveals a few others dealing with attempts to establish accountability for push-backs and pullbacks in the Central Mediterranean. These attempts have been made at the domestic as well as at the regional and international levels, and some still await judgments. Their results could be significant with regard to Italy's continued ability to circumvent its legal obligations towards sea migrants, as I will discuss in the following subsections.

A. Cases before the Italian Courts

One notable *criminal case against a non-state actor* is that of the *Asso 28* decided by the Court of Naples.[155] This is the only case after the *Hirsi* decision

[152] The rights that the Communication argues have been breached include: the right to life (Art 6(1)); the prohibition of torture or cruel, inhuman, or degrading treatment or punishment (Art 7), alone and in conjunction with the prohibition of collective expulsions (Art 13); the prohibition of slavery and forced or compulsory labour (Art 8); and the right to liberty (Art 8).

[153] Communication to the United Nations Human Rights Committee in the case of SDG against Italy (n 148) 40–41.

[154] A Pijnenburg and K van der Pas, 'Strategic Litigation against European Control Policies: The Legal Battleground of the Central Mediterranean Migration Route' (2022) 24 *European Journal of Migration and Law* 401, 424. For instance, see the case of HRC, 'Communication no 3042/2017, Decision (Malta, CCPR/C/130/D/3042/2017) and (Italy, CCPR/C/128/D/3043/2017) of 27 January 2021' discussed in ch 4, section V.B.

[155] Trib Napoli, Sentenza 13.10.2021, n 1643. See: Redattore Sociale, 'Migranti, Scoppia il Caso Asso 28. "Fatto Grave, è Respingimento"' *Redattore Sociale* (31 July 2018), available at: www.redattoresociale.it/article/notiziario/migranti_scoppia_il_caso_asso_28_fatto_grave_e_respingimento; Il Post, 'Il Caso della Asso 28, Spiegato' *Il Post* (1 August 2018), available at: www.ilpost.it/2018/08/01/asso-28-migranti-libia/; ASGI, 'Condanna di Asso 28: un Precedente che Può Scardinare la Prassi dei Respingimenti in Libia' (ASGI, 19 October 2021), available at: www.asgi.it/notizie/libia-condanna-respingimento/.

concerning an Italian ship that returned migrants back to Libya. The events took place in 2018, when the *Asso 28* – an Italian-flagged, private ship belonging to the Augusta Offshore Company, which was providing support to the Sabratha oil platform off the Libyan coast – rescued over 100 migrants, including women and children, in the international waters of the Libyan SAR zone. The shipmaster sailed to Tripoli, with the shipwrecked on board, on instructions from the Sabratha platform managers and unidentified Libyan authorities. In particular, the trip was conducted under the guidance of an embarked Libyan customs official – at any oil platform, there is a customs officer in charge of protecting national interests – and not the Libyan SAR authorities.[156]

The case was brought against the shipmaster of the *Asso 28* with the assistance of the NGO Open Arms. It was argued that the shipmaster had the duty to immediately inform the Libyan SAR authorities and, in the event of no answer, the IMRCC.[157] However, he failed to do so. The shipmaster only contacted the IMRCC while en route to Libya and then transported the migrants onto a Libyan Coast Guard vessel that disembarked them in Libya.

The Court of Naples, with the decision of 13 October 2021, convicted the shipmaster for the crimes of 'arbitrary disembarkation and abandonment of persons' (Article 1155 of the Navigation Code) and 'abandonment of minors' (Article 591 of the Criminal Code). The Court reasoned that Libya is not a safe place of disembarkation, and the return of migrants there occurred without the mandatory coordination of the competent SAR authorities. The orders given to the shipmaster were provided by an authority without the power to do so; thus, he could not be excused for having carried out a lawful order under Article 51 of the Criminal Code. The decision was then confirmed by the Court of Appeals of Naples[158] and the Court of Cassation.[159] This case is important because the courts took the view that Libya is an unsafe country and that arbitrarily disembarking migrants there can be an action of criminal relevance. However, the question that remains open is whether the decision could have reached a different outcome if the orders were given by the Libyan or Italian maritime authorities – in other words, whether the captain would have been convicted if he had disembarked the migrants in Libya upon the orders of the Libyan Coast Guard or the IMRCC.[160]

[156] Vassallo Paleologo, 'Il Tribunale di Napoli Condanna i Respingimenti in Libia' (n 46).
[157] See ch 4, section IV.A.
[158] App Napoli, Sentenza 10.11.2022, n 16696.
[159] Interview with Lawyer no 3, Milan (online, 27 October 2023).
[160] Cecilia Pagella, 'Caso Asso 28: La Corte d' Appello di Napoli Conferma la Condanna per Sbarco Arbitrario e Abbandono di Minori o Incapaci sulle Coste Libiche' (*Sistema Penale*, 8 May 2023), available at: www.sistemapenale.it/it/scheda/pagella-caso-asso-28-la-corte-dappello-di-napoli-conferma-la-condanna-per-di-sbarco-arbitrario-e-abbandono-di-minori-o-incapaci.

Among the civil cases, the *Osman* case[161] and the *Asso 29* case,[162] both before the Court of Rome, should be discussed.

Osman refers to events that occurred in the summer of 2009, when a group of Eritrean citizens was rescued by the Italian Navy in international waters. The migrants were subsequently transferred onto another vessel belonging to the Italian Navy and forcibly repatriated to Libya, despite having expressed their desire to seek asylum and obtain international protection. Thus, Amnesty International and ASGI (Associazione per gli Studi Giuridici sull' Immigrazione – Association for Legal Studies on Immigration) filed a case against the Ministry of the Interior, the Ministry of Defence, the Ministry of Foreign Affairs and the Presidency of the Council of Ministers on behalf of the affected migrants.

In 2019, the Court of Rome declared the unlawfulness of the Italian authorities' actions in violation of the non-refoulement principle and the prohibition on collective expulsions. Consequently, the Court recognised the right of the applicants to enter Italy to formalise their asylum application, in addition to granting each of them the compensation of €15,000. In other words, the public administration was ordered to allow the applicants, who in the meantime had fled from Libya and were held up for years in Israel, to enter Italy in order to exercise the right to apply for asylum in direct application of Article 10, paragraph 3 of the Constitution.[163] The Court emphasised that adherence to such a provision is mandatory even in maritime areas, as states are bound by their legal responsibilities, which encompass obligations derived from international law.[164] The principle does not allow any exception, although a state does not have the obligation to admit an asylum seeker into its own territory – the state

[161] Trib Roma, Sentenza 14.11.2019, n 22917; Rita Russo, 'Respingimenti Illeciti e Diritto d'Asilo: è Sufficiente il Risarcimento in Denaro? Nota a Trib. Roma, 28.11.2019 no 22917' (*Giustizia Insieme*, 5 February 2020), available at: www.giustiziainsieme.it/it/diritto-civile/858-respingimenti-illeciti-e-diritto-d-asilo-e-sufficiente-il-risarcimento-in-denaro-nota-a-trib-roma-28-11-2019-n-22917?hitcount=0; Amnesty International, '"Caso Osman": Tutte le Tappe che Hanno Portato alla Condanna del Governo Italiano' (Amnesty International, 31 August 2020), available at: www.amnesty.it/caso-osman-tutte-le-tappe-che-hanno-portato-alla-condanna-del-governo-italiano/. See ASGI, 'Storica Vittoria del Diritto di Asilo: un Visto d'Ingresso in Italia per Richiedere Protezione' (ASGI, 30 August 2020), available at: www.asgi.it/asilo-e-protezione-internazionale/vittoria-diritto-asilo-respinti-illegalmente-eritrei-oggi-in-italia-con-visto/.

[162] Rosita Rijtano, 'Respingimenti in Libia, Asso Ventinove a Processo' (*Lavialibera*, 15 February 2021), available at: lavialibera.it/it-schede-469-respingimenti_libia_asso_ventinove_processo; Luisiana Gaita, '"Marina Iitaliana Ha Coordinato Respingimento Illegale di Migranti in Libia": Cinque Eritrei Citano in Fiudizio Governo e un'Azienda Privata' *Il Fatto Quotidiano* (12 February 2021), available at: www.ilfattoquotidiano.it/2021/02/12/marina-italiana-ha-coordinato-respingimento-illegale-di-migranti-in-libia-cinque-eritrei-citano-in-giudizio-governo-e-unazienda-privata/6099643/.

[163] This principle has been implemented in Decreto Legislativo 25 luglio 1998, n 286, Testo unico delle disposizioni concernenti la disciplina dell'immigrazione e norme sulla condizione dello straniero (come modificato) (Testo Unico sull' Immigrazione – TUI) Art 19.

[164] Trib Roma, Sentenza 14.11.2019, n 22917, 8.

can choose to send the applicant to a safe third country. According to the Court, the MoU between Libya and Italy, invoked by the Italian authorities to justify their return of the migrants to Libya, does not constitute an express authorisation for pushbacks towards that country. To strengthen its decision on this point, the Court referred to the similar *Hirsi* case,[165] discussed in section II.B. As such, this is not only a rights-oriented judgment but also a clear attempt by the Court to restore the ROL.

In *Asso 29*, which is still pending before the Court of Rome,[166] the contested events took place in July 2018. The *Asso 29*, a ship flying the Italian flag and owned by Augusta Offshore Company, rescued about 150 people in the Libyan SAR area and then brought them back to Libya with the coordination of the Italian Navy authorities stationed in Tripoli and assisted by the Libyan authorities. The case was filed by five Eritrean nationals, with the help of ASGI and Amnesty International, against the Italian authorities, the Offshore Company Augusta, and the shipmaster of the *Asso 29*. The claimants' lawyers asked the Court to declare the pushback unlawful, as it had exposed the applicants to months of arbitrary detention and abuse in violation of various legal provisions, including the prohibitions of refoulement and collective expulsions and the right to seek asylum. In addition, they sought compensation for the damages suffered by the applicants and an injunction to prohibit the actors involved from repeating their conduct in the future. Among the issues at stake, the judge will have to address whether it was a coincidence that the Italian Navy coordinated a pushback to Libya or whether Italy played a central role in bringing people back to Libya.[167] In this respect, the decision will be decisive in terms of clarifying the practices taking place in the Mediterranean and the manner in which the operation was carried out. While the case is still pending, it is worth noting that one of the claimants, a Sudanese citizen stranded in Libya, filed an urgent interim injunction application with the Court in order to be allowed to enter Italy and apply for international protection. On 10 June 2023, the Court of Rome granted the request, reasoning that the claimant was under Italian jurisdiction when on board the *Asso 29*, and the Italian state breached the obligation to disembark him to a POS.[168] As in Libya the claimant's human rights were at risk, the Italian administration was ordered to make the necessary arrangements for the claimant to travel to Italy. However, the Italian embassy in Libya has failed to comply

[165] ibid 8, 9.
[166] Rijtano (n 162); Gaita (n 162).
[167] Luca Rondi, 'Respingimenti in Libia: Governo Italiano e Società Private a Processo' (*Altreconomia*, 13 February 2021), available at: altreconomia.it/respingimenti-in-libia-governo-italiano-e-societa-private-a-processo/.
[168] Trib Roma, Ordinanza 10.06.2023, RG 18757/2023.

with the Court's order, and a new procedure to ensure its execution has been started.[169]

Finally, in 2021, ASGI lodged a complaint with the prosecutor at the Regional Court of Auditors in Rome,[170] asking to investigate the use of public funds by some Italian NGOs in immigrant detention centres in Libya. In particular, the complaint highlights the need to obtain clarity on whether the money is being used in compliance with the statutory goals of cooperation and development for which it was allocated – and not, for example, being embezzled or diverted.[171]

It should be noted that, common to all these cases, jurisdiction was not an issue either because the ships involved flew the Italian flag and participated in the actions that breached the human rights of the migrants involved or because the funds were given to Italian NGOs. However, in many other cases, establishing that Italy had control over the pullbacks carried out by other actors is much more complex.

B. Regional and International Initiatives

At the regional level, in 2018, the Global Legal Action Network (GLAN) filed the case of *SS and others v Italy* with the ECtHR, where the issue at stake was whether Italy exercised decisive influence over a SAR operation performed by the Libyan Coast Guard which ended with a number of migrants being returned to Libya. In particular, the question to be decided was whether, as a consequence of its funding, training and supply of equipment to Libya, Italy bears responsibility for the human rights violations endured by the applicants.[172]

[169] Franz Berraggino, 'Migranti, Tribunale Impone L'Ingresso di un Sudanese Respinto in Libia: "Rischia Torture". Ma il Governo non Rispetta l'Ordinanza' *Il Fatto Quotidiano* (29 June 2023), available at: www.ilfattoquotidiano.it/2023/06/29/migranti-tribunale-impone-lingresso-di-un-sudanese-respinto-in-libia-rischia-torture-ma-il-governo-non-rispetta-lordinanza/7211152/.

[170] ASGI, 'ASGI Asks the Italian Court of Auditors for an Investigation into the Use of Public Funds in Detention Centres in Libya' (ASGI, 27 January 2021), available at: sciabacaoruka.asgi.it/en/asgi-asks-the-italian-court-of-auditors-for-an-investigation-into-the-use-of-public-funds-in-detention-centres-in-libya/. The complaint is available at ASGI, 'To the Regional Public Prosecutor's Office at the Court of Auditors, Section of Lazio Rome: Complaint' (ASGI, January 2021), available at: sciabacaoruka.asgi.it/wp-content/uploads/2021/03/Esposto-Corte-dei-Conti-ITA_ENG-1.pdf.

[171] ASGI, 'Esposto alla Procura Regionale presso la Corte dei Conti di Roma' (ASGI, January 2021), available at: sciabacaoruka.asgi.it/wp-content/uploads/2021/03/Esposto-Corte-dei-Conti-ITA_ENG-1.pdf.

[172] GS Goodwin-Gill, J McAdam and E Dunlop, 'The Principle of Non-refoulement – Part 2' in GS Goodwin-Gill and J McAdam (eds), *The Refugee in International Law*, 4th edn (Oxford, OUP, 2021); Andreina de Leo, 'S.S. and Others v Italy: Sharing Responsibility for Migrants Abuse in Libya' (*PILPG*, 6 January 2020), available at: www.publicinternationallawandpolicygroup.org/lawyering-justice-blog/2020/4/23/ss-and-others-v-italy-sharing-responsibility-for-migrants-abuses-in-libya; Müller and Slominski (n 28) 814. See ch 4, section II.C.

In the complaint, the 2017 MoU is referred to as the basis for Italy to support and finance the activities of the Libyan Coast Guard, arguably making Italy responsible for the human rights violations that result from Libyan and Italian vessel interceptions.[173]

Before ascertaining any violations of the ECHR by Italy, the ECtHR will first have to establish whether or not it has jurisdiction over the case.[174] Differently from *Hirsi*, in *SS and others* the migrants were intercepted by a Libyan Coast Guard vessel instead of an Italian vessel. Furthermore, Italy's engagement entailed partially coordinating the rescue operation through its IMRCC, by having donated the Libyan Coast Guard's vessel, and through the presence of an Italian helicopter at the location.[175] Finding jurisdiction in this case seems to be a difficult issue, as the Court would need to move away from its strict precedents, according to which 'Italy must exercise full and exclusive control over the migrants',[176] and thus adopt a lower threshold to find extraterritorial jurisdiction.[177]

However, it should be noted that in *Xhavara and others v Italy and Albania*, involving irregular migrants trying to reach Italy from Albania on the ship *Kater I Rades*, which sank due to a collision with the Italian warship *Sibilla* in the international waters of the Otranto Channel on 28 March 1997, the ECtHR determined that the *Kater I Rades* was under Italian jurisdiction.[178] To reach

[173] *SS and others v Italy* App no 21660/18 (ECtHR, 11 November 2019). The disputed facts occurred on 6 November 2017, when the Libyan Coast Guard intervened in a SAR operation concerning about 130 migrants off the Libyan coast. The operation had been initiated by the NGO ship Sea-Watch 3, and was partly coordinated by the IMRCC, with the logistical support of an Italian ship stationed in Tripoli (as part of the *Mare Sicuro* mission). The Libyan Coast Guard was also contacted by the IMRCC, and it is unclear and remains to be assessed whether it then intervened to coordinate the event on its own initiative or upon instruction from the IMRCC. Of the 17 applicants, 14 Nigerian citizens and the Ghanaian citizen were rescued and brought to Italy by the Sea-Watch 3, while 2 Nigerian citizens were brought back to Libya by the Libyan Coast Guard and later repatriated to Nigeria. The case was presented by 17 survivors through GLAN and ASGI against Italy for violation of Art 2 (right to life), Art 3 (prohibition of torture and inhuman and degrading treatment), and Art 4 of Protocol no 4 (prohibition of collective expulsions) of the ECHR. In the complaint, it is argued that the Libyan Coast Guard did not immediately intervene, that they engaged in some dangerous manoeuvres before rescuing the migrants, and that they beat up the migrants while on board. The court application exposes how the intervention of the Libyan Coast Guard follows the terms of the 2017 MoU between Italy and the Libyan Government of National Accord, according to which Italy enables and coordinates the Libyan response at sea – arguably making Italy legally responsible for the actions of Italian and Libyan vessels in the case. GLAN, 'Legal Action against Italy over its Coordination of Libyan Coast Guard Pullbacks Resulting in Migrant Deaths and Abuse' (n 147); A Fazzini, 'Il Caso S.S. and Others v Italy Nel Quadro dell'Esternalizzazione delle Frontiere in Libia: Osservazioni sui Possibili Scenari al Vaglio della Corte di Strasburgo' (2020) 2 *Diritto, Immigrazione e Cittadinanza* 86.

[174] Fazzini (n 173) 102.

[175] Pijnenburg, 'From Italian Pushbacks to Libyan Pullbacks' (n 147) 406.

[176] ibid 411, 426.

[177] ibid.

[178] Although the facts did not take place in the Central Mediterranean, the case is particularly important in the context of the debate on whether or not a state has jurisdiction for incidents occurring in international waters. *Xhavara and Fifteen Others v Italy and Albania* (Admissibility Decision) App no 39473/98 (ECtHR, 11 January 2001); S Trevisanut, 'Is there a Right to be Rescued at Sea? A Constructive View' (2014) 4 *Questions of International Law* 3, 9–10.

this conclusion, the Court reasoned that the incident occurred during operations conducted under a bilateral cooperation agreement signed by Italy and Albania on 25 March 1997. The ECtHR did not provide further explanation on the matter, but according to Trevisanut the mere presence of an agreement that grants enforcement powers to a state is enough to establish jurisdiction.[179] In any case, a case-by-case evaluation of the specific circumstances would still be necessary.

International legal initiatives include two communications to the prosecutor of the International Criminal Court (ICC), who must decide whether or not a preliminary assessment shall be carried out – a phase that precedes the opening of formal investigations.

The first such communication was submitted by two individual lawyers and several students of the Paris Institute of Political Studies in 2019[180] and argues that EU and EU Member State responses towards sea migrants in the Mediterranean and migrants in Libya between 2014 and 2019 involved crimes against humanity in violation of Article 7 of the Rome Statute.[181] According to Pasquero, it is unlikely that such a preliminary assessment will begin, mostly because an investigation of this type would threaten the legitimacy of the ICC – a judicial body which has among its strongest supporters the same countries that would need to be investigated.[182] Nevertheless, he points out that 'whatever its outcome, the Communication represents a landmark step in the political and legal debate on migration, breaking the taboo that has so far prevented public

[179] Trevisanut (n 178) 9–10.

[180] Pijnenburg and van der Pas (n 154) 415. See Communication to the Office of the Prosecutor of the International Criminal Court Pursuant to Article 15 of the Rome Statute (EU Migration Policies in the Central Mediterranean and Libya, 2014–2019), available at: www.statewatch.org/media/documents/news/2019/jun/eu-icc-case-EU-Migration-Policies.pdf.

[181] Some of the most important points in the Communication are the following: The present case concerns the legal duty to protect the right to life. This duty is based, in the exceptional circumstances of the present case, on various normative frameworks: international maritime, human rights and refugee law … According to international maritime law conventions, [which] all the relevant EU Member States are party to, EU and MS agencies and agents have a duty to render assistance to boats in distress, to conduct safe SAR [operations] and to ensure the survivors are disembarked in a safe port (points 606–07). To conclude, the European Union and its Member [State] agents and officials arbitrarily deprived and failed to protect the inherent right to life in the sense of the International Covenant on Civil and Political Rights, 'of … persons on whose enjoyment of the right to life it exercises power or effective control, [including] persons located outside any territory effectively controlled by the State, whose right to life is nonetheless impacted by its military or other activities in a direct and reasonably foreseeable manner'. It therefore violated its 'obligations under international law not to aid or assist activities undertaken by other States and non-State actors that violate the right to life' and to 'respect and protect the lives of individuals who find themselves in a situation of distress at sea, in accordance with their international obligations on rescue at sea' (point 620). Given the EU's effective control over the situation at the time of interception, the deportations violated asylum seekers' most fundamental, internationally protected human rights: dignity, life, liberty, physical and mental health, and their right to exit and seek asylum (point 774).

[182] A Pasquero, 'La comunicazione alla Corte Penale Internazionale sule Responsabilità dei Leader Europei per Crimini contro l'Umanità Commessi nel Mediterraneo e in Libia. Una Lettura Critica' (2020) 1 *Diritto, Immigrazione e Cittadinanza* 50, 50.

opinion from seeing European political leaders also as suspects of atrocious international crimes'.[183]

The second communication was filed by several NGOs to the prosecutor of the ICC on 23 November 2021. The communication addresses the commission of grave crimes against migrants in Libya and asks the prosecutor to investigate them.[184] As this communication is focused on Libyan rather than European actors, this author is of the view that it has better chances of proceeding to the next stage.

Other international attempts to establish Italy's accountability are those presented by a number of NGOs: (1) in 2020, to the UN Committee against Torture, to investigate Italy's role in pushbacks and pullbacks to Libya and the systematic torture of migrants in that country;[185] and (2) in 2021, to the UN Committee on the Elimination of Discrimination against Women, on behalf of two Nigerian women victims of trafficking exploited in Libya. The two women tried to reach Italy but were intercepted and returned to their country in violation of Article 2 (right to non-discrimination) and Article 6 (right to protection from the exploitation of prostitution) of the Convention on the Elimination of all Forms of Discrimination against Women[186] Both cases are pending.

In conclusion, whereas a number of civil society organisations have attempted to establish accountability for violations of migrants' rights and push a new and more expansive concept of jurisdiction, the outcomes are still unknown. However they are decided, the cases before the ECtHR and the ICC in particular may establish important precedents.

VI. CONCLUSION

In the absence of a common EU response to African migration, Italy has adopted a functionalist approach through a number of agreements with third countries to control immigration flows and secure its borders. Particularly relevant in this context are the agreements on immigration control that Italy has concluded

[183] ibid 78.

[184] International Federation for Human Rights (FIDH), European Center for Constitutional and Human Rights (ECCHR), Lawyer for Justice in Libya (LFJL), Communication to the Office of the Prosecutor of the International Criminal Court, 'Situation in Libya – Article 15 Communication on the Commission of Crimes against Migrants and Refugees in Libya' (19 November 2021), available at: www.fidh.org/IMG/pdf/20211119_executive_summary_libya_icc_final.pdf.

[185] Centre Suisse Pour la Défense des Droits des Migrants, 'Information Submitted under Article 20 of the Convention against Torture and Other Cruel, Inhuman or Degrading Treatment or Punishment Concerning Italy's Responsibility for the Torture of Migrants Pulled Back to Libya' (25 June 2020), available at: centre-csdm.org/wp-content/uploads/2020/07/CAT-Art.-20-Inquiry-CSDM-01.07.2020.pdf.

[186] ASGI, 'Press Conference: Italy and Libya Brought before the UN CEDAW Committee by Two Women Victims of Trafficking' (ASGI, 3 December 2021), available at: en.asgi.it/press-conference-italy-and-libya-brought-before-the-un-cedaw-committee-by-two-women-victims-of-trafficking/; Pijnenburg and van der Pas (n 154) 416.

with Libya – which is not even a functioning state – and Tunisia, given their role in pushbacks and pullbacks and thus their consequences for human rights and the ROL.

In order to evade the accountability laid down in the *Hirsi* judgment of 2012, Italy has established a legal loophole by entrusting border control to third nations through these accords. The 'contactless control' strategy, which aims to contain migrants indirectly, poses difficulties in establishing jurisdiction and consequently accountability for human rights violations.[187]

From a substantive point of view, the agreements affect a number of migrants' rights,[188] as they presume the safety of the cooperating country despite evidence of violations of the principle of non-refoulement and other fundamental rights. The aforementioned rights encompass the entitlement to personal freedom, the entitlement to freedom from inhumane and degrading treatment, the entitlement to seek asylum, and the entitlement to access to justice. As such, these agreements create a divide between those who are citizens, integrated in the state system, and those who are outside it and thus without access to rights.[189]

From a formal point of view, these agreements are characterised by general and vague terms that leave wide discretion concerning the obligations accepted by the signatory parties. Moreover, they take the form of atypical and non-legally binding instruments with uncertain legal effects that exclude both parliamentary control and publication in violation of the constitutional procedures.[190] However, the issue is complex and controversial, and the Italian government (as well as a few scholars) takes the view that an agreement concluded by the executive without parliamentary approval may nevertheless be valid – for example, if dealing with technical matters within the competence of some ministers,[191] or if based on constitutional custom or tacitly approved by Parliament. Regardless of these debates, what is clear is that the failure of Parliament to assert its checking powers could be taken to suggest that the majority's will is to support the executive's decisions in foreign policy.[192] On the other hand, given the subject matter of the agreements and the challenges to human rights that they pose, a 'cautious approach' should be taken.[193]

As far as accountability is concerned, there exists a dearth of transparency on the part of the Italian authorities, which have withheld information pertaining to the financial and technical assistance provided to the third countries entrusted

[187] Fazzini (n 173) 89–90. See also, Spagnolo (n 60) 210, 212.

[188] Spagnolo (n 60) 213.

[189] Although not in the context of these agreements, see G Agamben, *Means without End: Notes on Politics* (Minneapolis, MN, University of Minnesota Press, 2000) 18.

[190] Antonio Servedio, 'Gli Accordi in Forma Semplificata e i Soggetti di Diritto Internazionale' (*Ministro della Difesa, Carabinieri*, nd), available at: www.carabinieri.it/media---comunicazione/rassegna-dell-arma/la-rassegna/anno-2001/n-2---aprile-giugno/studi/gli-accordi-in-forma-semplificata-e-i-soggetti-di-diritto-internazionale; Olivito (n 61) 512–15; Cafaro (n 130) 7, 22–23.

[191] Spagnolo (n 60) 214–15.

[192] Raffiotta (n 55) 20.

[193] Spagnolo (n 60) 210.

with the responsibility of externalising immigration control. Furthermore, there is the absence of a monitoring mechanism to oversee the implementation of such agreements.[194] The EU and its Member States adopt an analogous approach and, in their respective attempts to avoid responsibility for migrants' protection, even seem to be in competition with each other.

Despite all these issues, the Italian Parliament did not intervene to challenge the agreements' legality due to political considerations. According to Savino, this is because parliaments are elected by citizens, whose interests might appear to be 'at odds with the full protection of migrants' liberties'.[195] Thus, it can be concluded that, in the context of sea migration, the Parliament's power-checking competence is weakened. Similarly, the Italian Constitutional Court has traditionally performed 'a "weak scrutiny" of legislation aimed at the control of migration flows'.[196]

Finally, besides relying on Libya and Tunisia to prevent the arrival of sea migrants, Italy has also assigned rescue operations to commercial ships rather than to NGOs as part of the strategy to delegate pullbacks to other actors and avoid the corresponding legal obligations.

In a few individual cases, the Italian courts have upheld the rights affected by the agreements and strategies discussed in this chapter, but the jurisdictional issue and other practical barriers to migrants' access to justice have had an impact on the number of cases that could be pursued. The same problems are reflected at regional and international fora. In this regard, whereas the case of *SS and others v Italy*, which is pending before the ECtHR, could be crucial in establishing Italy's direct responsibility for the ongoing pullbacks to unsafe countries, it also faces the thorny issue of jurisdiction, towards which the ECtHR has tended to adopt a cautious approach.

To conclude, it should be remembered that Italy's strategies are possible because they are backed and sometimes replicated at the EU level.[197] Despite all the discussions and media attention on the matter, the EU does not provide a comprehensive response to sea migration and remains focused on the security of borders,[198] whereas what is needed is a coordinated response based on the principles of the ROL.

[194] Ghebreigziabiher Ogbazghi (n 27) 44.

[195] M Savino, 'The Refugee Crisis as a Challenge for Public Law: The Italian Case' (2016) 17 *German Law Journal* 981, 1003.

[196] ibid. See also Golia (n 57) 84–85.

[197] Lisa O'Carroll, 'Italian MP Warns Migration an Issue for All of Europe on Lampedusa Visit' *Guardian* (17 September 2017), available at: www.theguardian.com/world/2023/sep/17/italian-pm-warns-migration-an-issue-for-all-of-europe-on-lampedusa-visit?CMP=Share_iOSApp_Other.

[198] Sea arrivals take place because there are no other ways to reach Europe, including for economic migrants. Cooperation with countries of origin and transit to expand circular labour migration is required to partially address the problem. Interview with Marco Borraccetti, Associate Professor of European Union Law, Università di Bologna, Italy (online, 2 May 2023).

6

Legal Provisions, Policies and Case Law on NGOs Engaged in SAR Activities

I. INTRODUCTION

IN THIS CHAPTER, I analyse legislation, policies, practices, and case law concerning non-governmental organisations' (NGOs) search and rescue (SAR) activities in the Central Mediterranean. Between 2015 and 2018, NGO vessels became important assets in SAR operations in the Mediterranean, to the point where the Italian Coast Guard came to regularly rely upon them. For instance, 'according to an inquiry by the Italian Senate, during the first six months of 2017 (1 January– 0 June), some 10 vessels deployed by NGOs'[1] saved more than a third of the migrants rescued in the Mediterranean (33,190 of 82,187 persons).[2] Throughout the year 2017 and right up until June 2018, according to the Italian Coast Guard, 'such NGO vessels carried out roughly 40 per cent of all rescues'.[3]

Whereas NGOs were initially praised for their SAR activities, the high number of disembarked migrants in 2016 and 2017 provoked political and media demands to prevent their arrival.[4] The reversal in the perception of NGOs' contribution was prompted by the fear that they acted as a pull factor for illegal immigration, on the basis of claims that such SAR operations encouraged

[1] Fundamental Rights Agency (FRA), 'Fundamental Rights Considerations: NGO Ships Involved in Search and Rescue in the Mediterranean and Criminal Investigations – 2018' (Report, FRA, 1 October 2018), available at: fra.europa.eu/en/publication/2019/fundamental-rights-considerations-ngo-ships-involved-search-and-rescue.

[2] Senato della Repubblica (XVII Legislatura 2013–2018), Documento XVII, n 9, 'Documento Approvato dalla 4a Commissione Permanente a Conclusione dell'Indagine Conoscitiva sul Contributo dei Militari Italiani al Controllo dei Flussi Migratori nel Mediterraneo e l'Impatto delle Attivita' delle Organizzazioni non Governative', available at: www.senato.it/leg/17/BGT/Schede/docnonleg/34327.htm.

[3] FRA, 'Fundamental Rights Considerations: NGO Ships Involved in Search and Rescue in the Mediterranean and Criminal Investigations – 2018' (n 1).

[4] E Cusumano and M Villa, 'From "Angels" to "Vice Smugglers": The Criminalization of Sea Rescue NGOs in Italy' (2021) 27 *European Journal on Criminal Policy and Research* 23, 29; F Pusterla, 'Legal Perspectives on Solidarity Crime in Italy' (2021) 59(3) *International Migration* 79, 84.

migrants to attempt their sea journeys[5] and claims that some NGOs were colluding with smugglers.[6]

In response to this changing context, Italian prosecutors and governments have criminalised NGOs and adopted a number of other practices and policies to directly or indirectly prevent their SAR activities.[7] Investigations and legal actions have been started against crew members and other private persons who participated in rescue operations aboard NGO ships.[8] Repeatedly, the courts have interceded on NGOs' behalf in line with rule of law (ROL) principles, but successive governments have found ways to bypass these rulings, effectively deterring NGOs' SAR activities. Similar measures to obstruct NGOs' SAR operations have been taken in other European Union (EU) countries, such as Malta, Greece, Spain, France, and also more recently in the UK.[9] A major reason for this trend is the EU's emphasis on combating migrant smuggling in its response to the refugee crisis that arose in 2015.[10] As a consequence, with the intention of preventing, investigating and prosecuting individuals involved in migrant smuggling, the EU adopted and modified a broad spectrum of EU policies and laws, as I explained in chapter three, section III and section V.[11] These policies have served to curtail the effective SAR resources in the Mediterranean.[12] Whereas there is extensive research

[5] L Masera, 'L' Incriminazione dei Soccorsi in Mare: Dobbiamo Rassegnarci al Disumano?' (2018) 2 *Questione Giustizia* 225, 226.

[6] ibid; Paola Barretta, 'Da Eroi a Trafficanti: le Accuse ai Protagonisti delle Operazioni di Ricerca e Soccorso in Mare' (*Questione Giustizia*, 4 July 2017), available at: www.questionegiustizia.it/articolo/da-eroi-a-trafficanti_le-accuse-ai-protagonisti-delle-operazioni-di-ricerca-e-soccorso-in-mare_04-07-2017.php.

[7] This is referred to by some authors as the 'policing of humanitarian assistance', where the use of criminal law is just one of the strategies adopted. F Alagna, 'The Continuation of Criminalization by Other Means: The Role of the Judicial Agency in the Italian Policing of Humanitarian Assistance at Sea' (2022) *Mediterranean Politics* 1, 2, available at: www.tandfonline.com/doi/full/10.1080/13629395.2022.2135072; S Carrera, J Allsopp and L Vosyliūtė, 'Policing the Mobility Society: The Effects of EU-Anti-Migrant Smuggling Policies on Humanitarianism' (2018) 4 *International Journal of Migration and Border Studies* 236, 239.

[8] Masera, 'L' Incriminazione dei Soccorsi in Mare' (n 5) 226; FRA, 'Fundamental Rights Considerations: NGO Ships Involved in Search and Rescue in the Mediterranean and Criminal Investigations – 2018' (n 1).

[9] J Allsopp, L Vosyliūtė and S Smilalowski, 'Picking "Low-Hanging Fruit" While the Orchard Burns: the Cost of Policing Humanitarian Actors in Italy and Greece as a Strategy to Prevent Migrant Smuggling' (2020) 27 *European Journal of Criminal Policy and Research* 65.

[10] S Carrera et al, 'Introduction' in S Carrera et al, *Policing Humanitarianism: EU Policies Against Human Smuggling and their Impact on Civil Society* (Oxford, Hart Publishing, 2019) 1.

[11] ibid.

[12] FRA, 'Fundamental Rights Considerations: NGO Ships Involved in Search and Rescue in the Mediterranean and Criminal Investigations – 2018' (n 1). On some of the challenges facing NGOs and the constraints that come from negotiating different interests in the Mediterranean, see P Cuttitta, 'Repoliticization through Search and Rescue, Humanitarian NGOs and Migration Management in the Central Mediterranean' (2018) 23 *Geopolitics* 632; Ċ Mainwaring and D DeBono, 'Criminalizing solidarity: Search and Rescue in a Neo-Colonial Sea' (2021) 39 *Environment and Planning C: Politics and Space* 1030, 1043; P Müller and P Slominski, 'Shrinking the Space for Civil Society: (De)Politicizing the Obstruction of Humanitarian NGOs in EU Border Management' (2022) 48) *Journal of Ethnic and Migration Studies* 4774.

on the negative outcomes that third-country nationals face when attempting irregular entry into the EU due to these policies,[13] as well as on the consequences for NGOs or family members who are accused of facilitating irregular immigration, the actual national implementations of these anti-smuggling policies have received limited attention, and it remains unclear to what extent their impact on civil society differs according to the country and actors involved.[14]

Against this background, I review the data in light of the strategies adopted by Italian governments between 2016 and 2023 to remove NGO ships from the international waters of the Central Mediterranean and thus prevent/repress their activities. Therefore, moving in roughly chronological order, I analyse Article 12 of Legislative Decree no 286/98, which was used to launch the first investigations against NGOs for aiding and abetting irregular immigration (section II);[15] the 2017 Code of Conduct, aimed at regulating NGOs' activities in order to prevent migrants in distress at sea from arriving in Italy (section III); the 2018 'closed ports' policy and the 2019 directives of the Minister of the Interior prohibiting the entry of NGO vessels into territorial waters (section IV); the government's amendments to Legislative Decree no 286/98 through Security Decree-bis (section V), Law Decree no 130/2020 (section VI), and Law Decree no 1/2023 (section X); the courts' responses concerning the application of Article 12 of Legislative Decree no 286/98 and its amendments (section VII); the measures adopted by the Italian Coast Guard on the grounds of the safety of navigation framework (section VIII); and the decrees issued during the Covid-19 pandemic (section IX).

As I show in this chapter, all these measures are particularly problematic from an ROL perspective, especially because they involve the use of special rather than general instruments to target NGOs – weakening the protection of human rights, the principles of equality before the law, legal certainty and legality. Moreover, these measures have sometimes been adopted in violation of the principle of separation of powers, creating tensions among the different state actors involved.

II. THE CRIMINALISATION OF NGOs FOR AIDING AND ABETTING IRREGULAR IMMIGRATION: ARTICLE 12 OF LEGISLATIVE DECREE NO 286/1998

The first investigations against NGOs for alleged contacts with smugglers started in 2017,[16] and were mostly carried out on the basis of Article 12 of Legislative Decree 286/1998 (Testo Unico sull' Immigrazione, TUI – Consolidated

[13] Carrera et al, 'Introduction' (n 10) 1.
[14] ibid.
[15] Decreto Legislativo 25 luglio 1998, n 286, Testo Unico delle disposizioni concernenti la disciplina dell'immigrazione e norme sulla condizione dello straniero (come modificato) (Testo Unico sull' Immigrazione – TUI).
[16] See section VII of this chapter.

Immigration Act), which criminalises the aiding and abetting of irregular immigration. Article 12 was amended several times over the years, allegedly to implement the Facilitators Package,[17] the UN Convention Against Transnational Organized Crime, and its Protocols, although its compliance with the latter is the subject of debate.[18]

Specifically, Article 12(1) TUI punishes

> the conduct of anyone … who promotes, directs, organizes, finances or carries out the transport of foreigners in the territory of the State, or carries out acts aimed at illegally procuring their entry … with imprisonment from one to five years and with a fine of €15,000 for each person.[19]

This sanction was applicable to all the proceedings discussed below in section VII, but with Law Decree no 20/2023 of 10 March 2023, the prison time was lengthened from two to six years.

Furthermore, Article 12(3) TUI provides for aggravating circumstances and for greater severity of the sentence – imprisonment from five to 15 years, more recently increased to six to 16 years with Law Decree no 20/2023 – in a number of situations, including when the number of foreigners exceeds five[20] or if international means of transport or forged or illegal documents have been used.[21] The penalty is further increased in the event of other aggravating circumstances[22] listed in Article 12(3-ter), including when the crime is committed with the intent to profit – *exceeding even the provisions of the Facilitators Package, which require Member States to adopt appropriate sanctions against the facilitation of illegal immigration but without contemplating aggravating circumstances*. Moreover, Article 12(4-ter) provides for the seizure of the means of transport used to commit the crime.

It is important to note that, in line with the EU provisions,[23] the purpose of profit is not a constitutive element of the crime of aiding and abetting illegal immigration to Italy. The profit element, which has been broadly defined to include even 'unfair advantage',[24] prompts an aggravating circumstance in relation to

[17] The Facilitators Package includes Council Directive 2002/90/EC of 28 November 2002, defining the facilitation of unauthorised entry, transit and residence [2002] OJ L328/17, and Council Framework Decision 2002/946/JHA of 28 November 2002 on the strengthening of the penal framework to prevent the facilitation of unauthorised entry, transit and residence OJ L328/1.

[18] For a discussion on these instruments, see ch 3, section V.

[19] G Savio, 'Favoreggiamento dell'Immigrazione Irregolare: Alcuni Dubbi di Costituzionalità. Nota a Margine dell'Ordinanza del Tribunale di Bologna 1.12.2020' (ASGI, 23 February 2021), available at: www.asgi.it/notizie/favoreggiamento-immigrazione-irregolare-costituzionalita-ordinanza-tribunale-bologna-1-12-2020. See cited case: Cass pen, sez I, Sentenza 22.05.2014, n 28819.

[20] TUI (n 15) Art 12(3)(a).

[21] ibid Art 12(3)(d).

[22] ibid Art 12(3-bis).

[23] See ch 3, section V.

[24] S Carrera et al, *Policing Humanitarianism: EU Policies against Human Smuggling and their Impact on Civil Society* (Oxford, Hart Publishing, 2019) 61.

the same crime.[25] As mentioned in chapter three, this is problematic because it exposes humanitarian actors to the risk of criminalisation for their activities. Indeed, Article 12 TUI has been the main provision used to prosecute NGOs for their SAR operations.[26] In light of this, Minetti points out that Article 12 TUI stands in contrast to the constitutional principle of the 'rehabilitative function of criminal law', which relies on criminal intent.[27] Also, from a procedural standpoint, the aggravating circumstances in Article 12(3-ter) TUI do not comply with the rule that requires them to be balanced against attenuating circumstances.[28]

'The safeguard in Article 1(2) of the Facilitation Directive, allowing Member States not to impose sanctions when irregular entry of migrants is facilitated for humanitarian purposes',[29] has been transposed in Article 12(2) TUI with some changes: only humanitarian rescue and assistance provided to foreigners *within Italy* does not constitute a crime.[30] As such, the Italian implementation of the humanitarian clause applies in very few cases, namely rescue activities carried out by ships flying the Italian flag or in Italian territorial waters – within 12 nautical miles of the Italian Coast.[31] The clause does not exempt NGO vessels flying foreign flags from the crime of facilitating illegal immigration when rescuing migrants in international waters, where most of the NGOs perform their SAR operations.[32] Moreover, it is reported that the clause is of very limited value, as it is usually not applied even to Italian vessels in the investigation phase and only considered at the judicial stage.[33]

The lawfulness of Article 12(3)(d) TUI was reviewed by the Constitutional Court with respect to the use of international transportation and false documents as an aggravating circumstance of the crime of aiding illegal immigration, which entailed a fivefold increase in the minimum penalty and threefold in the

[25] TUI (n 15) Art 12(3-ter)(b).

[26] See section VII of this chapter.

[27] M Minetti, 'The Facilitators Package, Penal Populism and the Rule of Law: Lessons from Italy' (2022) 11 *New Journal of European Criminal Law* 335, 345. The rehabilitative function of criminal law is also enshrined in Art 27 of the Constitution.

[28] This principle is established in Art 69 of the Criminal Code. The only exceptions that Art 12 allows concern cases where Arts 98 and 114 of the Criminal Code are applicable. According to Art 114 of the Criminal Code, a judge can decrease the punishment when the contribution of one of the persons involved in the crime has been of minimal importance in its preparation or execution. In relation to Art 98 of the Criminal Code, the criminal responsibility is established of any person who is at least 14 years of age but not yet 18, as long as he/she had full mental capacity, although the punishment shall be decreased. Savio (n 19); see Minetti (n 27) 345.

[29] Council Directive 2002/90/EC (n 17) Art 1(2); FRA, 'Fundamental Rights Considerations: NGO Ships Involved in Search and Rescue in the Mediterranean and Criminal Investigations – 2018' (n 1).

[30] It should be noted that the humanitarian justification has a broader scope than the state of necessity referred to in Art 54 of the Criminal Code; the latter requires the existence 'of present danger of serious harm to the person', whereas Art 12(2) requires the foreigner to be in a 'condition of need'.

[31] Interview with SAR NGO operator (online, 10 March 2023).

[32] ibid.

[33] Interview with immigration lawyer no 5, Rome (online, 3 April 2023).

maximum compared with the basic case – although not in cases concerning SAR NGOs. Specifically, the Court found a violation of the principle of equality and the re-educational purpose of the sentence in agreement with Articles 3 and 27(3) of the Constitution.[34] The Court pointed out that, whereas these sanctions could be justified when applied to traffickers, they are disproportionate in other situations, such as those involving family members, humanitarian assistance, or rescue operations.[35] Therefore, in the absence of other aggravating circumstances, the crime shall be punished by imprisonment for one to five years.

More recently, in July 2023, in a case concerning a Congolese asylum seeker who was charged under Article 12 TUI for facilitating illegal immigration after she, her daughter and niece entered Italy using forged documents, the Court of Bologna asked the European Court of Justice (ECJ) to assess the compatibility of Article 12 TUI and the Facilitators Package with the EU Charter of Fundamental Rights – the issue is whether EU and Italian legislation by not requiring the intent to profit as an element of the crime, and not requiring states to decriminalise persons who act for humanitarian or altruistic reasons, breaches fundamental rights.[36]

One final problem is that, in some cases, prosecutors have applied Article 12 TUI together with Article 416 of the Criminal Code on criminal association (*associazione a delinquere*) – when three or more persons come together to commit one or more crimes – which expands the preventive measures and investigative powers during the investigations.[37] Specifically, in cases involving both crimes, the legislator established the competence of the district prosecutor through Article 51 of the Code of Criminal Procedure, which concerns organised crime in general.[38] The District Prosecutor office is located at the Criminal Court of the capital in each region, where the anti-mafia prosecutors are also placed – called Direzione Distrettuale Antimafia (National Anti-Mafia District).[39] Besides the institutional organisation, which 'created a connection with anti-mafia

[34] The Tribunal of Bologna referred this question to the Constitutonal Court with ordinance 01.12.2020. See Corte Cost, Sentenza 10.03.2022, n 63. Stefano Zirulia, 'La Corte Costituzionale sul Favoreggiamento dell'Immigrazione Irregolare: Illegittima l'Aggravante che Parifica il Trattamento Sanzionatorio dei Trafficanti a Quello di Coloro che Prestano un Aiuto per Finalità Solidaristiche' (*Sistema Penale*, 23 March 2022), available at: www.sistemapenale.it/it/scheda/corte-costituzionale-2022-63-favoreggiamento-immigrazione-irregolare-aggravato-nota-zirulia#_ftnref3.

[35] Corte Cost, Sentenza 10.03.2022, n 63 (n 34).

[36] Trib Bologna, Ordinanza di Rinvio Pregiudiziale alla Corte di Giustizia dell'Unione Europea ex art. 267 TFEU, 17.07.2023, n 10034/2019, available at: www.sistemapenale.it/pdf_contenuti/1690355028_trib-bologna-sez-i-ord-rinvio-pregiudiziale-favoreggiamento.pdf; Iuventa Crew, 'European Court of Justice to Examine Legality of the Offence of Facilitating Unauthorised Migration' (*Iuventa Crew*, 25 July 2023), available at: iuventa-crew.org/en/2023/07/25/european-court-of-justice-to-examine-legality-of-the-offence-of-facilitating-unauthorised-migration/.

[37] Minetti (n 27) 343; Decreto Legislativo 6 Settembre 2011, n 159, Codice delle Leggi Antimafia e delle Misure di Prevenzione, nonché nuove disposizioni in materia di documentazione antimafia, a norma degli articoli 1 e 2 della Legge 13 agosto 2010, n 136.

[38] Codice penale 19 ottobre 1930, n 1398 (come modificato) Art 51(3-bis).

[39] Minetti (n 27) 343; Arci Porco Rosso and Alarm Phone, 'Dal Mare al Carcere. La Criminalizzazione dei Cosiddetti Scafisti' (*Dal Mare al Carcere*, 15 October 2021) 20–21, available at: dal-mare-al-carcere.info/.

prosecutorial activities',[40] the office of this prosecutor is 'shaped by a sort of an "anti-mafia mindset", which has facilitated – since a very early phase in the prosecution of migrant smuggling – an organized crime-oriented perception of the [SAR NGO] phenomenon'.[41] Moreover, the same Article 51 of the Code of Criminal Procedure triggers a special framework for the indicated crimes, including special extended investigative timelines;[42] covert operations; longer statutes of limitations; and delayed right of the accused to speak with an attorney.[43]

The focus on security and preventive measures – common also to Article 416-bis of the Criminal Code, which deals with the crime of mafia association – is highly controversial as it weakens the retributive and rehabilitative aspects of criminal law.[44] Apart from these technical features, attention must be brought to the wide scope of Article 12 TUI and the fact that it was meant to criminalise traffickers and smugglers and not humanitarian actors.[45] At the same time, Article 12 TUI must be understood in the EU context, as it implements EU legislation which on the one hand requires criminalising several actions in connection with aiding and abetting irregular immigration, and on the other, leaves discretion to states for introducing a humanitarian clause.[46]

III. THE 2017 CODE OF CONDUCT FOR NGOs ENGAGED IN SAR ACTIVITIES

The criminal investigations against NGOs were quickly instrumentalised by right-wing politicians and media for their own populist agendas. In response, in 2017, a Parliamentary Committee inquiry was set up to address accusations that NGOs aimed at 'the ethnic replacement of peoples by other peoples' and that their vessels patrolled 'too close to Libyan waters and even in Libyan waters, thus creating corridors for smugglers'.[47] Although the Committee did not find any evidence supporting such accusations, it concluded its mandate by recommending that NGOs' SAR activities be regulated.[48] Accordingly, the centre-left Gentiloni government adopted the 'Code of Conduct for NGOs Engaged in Search and Rescue Operations at Sea'[49] as a partial response.

[40] Alagna (n 7) 15.

[41] ibid.

[42] Codice di Procedura Penale 22 settembre 1988, n 447 aggiornato, da ultimo, alla Legge 24 maggio 23, n 60, art 407: the time line for the investigations is extended from 18 months to 2 years.

[43] Interview with Stefano Zirulia, Associate Professor of Criminal Law, Università degli Studi di Milano (online, 4 April 2023).

[44] Minetti (n 27) 345–46.

[45] Interview with Zirulia (n 43).

[46] ibid.

[47] Cuttitta (n 12) 649.

[48] ibid.

[49] Ministero dell'Interno, 'Codice di Condotta per le Ong Impegnate nelle Operazioni di Salvataggio dei Migranti in Mare' (2017) (Codice di Condotta) 1, available at: www.interno.gov.it/sites/default/files/codice_condotta_ong.pdf; E Cusumano, 'Straightjacketing Migrant Rescuers? The Code of Conduct on Maritime NGOs' (2019) 24 *Mediterranean Politics* 106.

The Code required the subscribing NGOs to undertake a number of commitments, including not entering 'Libyan territorial waters, except in situations of serious and imminent danger' which demand immediate intervention;[50] not to obstruct the Libyan Coast Guard;[51] not to transfer migrants to other ships and not to send light signals or communicate with ships in movement to facilitate the departure or embarkation of vessels carrying migrants;[52] to cooperate with the competent Maritime Rescue Coordination Centre (MRCC); to recognise Italian jurisdiction over ships flying foreign flags in international waters and/or Libyan waters,[53] and thus allow Italian police agents onto NGO ships to carry out investigations.

Besides the concerns surrounding its content, which has been criticised for violating the international law of the sea and human rights, scholars point out that the Code's legal value is weak given that it is a document concerning private subjects and laid down by the government, without any normative or regulatory rank,[54] and that its obligations are all one-sided.[55] According to Masera, the Italian government chose a soft-law instrument because legislation preventing SAR operations could have been more easily challenged. In contrast, this document could better evade judicial control, and at the same time communicate to the public that the government was changing its policy on NGOs.[56]

Despite the majority of NGOs signing the Code, several, like Médecins Sans Frontières and Jugend Rettet, did not, taking the position that they already complied with several of its requirements and that the Code imposed an unnecessary limitation on their rescue operations.[57] As a consequence of refusing to sign the Code, the Italian government threatened to bar these organisations from disembarking in Italy.[58] To prevent such a consequence, a few NGOs – for instance Sea-Watch and SOS Méditerranée – negotiated an Addendum to the Code with the Italian government. The Addendum clarified that police officers' investigations on board NGO ships could not infringe upon UNCLOS provisions establishing the 'exclusive jurisdiction' of the flag state over ships on the

[50] Codice di Condotta (n 49) 1.

[51] ibid.

[52] ibid 2.

[53] ibid 3.

[54] Masera, 'L'Incriminazione dei Soccorsi in Mare' (n 5) 227; I Papanicolopulu, 'Immigrazione Irregolare, Via Mare, Tutela della Vita Umana e Organizzazioni non Governative' (2017) 3 *Diritto, Immigrazione e Cittadinanza* 1, 22–29; LM Brigida, 'Ricerca e Soccorso in Mare: Questioni Giuridiche sulla Determinazione del Place of Safety' (Master's Thesis, University of Rome, 2020) 128.

[55] Papanicolopulu, 'Immigrazione Irregolare, Via Mare, Tutela della Vita Umana e Organizzazioni non Governative' (n 54) 22–29.

[56] Luca Masera, 'Il Contrasto Amministrativo alle ONG che Operano Soccorsi in Mare: Forme Mutevoli di una Politica Costante' (*Questione Giustizia*, 2021) 1, 5, available at: www.questionegiustizia.it/data/doc/2925/masera-contrasto-ong-2021.pdf.

[57] Médecins Sans Frontières, 'MSF Committed to Saving Lives on Mediterranean but Will Not Sign the Italian "Code of Conduct"' (Press Release, *Médecins Sans Frontières*, 31 July 2017), available at: www.msf.org/msf-committed-saving-lives-mediterranean-will-not-sign-italian-"code-conduct"; FRA, 'Fundamental Rights Considerations: NGO Ships Involved in Search and Rescue in the Mediterranean and Criminal Investigations – 2018' (n 1).

[58] Cusumano and Villa (n 4) 30.

high seas,[59] upon other relevant international law, or upon the captain's competences. Moreover, NGOs could not be required to follow the Libyan Coast Guard's instructions unless they were within the Libyan 12-mile sea zone – addressing concerns that the Code could force NGOs to cooperate with the Libyan authorities in conducting pushbacks or pullbacks.[60]

Regardless of whether they signed the Code or not,[61] all NGOs had their activities seriously limited given the uncertainty that it created. At the time of writing, however, its relevance has faded as the government has adopted different and more effective strategies to curtail NGOs' SAR operations,[62] as I explain in the next sections.

IV. SALVINI'S 2018 'CLOSED PORTS' POLICY AND 2019 MINISTERIAL DIRECTIVES AGAINST NGOs

In March 2018, the Northern League and Five Star Movement, which campaigned for stricter immigration laws, won the national elections.[63] In summer 2018, despite no formal law having been enacted, the newly appointed right-wing Italian Interior Minister Salvini announced a 'policy of closed ports'[64] consisting in the adoption of ad hoc prohibitions on specific vessels entering territorial waters or disembarking[65] – the first case even concerned the Coast Guard's vessel *Diciotti*.[66] The closed port policy marked a completely new approach to the treatment of NGO vessels, which until then the Italian MRCC had always allowed to disembark after rescue operations.[67] Salvini's strategy was meant to show his tough stance against irregular immigration and gain leverage in the EU so as to facilitate the relocation of those rescued to other countries.[68] Initially, this policy was carried out merely by virtue of the Ministry of the

[59] United Nations Convention on the Law of the Sea (Montego Bay, 10 December 1982) UN Doc A/CONF 1833 UNTS 397 (UNCLOS Convention) art 92(2). For a discussion on UNCLOS provisions, see ch 3, section II.

[60] Sea-Watch, 'Sea-Watch Comes to an Agreement Concerning the Code of Conduct' (Sea Watch, 18 October 2017), available at: sea-watch.org/en/sea-watch-comes-to-an-agreement-concerning-the-code-of-conduct/.

[61] Masera, 'Il Contrasto Amministrativo alle ONG che Operano Soccorsi in Mare' (n 56) 5; Cusumano and Villa (n 4) 30.

[62] Interview with Luciano Scalettavi, President of NGO ResQ People (online, 6 February 2023); Interview with Luca Masera, Professor of Criminal Law, Università degli Studi di Brescia (online, 2 February 2023).

[63] Cusumano and Villa (n 4) 30.

[64] Masera, 'Il Contrasto Amministrativo alle ONG che Operano Soccorsi in Mare' (n 56) 4–5.

[65] Cusumano and Villa (n 4) 30.

[66] See ch 4, section V.C, and ch 7, section V.B.

[67] Cusumano and Villa (n 4) 30.

[68] ibid. For example, in April 2019, 'Italy and Malta both denied the vessel Sea Eye port entry; the migrants ultimately disembarked in Malta with military patrol boats, to be distributed among four countries'. ÁJ García-Carriazo, 'Small Island, Big Issue: Malta and Its Search and Rescue Region – SAR' (2019) 7 *Paix et Sécurité Internationales* 299, 318.

Interior's competence according to the 'Standard Operating Procedures',[69] the only official document – although not binding – on the matter.

In 2019, to address concerns that the 'closed port' policy did not have any legal basis, Salvini adopted four ministerial directives addressed to the border authorities, aimed at preventing the entry of NGO vessels into Italian waters after they carried out SAR operations in international waters. The first, Directive 14100/141/8, dated 18 March 2019,[70] was general in character and made a number of statements with the aim to coordinate surveillance of maritime borders and combat illegal immigration.[71] In particular, the Directive highlighted the recognition of the Libyan authorities' responsibilities in the management of SAR operations.[72]

The three ad hoc directives, dated 4 April 2019 (targeting the *Alan Kurdi* of the NGO Sea-Eye), 15 April 2019 (targeting the *Mare Jonio* of the NGO Mediterranea Saving Humans), and 15 May 2019 (targeting the *Sea-Watch 3* of the NGO Sea-Watch),[73] issued on the occasion of specific NGO rescue missions in international waters, did not directly prohibit NGO ships from entering territorial waters. Rather, they communicated to the border and police authorities that the NGOs allegedly (1) engaged in 'non-inoffensive passage', causing harm to the peace, order, and security of the state (failing to meet the exception granted to foreign ships to sail in other states' territorial waters in accordance with Article 19 UNCLOS);[74] (2) misused international law;[75] and (3) cooperated with smugglers.[76]

The ministerial directives affected several principles of the ROL.[77] First, the directives placed the public interest in security and the fight against illegal immigration and terrorism on the same level as saving lives at sea, in violation of

[69] Ministero delle Infrastrutture e dei Trasporti, Comando Generale del Corpo delle Capitanerie di Porto – Guardia Costiera, Standard Operating Procedures SOP 009/15, settembre 2015. See ch 4, section II.C.

[70] Ministero dell'Interno, Direttiva 18 marzo 2019, n 14100/141/(8) (Direttiva per il Coordinamento Unificato dell'attivita di Sorveglianza delle Frontiere Marittime e per il Contrasto all'Immigrazione Illegale ex Art 11 del D Lgs n 286/1998 recante il Testo Unico in Materia di Immigrazione. Integrazione Concernente le Attività SAR Libia – Nota della Commissione Europea).

[71] The Directive states that traffickers seem to systematically use strategies that trigger NGO rescue operations and the consequent irregular entry of migrants into the Italian territory; ibid.

[72] ibid.

[73] Ministero dell'Interno, Direttiva 4 Aprile 2019 (Intervento dell'assetto 'Alan Kurdi' (ONG Sea Eye) iniziato in 3 April 2019), available at: www.interno.gov.it/sites/default/files/direttiva_4_aprile_2019.pdf; Ministero dell'Interno, Direttiva 15 Aprile 2019 (concerning the activities of the ship Mare Jonio), available at: www.interno.gov.it/sites/default/files/direttiva_del_ministro_n._141001418_15_aprile_2019.pdf; Ministero dell'Interno, Direttiva 15 Maggio 2019 (Intervento di Sea Watch 3 del 15 Maggio 2019 in area SAR libica) (Concerning the activities of Sea-Watch of 3 and 15 May 2019 in Libyan SAR zone), available at: www.interno.gov.it/sites/default/files/direttiva_15_maggio_2019.pdf.

[74] Ministero dell'Interno, Direttiva 15 Maggio 2019 (n 73); Marco Magri, 'Obbligo di Soccorso in Mare, Funzioni della Guardia Costiera e Respingimenti "Delegati": sui Poteri del Ministro dell'Interno' 2019 (1) *Istituzioni del Federalismo* 149.

[75] Ministero dell'Interno, Direttiva 4 Aprile 2019 (n 73).

[76] Ministero dell'Interno, Direttiva 15 Aprile 2019 (n 73); Cusumano and Villa (n 4) 31.

[77] S Romano, 'L'(Ab)uso del Diritto Penale Contro le Azioni di Soccorso delle ONG' (2021) XXI *Diritto e Questioni Pubbliche*, Special Issue 41 59; see also, Statewatch.org, 'Italy: UN Special Rapporteurs Call for Withdrawal of Salvini Decree Criminalizing Search and Rescue Activities' (Statewatch.org, 22 May 2019), available at: www.statewatch.org/news/2019/may/italy-un-special-rapporteurs-call-for-withdrawal-of-salvini-decree-criminalising-search-and-rescue-activities/.

migrants' human rights. Second, the directives required the border authorities to recognise the legitimacy of the Libyan SAR zone and Libyan authorities,[78] despite the non-refoulement principle. Third, the directives breached the principle of separation of powers by interfering with the 'prerogatives of the Judicial Authority'.[79] By acting as a crime report and by reason of the principle of mandatory criminal investigation, each disembarkation following a ministerial directive necessarily triggered the opening of criminal proceedings against those responsible for the rescue and the seizure of the rescuers' ship,[80] as mandated by Article 3(4-ter) TUI. Therefore, 'the directives aimed at a priori attributing the nature of a crime to rescue operations at sea concluded by humanitarian actors, ordering the national police and the national coordinating authority, to prevent "the illegal entry of immigrants into the national territory"'.[81]

In addition, the directives created confusion about the competences of the ministries involved: the power to adopt a directive on this matter and on SAR operations belonged to the Minister of Infrastructure and Transport as the chief authority of the Coast Guard, rather than the Minister of the Interior.[82] Finally, the directives impacted matters regulated by primary and international legislation, in violation of the hierarchy of legal sources.[83]

In terms of their consequences, on the basis of the Directive of 18 March 2019 concerning the ship *Mare Jonio* and the Directive of 15 May 2019 targeting the *Sea-Watch 3*, the NGO ships were seized and investigations were opened for the alleged crime of aiding and abetting illegal immigration. However, the prosecutors dropped the charges in both cases.[84] More relevant is the judicial proceeding that followed the Directive of 4 April 2019 concerning the *Alan Kurdi*, which

[78] See ch 4, section III.B.

[79] Romano (n 77) 60; United Nations Human Rights Office of the High Commissioner, 'Joint Communication from Special Procedures' (OHCHR, 15 May 2019) 2–3, available at: www.avvenire.it/c/attualita/Documents/ONUdirittiViolati.pdf.

[80] Romano (n 77) 59.

[81] ibid 60.

[82] Brigida (n 54) 134; Fabio Caffio, 'La "Direttiva Salvini" sulle Frontiere Marittime' (*AnalisiDifesa*, 19 March 2019), available at: www.analisidifesa.it/2019/03/la-direttiva-salvini-sulle-frontiere-marittime/. See ch 4, section II.A.

[83] Brigida (n 54) 135.

[84] Mediterranea Saving Humans, 'New Judiciary Acquittal Coming for the "Mare Jonio" Ship' (Mediterranea Saving Humans, 20 October 2021), available at: mediterranearescue.org/en/news-en/new-judiciary-acquittal-coming-for-the-mare-jonio-ship-rescue-at-sea-cannot-be-criminalised-it-is-an-obligation/; Giorgio Ruta and Alessandra Ziniti, 'Migranti, la Mare Jonio Entra nel Porto di Lampedusa, la Gdf la Sequestra e Convoca il Comandante' *La Repubblica* (19 March 2019), available at: www.repubblica.it/cronaca/2019/03/19/news/gdf_nega_via_radio_ingresso_in_acque_territoriali_nave_mare_jonio_prosegue_verso_lampedusa_per_ripararsi_da_mare_mosso-221959028/; AGI, 'Il Braccio di Ferro tra Salvini e il PM di Agrigento sulla Sea-Watch 3' (*AGI*, 19 May 2019), available at: www.agi.it/cronaca/migranti_sea_watch_salvini_patronaggio-5510580/news/2019-05-19/; Il Post, 'Cos'è Successo con la Sea-Watch' *Il Post* (20 May 2019), available at: www.ilpost.it/2019/05/20/sea-watch-sbarco-migranti/; Melting Pot Europa, '65 Naufraghi Soccorsi dalla Sea-Watch Lasciati in Alto Mare per Quattro Giorni Senza un Porto Sicuro' (*Melting Pot Europa*, 17 May 2019), available at: www.meltingpot.org/2019/05/65-naufraghi-soccorsi-dalla-sea-watch-lasciati-in-alto-mare-per-quattro-giorni-senza-un-porto-sicuro/.

gave rise to an opposite situation. The case involved a rescue carried out on 3 April 2019 in the Libyan SAR area, and the subsequent request for permission to disembark at an Italian port. With the adoption of Directive 4 April 2019 addressed to the MRCC Rome, the *Alan Kurdi* could only disembark in Malta on 13 April, upon an agreement between Italy and other EU states which also provided for the distribution of the migrants among different countries.[85] As a consequence, the prosecutor of Agrigento opened investigations against Minister of the Interior Salvini and his Head of Cabinet, in relation to the crimes of omission of official acts,[86] abuse of office[87] and failure to rescue at sea.[88] However, the Prosecutor's Office at the Court of Ministers of Rome,[89] competent to deal with ministerial crimes, asked for the case to be dismissed.[90] On 21 November 2019, the Court of Ministers of Rome ordered the dismissal of the criminal proceedings, holding that in the case at issue the accused did not have any obligation to provide a 'place of safety' (POS).[91] According to the Court, the obligation to provide a POS exists only when state authorities directly carry out SAR operations. Such an obligation does not exist when rescues are carried out by ships belonging to NGOs and acting autonomously. The Court noted that the issue at stake is not regulated by any provision – the relevant legislation was not drafted to address the current events occurring in the Mediterranean. As such, the Court held that the Minister of the Interior and his Head of Cabinet's actions did not fall under Article 323 and Article 328 of the Criminal Code, which require the violation of mandatory provisions concerning public functions. Regarding the issue of omission of help, the Court reasoned that Article 1113 of the Navigation Code applies only when the competent MRCC requests a ship to rescue persons in danger and the ship fails to comply with the request – a situation differing from that under examination.[92]

Zirulia and De Vittor have been critical of the decision. According to them, the SAR and SOLAS Conventions do actually set out an obligation of cooperation incumbent on 'all the States involved. Although this obligation to cooperate

[85] Ministero dell'Interno, Direttiva 4 Aprile 2019 (n 73) 2–3; Brigida (n 54) 230.

[86] Codice penale (n 38) Art 328(1).

[87] ibid Art 323.

[88] Codice della navigazione, 30 marzo 1942 n 327 (Edizione 2020) art 1113. See Trib Roma, Collegio per i Reati Ministeriali, Ordinanza di Archiviazione 21.11.2019, n 6; Stefano Zirulia and Francesca De Vittor, 'Il Caso della Nave Alan Kurdi: Profili di Diritto Penale e Internazionale in Punto di Omessa Assegnazione di un Porto Sicuro' (*Sistema Penale*, 5 December 2019), available at: www.sistemapenale.it/it/scheda/caso-nave-alan-kurdi-diritto-penale-diritto-internazionale-omessa-assegnazione-porto-sicuro.

[89] As explained in ch 4, section V.C, the Court of Ministers is a specialised section of the Court located in the capitals of the regions, and is competent to decide on cases involving crimes committed by the ministers and Prime Minister in the exercise of their functions (called 'ministerial crimes'). Legge Costituzionale 16 gennaio 1989, n 1.

[90] Trib Roma, Procura della Repubblica, 22.07.2019, Richiesta di archiviazione, RGNR 21925/19, available at: www.sistemapenale.it/pdf_contenuti/1575492096_richiesta-archiviazione-alan-kurdi-salvini-piantedosi.pdf.

[91] Trib Roma, Collegio per i Reati Ministeriali, 21.11.2019, Ordinanza n 6; Zirulia and De Vittor (n 88).

[92] Trib Roma, Collegio per i Reati Ministeriali, 21.11.2019, Ordinanza n 6; Zirulia and De Vittor (n 88).

can be qualified as an obligation of means and not of results … each State involved is bound to act in good faith in order to achieve the desired result'.[93] Accordingly, the question would be whether the authorities' failure to carry out official obligations could be found 'not so much in not having granted a POS, but in not having actively cooperated with the other States involved to reach a quick solution'.[94] At the same time, Zirulia notes how this decision has limited impact, as it was issued in the pre-trial stage where the facts under consideration only underwent a first preliminary assessment.[95]

The directives' hostile approach towards NGOs was then strengthened with the adoption of the subsequent Decree Law no 53 of July 2019,[96] as explained in the next section.

V. LEGAL BASIS FOR THE CLOSED PORT POLICY: LAW DECREE NO 23/2019

In June 2019, the Italian government adopted Law Decree no 23/2019 – also known as 'Salvini-bis' or 'Security Decree-bis'[97] – in the belief that it could address the problems of legality raised by the ministerial directives discussed in the former section and, at the same time, obtain public support by showing hostility towards NGOs.[98]

Essentially, Law Decree no 23/2019 amended Article 11 of Legislative Decree no 286/1998 (TUI) *by granting the Minister of the Interior*, in agreement with the Minister of Defence and the Ministry of Infrastructure and Transport, after having informed the Prime Minister, *the power to issue orders to limit or prohibit vessels' entry, transit, or docking in territorial waters* – except for military ships or state-owned ships – *for public order and safety reasons or breaches of immigration laws*.[99] In case of violations of the Minister's order – in addition to the criminal sanctions for aiding and abetting illegal immigration when the actions amount to a crime – the shipmaster and the shipowner[100] could be subject to an administrative sanction ranging between €10,000 and €50,000. Moreover, in case of reiterated offences, the vessel could be confiscated.[101] Law no 77 of 8 August 2019, converting Law Decree no 53/2019 into law, significantly increased

[93] Zirulia and De Vittor (n 88).
[94] ibid.
[95] Interview with Zirulia (n 43).
[96] Romano (n 77) 60.
[97] Decreto Legge 14 giugno 2019, n 53, Disposizioni urgenti in Materia di ordine e sicurezza pubblica.
[98] Pusterla (n 4) 86.
[99] Decreto Legge 14 giugno 2019, n 53 (n 97) art 1; TUI (n 15) Art 11.
[100] For a discussion on the joint liability of the shipowner, see G Marchiafava, 'The Impact of the New Italian Security Regulation on the Search and Rescue of Migrants at Sea' (2020) 174 *Comparative Maritime Law* 133, 148.
[101] TUI (n 15) Art 12(6-bis).

the administrative sanction from €150,000 up to a maximum of €1 million, and introduced the immediate precautionary seizure of the vessel.[102]

The practical effect of these provisions was to provide a legal basis for the entry bans and more severe penalties for their violations. One of the main problems was that they interfered with the power of the judiciary and of the Minister of Infrastructure and Transport. As Masera explains, they attributed 'the sanctioning power to the administrative authority (the prefects hierarchically under the authority of the Minister of the Interior)'[103] and made the judicial authority's check only subsequent to the appeal of the affected NGO.[104] In other words, these measures were meant to reduce criminal judges' involvement, as they would be less likely than the administration to seize NGO ships – as will be explained in section VII, judges showed caution in applying penalties to the rescuers. On the contrary, prefects were expected to apply the new administrative measures, and it was up to the NGOs to challenge them before the judicial authorities, if they were to be challenged at all.[105] Moreover, the Minister of the Interior's powers overlapped with those of the Minister of Infrastructure and Transport in similar matters.[106] Given that the Minister of the Interior is competent in issues of public security and the Minister of Infrastructure and Transport is responsible for safety of navigation, it could be difficult to effectively determine who had the relevant authority to adopt a specific measure in the context of rescues.[107]

Besides these problematic aspects, Law Decree no 23/2019 violated the principle of legality because it lacked the extraordinary necessity and urgency requirements in accordance with Article 77 of the Constitution that urgent decrees must meet.[108] As Zirulia points out, the 'extraordinary necessity and urgency' condition is not met by Decree Law no 23/2019, as it only broadly refers to the generic aim of protecting security and public order, and the government

[102] Legge 8 Agosto 2019, n 77, Conversione in Legge, con modificazioni, del Decreto Legge 14 giugno 2019, n 53, Recante disposizioni urgenti in materia di ordine e sicurezza pubblica, Allegato.

[103] Masera, 'Il Contrasto Amministrativo alle ONG che Operano Soccorsi in Mare' (n 56) 8.

[104] ibid 8.

[105] ibid.

[106] Brigida (n 54) 139. According to Art 83 of the Navigation Code, 'The Minister of Transport and Navigation may limit or prohibit the transit and stop of merchant ships in the territorial sea, for reasons of public order, safety of navigation and, in agreement with the Minister of the Environment, for reasons of protection of the marine environment, determining the areas to which the ban applies'.

[107] 'An extreme situation could correspond to the case in which migrants, in opposing the decision of the commander of the rescuing ship, take control of the latter, thus generating a hypothesis of danger for the safety of navigation due to their inexperience'. The case involving the commercial Italian ship *Vos Thalassa*, which I discussed in ch 5, section II.C, 'has come close to this hypothesis'. Brigida (n 54) 141; see also, L Masera, 'La Legittima Difesa dei Migranti e l'Illegittimità dei Respingimenti verso la Libia (Caso Vos Thalassa)' (*Diritto Penale Contemporaneo*, 24 June 2019), available at: archiviodpc.dirittopenaleuomo.org/d/6754-la-legittima-difesa-dei-migranti-e-lillegittimita-dei-respingimenti-verso-la-libia-caso-vos-thalassa.

[108] S Zirulia, 'Decreto Sicurezza-bis: Novità e Profili critici. Decreto Legge 14 giugno 2019, n 53, recante Disposizioni urgenti in materia di ordine e sicurezza pubblica (G.U. n 138 del 14 giugno 2019)' *Diritto Penale Contemporaneo* (18 giugno 2019), available at: archiviodpc.dirittopenaleuomo.org/d/6738-decreto-sicurezza-bis-novita-e-profili-critici.

could have followed the normal parliamentary legislative process. Thus, 'the role of Parliament is reduced to a mere vote of confidence, with the ultimate result of completely eliminating the political debate around regulatory interventions destined to have a profound impact on fundamental rights'.[109]

Mattarella, the President of Italy, upon signing the conversion Law no 77 of 8 August 2019, also raised doubts as to the legality and lawfulness of Law Decree no 23/2019. In particular, the President noted the failure to make any distinction in treatment between types of vessels or actions involved and in relation to the reasons for transporting migrants.[110] According to him, the general language used could affect both the safety of citizens and the certainty of the law.[111] Moreover, the principle of proportionality between sanctions and behaviours, as requested by the Italian Constitution, was disregarded.[112] Finally, the international obligation imposed by UNCLOS on ship captains to save people in distress at sea[113] was weakened in violation of the hierarchy of legal sources, which requires national rules to comply with international law. However, such concerns were not considered by the political majority, and the government's legislative power contributed to an 'incremental undermining of migrants' rights'.[114]

In any case, the administrative sanctions only found application in summer 2019. In fact, the Minister of the Interior exercised the power to prohibit entry into Italian territorial waters on the day of the entry into force of Law Decree no 53/2019 against the *Sea-Watch 3*,[115] and in the following weeks against the *Open Arms*,[116] *Mare Jonio*,[117] *Eleonore*[118] and *Ocean Viking*. In all these cases,

[109] ibid.

[110] Marchiafava (n 100) 154–55.

[111] Masera, 'Il Contrasto Amministrativo alle ONG che Operano Soccorsi in Mare' (n 56) 7 ft 19.

[112] Presidenza della Repubblica, 'Decreto Sicurezza bis: Mattarella Promulga e Invia la Lettera ai Presidenti di Senato, Camera e del Consigli dei Ministri' (8 agosto 2019), available at: www.quirinale.it/elementi/32099.

[113] Masera, 'Il Contrasto Amministrativo alle ONG che Operano Soccorsi in Mare' (n 56) 7, fn 19.

[114] S Zirulia and G Martinico, 'Criminalising Migrants and Securitising Borders: The Italian "No Way" Model in the Age of Populism' in V Stoyanova and S Smet (eds), *Migrants' Rights, Populism and Legal Resilience in Europe* (Cambridge, CUP, 2022) 268.

[115] Marchiafava (n 100) 151. This gave rise to the case concerning Captain Carola Rackete, discussed in section VII.B of this chapter.

[116] Marchiafava (n 100) 150; TAR Lazio, sez I ter, Decreto 14.08.2019, n 5479.

[117] ANSA, 'Mare Jonio Ship Seized' (*ANSA*, 3 September 2019), available at: www.ansa.it/english/news/2019/09/03/mare-jonio-ship-seized_9e60fc4b-41c6-4ffa-8fa4-808a27c0c46c.html.

[118] FQ, 'Migranti, Indagati il Capitano e Capo Missione della Nave Eleonore: "Favoreggiamento dell'Immigrazione Clandestina"' *Il Fatto Quotidiano* (3 September 2019), available at: www.ilfattoquotidiano.it/2019/09/03/migranti-indagati-capitano-e-capo-missione-della-nave-eleonore-favoreggiamento-dellimmigrazione-clandestina/5427209/; FQ, 'Elenonore, Sbarcati i 104 naufraghi a Bordo. La Nave Aveva Violato il Divieto d' Ingresso: Sequestrata dalla Guardia di Finanza' *Il Fatto Quotidiano* (2 September 2019), available at: www.ilfattoquotidiano.it/2019/09/02/eleonore-sbarcati-i-104-naufraghi-a-bordo-la-nave-aveva-violato-il-divieto-dingresso-sequestrata-dalla-guardia-di-finanza/5424237/; Trib Ragusa, Sentenza 16.06.2021, NRG 1147/2020, available at: www.sistemapenale.it/pdf_contenuti/1626027786_tribunale-di-ragusa-sentenza-eleonore.pdf; Mauro Indelicato, 'L'Ultimo Regalo dei Giallorossi: le Toghe Liberano le ONG' *Il Giornale* (18 June 2021), available at: www.ilgiornale.it/news/cronache/lultimo-regalo-dei-giallorossi-toghe-liberano-ong-1955664.html.

the vessels obtained authorisation to disembark after an average stand-off of 14 days at sea,[119] following which they were subject to immediate seizure and criminal investigations. The *Ocean Viking* was the only one allowed to disembark in Malta after 13 days.[120]

Importantly, a few days after the conversion law, the administrative judge of the Lazio Administrative Tribunal (Tribunale Amministrativo Regionale – TAR) declared the application of Law no 77 of 8 August 2019 unlawful in the case against Open Arms, in relation to the ministerial order of 1 August 2019 prohibiting the ship from entering into territorial waters. The facts involved the rescue of about 150 migrants in international waters by the vessel *Open Arms*, which was then refused permission to disembark in the closest safe countries, Italy and Malta.[121] Consequently, on 13 August, Open Arms filed a complaint with the Lazio TAR, 'arguing that the denial of permission to enter Italian waters violated international law and the human rights of the migrants on board'.[122]

The judge reasoned that the ministerial order adopted by force of Law no 77 of 8 August 2019 did not comply with the international legislation on rescue at sea of distressed vessels and disembarkation of rescued people in a safe place, which are hierarchically superior to national provisions.[123] Therefore, the order had to be lifted. Nevertheless, Salvini refused to do so. Moreover, he declined to follow the instruction by Conte, the Prime Minister at the time, that disembarkation had to be allowed because the *Open Arms* was located near territorial waters, and doing otherwise could breach not only the law of the sea but also the prohibition on collective expulsions.[124] Disembarkation was possible only on 20 August 2019, upon the Prosecutor of Agrigento's intervention. With the start of the investigations against Salvini – for the crimes of unjustified refusal to carry out official acts/measures in accordance with Article 328 of the Criminal Code, and kidnapping according to Article 605 of the Criminal Code – the ship was seized, which indirectly triggered the disembarkation of the migrants.[125]

Subsequently, with reference to the same episode, in April 2021, the Palermo Judge for Preliminary Investigations indicted Salvini for the crimes of kidnapping, omission of official acts and abuse of office,[126] and the case remains

[119] Cusumano and Villa (n 4) 31.

[120] ibid.

[121] Jason Horowitz, 'Salvini's Standoff at Sea Highlights Italy's War on Rescue Ships' *New York Times* (16 August 2019), available at: www.nytimes.com/2019/08/16/world/europe/salvini-italy-migrants-open-arms.html.

[122] ibid.

[123] TAR Lazio 14.08.2019, n 5479 (n 116).

[124] Internazionale, 'Tutto Quello che C'e' da Sapere su Salvini e il Caso Open Arms' *Internazionale* (30 July 2020), available at: www.internazionale.it/notizie/2020/07/30/open-arms-senato-processo-salvini.

[125] Zirulia and Martinico (n 114) 270.

[126] In the case against Open Arms, the Tribunal of Ministers of Palermo obtained permission from the Senate to continue investigating the case. The case should not be confused with the *Gregoretti* case, involving a Navy ship. The latter case had already ended with the acquittal of the former Minister Salvini. See ch 4, section V.C, and ch 7, section V.B.

pending before the Tribunal of Ministers of Palermo.[127] Accordingly, this case is especially significant for having prompted serious consequences for Italian politics and a conflict of powers among the institutional actors involved. More broadly, it negatively impacted public confidence in the Italian government's ability to respect human rights and to be in control of migration influxes,[128] contributing to 'a crisis of legitimacy'[129] in national and European politics.

The decision of the Lazio TAR, as well as the judicial decisions in the context of criminal allegations against NGOs explained below in section VII, along with the fall of the government that had approved the Security Decree-bis, opened the doors to a season of reforms which were aimed to mitigate the impact of Salvini's divisive anti-immigration policies.[130]

VI. CHANGES WITH LAW DECREE NO 130/2020: 'LAMORGESE REFORM'

The new Minister of the Interior Lamorgese of the Conte II government (supported by the populist Five Star Movement and the centre-left) no longer prohibited the entry of NGO ships into Italian territorial waters by way of Legislative Decree no 53/2019, which she repealed with Law Decree no 130/2020.[131] With the adoption of Law Decree no 130/2020,[132] the Minister of the Interior intended to communicate to the public that the Salvini-bis Decree against NGOs was repealed, although retained the power, in agreement with the Minister of Defence and the Minister of Infrastructure and Transport, after having informed the Prime Minister, to limit and prohibit the transit and docking of vessels in the territorial sea for public security reasons or violation of immigration laws. Nevertheless, such power could not be exercised in cases where the vessel engaged in the SAR operation immediately communicated with the competent MRCC and followed 'the instructions given by the competent authority in compliance with the international obligations'[133] of the law of the sea, the European Convention on Human Rights (ECHR), and refugee protection, as well as with the international anti-trafficking provisions.[134] Failure to

[127] Fulvio Vassallo Paleologo, 'Maggioranze di Governo e Processi Penali' (ADIF, 30 October 2021), available at: www.a-dif.org/2021/10/30/maggioranze-di-governo-e-processi-penali/; Melting Pot Europa, 'Open Arms, Terza Udienza del Processo Salvini' (*Melting Pot Europa*, 15 May 2022), available at: www.meltingpot.org/2022/05/open-arms-terza-udienza-del-processo-salvini/. See ch 4, section V.C, for an explanation of the procedure concerning ministerial crimes.

[128] V Moreno-Lax et al (eds), 'The EU Approach on Migration in the Mediterranean' (Study, European Parliament's Policy Department for Citizens' Rights and Constitutional Affairs, June 2021) 107, available at: www.europarl.europa.eu/thinktank/et/document/IPOL_STU(2021)694413.

[129] P Castelli Gattinara, 'The "Refugee Crisis" in Italy as a Crisis of Legitimacy' (2017) 9 *Contemporary Italian Politics* 318, 331.

[130] Masera, 'Il Contrasto Amministrativo alle ONG che Operano Soccorsi in Mare' (n 56) 11.

[131] ibid 9; Cusumano and Villa (n 4) 32.

[132] Decreto Legge 21 ottobre 2020, n 130.

[133] Decreto Legge 21 ottobre 2020, n 130, art 1(2).

[134] ibid.

follow the Minister of the Interior's order or this provision triggered a criminal and a pecuniary penalty:[135] punishment could involve cumulative imprisonment of up to two years and a fine of between €10,000 and €50,000.[136]

Therefore, the new decree did not address the issue of conflicting powers between the Minister of the Interior and the Minister of Transport, which could result in contradictory measures.[137] Moreover, it criminalised behaviour that before was only administratively sanctioned, although the message of the media to the public was that the new provisions were less excessive and arbitrary than those of the Salvini-bis Decree. On the other hand, it removed the Prefects' powers to apply administrative sanctions and reintroduced the competence of the criminal courts in cases where entry bans are violated. In practice, this afforded more guarantees to NGOs, which could avail themselves of the justifications of state of necessity and/or compliance with a duty – thus making the application of the penalties less likely.[138]

Regarding the exception made for rescue operations at sea when conducted in line with Law Decree no 130/20, Vassallo Paleologo commented that it has remained almost irrelevant, as it has not been applied in practice.[139] In addition, the exception could be triggered only if SAR operations were carried out in compliance with the instructions of the competent SAR authorities, including those of the Libyan Coast Guard, which NGOs refuse to follow.

However, *Lamorgese avoided the adoption of orders against NGOs on the grounds of Law Decree no 130/2020*, in part because she intended to mark a discontinuity with the policy of the former governments, but also because of the development of the judicial cases, especially the *Rackete* case, which clarified the legal provisions at stake, as discussed in the next section.

VII. INVESTIGATIONS AND CRIMINAL PROCEEDINGS FOR SAR OPERATIONS

In conjunction with the governments' directives, policies and decrees intended to curtail NGOs' SAR activities, prosecutors launched criminal investigations against these organisations. On the one hand, these may have dampened NGOs' activity. On the other hand, the attempt to criminalise them was rebuffed by the courts, that made it clear that in the event of a clash between Article 12 TUI and the duty to save lives, the latter shall be given higher importance.[140]

135 See Codice della navigazione (n 88) Art 1102.
136 Decreto Legge 21 ottobre 2020, n 130, art 1(2).
137 Marchiafava (n 100) 161.
138 Masera, 'Il Contrasto Amministrativo alle ONG che Operano Soccorsi in Mare' (n 56) 14.
139 Fulvio Vassallo Paleologo, 'Come si Trasformano i Soccorsi delle ONG in "Eventi Migratori"' (ADIF, 11 November 2021), available at: www.a-dif.org/2021/11/11/come-si-trasformano-i-soccorsi-delle-ong-in-eventi-migratori.
140 Minetti (n 27) 348.

A. Criminal Accusations against NGOs and Courts' Responses

An analysis of the reports and tables published by the Fundamental Rights Agency[141] as well as of the judicial decisions and documents publicly available online reveals that, between 2017 and 2020, prosecutors – especially Sicilian prosecutors, whose territorial competence is established by the place of NGO vessels' disembarkation – launched numerous investigations against various vessels and personnel of NGOs, including Open Arms, Save the Children, Jugend Rettet and Sea-Watch, for the crime of aiding irregular immigration.[142] Some of these cases were based on the so-called *Teorema Zuccaro* ('Zuccaro Theorem') – named after the prosecutor Carmelo Zuccaro of the Tribunal of Catania, who played a prominent role in the start of investigations[143] – aiming to prove collusion between Libyan traffickers and NGOs operating in international waters, which were said to work as 'sea taxis'.[144] Namely, the accusation was that some NGOs would rescue the motor boats and return them to the traffickers in exchange for profit.[145]

[141] Fundamental Rights Agency (FRA), 'June 2023 Update – Search and Rescue Operations in the Mediterranean and Fundamental Rights' (FRA, 11 October 2023), available at: fra.europa.eu/en/publication/2023/2023-update-ngo-ships-sar-activities?page=4&pid=7f3e5da6-0a39-46fe-a936-ec92c3377c59; FRA, 'December 2021 Update – Search and Rescue (SAR) Operations in the Mediterranean and Fundamental Rights' (FRA, 17 December 2021), available at: fra.europa.eu/en/publication/2021/december-2021-update-ngo-ships-sar-activities; FRA, 'Table 1: NGOs Involved in SAR Activities in the Mediterranean and Vessels/Aircrafts Deployed by Them (2015–2018)' (FRA, 1 October 2018), available at: fra.europa.eu/sites/default/files/fra_uploads/fra-2018-ngos-sar-mediterranean_en.pdf; FRA, 'Table 2: Legal Proceedings by EU Member States against Private Entities Involved in SAR Operations in the Mediterranean Sea' (FRA, June 2022), available at: fra.europa.eu/sites/default/files/fra_uploads/table-2-legal-proceedings-ngos-sar-operations-june-2022.pdf; FRA, 'June 2022 Update – Search and Rescue (SAR) Operations in the Mediterranean and Fundamental Rights' (FRA, 20 June 2022), available at: fra.europa.eu/en/publication/2022/june-2022-update-ngo-ships-sar-activities#publication-tab-0.

[142] Romano (n 77) 55.

[143] ibid. In a parliamentary hearing on the implementation of the Schengen Agreement that took place on 22 March 2017, Zuccaro presented a theory that has been considered more political than judicial. He raised the suspicion that some NGOs could afford the high cost for their operations because they were profiting from agreements made with traffickers. Although Zuccaro was unable to show any admissible court evidence in support of his statements, his accusations were used by politicians and the media to support their campaign and measures against NGOs. Comitato Parlamentare di Controllo sull'attuazione dell'Accordo di Schengen, di Vigilanza sull'attività di Europol, di Controllo e Vigilanza in Materia di Immigrazione, 'Indagine Conoscitiva Sulla Gestione Del Fenomeno Migratorio Nell'Area Schengen, Con Particolare Riferimento Alle Politiche Dei Paesi Aderenti Relative Al Controllo Delle Frontiere Esterne E Dei Confini Interni' (XVII, Legislatura, 22 Marzo 2017); D Facchini, *Alla Deriva: I Migranti, le Rotte del Mar Mediterraneo, le Ong: il Naufragio della Politica, che Nega i Diritti per Fabbricare Consenso* (Milano, Altra Economia 2018) 177–79. As a consequence of such accusations, in the spring of 2017, the Italian Senate Defence Committee carried out a parliamentary inquiry and in the end dismissed such allegations. It found that NGOs were not involved directly or indirectly in migrant smuggling, but recommended better coordination of their work with the Italian Coast Guard. Senato della Repubblica, XVII Legislatura, 'Documento XVII n 9'; FRA, 'Fundamental Rights Considerations: NGO Ships Involved in Search and Rescue in the Mediterranean and Criminal Investigations – 2018' (n 1). Thus, the Italian government of Prime Minister Gentiloni adopted the Code of Conduct for NGOs, as discussed in section III of this chapter.

[144] This expression was used by the Italian media. Brigida (n 54) 124, ft 490.

[145] Facchini (n 143) 179.

Almost all cases involved the accusations of aiding and abetting illegal immigration and/or collusion with smugglers. In a few of them, the charges concerned the alleged offences of disobedience to maritime authorities' orders, disobedience to warships' orders, the aggravated ground of association with a criminal organisation,[146] and illegal management of waste of the vessel. In all criminal proceedings, measures against NGOs entailed financial prevention measures, especially seizure of the vessels – and therefore the consequent cessation of activities at sea and damage to the NGOs' image.

Although precise statistics are unavailable concerning the number of criminal proceedings against NGOs, it seems that they amounted to at least four in 2017, five in 2018, nine in 2019,[147] two in 2020 and none between 2021 and June 2023.[148] Some vessels and crews were subject to more than one proceeding in relation to different SAR events. Most cases were discontinued at the pre-trial stage for lack of incriminating evidence, often requested by the same prosecutors who had initiated the investigations,[149] and as of June 2023, six remain pending – those involving the *Iuventa*, *Vos Hestia*, *Vos Prudence*,[150] *Open Arms*, *Mare Jonio* and *Aquarius*.[151]

As of November 2023, no NGO has been convicted, and only one case – concerning the *Iuventa*, a vessel flying the Dutch flag and run by the German NGO Jugend Rettet – has reached the trial stage.[152] The *Iuventa* was the first case and also one of the most important investigations against SAR NGOs. The charges concerned three different rescue operations (one on 10 September 2016 and two on 18 June 2017) where the *Iuventa* saved several migrants in international waters and then transferred them to the *Vos Hestia* of Save The Children and *Vos Prudence* of Médecins Sans Frontières, which later disembarked them in Sicily. The investigations, started in 2017 by the prosecutors of Trapani, involved the alleged crimes of aiding and abetting illegal immigration to Italy according

[146] For instance, this occurred in the case against Open Arms for the SAR events of 15 March 2018. See Trib Catania, Giudice per le indagini preliminari, Decreto di sequestro preventivo 27.03.2018, n 2474/19 l, available at: www.questionegiustizia.it/data/doc/1600/decreto_convalida_sequestro_preventivo_tribunale_catania.pdf. However, in 2019, the prosecutor dropped these charges and only continued the investigation for the crime of aiding and abetting illegal immigration. Trib Ragusa, Procura della Repubblica, Avviso di Conclusione delle Indagini Preliminari 03.12.2019.

[147] This is confirmed by Cusumano and Villa (n 4) 32.

[148] FRA, 'June 2023 Update' (n 141).

[149] See also, Asylum Information Database (AIDA) and European Council on Refugees and Exiles (ECRE), 'Country Report: Access to the Territory and Push Backs' (AIDA, 20 May 2022), available at: asylumineurope.org/reports/country/italy/asylum-procedure/access-procedure-and-registration/access-territory-and-push-backs/#_ftnref70.

[150] *Iuventa*, *Vos Hestia* and *Vos Prudence* are jointly pending before the same judge.

[151] FRA, 'June 2023 Update' (n 141).

[152] See Alagna (n 7) 8, 16. It should be noted that in the Italian system, pre-trial judges decide whether there are sufficient grounds and evidence to go to trial. Trial judges are in charge of adjudicating the case.

to Article 12 TUI and collusion with traffickers according to Article 416 of the Criminal Code.[153] In particular, the crew members were accused of having agreed to handovers of migrants with traffickers. Consequently, the prosecutor argued that 'the legal justification for the fulfilment of the duty to rescue at sea'[154] does not apply – in other words, the *Iuventa* did not provide assistance in a situation of distress, but planned the entry of irregular migrants into Italy. The precautionary seizure of the vessel went through different reviews, and reached the Supreme Court of Cassation (Corte Suprema di Cassazione), the highest court in Italy on matters of interpretation of law. All the courts upheld the lawfulness of the seizure, as they accepted the prosecutor's argument concerning the existence of serious circumstantial evidence of the crimes.[155] The courts also confirmed the jurisdiction of the Italian courts because part of the crime took place in Italian territorial waters and territory, ie, where the disembarkation of illegal immigrants occurred. In March 2021,[156] and later in December 2021,[157] the prosecutor closed the investigation against some of the defendants, dropped the charges for criminal association to commit a crime, and continued the case only concerning the offences of aiding and abetting illegal immigration.[158] The trial, which remains pending on the merits,[159] has received intense media attention. Scholars have noted the unusual use of powers and resources similar to those used in the investigations of mafia crimes, including

[153] Trib Trapani, Procura della Repubblica, Richiesta di sequestro preventivo 06.05.2017, NRG 4060/16; F Vassallo Paleologo, 'Caso Iuventa, Anomalie di un'Inchiesta Politico-giudiziaria' (ADIF, 19 May 2022) www.a-dif.org/2022/05/19/caso-iuventa-anomalie-di-uninchiesta-politico-giudiziaria/. See also, Twitter, Iuventa Crew (*Twitter*, 17 June 2019), available at: mobile.twitter.com/iuventacrew/status/1140829739734540288. The case also involves Doctors Without Borders and Save the Children.

[154] S Zirulia, 'Is that a Smuggler? The Blurring Line between Facilitating Illegal Immigration and Providing Humanitarian Assistance at the European Borders' in GL Gatta, V Mitsilegas and S Zirulia (eds), *Controlling Immigration through Criminal Law: European and Comparative Perspectives on 'Crimmigration'* (Oxford, Hart Publishing 2020) 243; Trib Trapani, Giudice per le indagini preliminari, Decreto di sequestro preventivo 02.08.2017, n 216/2017.

[155] Trib Trapani, Giudice per le indagini preliminari, Decreto di sequestro preventivo 02.08.2017, n 216; Cass pen, sez I, Sentenza 24.04.2018, n 56138.

[156] Romano (n 77) 56; Fulvio Vassallo Paleologo, 'Archiviata una parte dell'indagine Iuventa. Quali prove contro MSF e Save The Children?' (ADIF, 27 May 2022), available at: www.a-dif.org/2022/05/27/archiviata-una-parte-dellindagine-iuventa-quali-prove-contro-msf-e-save-the-children/.

[157] Vassallo Paleologo, 'Archiviata una parte dell'indagine Iuventa' (n 156); P Lambruschi, 'Migranti. Cinque Anni di Indagini e Menzogne: Cadono tutte le Accuse per Don Zerai' *Avvenire* (27 May 2022) www.avvenire.it/attualita/pagine/don-zerai-cadono-tutte-le-accuse-dopo-5-anni-di-indagini.

[158] Cusumano and Villa (n 4) 32.

[159] See Fulvio Vassallo Paleologo, 'Indagini sul Caso Iuventa (con Save the Children e MSF): a Trapani un Ritorno alla Giurisdizione?' (ADIF, 23 May 2022), available at: www.a-dif.org/2022/05/23/indagini-sul-caso-iuventa-con-save-the-children-e-msf-a-trapani-un-ritorno-alla-giurisdizione/; Iuventa Crew, 'Whether in Ports or Courtrooms, Italy Disregards Basic Rights' (*Iuventa Crew*, 12 November 2022), available at: iuventa-crew.org/en/2022/11/12/whether-in-ports-or-courtrooms-italy-disregards-basic-rights/; Fulvio Vassallo Paleologo, 'ONG a Giudizio, il Caso IUVENTA Non è Chiuso' (ADIF, 21 February 2022) www.a-dif.org/2022/02/21/ong-a-giudizio-il-caso-iuventa-non-e-chiuso/.

undercover investigations and wiretapping of journalists, lawyers and academics during their conversations with the accused NGOs.[160]

Scholars have commented that criminal investigations against NGOs are 'difficult to classify'[161] and seem in line with the 'closed port' policy.[162] Cusumano and Villa discuss that

> [a]lthough the independence of the judiciary from the executive branch is firmly embedded in the Italian political system, the wider climate of suspicion against NGOs is likely to have affected public prosecutors' decision to initiate investigations ... These proceedings resonate with the government stance towards NGOs.[163]

Minetti agrees with this view, but also points out that it is necessary to consider the Constitutional principle of mandatory prosecution: given that the offence of facilitating illegal immigration entails bringing irregular migrants to Italy, prosecutors have the obligation to establish whether or not an offence has been committed in the first place. On the other hand, she discusses how some prosecutors have shown unjustified persistence in pursuing the proceedings.[164] Thus, scholars argue that the prosecutors' approach may have been influenced by 'the narrative spread by the populists'.[165]

However, Cusumano and Villa acknowledge

> that not all investigations were motivated by the conviction that NGOs were involved in wrongdoings or the attempt to stop their activities. When rescue ships were denied the authorization to dock, some prosecutors who considered it illegal to leave migrants at sea for too long arguably enacted a strategy of seizing ships in order to facilitate the disembarkation of those on board. This was the case for Sea-Watch 3 in May 2019 and Open Arms in August 2019, both impounded and released soon thereafter.[166]

On the other hand, in proceedings against NGOs, the response of the judges has been to find the existence of the objective and subjective elements of the crime of aiding irregular immigration (Article 12(1) and Article 13(3) TUI), but at the

[160] In particular, the transcripts of the conversations were deposited with the Court and thus became publicly accessible. This conduct violated the protection afforded by Art 103 of the Code of Civil Procedure – protection of privacy and the sources of journalists. Annalisa Camilli, 'L'Inchiesta Anomala della Procura di Trapani sulle ONG' *Internazionale* (9 April 2021), available at: www.internazionale.it/notizie/annalisa-camilli/2021/04/09/ong-giornalisti-procura-trapani-migranti; Romano (n 77) 56; Giuseppe Sambataro, 'The Protection of Journalist Sources in Italian Criminal Proceedings: The Iuventa Case' (*Global Freedom of Expression*, Columbia University, 8 July 2022), available at: globalfreedomofexpression.columbia.edu/updates/2022/07/the-protection-of-journalistic-sources-in-italian-criminal-proceedings-the-trapani-case/.

[161] Zirulia and Martinico (n 114) 272.

[162] ibid.

[163] Cusumano and Villa (n 4) 32.

[164] Interview with Marta Minetti, PhD Candidate, Queen Mary University of London (online, 9 February 2023); see also, Zirulia and Martinico (n 114) 272.

[165] ibid 273.

[166] Cusumano and Villa (n 4) 32.

same time of justifications for such actions. More precisely, the judges found that the exceptions governed by Article 51 of the Criminal Code (exercise of a right or fulfilment of a duty) and/or Article 54 of the Criminal Code (state of necessity) were applicable.[167] Regarding the 'fulfilment of a duty', the judges clarified that there is an obligation to rescue at sea provided for by international custom and international law, which establishes that states must adopt measures to ensure ship captains' fulfilment of their obligation to rescue at sea in cases of 'distress at sea'.[168]

In addition, the judicial trend has been to interpret 'place of safety' as a place where human rights are guaranteed according to international law.[169] Specifically, in the case against Open Arms, the Judge for Preliminary Investigations of the Court of Ragusa ruled that the duty to rescue was justified not because the dinghies were in distress – although overcrowded, they 'were in a good state of buoyancy and the weather conditions were stable'[170] – but because they would have been 'intercepted by the Libyan Coast Guard and taken back to a country where, admittedly, no safe ports exist, and indeed migrants are subjected to serious and documented human rights violations'.[171] Thus, the concept of POS implies a place where human rights and prohibition of non-refoulement are guaranteed.[172]

In September 2020, the Judge for Preliminary Investigations of the Tribunal of Agrigento followed a similar approach in the cases initiated in March 2019 against the shipmaster as well as the head of the mission of the ship *Mare Jonio*, operated by Mediterranea Saving Humans.[173] The judge stressed that the obligation to save lives at sea imposed upon states overrides provisions and bilateral agreements adopted to fight illegal immigration. Such an obligation imposes the

[167] Romano (n 77) 46; see, for instance, Trib Ragusa, Ufficio Giudice per le indagini preliminari, Decreto 16.04.2018, n 1182/18, available at: newsmagnify.it/wp-content/uploads/2018/08/Decreto-di-rigetto-di-richiesta-di-sequestro-preventivo-GIP-di-Ragusa-16-Aprile-2018.pdf.

[168] Romano (n 77) 46.

[169] eg, this was the reasoning in the case against Open Arms initiated in 2018. Trib Ragusa, Giudice per le indagini preliminari, Decreto 16.04.2018, n 1182/18, 13–14.

[170] Zirulia, 'Is that a Smuggler?' (n 154) 245. 'On 15 March 2018, three overcrowded dinghies had been sighted in Libyan SAR waters. Given that the Libyan Coast Guard had formally taken charge of the rescue operations, the Italian Coast Guard had ordered the NGO not to intervene … The crew had disregarded the order and carried out the rescue of over two hundred people, having arrived before the Libyans at the scene of the incident … [T]he NGO had sailed onwards to the Italian coast on its own initiative, where it was finally authorised to dock at Pozzallo. The Catania Preliminary Investigations Judge had initially ordered the seizure of the ship due to it having facilitated illegal entry, ruling out the justification of the duty of rescue at sea'; ibid 244.

[171] ibid 243; Trib Ragusa, Giudice per le indagini preliminari, Decreto 16.04.2018, n 1182/18, 13–14. The case against Open Arms was started in March 2018 and involves the accusations of aiding and abetting illegal immigration in violation of Art 12 TUI. It is to be distinguished from the case involving Open Arms against Salvini, which I mentioned in section V of this chapter.

[172] Trib Ragusa, Giudice per le indagini preliminari, Decreto 16.04.2018, n 1182/18, 13–14.

[173] Romano (n 77) 62; Ruta and Ziniti (n 84).

duty to disembark at a place where the lives of the rescued persons will no longer be in danger and where fundamental needs such as food, shelter and medical care are met. As a consequence, orders to hand migrants over to the Libyan authorities or disembark in Libya are unlawful and cannot constitute legally required actions.[174] However, the turning point occurred with the decision of the Supreme Court of Cassation in the *Rackete* case, as explained below.

B. The Supreme Court of Cassation's Decision in *Rackete*

The sentence of the Supreme Court of Cassation no 6626 of 2020 regarding the arrest of captain Carola Rackete of the *Sea-Watch 3* further strengthened the judicial approach.[175] In June 2019, after having rescued 53 migrants in distress in the Libyan SAR area, Rackete disregarded the order of the Libyan authorities to disembark them in Tripoli, and sailed from international waters towards Italy.[176] Despite the ban on entering Italian territorial waters issued by the Minister of the Interior Salvini according to the Security Decree-bis, after a two-week stand-off with the Italian authorities, Rackete broke an Italian naval blockade of the Guardia di Finanza (Finance Police) that was trying to block the *Sea-Watch 3*, and finally docked the vessel in Lampedusa.[177] Accordingly, after disembarking the migrants, Rackete was arrested on charges of resistance to a public official (Article 337 of the Criminal Code) and committing an act of violence against a warship (Article 1100 of the Navigation Code). A second separate criminal proceeding was started against her for aiding illegal immigrants – a strategy which, according to Minetti, attempted to maximise the chances to indict the accused and points to an excessive prosecutorial will.[178]

After the Judge for Preliminary Investigations of the Court of Agrigento[179] refused to confirm the arrest because Rackete acted according to the duty to save lives at sea and because the vessel of the Guardia di Finanza could not be categorised as a warship, the prosecutor appealed to the Supreme Court of Cassation. The Supreme Court of Cassation found the arrest illegitimate and dismissed the case,[180] in line with the lower court.

[174] Romano (n 77) 62.
[175] Cass pen, sez III, Sentenza 16.01.2020, n 6626; Romano (n 77) 62.
[176] Brigida (n 54) 231.
[177] Lorenzo Tondo, 'Rescue Ship Captain Arrested for Breaking Italian Blockade' *Guardian* (29 June 2019), available at: www.theguardian.com/world/2019/jun/29/sea-watch-captain-carola-rackete-arrested-italian-blockade.
[178] Interview with Minetti (n 164).
[179] Trib Agrigento, Giudice per le indagini preliminari, Ordinanza 02.07.2019, available at: www.giurisprudenzapenale.com/wp-content/uploads/2019/07/Rachete-Carola-Ordinanza-sulla-richiesta-di-convalida-di-arresto.pdf.
[180] Cass pen, sez III, Sentenza 16.01.2020, n 6626 (n 175).

One of the main issues in the case concerned the content of the duty to rescue.[181] The Supreme Court of Cassation stated that the duty to rescue mandated by international law includes not only taking people aboard but their subsequent disembarkation to a POS. The Supreme Court of Cassation reasoned that, according to the IMO Guidelines on the Treatment of Persons Rescued at Sea (2004 IMO Guidelines),[182] a safe place is a place where the rescued people are physically safe and their fundamental rights guaranteed.[183] Consequently, a ship cannot be considered a POS because it is at the mercy of adverse weather, does not guarantee fundamental rights, and does not allow the rescued persons to lodge an application for international protection.[184] Strengthening its decision by referring to international law and fundamental rights, the Supreme Court of Cassation pointed out the centrality of the person, the absolute right to life and personal dignity, and the principle of solidarity inherent in the nature of the obligation to rescue at sea.

In considering the unreasonableness of the arrest, the Supreme Court of Cassation also admonished the Guardia di Finanza, noting that the provisions to save lives at sea are well known not only to people who carry out rescue operations, but also to those engaged in maritime police activities.[185] 'In other words … the very officials who should have been the most acutely aware of the duty to save lives at sea, were the ones who ignored this duty in their efforts to arrest a master for acting in compliance with it'.[186]

Finally, according to Zirulia,

> by considering justified a conduct that consisted in forcing the blockade of entry into territorial waters and hitting a patrol boat that was obstructing the docking manoeuvre, the Court of Cassation assigned a sort of 'right of resistance' to whoever, acting in accordance with the law, opposes the conduct of the public forces that might jeopardise the fundamental rights of persons, including (given the explicit reference to the Geneva Convention) the right to seek asylum.[187]

Regarding the charge of having committed an act of violence against a warship, in dismissing it, the Supreme Court of Cassation confirmed that the Guardia di Finanza's vessel was not a warship but rather a military vessel.[188]

[181] I Papanicolopulu, 'Duty to Rescue and Entry into Port: The *Carola Rackete* Decision' (2020) 30 *International Yearbook of International Law* 453, 455–56.

[182] Maritime Safety Committee, Guidelines on the Treatment of Persons Rescued at Sea, UN Doc MSC 78/26/Add.2, Res MSC167(78) (20 May 2004) (2004 IMO Guidelines). See ch 3, section II.D.

[183] Romano (n 77) 63; Cass pen, sez III, Sentenza 16.01.2020, n 6626 (n 175) 11.

[184] Romano (n 77) 63. Cass pen, sez III, Sentenza 16.01.2020, n 6626 (n 175).

[185] Papanicolopulu, 'Duty to Rescue and Entry into Port' (n 181) 458.

[186] ibid.

[187] Zirulia, 'Is that a Smuggler?' (n 154) 248.

[188] A warship vessel 'must belong to the armed forces of the State; it must bear the external distinctive markings of military vessels; its crew must be subject to military discipline; and, finally, it must be under the command of a naval officer at the service of the State and registered in the specific role of officials. The latter condition, according to the Corte di Cassazione, was not demonstrated', as the *Guardia di Finanza*'s vessel was under the orders of a '*maresciallo*' rather than a naval officer. Papanicolopulu, 'Duty to Rescue and Entry into Port' (n 181) 456.

Thus, the decision of the Supreme Court of Cassation elucidated that the duty to save lives at sea prevails over the interest of protecting national borders.[189] Although the case concerned Rackete's arrest for resisting public officials and an act of violence against a warship, the findings 'seem to have a broader scope, capable of justifying the commission of a wide array of offenses (including the one of facilitating illegal immigration), when necessary to fulfil the duty of assistance'.[190] In fact, in 2021, the prosecutor discontinued the other case against Rackete for aiding and abetting illegal immigration.[191] Additionally, after the *Rackete* case, criminal accusations against NGOs for facilitating irregular immigration have been less frequent.

Rossi, however, takes a critical view of the Judge for Preliminary Investigations of Agrigento and the Supreme Court of Cassation's decisions in the *Rackete* case. First, according to him, the SAR and SOLAS Conventions do not provide any guidance on where to disembark rescued persons, and leave such a choice to the cooperation of the contracting state parties. These conventions do not state that a shipmaster must disembark to the *nearest* POS,[192] but only to a 'place of safety' within a reasonable time.[193] Moreover, he points out that international law gives the port state the power to control and give access to its ports. There is neither a specific provision imposing a duty on a shipmaster of a private vessel to disembark the migrants to a POS, nor to disembark at the nearest port to the rescue.[194] The SAR Convention only refers to an obligation upon states to deliver the rescued persons to a POS.[195] As such, the correct question to ask was whether the *Sea-Watch could*, and not whether it *should*, enter the Italian port. Rossi acknowledges that a coastal state's right to prohibit access to its ports encounters an exception in cases of a state of necessity, 'that is in situations that threaten people's lives aboard the vessel'.[196] Nevertheless, he argues that in the case of the *Sea-Watch* the state of necessity exception did not apply because the

[189] Minetti (n 27) 348.

[190] Zirulia and Martinico (n 114) 274.

[191] Interview with Minetti (n 164); Stefano Zirulia, 'Caso Sea Watch (Carola Rackete): Archiviate le Accuse di Favoreggiamento dell'Immigrazione Irregolare e Rifiuto di Obbedienza a Nave da Guerra' (*Sistema Penale*, 17 January 2022), available at: www.sistemapenale.it/it/scheda/caso-sea-watch-carola-rackete-archiviate-le-accuse-di-favoreggiamento-dellimmigrazione-irregolare-e-rifiuto-di-obbedienza-a-nave-da-guerra.

[192] P Rossi, 'Politica dei "Porti Chiusi" e Diritto Internazionale: il Caso della Sea Watch 3' (2019) 6 *Osservatorio Costituzionale* 48, 62, 64.

[193] Adoption of Amendments to the International Convention on Maritime Search and Rescue, 1979, as amended, MSC Res.155(78), 78th sess, Agenda Item 26, IMO Doc MSC 78/26/Add 1 Annex 5 (4 June 2004, adopted 20 May 2004) (2004 Amendments to the SAR Convention) Annex, ch 3, para 3.1.9; Adoption of Amendments to the International Convention on Safety of Lives at Sea, 1974, as amended, MSC Res.153(78), 78th sess, Agenda Item 26, IMO Doc MSC 78/26/Add 1 (4 June 2004, adopted 20 May 2004) (2004 Amendments to the SOLAS Convention) Annex, ch V, Reg 33.4 (1–1); see ch 4, section II.C.

[194] Rossi (n 192) 64. See ch 3, section II.C.

[195] Ch 3, section II.C; Rossi (n 192) 64–65.

[196] This is a consuetudinary rule of international law. Rossi (n 192) 65.

migrants who needed urgent medical conditions were disembarked. Moreover, the European Court of Human Rights (ECtHR), upon urgent request by the *Sea-Watch 3* to adopt interim measures, refused to do so on the grounds that there was no 'risk of urgent or irreparable harm'.[197] Therefore, according to Rossi, Italy did not have a legal obligation to allow disembarkation.[198]

On the other hand, although not binding, the 2004 IMO Guidelines, applicable to both states and all shipmasters, clarify that 'coastal States should relieve the ship as soon as practicable'.[199] They also add that states 'should make every effort to minimize the time survivors remain aboard the assisting ship'.[200] Whereas Rossi underlines that the Guidelines state that shipmasters may have to be ready to deal with 'inevitable delays'[201] in the disembarkation phase, it is difficult to believe that delays due to disputes on where to disembark may be considered 'inevitable'.

Also, given that the *Sea-Watch 3* was in front of the Lampedusa port, it seemed reasonable to allow disembarkation rather than tranship the migrants and take them to another state (which also had to give authorisation to enter its ports),[202] as the time required to do so would have caused the situation on the vessel to degenerate,[203] assuming it had not yet degenerated.

Second, Rossi discusses that the principle of non-refoulement prohibits one from returning an individual to a place where he or she could face a risk of persecution, but does not create the right to enter a state.[204] While this is a correct statement, he fails to take into account that the Italian Constitution

[197] Rossi (n 192) 66. See *Rackete and others v Italy* App no 32969/19 (ECtHR, 25 June 2009); Registrar of the European Court of justice, 'The Court Decides Not to Indicate an Interim Measure Requiring that the Applicants Be Authorised to Disembark in Italy from the Ship Sea-Watch 3' (Press Release, 25 June 2019), available at: hudoc.echr.coe.int/app/conversion/pdf/?library=ECHR&id=003-6443361-8477507&filename=Rackete%20and%20Others%20v.%20Italy%20-%20request%20for%20interim%20measure%20refused%20in%20the%20case%20of%20Sea%20Watch%203.pdf. The Court noted that 10 vulnerable people had already been allowed to disembark, and therefore it did not deem the other migrants on board to be facing an emergency situation. According to Rossi, the refusal of the ECtHR to issue the interim measure is an additional element to support the view that the migrants on the Sea-Watch were not in a situation of distress, that is a situation of extreme danger to life. Interview with Pierfrancesco Rossi, Adjunct Professor of International Law, Università degli Studi della Calabria (online, 15 June 2023).

[198] However, the situation would be different if the ship was already in the waters of an Italian port, where delays in disembarking would trigger violations of international law – this occurred, for example, in the *Diciotti* case; ibid; see ch 7, section V.B.

[199] 2004 IMO Guidelines (n 182) s 6.3.

[200] ibid para 6.8.

[201] ibid para 6.9.

[202] Rossi agrees that allowing disembarkation was the most reasonable solution given the situation. Interview with Rossi (n 197).

[203] Alessandro Gamberini, 'Migrazione: Dichiarazioni alla Stampa dall'Avvocato Gamberini, Legale della Comandante della Sea Watch 3, Carola Rackete' *Radio Radicale* (Video Recorded Interview, 1 July 2019), available at: www.radioradicale.it/scheda/578535/migrazione-dichiarazioni-alla-stampa-dellavvocato-alessandro-gamberini-legale-della.

[204] Rossi (n 192) 67–68; S Trevisanut, 'The Principle of Non-Refoulement and the De-Territorialization of Border Control at Sea' (2014) 27 *Leiden Journal of International Law* 661, 661.

provides for a wider right to seek asylum, which also entails the right to enter the Italian territory.[205]

In conclusion, the courts overturned the security-oriented approach of the ministerial provisions and policies, and instead adopted a perspective focused on the rights of individuals,[206] which has had wider effects than in the single cases before them.[207] Nevertheless, the government's strategy against NGOs has changed and been refined by the use of administrative sanctions for the alleged failure of NGO vessels to meet a number of technical requirements.[208]

VIII. APPLICATION OF SAFETY OF NAVIGATION PROVISIONS AGAINST SAR NGOs AND THE ECJ'S DECISION IN *SEA-WATCH 3* AND *SEA-WATCH 4*

As a consequence of judicial decisions which made the criminalisation of NGOs more and more difficult, Lamorgese started favouring the Port Authorities' use of the administrative inspection tool to check on the compliance of NGO ships with international and national legislation on safety of navigation,[209] namely the Paris Memorandum of Understanding on Port State Control (Paris MoU),[210] Directive 2009/16,[211] and the implementing Legislative Decree no 53 of 2011.

As explained in chapter three, section VI, according to these instruments, vessels navigating in international waters need to have a 'classification certificate' issued by the flag state ensuring that they meet navigation standards in light of the services they provide.[212] Given the absence of a specific category that can be assigned to NGO vessels engaged in SAR activities, in practice they are classified in different ways – sometimes as cargo ships, sometimes as tug boats and others as fishing vessels.[213] In light of this gap, on several occasions, the Port Authorities

[205] See ch 5, section V.A.

[206] Romano (n 77) 62; Zirulia, 'Caso Sea-Watch (Carola Rackete)' (n 191).

[207] For a general discussion on the influence of courts' decisions, see M Galanter, 'The Radiating Effects of Courts' in KD Boyum and L Mather (eds), *Empirical Theories of Courts* (New York, Longman, 1983).

[208] Romano (n 77) 64; Interview with Eugenio Cusumano, Lecturer in International and European Studies, University of Leiden (telephone, 14 June 2023).

[209] Lamorgese did not adopt any formal or precise provision in this regard – it would have been difficult to do otherwise. Interview with Masera (n 62).

[210] The Paris Memorandum of Understanding on Port State Control, adopted in Paris on 26 January 1982, has been signed by the majority of EU Member States and Canada. See Paris MoU, available at: www.parismou.org/inspections-risk/library-faq/memorandum; F De Vittor, 'Il Port State Control sulle Navi delle ONG che Prestano Soccorso in Mare: Tutela della Sicurezza della Navigazione o Ostacolo alle Attività di Soccorso?' (2021) 15 *Diritti Umani e Diritto Internazionale* 103. See ch 3, section VI.

[211] Council Directive 2009/16/EC of the European Parliament and of the Council of 23 April 2009 on Port State Control [2009] OJ L131/57. The Directive reproduces the content of the Paris MoU and its annexes. See ch 3, section VI.

[212] Directive 2009/16/EC, Art 3; De Vittor (n 210) 95.

[213] De Vittor (n 210) 95.

have claimed that NGOs systematically use vessels which do not have the necessary certificate of suitability to carry out SAR activities and are therefore dangerous.[214] They have also argued that cargo ships can carry out rescues only in exceptional and unforeseen cases.[215] Similar arguments have been made by the authorities in other EU states, such as Malta, Spain, Germany and the Netherlands.[216]

On their end, NGOs have pointed out that neither international or European, nor national legislation sets out the requirements for private vessels to meet when engaged in SAR operations.[217] Moreover, the international law of the sea establishes the shipmaster's obligation to save any person in distress at sea,[218] regardless of whether the vessel is intended to provide SAR services or not and of who is being rescued.[219] As such, they have raised concerns regarding both the expectation that their vessels meet the same safety requirements as established for commercial ships transporting passengers,[220] and the legality of the systematic inspections and seizures.[221]

According to some scholars, the Port Authorities' practice is in breach of the principle of mutual recognition of safety certificates issued by flag states, as recognised by the Paris MoU and Directive 2009/16/EC,[222] as it disregards the fact that NGO ships have already passed checks required by the legislation of their flag countries. Any issue relating to certificates or safety shall be brought to the attention of the competent flag state. Only if the flag state does not adopt the necessary measures according to the international provisions can the port state require additional measures, including seizing the vessels.[223]

[214] ibid 122.

[215] For more information on the administrative seizures, see FRA, 'Table 2: Legal Proceedings by EU Member States against Private Entities Involved in SAR Operations in the Mediterranean Sea' (n 141); Masera, 'Il Contrasto Amministrativo alle ONG che Operano Soccorsi in Mare' (n 56) 10; De Vittor (n 210) 103, 118.

[216] FRA, 'June 2023 Update' (n 141).

[217] De Vittor (n 210) 103, 128.

[218] UNCLOS, art 98; SOLAS, Ch V, reg 33.1.

[219] De Vittor (n 210) 103, 127.

[220] Vassallo Paleologo, 'Come si Trasformano i Soccorsi delle ONG in "Eventi Migratori"' (n 139); De Vittor (n 210) 103.

[221] The lack of provisions regulating NGO ships engaged in SAR operations has been confirmed by the TAR of Palermo in the cases *Sea-Watch EV c Ministero delle Infrastrutture e dei Trasporti e Capitaneria di Porto di Palermo*, ricorso n 1596/2020 and *Sea-Watch EV c Ministero delle Infrastrutture e dei Trasporti e Capitaneria di Porto Empedocle*, ricorso n 1864/2020, Ordinanza 02.03.2021. De Vittor (n 210) 103, 124, fn 77; L Gennari, 'Navi in Porto, Naufragi nel Mediterraneo: la Dimensione Amministrativa del Contrasto alle Operazioni di Soccorso' (2021) XXI *Diritto e Questioni Pubbliche*, Special Issue 83, 85.

[222] Masera, 'Il Contrasto Amministrativo alle ONG che Operano Soccorsi in Mare' (n 56) 10 ft 26. For example, upon communication of the detention of *Sea-Watch 3*, *Sea Watch 4* and *Ocean Viking* to their flag states – Germany and Norway, respectively – these countries confirmed the validity of their safety certificates and conformity with international provisions and their awareness of the systematic SAR activities of the vessels. De Vittor (n 210) 103, 112, 117, 124.

[223] De Vittor (n 210) 103, 122.

In response to the Port Authorities' inspections, in most cases, NGOs have agreed to rectify the 'irregularities' of their vessels in order to be able to sail again.[224] At the time of writing, NGOs have judicially challenged their vessels' seizure before the competent Tribunale Amministrativo Regionale (TAR – Regional Administrative Tribunal) in only two cases, and the issue was decided on the merits.[225] Both cases were initiated by the NGO Sea-Watch before the TAR of Palermo, challenging the seizure of the *Sea-Watch 3* and *Sea-Watch 4* imposed on 8 July 2020 and 19 September 2020 respectively. The TAR made a preliminary reference to the ECJ which in essence posed the question of whether the Italian Port Authorities' controls on NGO ships flying a foreign flag exceed the powers conferred by EU legislation.[226]

In August 2022, the ECJ[227] ruled that NGO ships systematically carrying out SAR activities are covered by Directive 2009/16 and may be subject to controls by port states. However, port states must show, in each specific case, that the inspection is justified because there is a clear risk to safety, health, or the environment. Among the elements of risk, the port state may consider that NGO vessels registered as cargo ships are being used for SAR purposes. Nevertheless, the fact that rescued vessels may transport a higher number of persons than that indicated in their certificates constitutes an 'overriding factor' according to Article 11 of Directive 2009/16,[228] and in itself cannot be used to justify port controls: rescued people cannot be considered as 'passengers'. In addition, port states cannot require NGO vessels to be in possession of different safety certificates from those issued by the flag state, nor that they meet all the requirements for different ships' classification. Should the port state find the existence of a risk, it can adopt all the measures that it deems necessary – as long as they are adequate, reasonable and proportionate. Finally, the Court stressed the importance of the principle of good faith collaboration among the interested states in order to address the issues that arise in this context,[229] and

[224] This conclusion can be reached by a reading of the data found in: FRA, 'Table 2: Legal Proceedings by EU Member States against Private Entities Involved in SAR Operations in the Mediterranean Sea' (n 141).

[225] Masera, 'Il Contrasto Amministrativo alle ONG che Operano Soccorsi in Mare' (n 56) 8, 10–13; see FRA, 'Table 2. Legal Proceedings by EU Member States against Private Entities Involved in SAR Operations in the Mediterranean Sea (n 141); Interview with Irini Papanicolopolu, British Academy Global Professor of International Law, SOAS University of London (online, 10 May 2023).

[226] TAR Palermo, III sez, Sea-Watch EV c Ministero delle Infrastrutture e dei Trasporti e Capitaneria di Porto di Palermo, Ordinanze 22.12.2020, n 2974/2020 e n 2994/2020.

[227] Joined Cases C-14/21 and C-15/21 *Sea-Watch EV c Ministero delle Infrastrutture e dei Trasporti casi* (C-14/21 and C-15/21), *Capitaneria di Porto di Palermo caso* (C-14/21), *Capitaneria di Porto di Porto Empedocle caso* (C-15/21) [2022] C 424/8. For a commentary on the case, see Efthymios Papastavridis, 'Sea Watch Cases Before the EU Court of Justice: An Analysis of International Law of the Sea' (*Odysseus Network*, 12 December 2022), available at: eumigrationlawblog.eu/sea-watch-cases-before-the-eu-court-of-justice-an-analysis-of-international-law-of-the-sea/.

[228] Joined Cases C-14/21 and C-15/21 *Sea-Watch EV* (n 227) paras 15, 19(2), 39, 47, 66(2).

[229] The national controversy came to an end with the release of the vessels and thus termination of the subject matter of the case before the Italian judge. Interview with immigration lawyer no 5 (n 33).

that the Directive must be interpreted in light of international law, including the conventions on the law of the sea.

Vassallo Paleologo has remarked on the importance of the ECJ decision, as it sets forth the principle that, for the port state to carry out inspections, it must prove serious safety problems in each specific case rather than carrying them out systematically following the same general motivations,[230] thus limiting the exercise of arbitrary power. On the other hand, although the decision limits the power of the Italian Coast Guard, it has not yet been taken seriously and has not prevented them from carrying out new POS inspections on NGO vessels, including the *Sea-Watch 3*.[231] Whereas it may be possible to legally challenge these practices, according to Papanicolopulu, the government relies on the long wait times involved in administrative justice, which discourage NGOs from pursuing judicial cases.[232]

Thus, as Cusumano and Villa comment, whereas criminal investigations and prohibitions on disembarkation decreased by late 2020, the 'broader discursive stigmatization of non-governmental rescue did not completely subside'[233] and governments used other, more subtle strategies to prevent NGOs' SAR activities.[234]

IX. INTER-MINISTERIAL DECREES AND DISEMBARKATION ISSUES DURING THE COVID-19 PANDEMIC

The Covid-19 pandemic had a notable impact on SAR operations in the Central Mediterranean in 2020. As a result of Covid-19 response measures,

[230] It should be noted that the Palermo TAR, which referred the case to the ECJ, had ordered that the detention of the *Sea-Watch 3* and *Sea-Watch 4* ships be lifted. The judge reasoned that safety of navigation is within the competence of the flag state and of the shipmaster in cases requiring emergency actions, underlining how – in any case – the transportation of rescued migrants is limited to the time strictly necessary to take them to a POS. Fulvio Vassallo Paleologo, 'La Corte Giustizia EU Pone Limiti alla Prassi dei Fermi Amministrativi' (*Melting Pot Europa*, 2 August 2022), available at: www.meltingpot.org/2022/08/la-corte-di-giustizia-ue-pone-limiti-alla-prassi-dei-fermi-amministrativi-chi-risarcira-i-danni-per-i-mancati-soccorsi/; Sea-Watch, 'Il TAR di Palermo Sospende il Fermo delle Navi di Sea-Watch' *Pressenza International Press Agency* (2 March 2021), available at: www.pressenza.com/it/2021/03/Il-tar-di-palermo-sospende-il-fermo-delle-navi-di-sea-watch/. However, upon appeal of the Minister of Infrastructure and Transport of the Draghi Government, the Council of Administrative Justice of the Region of Sicily (Consiglio di Giustizia Amministrativa della Regione Sicilia) overturned the Palermo TAR's decision. According to the Council, SAR operations shall be carried out considering the safety of the rescued and of the crew (including the adequate provisions of toilets and staff shifts), safety of navigation and the environment. These conditions that are not satisfied by the Sea-Watch 3 and Sea-Watch 4. Consiglio di Giustizia Amministrativa per la Regione Siciliana, Ordinanza 08.05.2021, REG RIC 341/2021; Fulvio Vassallo Paleologo, 'Ancora un Fermo Amministrativo per Bloccare i Soccorsi Umanitari nel Mediterraneo Centrale' (ADIF, 6 June 2021), available at: www.a-dif.org/2021/06/06/ancora-un-fermo-amministrativo-per-bloccare-i-soccorsi-umanitari-nel-mediterraneo-centrale/.

[231] Interview with immigration lawyer no 5 (n 33). For example, on 21 September 2022, after the *Sea-Watch 3* had rescued 428 sea migrants, the Italian authorities stopped the vessel again and performed a detailed safety inspection. Sea-Watch 3, 'Sea-Watch 3 – Italy Ignores ECJ Ruling' (Sea Watch, 23 September 2022), available at: sea-watch.org/en/sea-watch-3-blockade/.

[232] Interview with Papanicolopulu (n 225).

[233] Cusumano and Villa (n 4) 34.

[234] ibid; interview with Cusumano (n 208).

some states such as Italy and Malta refused to provide a secure port for NGO vessels engaged in SAR and placed limitations on their activities.[235] Specifically, in Italy, with Inter-ministerial Decree no 150 of 7 April 2020, the Ministry of Infrastructure and Transport, in agreement with the Ministry of Foreign Affairs and Cooperation, as well as the Ministry of the Interior and the Health Ministry closed the Italian ports by declaring them 'unsafe' for ships flying foreign flags outside the Italian SAR area and for the entire duration of the health emergency declared on 31 January 2020.[236] The Decree was adopted shortly after the German ship *Alan Kurdi* rescued 150 migrants in the international waters of the Libyan SAR zone and requested permission to disembark them in Lampedusa.[237] In line with this strategy, the Head of the Civil Protection Department adopted Decree no 1287 on 12 April 2020, imposing a period of mandatory quarantine on Italian ships[238] rather than on land for people who were rescued at sea and for whom it was not possible to identify a POS.

Inter-ministerial Decree no 150/2020 is problematic in relation to both substantive and formal aspects of ROL principles. From a substantive point of view, the Decree set forth an unjustifiably discriminatory treatment on the basis of nationality, as it provided that Italian ports are unsafe for some migrants – only those saved by foreign ships outside the Italian SAR zone. In contrast, Italian ports remained safe for people reaching the Italian coast on their own or by Italian vessels.[239] In light of this, the Commissioner for Human Rights of the

[235] M Stierl and D Dadusc, 'The "Covid Excuse": European Border Violence in the Mediterranean Sea' (2022) 45(8) *Ethnic and Racial Studies* 1453.

[236] Decreto del Ministro delle Infrastrutture e dei Trasporti di concerto con il Ministro degli Affari Esteri e della Cooperazione Internazionale, il Ministro dell'interno, e il Ministro della salute, del 7 aprile 2020, n 150; Fulvio Vassallo Paleologo, 'Il Governo Inasprisce il Decreto Sicurezza Bis di Salvini e Criminalizza il Soccorso Umanitario' (ADIF, 8 April 2020), available at: www.a-dif.org/2020/04/08/il-governo-inasprisce-il-decreto-sicurezza-bis-di-salvini-e-criminalizza-il-soccorso-umanitario/; Masera, 'Il Contrasto Amministrativo alle ONG che Operano Soccorsi in Mare' (n 56) 10; AM Pelliconi and M Goldoni, 'La Banalità dei Porti Chiusi per Decreto. Osservazioni sui Profili di Legittimità del Decreto Interministeriale 150/2020' (2020) 2 *Diritto, Immigrazione e Cittadinanza* 219; Laura Lo Verde, 'Le "Navi Quarantena": una Misura Temporanea o un Nuovo Approccio Oltre l'Emergenza?' (*Border Criminologies Blog*, 9 June 2021), available at: www.law.ox.ac.uk/research-subject-groups/centre-criminology/centreborder-criminologies/blog/2021/06/le-navi.

[237] The Maltese authorities adopted a similar approach to that taken by Italy in declaring their ports 'unsafe' due to the pandemic. ECRE, 'Med: 150 Stranded at Sea as Malta and Italy Declare Ports "Unsafe"' (ECRE, 10 April 2020), available at: ecre.org/med-150-stranded-at-sea-as-malta-and-italy-declare-ports-unsafe/.

[238] Decreto del Capo Dipartimento della Protezione Civile 12 aprile 2020 n 1287; ASGI, Report 'Diritti in Rotta. L'Esperimento delle Navi Quarantena e i Principali Profili di Criticità' (ASGI, 23 April 2021), available at: www.asgi.it/notizie/report-diritti-in-rotta-navi-quarantena/.

[239] A Pitino, 'Controllo delle Frontiere Italiane e Immigrazione nell'Emergenza Sanitaria Covid-19: tra *Soft Law* dell'Unione Europea e Misure Nazionali' (2021) *Corti Supreme e Salute* 1, 22–25; Vassallo Paleologo, 'Il Governo Inasprisce il Decreto Sicurezza Bis di Salvini e Criminalizza il Soccorso Umanitario' (n 236). As Borg Olivier of the NGO Repubblika noted in an interview, the closure of ports in Malta was likewise 'not complete', and the COVID restrictions did not apply to all ships equally. Krista Bonello Rutter Giappone, interview with Paul Borg Olivier, Lawyer with Repubblika, Malta (online, 10 December 2021).

Council of Europe prepared a communication in which he invited the authorities to fulfil the international obligation to disembark in a safe place for people rescued at sea while ensuring the protection of their health.[240]

From a formal point of view, the Ministry of Infrastructure and Transport did not have the competence to regulate the matter of sailing, transit and entry of ships into the territorial waters for reasons linked to public order and security. Such competence belongs to the Ministry of the Interior as the public authority in charge of public safety and security.[241] Moreover, according to the hierarchy of legal sources set out in the Constitution, matters regulated by law and international treaties – such as the provisions on disembarkation and the right to seek asylum – cannot be derogated from by administrative acts such as ministerial decrees.[242] However, attempts to challenge Inter-ministerial Decree no 150/2020 on the ground that it did not satisfy the legal requirements of extreme severity and urgency required for emergency legislation failed, as the TAR found the motivation supporting the Decree to be plausible given the health emergency situation.[243]

Finally, even if the health emergency was not extended after 31 March 2022, the government tried to 'normalise' the use of quarantine ships to better control sea migrants arriving in Italy, as well as to address the lack of space in reception centres in some places in Sicily.[244] This attempt, however, was broken off upon criticisms of unconstitutionality for breaching the time limit of the state of emergency set by law, as well as the period of validity of Inter-ministerial Decree no 150/2020, which constituted its legal basis.[245] Therefore, the quarantine ships were decommissioned on 1 June 2022.[246]

[240] Council of Europe, Commissioner for Human Rights, 'States Should Ensure Rescue at Sea and Allow Safe Disembarkation During the COVID-19 Crisis' (Statement, Commissioner for Human Rights, Council of Europe, 16 April 2020), available at: go.coe.int/6Bzqo.

[241] Pitino (n 239) 23; Irene di Valvasone, 'Sull'Attuale Illegalità delle Navi Quarantena' (*Melting Pot Europa*, 23 May 2022), available at: www.meltingpot.org/2022/05/sullattuale-illegalita-delle-navi-quarantena.

[242] Vassallo Paleologo, 'Il Governo Inasprisce il Decreto Sicurezza Bis di Salvini e Criminalizza il Soccorso Umanitario' (n 236); Cass pen, sez III, Sentenza 20.02.2020, n 6626; Pelliconi and Goldoni (n 236) 221–22; Pitino (n 239) 24; di Valvasone (n 241).

[243] TAR Lazio, sez III, 22.04.2020, n 3066 (holding that the decree was motivated by plausible arguments connected with the emergency situation); TAR Lazio, sez III, 07.10.2020, n 10152 (dismissing the legal action for lack of standing); Pitino (n 239) 26.

[244] Fulvio Vassallo Paleologo, 'Guerre Ibride e Sistemi di Accoglienza' (ADIF, 17 April 2022), available at: www.a-dif.org/2022/04/17/guerre-ibride-e-sistemi-di-accoglienza/; in this regard, it is also possible to listen to the interview of Annapaola Ammirati and Sami Aidoudi, 'Le "Navi Quarantena": l' Emergenza si fa Norma?' (*Melting Pot Europa*, 23 April 2022), available at: www.meltingpot.org/2022/04/le-navi-quarantena-lemergenza-si-fa-norma/.

[245] Decreto Legislativo 2 gennaio 2018, n 1; Codice della Protezione Civile, adottato con Decreto Legislativo 2 gannaio 2018, n 1, art 24.

[246] Fulvio Vassallo Paleologo, 'Dalle Navi Quarantena alla Detenzione Amministrativa Informale' (ADIF, 2 June 2022), available at: www.a-dif.org/2022/06/02/dalle-navi-quarantena-alla-detenzione-amministrativa-informale/.

X. LAW DECREE NO 1/2023 ('PIANTEDOSI DECREE') AND RELATED RESTRICTIONS ON NGOs' ACTIVITIES

On 2 January 2023, shortly after the start of its mandate, the right-wing Meloni government, which includes Salvini as the Minister of Infrastructure and Transport, adopted Law Decree no 1/2023, converted into Law no 15 of 24 February 2023, to further regulate and limit NGOs' SAR activities. The need to adopt new provisions to regulate NGOs emerged with two episodes that occurred shortly after the new mandate. The first concerned the vessels *Geo Barents* (belonging to Médecins Sans Frontières) and *Humanity 1* (belonging to SOS Humanity) in October 2023, when the authorities allowed only women and children to disembark in Catania. The other migrants were disembarked upon intervention of the health authorities a few days later.[247] The second event involved the *Ocean Viking* (belonging to SOS Méditerranée), which in November 2022, after rescuing over 230 migrants, was prohibited from entering territorial waters and forced to stay at sea for three weeks. Eventually, the vessel sailed towards France and docked in a southern port, causing a dispute between Italy and France.[248]

The new decree partially modifies Law Decree no 130/2020 concerning the power of the Minister of the Interior, in agreement with the Minister of Defence and the Minister of Infrastructure and Transport, after having informed the Prime Minister, to issue orders to 'limit or prohibit transiting or docking of vessels in the territorial sea'.[249] Specifically, the decree introduces a new limitation to such power and states that it cannot be exercised if a number of conditions are met, including: where vessels systematically engaged in SAR activities are in possession of the authorisations issued by the flag state and meet the safety requirements to navigate; where the rescued migrants are immediately informed of the possibility to apply for asylum, and information is collected and then provided to the relevant authorities; where the rescuing vessel immediately requests a port to disembark; and where the vessel reaches the port of disembarkation without delays.[250]

As such, the text of the decree presents a number of issues. First, the condition applying only to NGO vessels seems to require specific authorisations and

[247] Luca Masera, 'Il D.L. Piantedosi sulle Operazioni di Soccorso in Mare: L' Ennesimo Tentativo di Impedire Cio' che il Diritto Internazionale Impone e il Problema della Depenalizzazione come Fuga dalla Giurisdizione' (*Sistema Penale*, 13 February 2023), available at: www.sistemapenale.it/it/scheda/masera-il-dl-piantedosi-sulle-operazioni-di-soccorso-in-mare-lennesimo-maldestro-tentativo-di-impedire-cio-che-il-diritto-internazionale-impone-e-il-problema-della-depenalizzazione-come-fuga-dalla-giurisdizione.

[248] Masera, 'Il D.L. Piantedosi sulle Operazioni di Soccorso in Mare' (n 247); Euronews, 'Ocean Viking: Migrant Rescue Ship Allowed to Dock in France after Italy's Refusal' *Euronews* (11 November 2022), available at: www.euronews.com/2022/11/10/ocean-viking-migrant-rescue-ship-allowed-to-dock-in-france-after-italys-refusal.

[249] Decreto Legge 2 gennaio 2023, n 1, art 1(1).

[250] ibid.

characteristics in relation to SAR activities, in addition to those imposed by the flag state, despite the recent ECJ decision regarding the *Sea-Watch 3* and *Sea-Watch 4* which prohibited exactly these types of administrative measures.[251]

More generally, the provisions are vague, must be read together with other pieces of legislation to which they refer,[252] and leave wide room for arbitrary decisions, in violation of the principles of legality and legal certainty – for instance, it is unclear what the terms 'immediately' and 'without delays' mean in relation to having requested a port for disembarkation and sailing to the indicated port, respectively.

The obligations imposed on ship captains to proceed immediately to an assigned port entail a prohibition on NGO vessels staying in international waters after a first rescue has been carried out and waiting in case other rescue operations are necessary. They do not prohibit these vessels from carrying out multiple rescues per se, which would be in clear contradiction to the obligation to assist anyone in distress at sea[253] and in conflict with the international conventions on the law of the sea and human rights – the obligation to rescue is absolute in character, and applies regardless of whether the persons to be saved are migrants or not.[254] By contrast, on this point, international law does not provide clear guidance.[255] Also, the other listed conditions for NGOs to meet are not exhaustive and aim to identify a number of reasons to justify the intervention of the Minister of the Interior. According to Masera, this approach recalls that of the 2017 Code of Conduct, but is now enforceable.[256]

The new decree also adds two types of sanctions, which are issued by the Prefect who has territorial competence over a case.[257] In the event of violation of the ministerial order, the penalties applied are administrative fines ranging between €10,00 and €50,000 on ship captains and shipowners, as well as the accessory administrative sanction of administrative detention of the vessel used to commit the violation for two months – besides the applicable criminal penalties if a crime is committed.[258] In case of violation of the requirement to provide information to the authorities or failure to comply with their requests, a fine of between €2,000 and €10,000 is applied, together with administrative detention of the vessel for 20 days.[259] In both scenarios, for repeated breaches of these

[251] I Papanicolopulu and G Losi, 'La Sea Watch Davanti alla Corte di Giustizia dell'Unione European: Rapporti tra Fonti, Rapporti tra Stati e Regolazione (Indiretta) delle Attivita' di Soccorso in Mare' (2023) 1 *Diritto, Immigrazione e Cittadinanza* 235, 254.

[252] Interview with Giulia Losi, PhD Candidate, Università di Milano Bicocca, Milano (2 May 2023).

[253] Middle East Monitor, 'NGOs: Italy's New Decree "Obstructs" Migrant Rescue Operations' (*Middle East Monitor*, 6 January 2023), available at: www.middleeastmonitor.com/20230106-ngos-italys-new-decree-obstructs-migrant-rescue-operations-in-mediterranean/.

[254] See ch 3, sections II.A, II.B and III.A.

[255] Masera, 'Il D.L. Piantedosi sulle Operazioni di Soccorso in Mare' (n 247) 16.

[256] ibid 10.

[257] Decreto Legge 2 gennaio 2023, n 1, arts 1(2-quater), 1 (2-septies).

[258] ibid art 1 (2-quater).

[259] ibid art 1 (2-sexies).

provisions, as an accessory administrative sanction, it is possible to confiscate the ship[260] and immediately seize the vessel as a precaution,[261] which could further hinder NGOs' SAR operations. Therefore, the decree again changes the regime of sanctions applicable to NGOs by switching from criminal to administrative law, circumventing judicial control over the executive's power and orders.

In practice, the decree has created three types of problem. First, after NGOs receive orders to disembark at a specified port, they are left with no instructions on what to do if they need to carry out additional rescues (it is reported that the Italian MRCCs do not reply to NGO calls after they have assigned the port for disembarkation) and thus are left in an uncertain situation – torn between the obligation to rescue on one hand and the new provisions on the other.

Second, the Italian MRCCs have assigned ports far from the area of the rescue – according to NGOs, on more than 60 occasions between December 2022 and the end of August 2023[262] – sometimes in another Italian region, such as Ancona, La Spezia, or Ravenna, wasting NGO resources and placing the strained migrants under additional stress due to the longer navigation times.[263] NGOs have criticised this practice for violating the law of the sea and specifically the provisions on disembarkation, and for discriminating against NGO vessels, considering that other ships are allowed to disembark in Sicily or Calabria. In response, the government has argued that such a practice is necessary because the reception system in Sicily is under stress and there are not enough services for all the arrivals.[264]

Third, the new provisions seem to have allowed the authorities to expect access to NGOs' information, including informatic data, without any previous judicial authorisation.[265]

[260] Paolo Gentilucci, 'Il Nuovo Decreto Immigrazione e il Ruolo delle ONG' (*Diritto*, 5 January 2023), available at: www.diritto.it/il-nuovo-decreto-immigrazione-e-il-ruolo-delle-ong/. Decreto Legge 2 gennaio 2023, n 1, art 1 (2-quinquies).

[261] Decreto Legge 2 gennaio 2023, n 1, art 1(2-quinquies). Administrative detention (*fermo amministrativo*) is time limited and is used to allow inspections to be carried out. It differs from seizure (*sequestro*) of the vessel because it does not have a precautionary nature. The seizure is necessarily provisional, adopted while a decision is taken on whether to confiscate (*confisca*) the property. Confiscation is an accessory penalty which is imposed following a conviction and which consists of an actual expropriation in favour of the state.

[262] Statewatch.org, 'Urgent Warning: More Deaths at Sea, NGO Ships Blocked' (*Statewatch*, 30 August 2023), available at: www.statewatch.org/news/2023/august/urgent-warning-more-deaths-at-sea-ngo-ships-blocked/.

[263] Interview with Giulia Crescini, Immigration lawyer, Rome (online, 8 May 2023); interview with Marco Borraccetti, Associate Professor of European Union Law, Università di Bologna (online, 2 May 2023).

[264] Alessandra Ziniti, 'Intervista al Ministro dell'Interno. Piantedosi: "I Soccorsi in Mare Garantiti dallo Stato. Le ONG Fanno la Spola Solo con la Tripolitania. Come Mai?"' *La Repubblica* (31 December 2022), available at: www.repubblica.it/cronaca/2022/12/31/news/decreto_rave_migranti_piantedosi-381380862.

[265] Interview with Crescini (n 263).

Some NGOs, such as the German Sea-Eye, have stated that they will not comply with the new provisions.[266] In particular, Sea-Eye argues that the new provisions seek to regulate foreign ships' activities in international waters and apply sanctions upon arrival in the Italian territorial sea. However, such activities can only be regulated by the flag state. Moreover, although Italy can coordinate and give instructions on SAR operations in its SAR area, their enforcement remains with the flag state, according to both international and German law. As such, they argue that Italy is violating the principle of freedom of navigation as recognised by article 87 of UNCLOS.[267] Recently, on 30 June 2023, Sea-Eye filed a lawsuit at the Civil Court of *Chieti against Italy* for the 20-day long administrative detention of their *Sea-Eye 4* vessel and a related fine.[268] The penalties were imposed because the *Sea-Eye 4* rescued migrants from two different vessels in the course of the same operation, in breach of the new provisions. Tensions rose between Italy and Germany when Germany's intervention in the episode, as the flag state of the *Sea-Eye 4*, was disregarded.[269] The controversy between Italy and Germany further escalated in September 2023, after the German government granted funding to two NGOs active in the Mediterranean.[270]

In addition to the Sea-Eye's lawsuit, it should be noted that, in July 2023, Médecins Sans Frontières and a number of other NGOs have filed a complaint with the European Commission arguing that Law no 15/2023 and the related practice of the Italian authorities to assign distant ports for disembarkation, are in breach of EU provisions and international law.[271]

In conclusion, this decree is at the centre of new controversies and represents only one of the deterrence measures that the Italian government is taking against migrants[272] and humanitarian actors. Considering its recent adoption, it

[266] Angela Giuffrida, 'Sea Rescue Charities Rebel against Italian Anti-immigration Rules' *Guardian* (30 December 2022), available at: www.theguardian.com/world/2022/dec/30/sea-rescue-charities-rebel-against-italian-anti-immigration-rules.

[267] Sea-Eye, 'Sea-Eye Criticizes Italy's New Code of Conduct for Sea Rescue NGOs' (Sea Eye, 30 December 2022), available at: sea-eye.org/en/sea-eye-criticizes-italys-new-code-of-conduct-for-sea-rescue-ngos/.

[268] Sea-Eye, 'Sea-Eye Sues Italy for Unlawful Detention of Sea-Eye 4' (Sea-Eye, 3 July 2023), available at: sea-eye.org/en/sea-eye-sues-italy-for-unlawful-detention-of-sea-eye-4/.

[269] ibid.

[270] Reuters, 'Italy Criticises Germany for Funding Migrant Charity Groups' *Reuters* (22 September 2023), available at: www.reuters.com/world/europe/italy-criticises-germany-funding-migrant-charity-groups-2023-09-24/.

[271] Filip Lamparter, 'Challanging Restrictions on NGO Search and Rescue Operations in Italy: MSF's Complaint to the European Commission' (*humanrightscenter*, 14 September 2023), available at: www.humanrightscentre.org/blog/challenging-restrictions-ngo-search-and-rescue-operations-italy-msfs-complaint-european. Within 12 months, the Commission will have to decide whether or not to start an infringement procedure against Italy for breaching EU law.

[272] For instance, in September 2023, the Ministry of Interior issued a decree requiring asylum seekers to pay a bail of €4,938 to avoid detention. Decreto Interministeriale 14 Settembre 2023. However, shortly after its entry into force, the Specialised Section of the Court of Catania did not uphold the detention of a Tunisian asylum seeker, disapplying the Decreto Interministeriale 14 Settembre 2023. According to the Court, the decree is unlawful because it breaches EU law and the Italian Constitution. Trib Catania, Ordinanza 29.09.2023, NRG 10461/2023. In October 2023, in a similar case, the Specialised Section of the Court of Potenza reached the same conclusion. Trib Potenza, Ordinanza 12.10.2023, NRG 3698/2023.

remains to be seen how the courts and the European Commission will respond to its application.

XI. CONCLUSION

In this chapter I have discussed how, since 2017, the successive Italian governments have expanded and shifted their range of strategies for limiting the activities of NGOs in the Mediterranean, including adopting new provisions of various kinds to target NGO vessels and their crews, launching criminal investigations, seizing their boats, carrying out administrative inspections, and damaging their reputation. Overall, although these responses have involved a mix of criminal and administrative measures, they are characterised by a 'theological continuity, all inspired by a substantial diffidence towards humanitarian actors'.[273]

This assault on NGOs represents part of a trend in the EU and its Member States to criminalise and police solidarity with migrants on the grounds of anti-smuggling policies.[274] Arguably, the Italian government has been the main trendsetter. Of the 63 administrative or criminal proceedings faced by civil society actors involved in SAR operations between 2017 and October 2023 in Germany, Italy, Malta, the Netherlands and Spain, the large majority have taken place in Italy.[275] In particular, Article 12 TUI has been a powerful tool in the hands of prosecutors due to the 'lack of financial gain element of the crime' of aiding and abetting illegal immigration.[276] Also, the related provisions similar to those used against mafia crimes[277] have allowed its 'over-extensive reach'.[278] Thus, in Italy, complying with the duty to rescue has exposed shipmasters and crews to a number of charges, including for facilitating illegal immigration and association with criminal organisations.[279] However, most cases have been discontinued either for lack of evidence or because the Italian judges established that the duty to save lives at sea prevails over security and immigration control interests.

Despite this, and although no investigation to date has established NGOs' direct association with smugglers,[280] Italian populist parties and media continue to take the view that NGOs indirectly facilitate irregular immigration, and therefore continue to adopt new approaches to limit their activities. Some officials also see ambiguity as to the legality of certain SAR NGO practices, such as systematically navigating in the Libyan SAR zone and requesting to disembark

[273] Masera, 'Il D.L. Piantedosi sulle Operazioni di Soccorso in Mare' (n 247).
[274] Moreno-Lax et al (n 128) 96.
[275] FRA, 'June 2023 Update' (n 141).
[276] Minetti (n 27) 343.
[277] ibid.
[278] ibid.
[279] L Carballo Piñeiro, 'Occupational Hazards in the Light of the Maritime Migration Challenge' in PK Mukherjee et al (eds), *Maritime Law in Motion* (Cham, Springer International Publishing, 2020) 85.
[280] Cusumano and Villa (n 4) 24.

in Italy rather than their vessels' flag state.[281] Overall, these initiatives against NGOs have had repercussions, both in terms of reducing NGOs' presence at sea and compromising ROL principles. In this regard, previous discussions have pointed out how such criminalisation policies have far-reaching consequences on society, justifying illiberal policies that affect not only migrants but also other minority groups[282] and general trust in national and EU responses.

In particular, the principles of legality, legal certainty, separation of powers, equality before the law, and compliance with human rights have all been affected in this context. First, NGOs operate in the absence of a clear legal framework that takes into consideration their contribution to states' SAR systems. Some authors have commented that they 'constitute a *tertium genus* compared to public or private ships': on the one hand, they are not subject to several provisions applicable to state ships and on the other, although they are similar to private ships, they differ because their only reason for navigating is rescuing human lives.[283] Therefore, such a legal gap contributes to triggering informal and sometimes unlawful responses and practices on the side of the relevant authorities.

Second, some governments, ministers and prosecutors have abused their powers on several occasions, including by adopting measures in breach of the principle of hierarchy of legal sources for political aims; by exploiting the application of Article 12 TUI and the related provisions to investigate NGOs and prevent their activities at sea; by adopting 'emergency' legislation despite the absence of the legal prerequisites; and by claiming competences belonging to other state actors.

Third, the principle of equality before the law has been affected by the adoption of ad hoc measures that especially target NGOs, such as the directives adopted by Salvini, but also the emergency decrees during the Covid-19 pandemic, the application of safety of navigation measures, and Law Decree no 1/2023.

Finally, the overall outcome has been that of weakening migrants' human rights, as well as the certainty of the law,[284] for example where the discourse of securitisation competes with and overrides humanitarian concerns.[285] It should

[281] Cuttitta (n 12) 649; Romano (n 77) 45; interview with former ship captain of unit participating in Mare Nostrum (email, 15 February 2023); interview with Italian Coast Guard official (email, 28 June 2023).

[282] S Carrera et al, 'The Three Faces of Policing the Mobility Society in the EU' in S Carrera et al, *Policing Humanitarianism: EU Policies Against Human Smuggling and their Impact on Civil Society* (Oxford, Hart Publishing, 2019) 179.

[283] Brigida (n 54) 124.

[284] E Cusumano and K Gombeer, 'In Deep Waters: The Legal, Humanitarian and Political Implications of Closing Italian Ports to Migrant Rescuers' (2020) 25 *Mediterranean Politics* 245, available at: www.tandfonline.com/doi/full/10.1080/13629395.2018.1532145?scroll=top&needAccess=true.

[285] For a general discussion of Salvini's strategy of closing ports before the Covid emergency, see: V Moreno-Lax, D Ghezelbash and N Klein, 'Between Life, Security and Rights: Framing the Interdiction of "Boat Migrants" in the Central Mediterranean and Australia' (2019) 32 *Leiden Journal of International Law* 715.

also be highlighted how domestic actors' use of 'law and order' arguments to justify their policies has instead created tensions between democratic institutions. Meanwhile, the policies themselves have proven to be largely ineffective in preventing irregular sea arrivals.

On the other hand, the courts have reacted by clarifying that, even in cases where NGOs could be found to have committed the crime of aiding and abetting illegal immigration, these actions could be justified by the state of necessity or fulfilment of a duty – the duty to save lives at sea. Therefore, the courts have intervened by making 'a clear statement of the position of the judiciary in this uncertain climate'.[286] However, Salvini's closed port policy and orders remain under judicial review in the case against Open Arms as to whether his actions were legitimate, thus illustrating how the ongoing national and international ad hoc responses to sea migration are not only ineffective but also the cause of institutional tensions.[287] In other areas, such as that concerning the safety of navigation provisions, a number of issues remain unaddressed, and the courts have been able to give only partial answers.[288]

[286] Minetti (n 27) 349.

[287] Luca Masera, 'La Cassazione sul caso Rackete: la strategia dei porti chiusi è contraria alla disciplina dei soccorsi in mare' (*Questione Giustizia*, 26 February 2020), available at: www.questionegiustizia.it/articolo/la-cassazione-sul-caso-rackete-la-strategia-dei-porti-chiusi-e-contraria-alla-disciplina-dei-soccorsi-in-mare_26-02-2020.php.

[288] Papanicolopulu and Losi (n 251) 254.

7

Final Reflections

I. INTRODUCTION

THIS BOOK DEMONSTRATES that, from the perspective of the rule of law (ROL), the current national and regional responses to sea migration in the Mediterranean are a cause of serious concern and need to be replaced by methods that are more sophisticated, better coordinated and free from political interference.

In particular, these responses are marked by a complex and fragmented system of laws and policies that regulate different actors, interests and activities. The research confirms that these responses are characterised by a 'multiplication of legal, policy and operational developments'[1] that cause diverse areas and levels of regulation to interact and sometimes conflict, creating uncertainty about rights and duties as well as tensions among the actors involved (eg, between states or different authorities within the same state as well as between NGOs and states).

Moreover, the informal, sometimes unlawful practices of states involving pushbacks at the external borders[2] and the lack of implementation of international and national law due to political considerations[3] raise important questions of accountability and institutional governance. This scenario has prompted legal challenges and led to numerous judicial cases wherein the courts, tasked with implementing the ROL and constraining the abuse of power, have a multifaceted role. While in some areas, the courts have reinstated the ROL and upheld

[1] S Carrera and L den Hertog, 'Whose *Mare*? Rule of Law Challenges in the Field of European Border Surveillance in the Mediterranean' (Paper in *Liberty and Security in Europe* no 79/January 2015, Brussels, CEPS) 1.

[2] S Fine, 'All at Sea: Europe's Crisis of Solidarity on Migration' (Policy Brief, European Council on Foreign Relations, October 2019), available at: ecfr.eu/wpcontent/uploads/all_at_sea_europes_crisis_of_solidarity_on_migration.pdf; J Virkkunen and M Piiponen, 'Informal Practices and the Rule of Law: Russia, Migration and the "Arctic Route"' in R Turaeva and R Urinboyev (eds), *Labour, Mobility and Informal Practices in Russia, Central Asia and Eastern Europe: Power, Institutions and Mobile Actors in Transnational Space* (London, Routledge, 2021).

[3] S Klepp, 'Malta and the Rescue of Unwanted Migrants at Sea: Negotiating the Humanitarian Law of the Sea and the Contested Redesigning Borders' in H Schwenken and S Ruß-Sattar (eds), *New Border and Citizenship Politics* (London, Palgrave Macmillan, 2014); FL Gatta, 'Migration and the Rule of (Human Rights) Law: Two "Crises" Looking in the Same Mirror' (2019) 15 *Croatian Yearbook of European Law & Policy* 99.

individual rights, in others they have been very cautious not to overstep their competence. Another restraining factor upon the influence of the courts are the practical and legal limits on sea migrants' access to justice.

Finally, the ROL framework reveals that anti-migrant practices and agreements in the name of 'security' can in fact undermine the very foundations of 'law and order'. As the case of Italy shows, they not only provide inefficient, confusing and divisive answers to the questions posed by sea migration, they also weaken human rights, create imbalances between the branches of government, legitimise emergency rule and weaken constitutional guarantees.

In this chapter, after providing a summary of the main ROL issues concerning the responses to sea migration (section II), I focus on how the relevant multi-level regulatory framework (section III) makes it difficult to establish a coherent system, and how the multiple actors involved (section IV) produce contradictions that challenge the ROL. Then I discuss the role of the courts and the limited access to justice for migrants whose rights have been breached (section V). I also reflect on the limitations of the ROL framework in the context of sea migration (section VI) and draw some final conclusions (section VII). Besides summarising and providing commentary on the Italian case, the chapter points to its relevance from a broader international perspective.

II. SUMMARY OF MAIN ROL ISSUES AFFECTED BY RESPONSES TO SEA MIGRATION

In all three thematic areas explored in this book – states' failures to carry out effective and coordinated search and rescue (SAR) operations (chapter four); pushbacks and pullbacks of intercepted migrants to unsafe places (chapter five); and the adoption of measures criminalising and preventing NGOs' SAR operations (chapter six) – I note how ROL issues are closely interlinked. Moreover, each thematic area is characterised by multi-level frameworks involving the action and interaction of several actors with different aims, as well as by critical litigation which has occasionally upheld individual rights but at the same time been restrained by the limits of judicial competence. Furthermore, access to justice is complicated by other factors, such as jurisdictional and objective barriers relating to the physical space of the sea and the particular obstacles that may be faced by migrants, such as language barriers, lack of knowledge of the legal system and few or no means to instruct a lawyer.

The analysis of SAR operations and services in the Central Mediterranean in chapter four reveals several episodes where the arbitrariness of responses as well as lawlessness (ie, poor application of international and national legal norms) led to uncertainty and unpredictability. Whereas legislation and written policies exist on how to respond to vessels in distress, a few legal gaps remain and practices are not always lawful. This is especially true when, in the absence of a common EU approach on the matter, SAR activities take place in the overlapping SAR regions of Italy and Malta and when the respective authorities engage in disputes over where disembarkation shall take place[4] or who shall coordinate operations in international waters. These disagreements prejudice the provision of immediate assistance and leave migrants 'dependent [on] the political goodwill of States'.[5] The complexity of the circumstances is aggravated by interstate relations which are characterised by functional (rather than territorial) boundaries and which frequently elude judicial checks.[6]

Complicating the matter is a major legal gap arising from the fact that Malta did not sign the amendments to the 2004 SOLAS and SAR Conventions. This allows Malta to justify its avoidance of SAR activities and to apply a different interpretation of relevant legal terms. As a consequence, the responses to incidents at sea diverge according to which state is involved. For instance, Malta's interpretation of the term 'distress' 'calls for a situation of imminent danger whereby failure of immediate assistance would lead to injury or death. Conversely, Italy classifies all unseaworthy vessels as being in distress'.[7] Therefore, many operations and disembarkation activities in the joint SAR zone with Malta are based on ad hoc solutions between the two countries,[8] with serious consequences for the principle of legality.

Additionally, the failure to provide assistance to distressed migrants at sea without delay reveals an issue of discrimination. The law on SAR aims to protect the life of all sea travellers without any distinction as to their immigration status. However, in practice, the disembarkation of sea migrants has proven to be more difficult than for other seafarers.[9] As Spijkerboer has commented, many sea migrants die 'not because they may be targeted by states of destination, but because they are ignored'.[10] Discrimination in the decisions on whether or not to render such assistance or failures to coordinate and cooperate with other states and actors to provide assistance is, however, difficult to link to specific acts of individuals.[11] As such, accountability is hard to establish.

[4] ÁJ García-Carriazo, 'Small Island, Big Issue: Malta and its Search and Rescue Region – SAR' (2019) 7 *Paix et Securité Internationales* 299, 319.

[5] ibid.

[6] G Palombella, 'The Rule of Law and its Conception between "National" and "International"' in B Faedda (ed), *Rule of Law: Cases, Strategies and Interpretations* (Vicenza, Ronzani Edizioni Scientifiche, 2021) 79.

[7] International Convention for the Safety of Life at Sea (London, 1 November 1974) 1184 UNTS 278 (SOLAS Convention), Annex, ch V, reg 33-1; S Aquilina, 'The Application of Human Rights Law and Refugee Law at Sea: A Focus on Search and Rescue Operations' (Master's Thesis, University of Malta, 2021) 19.

[8] S Klepp, 'A Double Bind: Malta and the Rescue of Unwanted Migrants at Sea, a Legal Anthropological Perspective on the Humanitarian Law of the Sea' (2011) 23 *International Journal of Refugee Law* 538, 550.

[9] T Spijkerboer, 'Wasted Lives. Borders and the Right to Life of People Crossing Them' (2017) 86 *Nordic Journal of International Law* 1, 17.

[10] ibid 27.

[11] ibid.

In chapter five, I discussed how Italy stopped engaging in direct pushbacks after the *Hirsi* case. However, Italy has adopted a strategy of delegating pullbacks to other authorities. In particular, to this end, Italy has entered into cooperation and externalisation agreements with North African countries in order to enhance border controls. These do not comply with the legal procedures requiring such agreements to undergo scrutiny by Parliament and to be published. Furthermore, the agreements delegate pullbacks to entities that do not guarantee human rights and make it difficult to establish states' accountability.[12] In particular, the agreement with Libya has been reinforced through the creation of a large Libyan SAR zone, despite Libya's lack of recognition as either a legitimate state or a place of safety (POS).[13] The opacity on this matter is exacerbated by the role of the European Union (EU) and other Member States in the facilitation of operational collaboration with North African countries.[14]

In chapter six, I analysed how various Italian governments have adopted strategies to prevent non-governmental organisations (NGOs) from engaging in SAR operations and disembarking migrants to a safe place. These strategies include criminalising their activities, bringing charges against them, using administrative measures within the Port State Control framework,[15] exploiting the state of emergency during the pandemic to prohibit the entry of foreign vessels into territorial waters, and more recently adopting Law Decree no 1/2023 to limit NGOs' rescue operations. Some of these measures did not comply with the formal legal requirements, such as Interministerial Decree no 150 of 7 April 2020, issued in the context of the Covid-19 health emergency,[16] and the 2018 ministerial directives aimed at preventing the disembarkation of migrants from NGO vessels. Besides being adopted by authorities without the legal competence to do so,[17] these instruments violated the SAR Convention, its implementing Law no 147/1989, migrants' human rights, and the principle of non-discrimination on the ground of nationality, as they targeted migrants saved by foreign vessels outside the Italian SAR zone. Others, such as Law Decree no 53 of 14 June 2019, entailed the attribution of new competencies to the Minister of Interior, introducing the power to prohibit foreign vessels

[12] A Sciurba, 'Quel che Accade nel Mediterraneo Centrale come Emblema del Lato Oscuro del Diritto' in A Sciurba and M Starita (eds), 'Il Lato Oscuro della Criminalizzazione' (2021) XXI *Dirutto e Questioni Pubbliche*, Special Issue 7, 9.

[13] ibid.

[14] A Sánchez Legido, 'The Walls of Fortress Europe: Externalization of Migration Control and the Rule of Law' (2019) 23 *Spanish Yearbook of International Law* 345, 349.

[15] Sciurba (n 12) 11. See ch 3, section VI and ch 6, section VIII.

[16] A Pitino, 'Controllo delle frontiere italiane e immigrazione nell'emergenza sanitaria Covid-19: tra *soft law* dell'Unione europea e misure nazionali' (2021) 1 *Corti Supreme e Salute* 1, 22–25. See also, AM Pelliconi and M Goldoni, 'La Banalità dei Porti Chiusi per Decreto. Osservazioni sui Profili di Legittimità del Decreto Interministeriale 150/2020' (2020) 2 *Diritto, Immigrazione e Cittadinanza* 219, 221; ASGI, 'Diritti in Rotta. L'Esperimento delle Navi Quarantena e i Principali Profili di Criticità' (ASGI, 23 April 2021) 9, available at: inlimine.asgi.it/lesperimento-delle-navi-quarantena/.

[17] Pitino (n 16) 22–25.

that have carried out rescue operations from entering Italian waters – a power belonging to the Minister of Infrastructure and Transport.[18] Other EU countries, similarly under the sway of populist narratives, have also adopted measures to prevent NGOs' activities in the Mediterranean, contributing to a decrease in SAR operations.[19]

All the provisions and policies applied or adopted against NGOs raise issues as far as the principle of legality is concerned: the abuse of criminal law represented by the several investigations launched into the alleged crimes of aiding and abetting illegal immigration and even criminal association to commit crimes; the unjustified persistence of some prosecutors in pursuing these cases; and the misuse of administrative law on the part of the Port Authorities when ordering the detention of NGO vessels based on the Port State Control provisions.[20]

In conclusion, drawing on the ROL concept, my analysis of the aforementioned themes reveals that Italy's responses to sea migration have affected not only migrants' rights, but the domestic and international legal systems and the foundations of the state. In the next section I reflect on how the fragmented regulatory framework creates room for arbitrary decisions, policies and tactics.

III. MULTI-LEVEL REGULATORY FRAMEWORK: OVERLAPPING AND CONFLICTING PROVISIONS CAUSING UNCERTAINTY AROUND THE LEGAL OBLIGATIONS

The framework applicable to sea migration comprises a complex web of rules found in distinct areas of law, which is strongly shaped by international and EU law. Moreover, at the national level, the provisions implementing international and EU obligations are found in differently hierarchised laws belonging to distinct legal areas.[21] Some scholars point out that the provisions of the law of the sea are 'state-centred': they are drafted for regulating maritime navigation[22] rather than for rescuing sea migrants. Some instruments, such as the SAR Convention, were adopted in a different historical context, without the phenomenon of sea migration in mind.[23] For this reason, Papanicolopulu notes

[18] Sciurba (n 12) 11.

[19] I Lloyd-Damnjanovic, 'Criminalization of Search-and-Rescue Operations in the Mediterranean Has Been Accompanied by Rising Migrant Death Rate' (Report, Migration Policy Institute, 9 October 2020), available at: reliefweb.int/report/world/criminalization-search-and-rescue-operations-mediterranean-has-been-accompanied-rising; FRA, 'June 2022 Update – Search and Rescue (SAR) Operations in the Mediterranean and Fundamental Rights' (FRA, 20 June 2022), available at: fra.europa.eu/en/publication/2022/june-2022-update-ngo-ships-sar-activities.

[20] Sciurba (n 12) 11.

[21] M d'Amico and C Siccardi, 'La Tutela die Diritti Costituzionali dei Migrant ai Confini' in M Ambrosini, M d'Amico and E Perassi (eds), *Migrazioni, Confini, Diritti Umani* (Milano, Milano University Press, 2022) 25–26.

[22] I Papanicolopulu, 'Human Rights and the Law of the Sea' in D Joseph Attard et al (eds), *The IMLI Manual on International Maritime Law Volume I: The Law of the Sea* (Oxford, OUP, 2014).

[23] Sciurba (n 12) 8.

how the formulation of the law of the sea primarily revolves around the delineation of duties rather than the assertion of rights.[24] On the other hand, others argue that it is evident that the law of the sea aims to protect the lives of individuals, although this aim is not framed in terms of human rights. According to the UN Open-ended Informal Consultative Process on Oceans and the Law of the Sea, '[h]uman rights and refugee law principles are an important point of reference in handling rescue at sea situations'.[25] Furthermore, the UNCLOS and SAR Conventions refer, although in general terms, to the need to comply with other international obligations and rights.[26] Therefore, neither the law of the sea nor human rights should be seen as an autonomous regime.[27] However, Moreno-Lax notes how states often interpret the SAR obligations as being separate from those 'arising from refugee law and human rights',[28] and their relationship is debated. In situations such as this, some scholars have talked about 'fragmentation' of the legal framework,[29] as the relevant provisions are not within 'self-contained' bodies of laws[30] – a circumstance which I argue is detrimental to the principle of legal certainty.

The overlapping of anti-trafficking and anti-smuggling legislation with the duty to save lives at sea further complicates the scenario and generates contradictions, as the former places an emphasis on criminalisation and securitisation rather than protection.[31] This has been pointed out by authors such as Mitsilegas

[24] Papanicolopulu (n 22) 510.

[25] UNHCR, 'The Treatment of Persons Rescued at Sea: Conclusions and Recommendations from Recent Meetings and Expert Round Tables Convened by the Office of the United Nations High Commissioner for Refugees' Report of the Office of the UNHCR, UN Doc A/AC.259/17 (11 April 2008) para 8.

[26] See United Nations Convention on the Law of the Sea (Montego Bay, 10 December 1982) UN Doc 1833 UNTS 396 (UNCLOS Convention) last paragraph of Preamble and art 146 (referring to protection of human life); International Convention on Maritime Search and Rescue (Hamburg, 27 April 1979) 1405 UNTS 97 (SAR Convention) Art II.2.

[27] For a general discussion of human rights law not being a self-contained regime, see R Ferguson, 'The Fragmentation of International Law; the World Trade Organization and International Human Rights Regimes' in R Ferguson, *The Right to Food and the World Trade Organization's Rules on Agriculture* (Leiden, Brill, 2018) 46.

[28] V Moreno-Lax, 'Seeking Asylum in the Mediterranean: Against a Fragmentary Reading of EU Member States' Obligations Accruing at Sea' (2011) 23 *International Journal of Refugee Law* 174, 177.

[29] T Treves, 'Fragmentation of International Law. The Judicial Perspective' (2007) 23 *Comunicazioni e Studi* 821; regarding the issue of fragmentation between different areas of international law, see ILC, 'Fragmentation of International Law: Difficulties Arising from the Diversification and Expansion of International Law' Report of the Study Group of the ILC, UN Doc A/CN.4/L.682 (13 April 2006).

[30] Aquilina (n 7) 7; T Treves, 'Human Rights and the Law of the Sea' (2010) 28 *Berkeley Journal of International Law* 1; N Klein, 'A Case for Harmonizing Laws on Maritime Interceptions of Irregular Migrants' (2014) 63 *International & Comparative Law Quarterly* 787, 790.

[31] V Mitsilegas, 'Extraterritorial Immigration Control, Preventive Justice and the Rule of Law in Turbulent Times: Lessons from the Anti-Smuggling Crusade' in S Carrera, J Santos Vara and T Strik (eds), *Constitutionalising the External Dimensions of EU Migration Policies in Times of Crises: Legality, Rule of Law and Fundamental Rights Reconsidered* (Cheltenham, Edward Elgar Publishing, 2019) 293.

who have highlighted the transfer of 'security considerations of crime control to the field of migration'.[32] Reinforcing these provisions Regulation 2019/1896 introduced surveillance systems and cooperation with third countries to enable interceptions of illegal migrants in the context of Frontex's activities.[33]

In circumstances where different provisions of the same hierarchical weight overlap,[34] some commentators have discussed 'legal pluralism', which on occasion allows states to cherry-pick 'provisions that allow them to justify a securitised approach to protect state interests'.[35] This is illustrated by how the words 'POS' and 'distress' are subject to different interpretations depending on the country applying them. Critics of such practices argue that certain human rights are to be accorded a higher value in instances where there exists an overlap or conflict between them and other norms of international law.[36]

The domestic implementation of international and EU legislation has created additional issues. For instance, I have shown how under Article 12 of Legislative Decree no 286/1998, which criminalises the aiding and abetting of illegal immigration, humanitarian actors need to prove that they acted out of a state of necessity or exercised a legal duty, thus leaving room for legal uncertainty and the opening of judicial investigations.[37] Moreover, Article 12 of Legislative Decree no 286/1998 was framed to connect trafficking and smuggling to the fight against transnational crime, which tends to privilege 'a preventive rather than rehabilitative function'[38] of criminal law, allowing a number of prosecutors and politicians to misuse it to pursue an 'anti-immigration political agenda'.[39] According to Minetti, this has resulted in 'a diminishment of the Rule of Law'.[40] Similar measures to restrict NGOs' activities have been taken in other countries too, such as Greece, Spain and Hungary.[41]

[32] ibid, citing D Bigo, *Polices en Réseaux: L'Expérience Européenne* (Paris, Presses Sciences Po, 1996). See also, GL Gatta and S Zirulia, 'Introduction' in GL Gatta, V Mitsilegas and S Zirulia (eds), *Controlling Immigration through Criminal Law: European and Comparative Perspectives on 'Crimmigration'* (Oxford, Hart Publishing, 2020) 1–2.

[33] F Vassallo Paleologo, 'La Finzione della Zona SAR "Libica": Quale Giurisdizione sulle Acque Internazionali?' in G Bevilacqua (ed), *Sicurezza Umana negli Spazi Navigabili: Sfide Comuni e Nuove Tendenze – Human Security in Navigable Spaces: Common Challenges and New Trends* (Napoli, Editoriale Scientifica, 2021). See ch 3, section III.A.

[34] E Rigo, 'Arbitrary Law Making and Unorderable Subjectivities in Legal Theoretical Approaches to Migration' (2020) 14(2) *Nordic Journal of Applied Ethics* 71–88, 73.

[35] A Orav, 'Search and Rescue Efforts for Mediterranean Migrants' (Briefing, European Parliamentary Research Service, 2022) 9.

[36] Ferguson (n 27) 50. See also, d'Amico and Siccardi (n 21) 24.

[37] F Alagna, 'The Continuation of Criminalization by Other Means: The Role of the Judicial Agency in the Italian Policing of Humanitarian Assistance at Sea' (2022) *Mediterranean Politics* 1, 12, available at: www.tandfonline.com/doi/full/10.1080/13629395.2022.2135072.

[38] M Minetti, 'The Facilitators Package, Penal Populism and the Rule of Law: Lessons from Italy' (2022) 11 *New Journal of European Criminal Law* 335, 349.

[39] ibid.

[40] ibid.

[41] S Carrera et al, *Policing Humanitarianism: EU Policies against Human Smuggling and their Impact on Civil Society* (Oxford, Hart Publishing, 2019) 191.

Cooperation and readmission agreements with third countries may also compromise the ROL. While it may be argued that this approach is flexible and practical and reinforces the security of borders, one should also note the damage it has done to the principles of legality, legal certainty, access to justice and protection of human rights.[42] In Italy, these agreements have been adopted by the executive without ratification by Parliament and without ensuring transparency through publication. They are also worded in general terms, leaving ample discretion to the signatory parties, though the Italian Constitution does not allow the executive such wide freedom in the conclusion of international treaties.[43] Such generality and vagueness confer arbitrary power on the government, as the agreements can be bent to officials' will and used to escape accountability and judicial control.[44] Ultimately, they entrust the oversight of their external borders to third countries and facilitate the repatriation of migrants to the jurisdiction of the latter.[45] The approach that Italy has taken is not unique and is replicated at EU level, in particular with the EU–Turkey agreement.[46] As such, these agreements violate the principle that the government is bound by law to limit arbitrary power (including its own) and 'ensure public order and reasonable governance'.[47]

Furthermore, the Italian government has adopted several measures (discussed in chapter six) with regard to the policing of NGOs in the name of immigration control and security – ie, decree laws, interministerial decrees, ministerial orders – which intermingle or conflict with provisions included in international treaties or the Constitution. This approach, according to Alagna, reflects the tendency 'of the executivization of Italian policy-making, especially in the migration domain'.[48] On some occasions, the executive has used '"heterodox" tools' with 'unclear legal status' for matters that should be regulated by laws[49] and should comply with the generality requirement of the law. While such tools have the benefit of requiring little time to be adopted, they bypass the more complex

[42] For a similar argument concerning informal agreements between the EU and Turkey, see E Kassoti and N Idriz, 'The Informalisation of the EU's External Action in the Field of Migration and Asylum' in E Kassoti and N Idriz (eds), *The Informalisation of the EU's External Action in the Field of Migration and Asylum* (The Hague, TMC Asser Press, 2022) 4.

[43] C Siccardi, *I Diritti Costituzionali dei Migranti in Viaggio: Sulle Rotte del Mediterraneo* (Napoli, Editoriale Scientifica, 2021) 90.

[44] For a general discussion on when vagueness of the law contributes to a deficit in the ROL, see TAO Endicott, 'The Impossibility of the Rule of Law' (1999) 19(1) *Oxford Journal of Legal Studies* 1, 18.

[45] E Olivito, 'Il Cul-de-sac Costituzionale degli Accordi in forma Semplificata: Iniziativa Legislativa Parlamentare ed Esternalizzazione delle Politiche Migratorie' (2018) 24 *Diritto Pubblico* 435, 512; C Molinari, 'EU Readmission Deals and Constitutional Allocation of Powers: Parallel Paths that Need to Cross?' in E Kassoti and N Idriz (eds), *The Informalisation of the EU's External Action in the Field of Migration and Asylum* (The Hague, TMC Asser Press, 2022).

[46] The agreement aims to stop the flow of irregular migrants from Turkey into Europe. Olivito (n 45) 500.

[47] D Haljan, 'Is the Rule of Law a Limit on Popular Sovereignty?' in E Claes, W Devroe and B Keirsblick (eds), *Facing the Limits of the Law* (Berlin, Springer, 2009) 278–79.

[48] Alagna (n 37) 7.

[49] eg, the 2017 Code of Conduct and the directives against NGOs; ibid.

parliamentary procedure and thus 'limit the involvement of parliamentarians, public opinion and judicial review'.[50] Moreover, the executive has sometimes issued emergency decrees without proper justifications for situations that are not exceptional and that have become structural[51] – normalising the suspension of the ordinary operation of the law and creating, in Agamben's words, a way to govern based on 'the state of exception'.[52] In short, the executive has often misused its legislative power by ignoring the obligations of the law of the sea and human rights, undermining the principle of legal certainty, and disturbing the equilibrium between branches of government.

In conclusion, legal fragmentation in the context of sea migration is caused not only by the relevant EU and international legal provisions, but by their implementation at the national level, which increases the uncertainty of the law instead of clarifying the approach to take in cases of conflict between norms. In light of all this, the question is how to achieve coherence between the different levels and areas of legislation. Such coherence could be achieved or approached if the countries concerned were to adopt national legislation to clarify the most disputed issues. However, Kneebone has pointed out that legal systems tend to primarily represent their nationals and consider migrants as 'outsiders', and that the 'notion of territorial-parliamentary-state-sovereignty, which is represented by state borders and national jurisdictions, leads to a legal impasse'.[53] In other words, the same concept of nation is based upon members and boundaries, and membership is necessary even before issues of justice can be addressed.[54] As such, irregular migrants 'are most often outside the law altogether',[55] which leaves their interests underrepresented and their rights difficult to uphold.

The application, interpretation and coherence of the discussed provisions become even more problematic due to the numerous actors involved and their different agendas, as explained in the next section.

IV. MULTIPLE ACTORS, INFORMAL PRACTICES AND ABUSE OF POWER

From chapters four to six, it emerges that responses to sea migration are characterised by the interaction of several state and non-state actors – including migrants, NGOs, commercial vessels, and even different authorities within the same country – which operate according to diverging aims and prevent a

[50] ibid.

[51] d'Amico and Siccardi (n 21) 26.

[52] G Agamben, *Lo Stato di Eccezione* (Torino, Bollati Boringhieri, 2003).

[53] S Kneebone, 'Conclusions on the Rule of Law' in S Kneebone (ed), *Refugees, Asylum Seekers and the Rule of Law: Comparative Perspectives* (New York, CUP, 2009) 304.

[54] M Walzer, *Spheres of Justice: A Defense of Pluralism and Equality* (New York, Columbia University Press, 1996); C Dauvergne, 'Sovereignty, Migration and the Rule of Law in Global Times' (2004) 67 *Modern Law Review* 588, 591.

[55] Dauvergne, 'Sovereignty, Migration and the Rule of Law in Global Times' (n 54) 611–12.

uniform application of the law of the sea and human rights. Some of these actors are located in other jurisdictions and are subject to distinct legal obligations. This 'multiple actors' scenario prevents a uniform application of the law of the sea and human rights. Moreover, these actors often function according to informal practices which become blurred, cause uncertainty and circumvent accountability[56] – an aspect conceptualised by Thompson as 'the problem of many hands'.[57]

Whereas separate studies would be needed to investigate the role of these actors and their joint responsibility in more detail, here I limit the analysis to highlighting that, as concerns *non-state actors*, the public task of carrying out SAR operations has been partially performed since 2017 by commercial vessels and NGOs, which do not have sufficient institutional power or financial resources to rescue large numbers of migrants. A number of issues continue to affect their ability to provide assistance to sea migrants, especially the frequent failure of states to promptly coordinate or allow disembarkation to a place of safety. When rescues occur outside their SAR zone, Italy (among other EU states) has been shown to adopt ad hoc responses[58] that jeopardise the principle of legal certainty.[59] Moreover, NGOs' lack of 'legitimisation'[60] for their systematic SAR activities is a grey area, as they are not formally part of the legal framework of the law of the sea. Both the international sea conventions and the relevant national legislation indicate that the intervention of non-state actors is to be relied upon only in exceptional cases rather than routinely, as is currently the case. The ROL cannot be realised without integrating provisions on NGOs' activities into the current legal framework. A redefinition of NGOs' role may be needed to avoid the further restriction of their work, which remains dependent upon the political forces in power. Any national or regional legislative intervention regulating NGOs' SAR activities will have to face the main challenge of considering their structures and rights and give them the appropriate freedom and means to carry out their missions.[61]

[56] C Costello and I Mann, 'Border Justice: Migration and Accountability for Human Rights Violations' (2020) 21 *German Law Journal* 311, 313.

[57] DF Thompson, *Restoring Responsibility* (Cambridge, CUP, 2010) ch 1, as also cited by M Gkliati, 'Nexus Theory and the Multi-actor Reality of the EU External Borders: Testing the Efficacy of Non-Judicial Accountability Mechanisms' (Presentation at 'Shared Responsibility at the EU's External Borders' Conference, Barcelona, 29 September 2023).

[58] K Neri, 'The Challenges Faced by Private Ships in Large-scale Rescue Operations at Sea' in G Bevilacqua (ed), *Sicurezza Umana negli Spazi Navigabili: Sfide Comuni e Nuove Tendenze – Human Security in Navigable Spaces: Common Challenges and New Trends* (Napoli, Editoriale Scientifica, 2021) 105.

[59] ibid 108.

[60] S Bellezza and H Sadik, 'Humanitarian Engagement in Maritime Rescue and Migrants Relocation' in G Bevilacqua (ed), *Sicurezza Umana negli Spazi Navigabili: Sfide Comuni e Nuove Tendenze – Human Security in Navigable Spaces: Common Challenges and New Trends* (Napoli, Editoriale Scientifica, 2021) 80.

[61] The role and strategies of migrants and smugglers are also important in this context, but I have not analysed them here to keep the work within reasonable boundaries. However, this is an area where future research is needed.

Regarding *state actors*, several authorities are involved at different levels of power. In the last chapters I focused on the various initiatives of the Italian government to prevent sea migrants' arrival, and showed how it has often acted arbitrarily, transgressing the relevant substantive and procedural limits in the name of security and border control. Such initiatives have also affected the principle of equality, as the response is not the same for migrants and refugees as it is for regular passengers, showing how the concepts of distress and safety have not been applied evenly.

I also discussed how, in some cases, members of right-wing governments have willingly breached the law in defiance of the current EU system, which fails to provide for shared responsibility for migrants upon their disembarkation.[62] In this regard, Tsourdi has noted how 'the non-implementation of asylum-related obligations' has been an 'act of defiance motivated by ideological disagreement with the goal of asylum provision'.[63] However, in general, regardless of the 'political colour'[64] of the parties in charge, all Italian governments have continuously followed a conservative approach as far as responses to sea migration are concerned. The situation has been complicated by relations among states and their strategies for neglecting human rights without denying them overtly, which often amount to arguing that someone else is responsible[65] and thereby creating ambiguity and avoiding accountability.[66]

Sometimes the government's approach to sea migration has been made possible through the cooperation of states or entities whose systems are not based on democracy and the ROL – such as Libya – as well as through delegation of 'operational cooperation of EU Member States' border controls' to Frontex.[67] Though Frontex's SAR activities at sea are limited,[68] its aerial surveillance of migrants' vessels in the Central Mediterranean and consequent communication of their location to state authorities, especially to the Libyan Coast Guard, is highly relevant in this context.[69] Frontex's role and responsibility in the framework of interceptions and pullbacks to unsafe places remains unaddressed and begs for further enquiry.[70]

[62] E Tsourdi, 'Asylum in the EU: One of the Many Faces of Rule of Law Backsliding?' (2021) 17 *European Constitutional Law Review* 471, 481. For example, in the case of the Closed Port Policy discussed in ch 6, ss 4 and 5.

[63] Tsourdi (n 62) 485.

[64] Alagna (n 37) 7.

[65] D Guilfoyle, 'Jurisdiction at Sea. Migrant Interdiction and the Transnational Security State' in T Gammeltoft-Hansen and J Vedsted-Hansen (eds), *Human Rights and the Dark Side of Globalisation: Transnational Law Enforcement and Migration Control* (Abingdon, Routledge, 2017) 114–37, 128.

[66] ibid 129.

[67] Mitsilegas (n 31) 293.

[68] See ch 3, section III.

[69] In 2021, Frontex's aerial surveillance helped the Libyan Coast Guard to intercept about 10,000 migrants, nearly one third of the 32,000 returned to Libya. D Lohmüller, 'EU: Frontex Complicit in Abuse in Libya' (Human Rights Watch, 12 December 2022), available at: www.hrw.org/news/2022/12/12/eu-frontex-complicit-abuse-libya.

[70] Lohmüller (n 69); Benjamin Bathke, 'Frontex Says It Used More Airplanes for Border Control in 2020' (*InfoMigrants*, 27 March 2021), available at: www.infomigrants.net/en/post/31805/frontex-says-it-used-more-airplanes-for-border-control-in-2020; Vassallo Paleologo (n 33).

The judiciary, which in Italy is composed of both prosecutors and judges, has played an important but 'ambivalent'[71] part in the investigations against NGOs, as one must distinguish the role of the prosecutors from that of the judges. On the one hand, some prosecutors have engaged in 'efforts to counter, and especially to prevent' NGOs' SAR activities[72] to such an extent that their investigations have been labelled a form of 'prosecutorial populism'.[73] This approach has revealed some prosecutors' willingness to adopt a political stance,[74] which is problematic from the point of view of the separation of powers. In this regard, Alagna draws attention to the 'existence of judicial factions [*correnti*]' among prosecutors who have been influenced by the political debate.[75] According to him, in some cases, 'such discretion became extremely relevant – from the decision to [exert] jurisdiction in high seas to the use of specific investigative protocols', although the prosecutors he interviewed 'tend[ed] to interpret their agency in this context as the mere application of the law, while refusing the idea of exercising a discretional power'.[76] Alagna also explains that some Sicilian prosecutors may have been influenced both by their personal experience in mafia cases and by the culture of their offices – the Direzioni Distrettuali Antimafia (District Anti-mafia Prosecutor's Offices) – which usually investigate instances where a criminal organisation is suspected to be engaged in smuggling.[77]

On the other hand, the judges have dismissed these cases in pre-trial hearings (apart from the *Rackete* case, which went before the Supreme Court of Cassation, but this only concerned the issue of validation of the captain's arrest) and responded by reaffirming the rights of NGOs and sea migrants. In this way, the judiciary has been an 'enabler of both expansive and repressive dynamics'.[78] Nevertheless, as Alagna explains, the 'de-criminalization process' did not end the policing of NGOs, but rather led to its 'adaptation',[79] especially 'in terms of bottom-up dynamics'. According to him, the new responses that governments have taken following the judicial decisions recall what the

[71] Alagna (n 37) 8.
[72] Minetti (n 38) 346.
[73] ibid.
[74] Interview with Luca Masera, Professor of Criminal Law, Università degli Studi di Brescia (online, 2 February 2023); J Allsopp, L Vosyliūtė and S Smilalowski, 'Picking "Low-Hanging Fruit" While the Orchard Burns: The Cost of Policing Humanitarian Actors in Italy and Greece as a Strategy to Prevent Migrant Smuggling' (2021) 27 *European Journal of Criminal Policy and Research* 65, 67, 73–74.
[75] Alagna (n 37) 8.
[76] ibid 9.
[77] ibid 15–16; interview with Federico Alagna, Adjunct Professor of Political Science, Department of Political and Social Sciences, Università di Bologna (online, 11 May 2023); see ch 6, section II and section VII.A.
[78] Alagna (n 37) 1.
[79] ibid 17.

constructivist socio-legal scholarship has described as a 'radiating effect'[80] – referring to the broader, sometimes unintended impact of judicial decisions.

Moreover, Zirulia and Martinico argue that even if proceedings were dismissed, the criminalisation of NGOs has been problematic because of deterrent effects on humanitarian assistance, 'resulting in further deterioration of social and human ties between citizens and foreigners'.[81] Furthermore, some politicians strongly criticised the judges for their decisions in favour of NGOs, to the point that the UN Special Rapporteur on the independence of judges and lawyers raised concerns about the weakening of judicial power and autonomy.[82]

With regard to judicial decisions concerning the Port State Control framework, I explained in chapter six, section VIII, how the European Court of Justice (ECJ) has given only a partial response as far as its application to NGOs is concerned. The ECJ's ruling is nevertheless important, and it is necessary to see what effect it has had in practice. In areas unrelated to NGOs, the impact of the courts has been more limited in terms of providing an effective remedy, but also more diverse and complex, and I therefore discuss it separately in the next section.

Against this background, it is important to underline the ways in which the EU has influenced the dynamics in Italy. First, the EU legislation and stance towards immigrant smuggling has in practice enabled 'the emergence of cases of criminalization of humanitarian actors'[83] – similarly to what has occurred in other EU countries.[84] Second, the EU has supported Italian measures against NGOs, such as the 2017 Code of Conduct,[85] as well informal cooperation agreements with North African countries[86] and the creation of a Libyan SAR zone.[87]

[80] ibid 9, citing M Galanter, 'The Radiating Effects of Courts' in K Boyum and L Mather (eds), *Empirical Theories of Courts* (New York, Longman, 1983). Galanter discusses how courts' decisions may not only impact the parties of a specific case, but also have general effects ('radiating effects') on others' behaviour.

[81] S Zirulia and G Martinico, 'Criminalising Migrants and Securitising Borders. The Italian "No Way" Model in the Age of Populism' in V Stoyanova and S Smet (eds), *Migrants' Rights, Populism and Legal Resilience in Europe* (Cambridge, CUP, 2022) 275.

[82] Allsopp, Vosyliūtė and Smilalowski (n 74) 7.

[83] Alagna (n 37) 5; S Carrera, J Allsopp and L Vosyliūtė, 'Policing the Mobility Society: The Effects of EU-Anti-Migrant Smuggling Policies on Humanitarianism' (2018) 4 *International Journal of Migration and Border Studies* 236.

[84] For instance, Malta, Spain and Greece have also misused the EU framework against smuggling to legitimise their policies against NGOs engaged in SAR operations in the Mediterranean. See ch 3, section V.

[85] Alagna (n 37) 5; European Parliament, 'Answer Given by Mr Avramopoulos on Behalf of the Commission' E-005646/2017(ASW) (17 January 2018).

[86] See ch 5, section II and section III. See also, European Council and Council of the European Union (Consilium), 'Migration Flows in the Central Mediterranean Route' (23 January 2023), available at: www.consilium.europa.eu/en/policies/eu-migration-policy/central-mediterranean-route/.

[87] Alice Cuddy, 'Prompted by EU, Libya Quietly Claims Right to Order Rescuers to Return Fleeing Migrants' *Euronews* (7 August 2018), available at: www.euronews.com/2018/07/06/prompted-by-eu-libya-quietly-claims-right-to-order-rescuers-to-return-fleeing-migrants.

Third, the EU approach to SAR, which focuses on internal security rather than saving lives,[88] leaves a gap in the Mediterranean which is partially filled by the Libyan Coast Guard – trained and financed by the EU.[89] In this regard, Alagna notes how some Italian politicians accuse the EU of lacking effective policies on sea migration, especially for relocating migrants arriving in Italian ports, and use these arguments to 'legitimize the policing of humanitarian actors'[90] and the adoption of controversial policies. Fourth, the EU has also adopted informal externalisation agreements with third countries to prevent migrant arrivals, such as the 2016 EU–Turkey agreement, whose legal nature is highly debated.[91]

Finally, the interaction of these different actors affects the ROL not only at the national, but also at the international and EU levels: the international ROL, which lays greater emphasis on states' external relations and obligations than the national ROL,[92] is also weakened in this context. A change would be possible only with collaboration and partnership between all the actors involved. The question of what conditions might enable such a change represents a crucial direction for future research.

V. THE ROLE OF COURTS AND LIMITATIONS ON ACCESS TO JUSTICE

In light of the data, I conclude that the challenges to the ROL posed by the responses to sea migration are also due to the fact that it is not always possible for migrants to access justice. While the courts have often shown themselves to be guarantors of individual rights, able to rein in the power of the authorities and provide redress in claims for justice by establishing the supremacy of human rights, this is only possible after a legal violation has occurred[93] and judicial

[88] Alagna (n 37) 6.

[89] European Council and Council of the European Union (n 86).

[90] Alagna (n 37) 6.

[91] The nature of the agreement, which was concluded between the European Council and Turkey, is debated, in particular whether it is an international agreement or not. The ECJ, presented with this question, answered that it

> 'was not an act or international agreement attributable to the European Council, but rather that the real authors were the heads of state or government of the EU member states and their Turkish counterparts. Consequently, the Court declared that it did not have jurisdiction to assess the pleas, because none of the EU institutions featured among the authors of the EU–Turkey Statement'.

S Carrera, L den Hertog and M Stefan, 'It Wasn't Me! The Luxembourg Court Orders on the EU–Turkey Refugee Deal' (CEPS Policy Insights no 2017/15, April 2017) 2, available at: www.ceps.eu/wp-content/uploads/2017/04/EU-Turkey%20Deal.pdf. See also, I Papanicolopulu, 'Informal Lawmaking in Maritime Migration' in N Klein (ed), *Unconventional Lawmaking in the Law of the Sea* (Oxford, OUP, 2022) 64; E Fassi and S Lucarelli, 'The EU Migration System and Global Justice: an Assessment' in M Ceccorulli, E Fassi and S Lucarelli (eds), *The EU Migration System of Governance* (online, Palgrave Macmillan, 2021) 259–77, 263.

[92] S Marochkin, 'National and International Rule of Law: Proclaimed Adherence and Real-Life Policies' (2019) 44 *Review of Central and East European Law*, Special Issue 305, 309.

[93] M Starita, 'Conclusioni I Lati Oscuri del Diritto Internazionale sul Soccorso in Mare' (2021) XXI *Diritto e Questioni Pubbliche*, Special Issue 133, 137.

proceedings are completed,[94] which may take time, resources and physical presence in the destination country, as discussed in the next subsection. Thus, effective access has been limited to a small number of cases. Furthermore, the government's strategies in response to the judicial decisions keep changing and pose persistent obstacles. As such, the courts continue to be faced with new and controversial issues.

Given the complexity of the general landscape emerging from the analysis, I gather my reflections into two separate subsections: one on cases concerning violations of the law of the sea and/or human rights; and the other on cases concerning the abuse of executive power.

A. Cases Concerning Violations of the Law of the Sea and/or Human Rights

In chapters four and five, I discussed how Italy and other states have at times failed to provide prompt rescue and disembarkation services, ending in the loss of lives. I also discussed episodes where migrants rescued in international waters and non-Italian SAR areas have been taken back to Libya or other unsafe locations. Some of these cases have been brought before Italian, regional and international bodies on the basis of the claim of violations of international and national law, including the obligations deriving from the SOLAS and SAR Conventions and the inviolable rights of the person, in particular the right to life and the principle of non-refoulement. A few of these cases are still pending, so only a partial picture of the judicial and quasi-judicial responses can be drawn here.

The criminal cases before the Italian courts aim to ascertain the commission of crimes by captains of Italian ships or by any other national authority involved in pushback or pullback operations.[95] The civil actions, on the other hand, which are brought by migrants with the support of NGOs, focus on establishing unlawful conduct and, if successful, quantifying the compensation for damages.[96] In terms of international avenues, migrants have appealed

[94] ibid.

[95] For instance, the case of the *Asso 28* before the Tribunal of Naples. Trib Napoli, Sentenza 13.10.2021, n 1643. See Redattore Sociale, 'Migranti, Scoppia il Caso Asso 28. "Fatto grave, è respingimento"' *Redattore Sociale* (Roma, 31 July 2018), available at: www.redattoresociale.it/article/notiziario/migranti_scoppia_il_caso_asso_28_fatto_grave_e_respingimento_; ASGI, 'Condanna di Asso 28: un Precedente che Può Scardinare la Prassi dei Respingimenti in Libia' (ASGI, 19 October 2021), available at: www.asgi.it/notizie/libia-condanna-respingimento/. See ch 5, section V.A.

[96] This was used, for example, in *Osman* and *Asso 29* discussed in ch 5, section V.A. Regarding *Osman*, see Trib Roma, Sentenza 14.11.2019, n 22917/2019. See Rita Russo, 'Respingimenti Illeciti e Diritto d'Asilo: è Sufficiente il Risarcimento in Denaro? Nota a Trib. Roma, 28.11.2019 no 22917' (*Giustizia Insieme*, 5 February 2020), available at: www.giustiziainsieme.it/it/diritto-civile/858-respingimenti-illeciti-e-diritto-d-asilo-e-sufficiente-il-risarcimento-in-denaro-nota-a-trib-roma-28-11-2019-n-22917?hitcount=0; Amnesty International, '"Caso Osman": Tutte le Tappe che Hanno Portato alla Condanna del Governo Italiano' (Amnesty International, 31 August 2020), available at:

to the European Court of Human Rights (ECtHR) to ascertain the violation of rights covered by the European Convention on Human Rights, to the United Nations Human Rights Committee to determine violations of the International Covenant on Civil and Political Rights, to the International Criminal Court to ascertain the commission of crimes against humanity, and to the United National Committee against Torture concerning violations of the Convention against Torture.[97]

In my review of the respective decisions, I note how to a certain extent both judicial and quasi-judicial bodies are acting in an area without much judicial precedent. Their influence has been modest, even though the evolutionary interpretation and application of the relevant provisions has led to a few condemnations of Italy for breaches of human rights and law of the sea provisions. Such condemnations have especially been possible in situations where jurisdiction was not an issue because the actions of the ship or crew were clearly under the control of Italy – usually because the rescue vessels were flying the Italian flag.

However, most of these decisions, with the notable exception of *Hirsi*, have not had a major impact beyond the individual cases in question. For instance, in *Osman*,[98] the Court of Rome held that, as a consequence of the Italian Navy's interception of a group of migrants in international waters and their transfer to Libya in violation of the non-refoulement principle, the applicants had the right to: (1) be compensated for damages; as well as (2) enter Italy in order to apply for asylum according to Article 10(3) of the Constitution.[99] Despite the Court's recognition that anyone outside the Italian territory has the right to enter and apply for protection[100] – in connection with the non-refoulement principle – such a right has not been implemented in subsequent Italian policies and practices.

Even in terms of individual cases, the effectiveness of the courts is restricted by issues of access. Given the factual circumstances of sea migrants' lives, it is complicated for them to take legal action for violations of their rights and

www.amnesty.it/caso-osman-tutte-le-tappe-che-hanno-portato-alla-condanna-del-governo-italiano/. See ASGI, 'Storica Vittoria del Diritto di Asilo: un Visto d'Ingresso in Italia per Richiedere Protezione' (ASGI, 30 August 2020), available at: www.asgi.it/asilo-e-protezione-internazionale/vittoria-diritto-asilo-respinti-illegalmente-eritrei-oggi-in-italia-con-visto/. For the *Asso 29* case, see Rosita Rijtano, 'Respingimenti in Libia, Asso Ventinove a Processo' (*Lavialibera*, 15 February 2021), available at: lavialibera.it/it-schede-469-respingimenti_libia_asso_ventinove_processo; Luisiana Gaita, '"Marina Italiana Ha Coordinato Respingimento Illegale di Migranti in Libia": Cinque Eritrei Citano in Fiudizio Governo e un'Azienda Privata' *Il Fatto Quotidiano* (12 February 2021), available at: www.ilfattoquotidiano.it/2021/02/12/marina-italiana-ha-coordinato-respingimento-illegale-di-migranti-in-libia-cinque-eritrei-citano-in-giudizio-governo-e-unazienda-privata/6099643/.

[97] See ch 5, section V.B, and ch 4, section V.B.

[98] See ch 5, section V.A. Trib Roma, Sentenza 14.11.2019, n 22917.

[99] M Giuffré, 'Esternalizzazione delle Frontiere e *Non-refoulement*: Accesso al Territorio e alla Procedure di Asilo alla Luce della Sentenza n. 22917/2019' (2020) 1 *Questione Giustizia* 190.

[100] This is also in line with former cases of the Supreme Court of Cassation: Cass civ, sez I, Sentenza 25.11.2005, n 25028.

follow through with the proceedings.[101] First, in most cases migrants have neither the knowledge nor the means to start the relevant procedures. Thus, access to remedies requires proactive intervention by civil society associations or NGOs to protect the victims of violations. The legal actions illustrated in the former chapters were initiated because of the involvement of associations and NGOs, which were able to contact the people concerned after they had been pushed or pulled back to Libya. Second, even when access to a remedy is possible thanks to the assistance of civil society organisations, in some cases the effectiveness of the judicial remedy is affected by the time required to reach a decision as well as the practical and legal difficulties of pursuing the proceedings, such as providing evidence and testimonies.[102] For instance, some migrants may still be on the move or not have a fixed address after the start of proceedings, and be difficult to reach when their active participation in the cases is needed.[103]

Another restriction on migrants' access to justice relates to jurisdiction. As sea migrants are often outside the destination state both in the sense of not being in the state's territory and in the sense of not being under the state's effective control,[104] it is sometimes impossible to establish the courts' competence. The need to ascertain jurisdiction is a critical first step in assessing states' accountability for violations of human rights and/or the law of the sea, as highlighted in the literature and as discussed in chapters three and four. Here I provide some final reflections on the importance of the topic with respect to the ROL.

The main principle of human rights enforcement is that states are responsible for those within their jurisdiction. Generally, migrants in international waters who have neither reached Europe nor come into contact with any EU state actors 'do not enjoy the protection granted by the human rights obligations of European states'.[105] As Mann argues, in the absence of jurisdiction, 'there are no human rights' or connected duties, nor actions or omissions that could violate these duties. As a consequence, in these cases, migrants may lose their lives not due to any legal violation but because they fall into a 'black hole'.[106] Following this line of argument, the culprit is 'the structure of international law', combined with migrants' own decisions to travel and the conditions that cause them to make such a decision.[107]

However, the limits of jurisdiction are subject to debate. Recently, the concept of jurisdiction has been expanded to encompass instances beyond

[101] Krista Rutter Bonello Giappone, Interview with former ECtHR Judge Giovanni Bonello (emails, 19–20 April 2022).

[102] A Pijnenburg and K van der Pas, 'Strategic Litigation against European Migration Control Policies: The Legal Battleground of the Central Mediterranean' (2022) 24 *European Journal of Migration and Law* 401, 422.

[103] Interview with Lawyer no 4 (online, 25 October 2023).

[104] Spijkerboer (n 9) 28.

[105] I Mann, 'Maritime Black Holes: Migration and Rightlessness in International Law' (2018) 29 *European Journal of International Law* 347, 357.

[106] ibid.

[107] ibid 367–68.

the geographical boundaries of a state, where the state nonetheless exercises effective authority over a region or effective control over an individual.[108] For example, in the *Hirsi* case (as mentioned in chapter five, section II.B), the ECtHR held that Italy was directly involved in pushbacks and had violated the principle of non-refoulement as well as the prohibition of collective expulsion. The Court reasoned that, by intercepting migrants in international waters and transferring them to Italian Navy ships, Italy's *de jure* and *de facto* jurisdiction over the migrants was established – it had control over them.[109]

Nevertheless, the complexity and the fragmentation of the subject matter make it difficult to provide a clear and uniform concept of jurisdiction from the point of view of the courts, and each situation should be evaluated individually, taking into account its unique circumstances. Moreover, issues concerning pullbacks are more complicated than pushbacks, as they are performed 'in the interest or on behalf of the putative receiving state' but without its direct participation.[110]

Whether the intended destination country exercises effective control on pullbacks remains debated[111] and is still to be decided in the case of *SS and others v Italy*.[112] Most scholars consider it improbable that the ECtHR will establish jurisdiction with respect to policies that encourage or delegate border controls to third countries.[113] Such interceptions are performed by agents of other states or entities, occur outside EU Member States' territories, 'involve multiple players',[114] and are 'contactless'.[115] For the ECtHR to decide otherwise, it would have to move beyond its consolidated case law.[116]

[108] Interview with Bonello (n 101); GS Goodwin-Gill, J McAdam and E Dunlop, 'The Principle of Non-refoulement – Part 2' in GS Goodwin-Gill and J McAdam (eds), *The Refugee in International Law*, 4th edn (Oxford, OUP, 2021) 315; T Gammeltoft-Hansen, *Access to Asylum: International Refugee Law and the Globalization of Migration Control* (Cambridge, CUP, 2011) 125; UNHCR, 'Advisory Opinion on the Extraterritorial Application of Non-Refoulement Obligations under the 1951 Convention Relating to the Status of Refugees and Its 1967 Protocol' (January 2007) para 43; A Fazzini, 'Il Caso S.S. and Others v Italy Nel Quadro dell'Esternalizzazione delle Frontiere in Libia: Osservazioni sui Possibili Scenari al Vaglio della Corte di Strasburgo' (2020) 2 *Diritto, Immigrazione e Cittadinanza* 87, 102–03.

[109] G Ciliberto, 'Libya's Pullbacks of Boat Migrants: Can Italy Be Held Accountable for Violations of International Law?' (2018) 4 *Italian Law Journal* 489, 518.

[110] ibid.

[111] See Alice Riccardi, 'Esternalizzazione delle frontiere italiane in Libia e Niger: una Prospettiva di Diritto Onternazionale' (*Questione Giustizia*, 2020) 1, available at: www.questionegiustizia.it/rivista/articolo/esternalizzazione-delle-frontiere-italiane-in-libia-e-niger-una-prospettiva-di-diritto-internazionale; G Bevilacqua (ed), *Sicurezza Umana negli Spazi Navigabili: Sfide Comuni e Nuove Tendenze* (Napoli, Editoriale Scientifica, 2021).

[112] See ch 5, section V.B; *SS and others v Italy* App no 21660/18 (ECtHR, 11 November 2019); Ciliberto (n 109) 521; Goodwin-Gill, McAdam and Dunlop (n 108) 315.

[113] See, for instance, Sánchez Legido (n 14) 355; A Pijnenburg, 'From Italian Pushbacks to Libyan Pullbacks: Is *Hirsi 2.0* in the Making in Strasbourg?' (2018) 20 *European Journal of Migration and Law* 396, 396; Ciliberto (n 109) 518.

[114] Sánchez Legido (n 14) 353.

[115] ibid.

[116] Pijnenburg (n 113) 396.

However, a few judges and scholars have suggested alternative models. For example, in his concurring opinion in *Al-Skeini*, Judge Bonello wrote:

> Jurisdiction means no less and no more than 'authority over' and 'control of'. In relation to [European] Convention obligations, jurisdiction is neither territorial nor extra-territorial: it ought to be functional – in the sense that when it is within a State's authority and control whether a breach of human rights is, or is not, committed, whether its perpetrators are, or are not, identified and punished, whether the victims of violations are, or are not, compensated, it would be an imposture to claim that, ah yes, that State had authority and control, but, ah no, it had no jurisdiction.[117]

Moreno-Lax, like Bonello, proposes a 'functional approach' and maintains that 'operational power projected and actioned abroad, like other methods of territorial and/or personal control, amounts to an exercise of jurisdiction'.[118] Operational power involves the 'exercise of public powers, such as those ordinarily assumed by a territorial sovereign, taking the form of policy delivery and/or operational action translating into "situational control"'.[119] This would include the 'remote management techniques' that Italy has adopted in cooperation with the local Libyan authorities, who act 'as a proxy'.[120]

Therefore, the challenges posed by migrants who are situated beyond the EU territory, and especially in international waters, reveal shortcomings in the ROL framework. The ROL is built upon sovereignty, and 'sovereignty entails exclusive law making and law enforcing authority in a territory'.[121] In other words, the ROL is dependent on the notion of state, which remains primarily responsible for its enforcement. Several international law provisions are applicable to sea migration, but there remains a critical gap 'concerning the nature of the space beyond the states'.[122] As Guilfoyle states '[w]hen public authority is exercised beyond territory, respect for rights, especially those of non-citizens, is clearly at risk'.[123] Moreover,

> although human rights are increasingly acknowledged to apply beyond territory in law, the ship at sea remains a challenging space to police in practice. Human rights obligations are difficult for courts to supervise in an entirely isolated and self-contained environment far from metropolitan territory.[124]

[117] *Al-Skeini v United Kingdom* App no 55721/07 (ECtHR, 7 July 2011) paras 12 and 13.
[118] V Moreno-Lax, 'The Architecture of Functional Jurisdiction: Unpacking Contactless Control – On Public Powers, S.S. and Others v Italy, and the "Operational Model"' (2020) 21 *German Law Journal* 385, 388.
[119] ibid 387.
[120] ibid.
[121] Dauvergne, 'Sovereignty, Migration and the Rule of Law in Global Times' (n 54) 611–14.
[122] Palombella, 'The Rule of Law and its Conception between "National" and "International"' (n 6) 77.
[123] Guilfoyle (n 65) 127.
[124] ibid 130.

In conclusion, there are different views on the matter of jurisdiction when it concerns the extraterritorial acts of state agents. In my opinion, the question of whether a state has jurisdiction requires a *case-by-case evaluation of the level of control that state agents exercise over individuals and circumstances*. The fact that some events occur in international waters should not in itself be a reason to discard states' obligations to respect human rights. In many cases, they should still be held responsible for omissions to rescue or for cooperation with state actors of third countries that are involved in human rights violations.[125] Failing to do so can cause unpredictability and arbitrariness.

B. Cases Concerning the Abuse of Executive Powers

In cases where the issue at stake was whether members of the executive breached their legal obligations and abused their powers, the outcome has brought to light the limits of access to justice when ministerial crimes are involved. The procedure to pursue ministerial crimes presents some shortcomings. While the Italian courts are undoubtedly independent and have shown themselves willing to assess the legality of the executive's actions, the Senate has to grant authorisation to proceed with investigations and the parliamentary phase can be open to bias.[126] Such decisions may be dependent on the political forces in power – as I showed with respect to the different outcomes of similar cases against Matteo Salvini, then Minister of the Interior: the *Diciotti* case on the one hand, where the authorisation to investigate was denied, and the *Gregoretti* and *Open Arms* cases on the other, where it was granted.[127]

Therefore, I conclude there are areas of executive discretion in Italy that are non-justiciable. This issue is part of a wider discussion on the relationship between politics and judicial control, and an extensive analysis is outside the scope of this work. Here it is sufficient to mention that according to some (as seen in *Diciotti*), certain matters should be dealt with by the executive and legislature rather than the courts.[128] In this regard, Rossi argues that, in Italy,

[125] R Pisillo Mazzeschi, *International Human Rights Law: Theory and Practice* (Cham, Springer, 2021) 173.

[126] Zirulia and Martinico (n 81) 270. It should be noted that the Senate has to decide whether or not the executive's action under scrutiny is exempted from judicial control because it was taken to pursue a public interest at a high constitutional level. A Jr Golia, 'Migration and the Janus Faces of Solidarity and the Rule of Law: Brief Remarks in the Light of the Italian Experience' in T Russo, A Oriolo and G Dalia (eds), *Solidarity and Rule of Law: European Union and its Neighbours in a Globalized World* (Cham, Springer, 2023) 104–05.

[127] See ch 4, section V.C, and ch 6, section V.

[128] For a discussion of this point, see P Rossi, 'The Role of National Courts for the International Rule of Law: Insights from the Field of Migration' (2019) 12 *European Journal of Legal Studies* 195, 218.

the 'doctrine of the so-called *atto politico*,[129] a form of judicial abstentionism',[130] is 'one of tradeoff between separation of powers and the rule of law. In shielding political acts from judicial review, this doctrine entails an obvious tension with the idea that the political branches should be held accountable for breaches of the law'.[131]

According to Rossi, however, seen from the perspective of the national dimension of the ROL, it cannot be said that there is any 'accountability gap. Parliament's refusal to authorize prosecution belongs to the physiology of the domestic legal system'.[132] This is because constitutional law dictates that, with an absolute majority, the Senate has the power to decline authorisation to proceed with investigations if it deems that the minister has undertaken actions with the objective of protecting a constitutional interest of the state or in the pursuit of a paramount public interest while exercising their governmental function.[133] Rossi points out that the Senate's determination is explicitly designated as exempt from external scrutiny. Consequently, it is the domestic constitutional structure that permits transgressions of the law when they are aimed at advancing significant public interests, and this authority is exclusively conferred upon the Parliament.[134]

However, Rossi's view seems to adopt a formal understanding of the ROL concept. As explained in chapter two, section II, formal theories do not take into account that some laws can be discriminatory or arbitrary or prevent access to justice.[135] According to Palombella,

> ultimately the *legal* protection against arbitrariness and to guarantee liberty starts with the conditions for the limitation of law through law, that is, preventing one-sidedness and 'domination' *through* law. I believe that it is important to characterize the RoL as a constraint on the law itself, not just or directly a constraint on 'power'.[136]

In other words, if we consider one of the aims of the ROL to be that of limiting arbitrary power, we cannot allow laws that permit the executive to evade accountability. While there are reasons to avoid judicial interference in the executive's actions, as the executive has discretionary authority to carry out its

[129] In this regard, Rossi cites the following: C dell'Acqua, *Atto Politico ed Esercizio di Poteri Sovrani* (Padova, CEDAM 1983); G Di Gaspare, *Considerazioni sugli Atti Politici dei Governo e sull'Atto Politico: l' Esperienza Italiana e Francese nello Stato Liberale* (Milano, Giuffrè 1984); G Pepe, 'Il Principio di Effettività della Tutela Giurisdizionale tra Atti Politici, Atti di Alta Amministrazione e Leggi-Provvedimento' (2017) 22 *Federalismi.it*, available at: www.federalismi.it/nv14/articolo-documento.cfm?artid=35191.

[130] Rossi (n 128) 218–19.

[131] ibid 219.

[132] ibid 223.

[133] Legge Costituzionale 16 gennaio 1989, n 1, art 9 (3)(1); see also Costituzione Italiana, Art 96.

[134] Rossi (n 128) 223.

[135] G Palombella, 'Two Threats to the Rule of Law: Legal and Epistemic (Between Technocracy and Populism)' (2019) 11 *Hague Journal on the Rule of Law* 383, 384.

[136] ibid 385.

mandate, such discretion must itself be limited and contained.[137] The executive cannot be accorded impunity, for it may exercise discretion in bad faith and for improper aims.[138] Moreover, to prevent arbitrariness, it is not enough to evaluate laws or indicators from an abstract point of view. On the contrary, it is necessary to consider the content, context and socio-political factors.[139]

In this vein, some scholars and lawyers (who seem to adopt a substantive theory of the ROL) have criticised the existing procedure for not effectively guaranteeing that the executive's power is subject to judicial oversight. Following this view, according to which the content of the law shall reflect justice and moral principles,[140] I argue that the procedure should thus be re-evaluated. Nevertheless, only political will and action can address this problem: legislative reforms are needed to ensure a balance between the independence of the executive and the protection of individuals who are subject to the executive's decisions. This is especially important where individuals' rights have been directly violated and some form of harm has been suffered as a consequence.[141] The issue is complex and has already been the subject of wide discussion in constitutional law scholarship,[142] but it deserves attention by future studies, which should look further into possible effective and alternative models.

VI. LIMITATIONS OF THE ROL FRAMEWORK OF ANALYSIS IN THE CONTEXT OF SEA MIGRATION

While this study demonstrates the usefulness of the ROL framework, it also exposes certain limitations besides the boundaries that circumscribe state authority and the practical issues of implementation and enforcement of the relevant legal provisions, namely: the potential for political forces to bend the notion of the ROL to justify anti-migratory policies; the limited impact of the international and EU ROL; and the need for the ROL to adapt to events beyond national borders.

First, similar to authoritarian parties in some Eastern European countries, Italian political leadership has employed populist, security and nationalist rhetoric to 'redefine' the rule of law as rule *by* law[143] instead of directly calling

[137] R Dworkin, *Taking Rights Seriously* (Cambridge, MA, Harvard University Press, 1977) 31.

[138] L Sossin, 'The Unjustified Project of Roncarelli v Duplessis: Justiciability, Discretion, and the Limits of the Rule of Law' (2010) 55 *McGill Law Journal* 661, 677, 682.

[139] Palombella, 'Two Threats to the Rule of Law' (n 135) 384.

[140] See ch 2, section II and section IV.

[141] For a discussion of the justiciability problem in Canada, see Sossin (n 138) 688.

[142] See, eg, A Mitrotti, 'L'Atto Politico: Riflessioni Intorno ad Un Istituto in Perenne "Tensione" Tra Scienza Costituzionale ed Amministrativa' (2020) 1 *Nomos. Le Attualità nel Diritto* 1; dell'Acqua (n 129); Di Gaspare (n 129); Pepe (n 129); E Cheli, *Atto Politico e Funzione d'Indirizzo Politico* (Milano, Giuffré, 1961).

[143] 'Rule *by* law' refers to situations where those in power can arbitrarily adopt the law and apply it vis-a-vis anyone, and avoid accountability. By contrast, the 'rule *of* law' means that the law applies

the ROL into question.[144] In so doing, they not only undermine but draw attention away from the substantive conception of the ROL supported by Bingham, the Venice Commission, and the European Commission, which includes well-established and fundamental values such as respect for human rights, clarity of the law, and the principle of equality, as I discussed in chapter two. More generally on this point, the scholarship on 'rule by law' suggests that the concept is favoured by rulers, as it gives them the law as a powerful tool without their being subject to it, while at the same time legitimising a 'rational-legal government'.[145] In this regard, Italian populist parties have used the idea of rule by law in the context of security-oriented narratives and approaches to governance in the field of migration.[146] Citing Agamben, Davitti notes how these situations involving security threats and dangers are perceived as ever-present and become incorporated into the governing techniques of the sovereign. As such, the state of exception risks becoming the modern norm for government in the domain of migration.[147] Usually, this is explained by the fact that, in emergency situations, the focus is primarily on immediate responses rather than delving into the root causes of the problem. Time constraints prevent thorough analysis, long-term solutions and adherence to legal frameworks.[148] As such, the findings also validate Gowder's perspective that the essence of the ROL lies in adhering to it and being dedicated to it. The ROL can only thrive if individuals within a political community understand how it upholds their equal rights and are willing to collectively enforce it, even against those in positions of power.[149]

Therefore, the externalisation and security-oriented measures to prevent irregular sea arrivals not only undermine migrants' rights by preventing their access to asylum and putting their lives at risk during dangerous journeys. They also undermine good governance principles at the heart of substantive conceptions of the ROL. Moreover, this approach adopted by Italy and supported by the EU to allegedly counter irregular migration and prevent deaths at sea has

equally to all, including those in power, and that the law must be general and knowable to all. J Raz, *The Authority of Law: Essays on Law and Morality* (Hong Kong, OUP, 1979).

[144] In the context of Eastern EU countries, see L Pech, 'The Rule of Law as a Well-Established and Well-Defined Principle of EU Law' (2022) 14 *Hague Journal on the Rule of Law* 107, 137. For a discussion of the parliamentary debates and the narratives used by populist parties in Italy, see S Aru, 'Battleship at the Port of Europe: Italy's Closed-Port Policy and Its Legitimizing Narratives' (2023) 104 *Political Geography* 1.

[145] A Bedner, 'An Elementary Approach to the Rule of Law' (2010) 2 *Hague Journal on the Rule of Law* 48, 57. See also, K Jayasurya, 'The Exception Becomes the Norm: Law and Regimes of Exception in East Asia' (2001) 2(1) *Asian-Pacific Law & Policy Journal* 108.

[146] While this approach is not new, it is reflected in the EU and other Member States and has become more prevalent in recent years. T Abdehharim, 'The Securitization of the EU's Migration Policies: What Consequences for Southern Mediterranean Countries and their Relations to the EU?' (2020) 9 *Euromed Survey* 96, 97.

[147] D Davitti, 'Biopolitical Borders and the State of Exception in the European Migration "Crisis"' (2019) 29 *European Journal of International Law* 1173, 1183.

[148] ibid 1185; Agamben (n 52).

[149] P Gowder, *The Rule of Law in the Real World* (New York, CUP, 2016) 5.

proven to be ineffective even in terms of such justifications, as the number of sea migrant arrivals in 2023 is the highest it has been since 2016.[150]

Second, this work corroborates previous research indicating that in instances where states fail to adhere to the ROL, international law cannot always be relied upon.[151] Whereas some argue that the 'errant state may be condemned in international organizations for failure to comply with the rule of law'[152] and that international organisations rely on '"*super partes* law", a law of the international community',[153] the impact of these organisations and their quasi-judicial supervisory bodies is limited, as they rely on 'political consensus' to function.[154] In addition, the role of international law has proven to be of little value in this context with respect to international cooperation and relations among the affected states. At the regional level, the situation is more complex. With the Council of Europe, there has been some progress, in particular with the ECtHR's *Hirsi* case, and it remains to be seen how the Court will decide in *SS and others v Italy*. By contrast, EU legislation and institutions have been weakening the ROL in relation to sea migration through externalisation policies and agreements, legislation allowing the criminalisation of NGOs, lack of coordination of effective SAR services, focus on securitisation rather than human rights, as well as the failure to fairly distribute migrants across all Members States. There is therefore a close relationship between the ROL deficit[155] in Italy and the EU approach: the EU is more part of the problem than part of the solution.[156]

Third, I acknowledge that in the context of evolving border practices, enforcing the ROL necessitates significant legal advancements. This is largely due to the fact that the human rights framework and the ROL concept were originally conceived from a conventional Westphalian standpoint, primarily addressing individuals residing within a nation's borders. Further insights on this point are given by Fitzpatrick, who discusses the tension between the ROL's function to establish legal certainty and predictability 'and its need to be adaptive and responsive'[157] in a globalised era in order to expand its potential.[158]

[150] IOM, 'Arrivals' (IOM, 12 November 2023), available at: dtm.iom.int/europe/arrivals.

[151] P Craig, 'The Rule of Law. National, International, and Regional Dimensions' in B Faedda (ed), *Rule of Law: Cases, Strategies, and Interpretations* (Vicenza, Ronzani Edizioni Scientifiche, 2021) 62.

[152] ibid.

[153] Palombella, 'The Rule of Law and its Conception between "National" and "International"' (n 6) 77.

[154] Craig (n 151) 62.

[155] According to Endicott, a 'community suffers from a deficit when it lacks the rule of law in some respect'. Endicott (n 44) 7.

[156] For a similar argument concerning migrants' human rights in the Mediterranean, see MR Pistone, A Gallaher and D Zammit, 'The Subject of Rights Immersed in a "Sea of Troubles"' (2007) 11 *Mediterranean Journal of Human Rights* 9, 13.

[157] Dauvergne, 'Sovereignty, Migration and the Rule of Law in Global Times' (n 54) 611–14; P Fitzpatrick, '"Gods Would Be Needed": American Empire and the Rule of (International) Law' (2003) 16 *Leiden Journal of International Law* 429.

[158] Dauvergne, 'Sovereignty, Migration and the Rule of Law in Global Times' (n 54) 611–14; Fitzpatrick (n 157) 429.

In this respect, Gowder contributes to the debate by looking for solutions to improve the ROL beyond states' territories and suggests two possible ways: (1) identifying and relying on 'direct ties' between migrants and members of the political community as a basis to include their interests in a concrete way in the community (for instance, in the case of immediate family members); and (2) applying universal norms to all people – although he acknowledges the limits of these norms when applied to heterogeneous communities.[159]

Providing an optimistic view, Dauvergne explains, citing Hirst and Thompson, that the significance of the ROL has become increasingly paramount in contemporary times, owing to the need to foster a sense of unity within and beyond national boundaries. The evolving approaches of courts in addressing migration issues indicate a progression in the ROL and consequently in the concept of sovereignty. These changes may be 'subtle, tentative',[160] and prospective in nature. Nevertheless, considering the seemingly insurmountable challenge that conventional sovereignty poses to the implementation of just and fair migration laws, Dauvergne argues that it is crucial to nurture any potential for reform.[161]

In other words, while acknowledging the significant link between the ROL and the concept of sovereignty, Dauvergne points out how the ROL is based on principles that can stand apart from a sovereign entity such as the state. Recent rulings and recommendations by various courts and entities may indicate caution, but they also show a slow decline in the respect conventionally accorded to the executive branch on matters concerning sea migration. This trend acknowledges the growing respect for the ROL beyond state borders, at a time when migration and sovereignty are becoming ever more intimately intertwined.[162]

In conclusion, despite its limitations and idealistic aspirations, I argue that the ROL remains a critical concept. It serves as a means to advance and safeguard a shared normative framework – a framework in which the exercise of authority is bound by mutually agreed-upon regulations, ensuring the preservation of every individual's fundamental rights.

VII. CONCLUSION

In this book I approached the responses to sea migration in the Central Mediterranean from an ROL perspective, focusing on failures to rescue migrants

[159] Gowder (n 149) 160–61; see also, MJ Lister, 'Can the Rule of Law Apply at the Border? A Commentary on Paul Gowder's the Rule of Law in the Real World' (2018) 62 *Saint Louis University Law Journal* 323, 328–29.

[160] Dauvergne, 'Sovereignty, Migration and the Rule of Law in Global Times' (n 54) 614–15; P Hirst and G Thompson, *Globalization in Question: International Economy and the Possibilities of Governance*, 2nd edn (Cambridge, Polity Press, 1999).

[161] Dauvergne, 'Sovereignty, Migration and the Rule of Law in Global Times' (n 54) 614–15; Hirst and Thompson (n 160).

[162] C Dauvergne, 'Challenges to Sovereignty: Migration Laws for the 21st Century' (New Issues in Refugee Research, Working Paper no 92, UNHCR, July 2033) 13.

at sea and delays in responding, pushbacks and pullbacks to unsafe countries, and measures taken against SAR NGOs, often justified by recourse to populist narratives. The combination of the ROL principles that I adopted offers a comprehensive picture of how the Italian legal system functions in the particular area of sea migration. It also helps to avoid the risk of seeing the ROL as an 'an "all-or-nothing" concept'.[163] As McCorquodale points out, 'the existence of the rule of law is a matter of degree, with all legal systems being on a spectrum with no rule at all at one end and a complete actualisation of the rule of law at the other'.[164] Thus, it is incorrect to say that 'states have or do not have the rule of law'.[165] By framing the Italian responses to sea migration as ROL issues and breaking these down into their elements, it has been possible to reflect on an empirical reality that is void of the qualities that should characterise modern and liberal democracies. It has also been possible to analyse the role of the courts as guarantors of the ROL and conclude that their role has been valuable, albeit limited. For one, they may intervene only after a breach has occurred and only after several practical and legal obstacles have been overcome. In addition, the political nature of some issues limits their power to intervene.

The challenges to the ROL in this context are connected to the EU's failure to relocate sea migrants across all Member States, leaving coastal states with the primary responsibility for them. While this complaint has been overused as an excuse by some of these states – especially Italy and Malta – to justify a number of measures, it is clear that there is a need for policy responses which redesign this responsibility. Instead, Italy, fellow Member States and the EU have focused on the externalisation of border control, often through soft law instruments which blur accountability even further.[166] At an even deeper level, the challenges to the ROL are linked to the failure to address the problem of irregular migration at its roots. While this is a complex matter which is outside the scope of this study, I would like to mention that the failure to develop lawful entry pathways, both for refugees and economic migrants, needs urgent consideration.[167]

Solutions are needed at the EU level. Without a common design, the failings of the ROL at the national level have an impact on EU values and the EU's ROL framework,[168] 'leading to violations of the duty of sincere cooperation' in Article 4(3) of the Treaty on European Union,[169] fundamental rights more

[163] R McCorquodale, 'The Rule of Law and Migration: Some General Themes' (Conference, Asilah, Morocco, 21 July 2010) 2, available at: www.biicl.org/files/5066_rule_of_law_and_migration1.pdf.

[164] ibid.

[165] ibid.

[166] Tsourdi (n 62) 497; Fassi and Lucarelli (n 91) 263, 268.

[167] For a discussion on lawful entry pathways, see, eg, MC Foblets and L Leboeuf (eds), *Humanitarian Admission to Europe* (Baden-Baden, Nomos/Hart, 2020); A Loxa, 'Complementary Pathways: Pledging Protection at the Edges of EU Law' (2023) 25 *European Journal of Migration and Law* 226.

[168] Tsourdi (n 62) 495.

[169] ibid 490.

generally, and the foundations of the EU. Rather than politically influenced, ad-hoc responses, the approach to sea migration must be long-term and focus on harmonisation of the fragmented legal framework[170] in order to ensure legal certainty. Responses should include the modification of the current SAR zones, such as the overlapping area between Italy and Malta, and the revision of disembarkation agreements among all EU countries. In addition, to counter populist narratives, these measures should be justified to the public according to a new understanding of migration – one that accepts it as a 'normal and necessary phenomenon'[171] and links it to migrants' contributions to society, political stability in the countries of origin, and the need to offer international protection to refugees, as well as to cultural and historical relationships between countries of origin and reception.

Although the case study of Italy has its own characteristics, it is suggestive of trends in the measures that states are adopting to prevent sea arrivals, which include closing their ports, criminalising NGOs for their SAR operations, and externalising immigration control by outsourcing border management controls to third states. EU legislation and policies have had an impact on Italy and other EU countries' approaches to migration: the EU action in the field of migration has been heavily characterised by a security approach and external border controls. Such an approach has also furthered the convergence of immigration law with criminal law, especially with respect to anti-smuggling legislation, resulting in a hybrid system that causes inconsistencies, ineffectiveness and violations of fundamental rights.[172] At the same time, it would be inaccurate to describe Italy's role as a merely passive one. Rather, as Geddes and Scholten explain, Italy has played an active role in shaping EU policies given its geographic location and the number of irregular arrivals. This applies especially to the periods of rule by populist parties – Salvini's Lega Nord, Grillo's Five Star Movement, and Meloni's Brothers of Italy.[173]

While Italy's treatment of sea migration has led to a weakening of the ROL, the question of whether such conclusions can be generalised will require more comparative approaches and similar studies of other countries.[174] The legislation, practices and case law of other EU countries, each determined by its own set of legal and political factors, warrant a systematic and detailed investigation through the lens of the ROL. While security concerns are not in

[170] Orav (n 35) 1.

[171] Fine (n 2) 11. For a discussion on the drivers of immigration to Europe, see A Geddes and P Scholten, *The Politics of Migration and Immigration in Europe* (London, SAGE Publications Ltd, 2016) 237–47.

[172] Gatta, Mitsilegas and Zirulia (n 32).

[173] A Geddes and P Scholten, 'Italy and Spain: Opening a Pandora Box?' in A Geddes and P Scholten (eds), *The Politics of Migration and Immigration in Europe* (London, Sage Publications Ltd, 2016). For instance, in 2023, Italy was particularly influential during the negotiations with Tunisia over the adoption of cooperation and return agreements (see ch 5, section III.A).

[174] eg, unlike Italy, Spain has consistently maintained a relatively liberal policy approach to admissions and migrants' rights, although there have been some policy changes depending on whether the centre-right or centre-left has been in power. Geddes and Scholten, 'Italy and Spain' (n 173).

themselves necessarily or inevitably anti-migrant, securitisation in its current forms has tended to be used to legitimise the closure of borders and other anti-migrant responses, as well as 'emergency' measures. If these investigations bear out similar results, they will confirm the findings of this book that the current securitising approach to migration (which in some ways has become virtually indistinguishable from a strategy of deflection) is short-sighted, inadequate and harmful not only to migrants' rights, but to the foundations of the state as well as the credibility of the EU.

Annex

NGOs' Vessels Active in SAR Operations in the Central Mediterranean Sea between 2016 and end of September 2023[1]

Vessel	Flag state	NGO and country of registration	Operational
Alan Kurdi	Germany	Sea-Eye, Germany	Started operations in 2018. Stopped in 2021.[2] Renamed ResQ People.[3]
Alex Mediterranea	Italy	Mediterranea Saving Humans, Italy	Started operations in 2019. Stopped operations in 2020.
Aita Mari	Spain	Humanitarian Maritime Rescue, Spain	Started operations in 2017. Operational.
Aquarius	Initially Gibraltar, then Panama – both states revoked their flags[4]	SOS Méditerranée and Médecins Sans Frontières, Germany, France, Italy, Switzerland, the Netherlands	Started operations in 2016. Stopped operations in 2018.
Astral	Sweden	Proactiva Open Arms, Spain	Started operations in June 2016. Under maintenance.
Aurora	United Kingdom	Sea Watch, Germany (supported by British SAR Relief)	Started operations in 2022. Blocked.

(continued)

[1] Most of the data is based on the following publications: Fundamental Rights Agency (FRA), 'June 2022 Update – Search and Rescue (SAR) Operations in the Mediterranean and Fundamental Rights' (FRA, 20 June 2022), available at: fra.europa.eu/en/publication/2022/june-2022-update-ngo-ships-sar-activities#publication-tab-1; FRA, 'June 2023 Update Search and Rescue (SAR) Operations in the Mediterranean and Fundamental Rights' (FRA, 11 October 2023), available at: fra.europa.eu/en/publication/2023/2023-update-ngo-ships-sar-activities; Médecins Sans Frontières, 'Vessels at Sea' (Médecins Sans Frontières, nd), available at: searchandrescue.msf.org/history.html; Sea Watch, 'What We Do' (Sea Watch, nd), available at: sea-watch.org/en/mission/sea-watch-3/; SOS Humanity, 'Our Mission' (SOS Humanity, nd), available at: sos-humanity.org/en/our-mission/saving-lives/.

[2] Sea-Eye, 'The Alan Kurdi' (Sea-Eye, nd), available at: sea-eye.org/en/inform/alan-kurdi/#:~:text=In%20July%202021%2C%20Sea%2DEye,with%20the%20SEA%2DEYE%204.

[3] Resq, Home Page (Resq, nd), available at: resq.it/en/il-progetto-resq-in-mare/.

[4] The Maritime Executive, 'Last NGO-Run Rescue Vessel in Med Finds New Flag State' (The Maritime Executive, 6 November 2018), available at: maritime-executive.com/article/last-migrant-rescue-vessel-finds-new-flag-state.

(Continued)

Vessel	Flag state	NGO and country of registration	Operational
Bourbon Argos	Luxemburg[5]	Médecins Sans Frontières, France	Started operations in 2015. Stopped operations in 2016.
Eleonore	Germany	Mission Lifeline, the Netherlands	Started operations in 2016. Stopped operations in 2019.
Geo Barents	Norway	Médecins Sans Frontières, Netherlands	Started operations in May 2021. Operational.
Golfo Azzurro	Panama, until moored	Proactiva Open Arms, Spain	Started operations in 2016. Stopped operations in 2017.
Humanity 1	Germany	SOS Humanity, Germany	Started operations in 2022. Operational.
Iuventa	The Netherlands	Jugend Rettet, Germany	Started operations in 2016. Stopped operations in 2017.
Louise Michel	Germany	Louise Michel, Germany	Started operations in 2020. Under maintenance.
Mare Jonio	Italy	Mediterranea Saving Humans, Italy	Started operations in 2018. Under maintenance.
Minden	Germany	LifeBoat, Germany	Started operations in 2016. Stopped operations in 2019.
Nadir	Germany	RESQSHIP, Germany	Started operations in June 2021. Operational.
Ocean Viking	Norway	SOS Méditerranée, Germany, France, Italy, Switzerland	Started operations in 2019. Operational.
Open Arms	Spain	Proactiva Open Arms, Spain	Started operations in July 2017. Operational.
Phoenix	Norway	Migrant Offshore Aid Station, Malta	Started operations in May 2015. Stopped operations in October 2015.

(continued)

[5] K Rokiciński, 'The Possibilities of Saving Illegal Immigrants, by Ships Owned by the Non-Governmental Organizations on the Mediterranean Sea' (2020) XIV *Rocznik Bezpieczeństwa Morskiego* 171.

(Continued)

Vessel	Flag state	NGO and country of registration	Operational
Rise Above	Germany	Mission Lifeline, Germany	Started operations in 2021. Operational.
ResQ People	Germany	ResQ – People Saving People, Italy	Started operations in August 2021. Operational.
Sea-Eye	The Netherlands – revoked[6]	Sea-Eye, Germany	Started operations in 2016. Stopped operations in 2018.
Sea-Eye 4	Germany	Sea-Eye, Norway	Started operations in May 2021. Blocked.
Sea Watch 3	Germany	Sea Watch, Germany	Started operations in 2017. Stopped operations in 2018.
Sea Watch 4	Germany	Sea Watch, Germany	Started operations in 2021. Stopped operations in 2022. In 2022, it was renamed Humanity 1 and donated to SOS Humanity.
Seefuchs	The Netherlands – revoked[7] – and changed to Germany	Sea-Eye, Germany	Started operations in 2017. Stopped operations after detention in Malta in 2018.
Vos Hestia	Italy[8]	Save the Children, UK	Started operations in 2016. Stopped operations in October 2017. Not operational.
Vos Prudence	Italy	Médecins Sans Frontières, Belgium	Started operations in March 2021. Stopped operations in October 2017.

[6] Sea-Eye, 'The Sea-Eye' (Sea-Eye, nd), available at: sea-eye.org/en/inform/sea-eye/.

[7] Sea-Eye, 'Seefuchs. The Second Rescue Ship' (Sea-Eye, nd), available at: sea-eye.org/en/inform/seefuchs/.

[8] Agenzia Italia, 'Da Dove Vengono le 9 ONG Impegnate nei Soccorsi ai Migranti' (Agenzia Italia, 2 July 2017), available at: www.agi.it/cronaca/migranti_navi_bandiere_soccorsi_9_ong-1917981/news/2017-07-02/.

Glossary

Asylum Seeker and Refugee: An asylum seeker is someone whose request for protection has not been processed yet.[1] A 'refugee' is a person who meets the eligibility requirements of the refugee definition under Article 1(2) of the Refugee Convention: a person who

> 'owing to well-founded fear of being persecuted for reasons of race, religion, nationality, membership of a particular social group or political opinion, is outside the country of his nationality and is unable or, owing to such fear, is unwilling to avail himself of the protection of that country'.[2]

In this book I use words 'asylum seeker' and 'refugee' interchangeably, as according to the UNHCR, refugee status determination is merely declaratory and 'a person is a refugee within the meaning of the 1951 Convention as soon as he or she fulfils the criteria contained in the refugee definition'.[3] In other words, 'a person does not become a refugee because of recognition, but is recognised because he or she is a refugee'.[4]

Interception Measures: As international law does not provide a uniform definition of 'interception measures', I refer to the meaning commonly used in the literature and the UNHCR which includes

> '(i) prevent[ing] embarkation of persons on an international journey without the required documentation; (ii) prevent[ing] further onward international travel by persons who have commenced their journey either by land, air or sea; or (iii) assert[ing] control of vessels where there are reasonable grounds to believe the vessel is transporting persons contrary to international or national maritime law'.[5]

[1] Whereas all refugees had been asylum seekers, not all asylum seekers are recognised to be refugees. UNHCR, 'Glossary' (UNHCR, nd), available at: www.unhcr.org/449267670.pdf.

[2] Convention Relating to the Status of Refugees (Geneva, 28 July 1951) 189 UNTS 150 (Refugee Convention) Article 1(2). It should be noted that the 1969 Protocol Relating to the Status of Refugees expanded the protection of the Refugee Convention to make it universally applicable (the Refugee Convention applied only to refugees from the Second World War and from Europe). Protocol relating to the Status of Refugees (Geneva, 31 January 1967) 606 UNTS 267. UNHCR, 'Glossary' (n 1).

[3] UNHCR, 'Advisory Opinion on the Extraterritoriality Application of *Non-Refoulement* Obligations under the 1951 Convention relating to the Status of Refugees and its 1967 Protocol' (UNHCR, 2007) 2, available at: www.unhcr.org/4d9486929.pdf.

[4] ibid.

[5] E Koka, 'Irregular Migration by Sea: A Critical Analysis of EU and EU Member States Extraterritorial Practice in the Light of International Law' (PhD Thesis, University of Kent, 2018) 60.

Maritime Zones: The United Nations Convention on the Law of the Sea (UNCLOS) defines the following key maritime zones:

- **Internal waters**: They include 'waters on the landward side of the baseline of the territorial sea'[6] which are under the coastal state jurisdiction.[7]
- **Territorial sea**: This extends up to 12 nautical miles from the baseline.[8] The coastal state holds jurisdiction over the territorial sea area, but foreign vessels may navigate through it under the concept of 'innocent passage'.[9] While 'international waters' is informally used to refer to all waters beyond the territorial seas, including contiguous zones and EEZs, it is not a defined term in UNCLOS. 'International waters' is a broader term than 'the high seas', as it includes contiguous zones and EEZs.[10]
- **Contiguous zone**: Within a 12 nautical mile extension beyond the territorial sea, the state has jurisdiction to enforce its laws on matters including customs, taxation, immigration, and pollution.[11]
- **Exclusive economic zone (EEZ)**: This extends up to 200 nautical miles from the baseline, where the state has sole authority over natural resources.[12]
- **Continental shelf**: Coastal states possess exclusive rights to explore and exploit the resources of the seabed and subsoil within a 200 nautical mile zone from the baseline.[13]
- **The high seas**: The high seas encompass all areas of the ocean that do not fall within the jurisdiction of a state's exclusive economic zone, territorial sea, or internal or archipelagic waters. These areas are accessible to all states, granting them various freedoms such as navigation, overflight, and the laying of submarine cables. It is important to note that no state can claim sovereignty over any part of the high seas.[14]
- **The 'Area'**: This denotes the seabed beyond the continental shelf and operates under the principle of the 'common heritage of mankind'. This principle

[6] United Nations Convention on the Law of the Sea (Montego Bay, 10 December 1982) 1833 UNTS 396 (UNCLOS Convention) art 8.
[7] ibid art 1.
[8] ibid art 3.
[9] ibid art 17.
[10] International Relations and Defence Committee, *UNCLOS: The Law of the Sea in the 21st Century: 2nd Report of Session 2021–22* (HL 2022, 159) paras 12–13, available at: hcommittees.parliament.uk/publications/9005/documents/159002/default/. See UNCLOS, art 2 (Territorial Sea); art 33 (Continuous Zone); art 36 (Exclusive Economic Zone (EEZ); art 76(1) (Continental Shelf); and arts 86–87 (High Seas).
[11] UNCLOS, art 33.
[12] ibid art 57.
[13] ibid art 76.
[14] House of Lords (n 10) paras 12–13.

mandates that activities in the Area should be carried out for the collective benefit of humanity.[15]

- **Migrant**: Any person who is outside a state of which he/she is a citizen or national, or in the case of a stateless person, his/her state of birth or habitual residence. The term includes a wide range of categories, including economic migrants, refugees, asylum seekers, victims of trafficking, and stateless persons.[16]

[15] ibid. See UNCLOS, art 2 (Territorial Sea); art 33 (Continuous Zone); art 36 (Exclusive Economic Zone (EEZ); art 76(1) (Continental Shelf); and arts 86–87 (High Seas).

[16] There is no universally accepted definition of 'migrant'. IOM, 'IOM Definition of "Migrant"'(IOM, nd), available at: www.iom.int/about-migration.

Bibliography

BOOKS, MONOGRAPHS, ARTICLES, CHAPTERS, REPORTS, PAPERS AND THESES

Aas, K and Gundhus, HOI (2015) 'Policing Humanitarian Borderlands: Frontex, Human Rights and the Precariousness of Life' 55 *British Journal of Criminology* 1.

Abdehharim, T (2020) 'The Securitization of the EU's Migration Policies: What Consequences for Southern Mediterranean Countries and their Relations to the EU?' 9 *Euromed Survey* 96.

Aditus Foundation (2022) 'Country Report: Malta' (European Council on Refugees and Exhiles).

Agamben, G (2000) *Means without End: Notes on Politics* (Minneapolis, MN, University of Minnesota Press).

—— (2003) *Lo Stato di Eccezione* (Torino, Bollati Boringhieri).

Alagna, F (2022) 'The Continuation of Criminalization by Other Means: The Role of the Judicial Agency in the Italian Policing of Humanitarian Assistance at Sea' *Mediterranean Politics* 1.

Allsopp, J, Vosyliūtė, L and Smilalowski, S (2021) 'Picking "Low-Hanging Fruit" While the Orchard Burns: The Cost of Policing Humanitarian Actors in Italy and Greece as a Strategy to Prevent Migrant Smuggling' 27 *European Journal of Criminal Policy and Research* 65.

Aquilina, S (2021) 'The Application of Human Rights Law and Refugee Law at Sea: A Focus on Search and Rescue Operations' (Master's Thesis, University of Malta).

Ardalan, S (2020) 'EU and US Border Policy: Externalisation of Migration Control and Violation of the Right to Asylum' in V Mitsilegas, V Moreno-Lax and N Vavoula (eds), *Securitising Asylum Flows: Deflection, Criminalisation and Challenges for Human Rights* (Leiden, Brill/Nijhoff) 282–318.

Arrouche, K, Fallone, A and Vosyliūtė, L (2021) 'Between Politics and Inconvenient Evidence: Assessing the Renewed EU Action Plan against Migrant Smuggling' (Policy Brief no 2021/01, Centre for European Policy Studies, Brussels).

Aru, S (2023) 'Battleship at the Port of Europe: Italy's Closed-Port Policy and its Legitimizing Narratives' 104 *Political Geography* 1.

Attard, FG (2020) *The Duty of the Shipmaster to Render Assistance at Sea under International Law* (Leiden, Brill/Nijhoff).

Bantekas, I and Oette, L (2020) *International Human Rights Law and Practice* (Cambridge, CUP).

Barber, N (2003) 'The Rechtsstaat and the Rule of Law' 53 *University of Toronto Law Journal* 443.

Barnard, C and Fraser Butlin, S (2020) 'The Rule of Law and Access to the Courts for EU Migrants' 58 *Journal of Common Market Studies* 1621.

Basaran, T (2014) 'Saving Lives at Sea: Security, Law and Adverse Effects' 16 *European Journal of Migration and Law* 365.

—— (2015) 'The Saved and the Drowned: Governing Indifference in the Name of Security' 46 *Security Dialogue* 205.

Beaulac, S (2009) 'The Rule of Law in International Law Today' in G Palombella and N Walker (eds), *Relocating the Rule of Law* (Oxford, Hart Publishing) 197–224.

Bedner, A (2010) 'An Elementary Approach to the Rule of Law' 2 *Hague Journal on the Rule of Law* 48.

Bellezza, S and Sadik, H (2021) 'Humanitarian Engagement in Maritime Rescue and Migrants Relocation' in G Bevilacqua (ed), *Sicurezza Umana negli Spazi Navigabili: Sfide Comuni e Nuove Tendenze – Human Security in Navigable Spaces: Common Challenges and New Trends* (Napoli, Editoriale Scientifica) 77–94.

Bendel, P (2018) 'Contemporary Politics of International Protection in Europe: From Protection to Prevention' in A Weinar, S Bonjour and L Zhyznomirska (eds), *The Routledge Handbook of the Politics of Migration in Europe* (London, Routledge) 293–302.
Berti, C (2000) 'Right-wing Populism and the Criminalization of Sea-rescue NGOs: The "Sea-Watch 3" Case in Italy, and Matteo Salvini's Communication on Facebook' 43 *Media, Culture, and Society* 532.
Bevilacqua, G (ed) (2021) *Sicurezza Umana negli Spazi Navigabili: Sfide Comuni e Nuove Tendenze – Human Security in Navigable Spaces: Common Challenges and New Trends* (Napoli, Editoriale Scientifica).
Bianchini, K (2018) *Protecting Stateless Persons: The Implementation of the Convention Relating to the Status of Stateless Persons across EU States* (Leiden, Brill/Nijhoff).
—— (2020) 'En Route to Protection: A Literature Review of Key Issues in Refugee Law' (Working Paper No 203, Halle, Max Planck Institute for Social Anthropology).
Bingham, T (2007) 'The Rule of Law' 66 *Cambridge Law Journal* 67.
—— (2010) *The Rule of Law* (London, Penguin Press).
Border Violence Monitoring Network (2022) 'Black Book of Pushbacks' (*Border Violence Monitoring Network*, vol 1, updated edn).
Boubakri, A (2021) 'A Law for the Incorporation of the International Convention on Maritime Search and Rescue, 1979, as Amended into the Laws of Tunisia and to Provide for the Effective Implementation Thereof' (Master's Thesis, International Maritime Law Institute, University of Malta).
Breen, D and United Nations High Commissioner for Refugees Regional Bureau for Europe (2019) 'Desperate Journeys: Refugee and Migrant Children Arriving in Europe and How to Strengthen their Protection. January to September 2019' (UNHCR).
Brigida, LM (2020) 'Ricerca e Soccorso in Mare: Questioni Giuridiche sulla Determinazione del Place of Safety' (Master's Thesis, University of Rome).
Buquicchio, M (1980) *Il Procedimento Costituzionale di Formazione dei Trattati* (Napoli, Jovene).
Byrnem R, Noll, G and Vedsted-Hansen, J (2020) 'Understanding the Crisis of Refugee Law: Legal Scholarship and the EU Asylum System' 33 *Leiden Journal of International Law* 871.
Cafaro, S (2018) 'La Ratifica dei Trattati Internazionali, Una Prospettiva di Diritto Comparato – Italia' (European Parliamentary Research Service, Direzione Generale dei Servizi di Ricerca Parlamentare, Brussels).
Cancellaro, F (2020) 'Dagli Hot-Spots ai "Porti Chiusi": Quali Rimedi per la Libertà "Sequestrata" alla Frontiera?' 3 *Diritto Penale Contemporaneo* 428.
Cantat, C (2016) 'Rethinking Mobilities: Solidarity and Migrant Struggles beyond Narratives of Crisis' 2(4) *Intersections: East European Journal of Society and Politics* 11.
Carballo Piñeiro, L (2020) 'Occupational Hazards in the Light of the Maritime Migration Challenge' in PK Mukherjee et al (eds), *Maritime Law in Motion* (Cham, Springer) 77–95.
Carrera, S et al, *Policing Humanitarianism: EU Policies Against Human Smuggling and their Impact on Civil Society* (Oxford, Hart Publishing, 2019).
Carrera, S et al, 'The Three Faces of Policing the Mobility Society in the EU' in S Carrera et al, *Policing Humanitarianism: EU Policies Against Human Smuggling and their Impact on Civil Society* (Oxford, Hart Publishing, 2019) 171–81.
Carrera, S, Allsopp, J and Vosyliūtė, L (2018) 'Policing the Mobility Society: The Effects of EU-Anti-Migrant Smuggling Policies on Humanitarianism' 4 *International Journal of Migration and Border Studies* 236.
Carrera, S and Cortinovis, R (28 June 2019) 'Search and Rescue, Disembarkation and Relocation Arrangements in the Mediterranean. Sailing Away from Responsibility?' (Centre for European Policy Studies, Papers in Liberty and Security in Europe, No 2019–10).
—— (October 2019) 'The Malta Declaration on SAR and Relocation: A Predictable EU Solidarity Mechanism?' (Paper no 2019–14, Centre for European Policy Studies, Brussels).

Carrera, S and Hertog, L den (January 2015) 'Whose *Mare*? Rule of Law Challenges in the Field of European Border Surveillance in the Mediterranean' (Paper, *Liberty and Security in Europe* no 79, Centre for European Policy Studies, Brussels).

Carrera, S, Hertog, L den and Stefan, M (April 2017) 'It Wasn't Me! The Luxembourg Court Orders on the EU–Turkey Refugee Deal' (Policy Insights no 2017/15, Centre for European Policy Studies, Brussels).

Carrera, S, Mitsilegas, V, Allsopp, J and Vosyliūtė, L (eds) (2019) *Policing Humanitarianism: EU Policies against Human Smuggling and their Impact on Civil Society* (Oxford, Hart Publishing).

Carrera S, Santos Vara, J and Strik, T (eds) (2019) *Constitutionalising the External Dimensions of EU Migration Policies in Times of Crises: Legality, Rule of Law and Fundamental Rights Reconsidered* (Cheltenham, Edward Elgar Publishing).

Carrera, S et al (2018) 'Fit for Purpose? The Facilitation Directive and the Criminalisation of Humanitarian Assistance to Irregular Migrants: 2018 Update' (Technical Report, European University Institute).

—— (2019) 'Introduction' in S Carrera et al (eds), *Policing Humanitarianism: EU Policies Against Human Smuggling and their Impact on Civil Society* (Oxford, Hart Publishing) 1–12.

Casiello, C and Venditti, M (2019) 'Il Caso Diciotti: tra Obblighi di Soccorso in Mare e Garanzia dei Diritti Fondamentali' 39(2) *Diritto Pubblico Comparato ed Europeo Online* 947.

Castelli Gattinara, P (2017) 'The "Refugee Crisis" in Italy as a Crisis of Legitimacy' 9 *Contemporary Italian Politics* 318.

Centro di Ateneo per i Diritti Umani Antonio Papisca, Università di Padova (2022) *Annuario Italiano dei Diritti Umani 2021* (Padova, Padova University Press).

Cheli, E (1961) *Atto Politico e Funzione d'Indirizzo Politico* (Milano, Giuffré).

Chevallier, J (2010) *L'État de Droit*, 5th edn (Paris, Montchrestien).

Ciliberto, G (2018) 'Libya's Pullbacks of Boat Migrants: Can Italy Be Held Accountable for Violations of International Law?' 4 *Italian Law Journal* 489.

Clayton, G and Firth, G (2018) *Immigration and Asylum Law*, 8th edn (Oxford, OUP).

Conforti, B (1993) *International Law and the Role of Domestic Legal Systems* (Dordrecht, Martinus Nijhoff Publishers).

Coppens, J (2013) 'Migrants at Sea: A Legal Analysis of a Maritime Safety and Security Problem' (PhD Thesis, University of Ghent).

—— (2013) 'The Essential Role of Malta in Drafting the New Regional Agreement on Migrants at Sea in the Mediterranean Basin' 44 *Journal of Maritime Law and Commerce* 89.

Costa, P and Zolo, D (2002) *Lo Stato di Diritto: Storia, Teoria, Critica* (Milano, Feltrinelli).

Costello, C and Mann, I (2020) 'Border Justice: Migration and Accountability for Human Rights Violations' 21 *German Law Journal* 311.

Costello, C and Mouzourakis, M (2016) 'The Common European Asylum System: Where Did It All Go Wrong?' in M Fletcher, E Herlin-Karnell and C Matera (eds), *The European Union as an Area of Freedom, Security and Justice* (London, Routledge) 263–300.

Council of Europe, Parliamentary Assembly (PACE), Committee on Migration, Refugees and Displaced Persons (2012) 'Lives Lost in the Mediterranean Sea: Who is Responsible?' (Report, PACE, Strasbourg).

Craig, P (2021) 'The Rule of Law. National, International, and Regional Dimensions' in B Faedda (ed), *The Rule of Law: Cases, Strategies and Interpretations* (Vicenza, Ronzani Edizioni Scientifiche) 61–65.

Cusumano, E (2017) 'Emptying the Sea with a Spoon? Non-governmental Providers of Migrants Search and Rescue in the Mediterranean' 75 *Marine Policy* 91.

—— (2019) 'Straightjacketing Migrant Rescuers? The Code of Conduct on Maritime NGOs' 24 *Mediterranean Politics* 106.

Cusumano, E and Gombeer, K (2020) 'In Deep Waters: The Legal, Humanitarian and Political Implications of Closing Italian Ports to Migrant Rescuers' 25 *Mediterranean Politics* 245.

Cusumano, E and Villa, M (2021) 'From "Angels" to "Vice Smugglers": The Criminalization of Sea Rescue NGOs in Italy' 27 *European Journal on Criminal Policy and Research* 23.

—— (November 2019) 'Sea Rescue NGOs: A Pull Factor of Irregular Migration?' (Policy Brief, Robert Schuman Centre).
Cuttitta, P (2008) 'The Case of the Italian Southern Sea Borders: Cooperation across the Mediterranean?' in P Cutitta et al (eds), *Immigration Flows and the Management of the EU's Southern Maritime Borders* (Barcelona, CIDOB Editions) 45–62.
—— (2018) 'Repoliticization through Search and Rescue, Humanitarian NGOs and Migration Management in the Central Mediterranean' 23 *Geopolitics* 632.
D'Amico, M and Siccardi, C (2022) 'La Tutela die Diritti Costituzionali dei Migrant ai Confini' in M Ambrosini, M d'Amico and E Perassi (eds), *Migrazioni, Confini, Diritti Umani* (Milano, Milano University Press) 17–45.
Dauvergne, C (2004) 'Sovereignty, Migration and the Rule of Law in Global Times' 67 *Modern Law Review* 588.
—— (July 2023) 'Challenges to Sovereignty: Migration Laws for the 21st Century' (Working Paper no 92, New Issues in Refugee Research, UNHCR).
Davitti, D (2019) 'Biopolitical Borders and the State of Exception in the European Migration "Crisis"' 29 *European Journal of International Law* 1173.
Dedov, D (2021) 'How State of Emergency Affects Democracy. Fair Trial for Political Activists' in M Elósegui, A Miron and I Motoc (eds), *The Rule of Law in Europe: Recent Challenges and Judicial Responses* (Cham, Springer) 21–31.
De Sardan, O (2015) *Epistemology Fieldwork and Anthropology* (New York, Palgrave Macmillan).
De Vittor, F (2021) 'Il Port State Control sulle Navi delle ONG che Prestano Soccorso in Mare: Tutela della Sicurezza della Navigazione o Ostacolo alle Attività di Soccorso?' 15 *Diritti Umani e Diritto Internazionale* 103.
Dell'Acqua, C (1983) *Atto Politico ed Esercizio di Poteri Sovrani* (Padova, CEDAM).
Di Blase, A, Bartolini, G and Sossai, M (2019) *Diritto Internazionale e Valori Umanitari* (Roma, RomaTrE-Press).
Di Bologna, C (2004) 'Accordi e Missioni Internazionali: la Prassi Governativa' in A Barbera and TF Giupponi (eds), *La Prassi degli Organi Costituzionali* (Bologna, Bononia University Press) 295–309.
Di Gaspare, G (1984) *Considerazioni sugli Atti Politici dei Governo e sull'Atto Politico: l' Esperienza Italiana e Francese nello Stato Liberale* (Milano, Giuffré).
Dimitrova, S (2023) 'Rethinking "Jurisdiction" in International Human Rights Law in Rescue Operations at Sea in the Light of *AS and Others v Italy* and *AS and Others v Malta*: A New Right to be Rescued at Sea?' 56 *Israel Law Review* 120.
Duval, A (2018) 'Publish (Tweets or Blogs) or Perish? Legal Academia in Times of Social Media' 23(1) *Tilburg Law Review* 91.
Dworkin, R (1977) *Taking Rights Seriously* (Cambridge, MA, Harvard University Press).
—— (1985) *A Matter of Principle* (Oxford, OUP).
Ehrenreich Brooks, R (2003) 'The New Imperialism: Violence, Norms and the "Rule of Law"' 101 *Michigan Law Review* 2275.
EASO (9 June 2021) '"Safe Country of Origin" Concept in EU+ Countries: Situational Update' (Situational Update, Issue no 3).
Endicott, T (1999) 'The Impossibility of the Rule of Law' 19 *Oxford Journal of Legal Studies* 1.
Facchini, D (2018) *Alla Deriva: I Migranti, le Rotte del Mar Mediterraneo, le Ong: il Naufragio della Politica, che Nega i Diritti per Fabbricare Consenso* (Milano, Altra Economia).
Faedda, B (2021) 'Introduction' in B Faedda (ed), *The Rule of Law: Cases, Strategies and Interpretations* (Vicenza, Ronzani Edizioni Scientifiche) 13–18.
Fallon, R (2007) '"The Rule of Law" as a Concept in Constitutional Discourse' 97 *Columbia Law Review* 6.
Fassi, E and Lucarelli, S (2021) 'The EU Migration System and Global Justice: An Assessment' in M Ceccorulli, E Fassi and S Lucarelli (eds), *The EU Migration System of Governance: Justice on the Move* (New York, Palgrave Macmillan) 259–78.

Fazzini, A (2020) 'Il Caso S.S. and Others v Italy Nel Quadro dell'Esternalizzazione delle Frontiere in Libia: Osservazioni sui Possibili Scenari al Vaglio della Corte di Strasburgo' 2 *Diritto, Immigrazione e Cittadinanza* 86.

Ferguson, R (2018) 'The Fragmentation of International Law; the World Trade Organization and International Human Rights Regimes' in R Ferguson, *The Right to Food and the World Trade Organization's Rules on Agriculture* (Leiden, Brill) 13–50.

Fine, S (October 2019) 'All at Sea: Europe's Crisis of Solidarity on Sea Migration' (Policy Brief, European Council on Foreign Relations).

Fitzpatrick, P (2003) '"Gods Would Be Needed": American Empire and the Rule of (International) Law' 16 *Leiden Journal of International Law* 429.

Foblets, MC and Leboeuf, L (eds), *Humanitarian Admission to Europe* (Baden-Baden, Nomos/Hart, 2020).

—— (2020) 'Introduction: Humanitarian Admission to Europe. From Policy Developments to Legal Controversies and Litigation' in MC Foblets and L Leboeuf (eds), *Humanitarian Admission to Europe* (Baden-Baden, Nomos/Hart) 11–45.

Foundez, I (2011) 'Legal Pluralism and International Development Agencies: State Building or Legal Reform?' 3 *Hague Journal on the Rule of Law* 18.

Franchini, M (1980) 'I Poteri del Governo nella Conclusione di Accordi Internazionali' 1 *Rivista Trimestrale di Diritto Pubblico* 36.

Frelick, B, Kysel, IM and Podkul, J (2016) 'The Impact of Externalization of Migration Controls on the Rights of Asylum Seekers and Other Migrants' 4 *Journal on Migration and Human Security* 190.

Friedell, S (1979) 'Compensation and Reward for Saving Life at Sea' 77 *Michigan Law Review* 1218.

Frontex (2018) 'Multipurpose Aerial Surveillance' (Publications Office of the European Union).

Fuller, L (1969) *The Morality of Law* (New Haven, CT, Yale University Press).

Galani, S (2021) 'Port Closures and Persons at Sea in International Law' 70 *International & Comparative Law Quarterly* 605.

Galanter, M (1983) 'The Radiating Effects of Courts' in K Boyum and L Mather (eds), *Empirical Theories of Courts* (New York, Longman) 117–42.

Gallagher, A and David, F (2014) *The International Law of Migrant Smuggling* (Cambridge, CUP).

Gammeltoft-Hansen, T (2011) *Access to Asylum: International Refugee Law and the Globalization of Migration Control* (Cambridge, CUP).

Gammeltoft-Hansen, T and Aalberts, T (2014) 'Sovereignty at Sea: The Law and Politics of Saving Lives in Mare Liberum' 17 *Journal of International Relations & Development* 439.

García-Carriazo, ÁJ (2019) 'Small Island, Big Issue: Malta and its Search and Rescue Region – SAR' 7 *Paix et Securité Internationales* 299.

Gatta, GL (2019) 'Migration and the Rule of (Human Rights) Law: Two "Crises" Looking in the Same Mirror' 15 *Croatian Yearbook of European Law & Policy* 99.

Gatta, GL, Mitsilegas, V and Zirulia, S (eds) (2020) *Controlling Immigration through Criminal Law: European and Comparative Perspectives on 'Crimmigration'* (Oxford, Hart Publishing).

Gatta, GL and Zirulia, S (2020) 'Introduction' in GL Gatta, V Mitsilegas and S Zirulia (eds), *Controlling Immigration through Criminal Law: European and Comparative Perspectives on 'Crimmigration'* (Oxford, Hart Publishing) 1–8.

Geddes A and Scholten, P, 'Italy and Spain: Opening a Pandora Box?' in A Geddes and P Scholten (eds), *The Politics of Migration and Immigration in Europe* (London, Sage Publications Ltd, 2016) 173–94.

—— (2016) *The Politics of Migration and Immigration in Europe* (London, Sage Publications Ltd).

Gennari, L (2021) 'Navi in Porto, Naufragi nel Mediterraneo: la Dimensione Amministrativa del Contrasto alle Operazioni di Soccorso' XXI *Diritto e Questioni Pubbliche*, Special Issue 83.

Ghebreigziabiher Ogbazghi, M (2022) 'The Italy–Libya Agreements: Controversial Cooperation. Assessing the Human Rights Violations on Matters of Refugees and Migrants Protection' (Master's Thesis, University of Macedonia).

Ghera, F (2006) 'Commento all' Articolo 80' in R Bifulco, A Celotto and M Olivetti (eds), *Commentario alla Costituzione* (Torino, Utet Giuridica) 1559–78.

Giuffré, M (2012) 'State Responsibility Beyond Borders: What Legal Basis for Italy's Pushbacks to Libya?' 24 *International Journal of Refugee Law* 692.

—— (2020) 'Esternalizzazione delle Frontiere e *Non-refoulement*: Accesso al Territorio e alla Procedure di Asilo alla Luce della Sentenza n 22917/2019' 1 *Questione Giustizia* 190.

—— (2020) *The Readmission of Asylum Seekers under International Law* (eBook, Hart Publishing).

Giuffré, M and Moreno-Lax, V (2019) 'The Rise of Consensual Containment: From "Contactless Control" to "Contactless Responsibility" for Migratory Flows' in S Singh Juss (ed), *Research Handbook on International Refugee Law* (Cheltenham, Edward Elgar Publishing) 82–108.

Gkliati, M (29 September 2023) 'Nexus Theory and the Multi-actor Reality of the EU External Borders: Testing the Efficacy of Non-Judicial Accountability Mechanisms' (Presentation at 'Shared Responsibility at the EU's External Borders' Conference, Barcelona).

Goldsmith, JL and Posner, EA (1999) 'A Theory of Customary International Law' 66 *University of Chicago Law Review* 1113.

Golia, AJ (2019) 'La Fortezza che Resiste. Potere Estero, Conflitto di Attribuzione e Prescrittività Costituzionale' 3(1) *La Democrazia A-Costituzionale* 47.

—— (2023) 'Migration and the Janus Faces of Solidarity and the Rule of Law: Brief Remarks in the Light of the Italian Experience' in T Russo, A Oriolo and G Dalia (eds), *Solidarity and Rule of Law: European Union and its Neighbours in a Globalized World* (Cham, Springer) 99–109.

Golub, S (2003) 'Beyond Rule of Law Orthodoxy: The Legal Empowerment Alternative' (Working Paper no 41, Carnegie Endowment for International Peace).

Goodwin-Gill, GS and McAdam, J (2007) *The Refugee in International Law*, 3rd edn (Oxford, OUP).

Goodwin-Gill, GS, McAdam, J and Dunlop, E (2021) 'The Principle of Non-refoulement – Part 2' in GS Goodwin-Gill and J McAdam (eds), *The Refugee in International Law*, 4th edn (Oxford, OUP) 307–49.

Gowder, P (2016) *The Rule of Law in the Real World* (Cambridge, CUP).

Guilfoyle, D (2017) 'Jurisdiction at Sea. Migrant Interdiction and the Transnational Security State' in T Gammeltoft-Hansen and J Vedsted-Hansen (eds), *Human Rights and the Dark Side of Globalisation: Transnational Law Enforcement and Migration Control* (London, Routledge) 114–37.

Guilfoyle, D and Papastavridis, E (2014) 'Mapping Disembarkation Options: Towards Strengthening Cooperation in Managing Irregular Movements by Sea' (UNHCR).

Gunatilleke, G (2021) 'Justifying Limitations to Freedom of Expression' 22 *Human Rights Review* 91.

Haljan, D (2009) 'Is the Rule of Law a Limit on Popular Sovereignty?' in E Claes, W Devroe and B Keirsblick (eds), *Facing the Limits of the Law* (Berlin, Springer) 273–99.

Hartig, S (2020) 'Frontex: From Coordinating Controls to Combating Crime' 2 *European Criminal Law Associations' Forum* 134.

Hayek, FA (1944) *The Road to Serfdom* (Chicago, IL, University of Chicago Press).

Heller, C, Pezzani, L and Studio, S (2012) 'Report on the "Left-To-Die Boat"' (Centre for Research Architecture, Goldsmiths, University of London).

Hendow, M (2013) 'Tunisian Migrant Journeys: Human Rights Concerns for Tunisians Arriving by Sea' 2 *Laws* 187.

Hertogh, M (2016) 'Your Rule of Law is *Not* Mine: Rethinking Empirical Approaches to EU Rule of Law Promotion' 14 *Asia Europe Journal* 43.

Hirst, P and Thompson, G (1999) *Globalization in Question: International Economy and the Possibilities of Governance*, 2nd edn (Cambridge, Polity Press).

International Commission of Jurists (22 April 2022) 'Criminalization of Humanitarian and Other Support and Assistance to Migrants and the Defence of their Human Rights in the EU' (Briefing Paper, International Commission of Jurists).

International Relations and Defence Committee, *UNCLOS: The Law of the Sea in the 21st Century: 2nd Report of Session 2021–22* (HL 2022, 159).

Italian Coast Guard (December 2017) 'Search and Rescue (S.A.R.), Activity in the Central Mediterranean Sea from January 1st to December 31st 2017'.

—— (December 2018) 'Search and Rescue (S.A.R.), Activity in the Central Mediterranean Sea from January 1st to December 31st 2018'.

Janer Torrens, JD (2020) 'Migrant Search and Rescue Operations in the Mediterranean by Humanitarian Organizations: Migrant Smuggling or Humanitarian Assistance?' 8 *Paix et Securité Internationales* 381.

Jaremba, U and Mak, E (May 2014) 'Interviewing Judges in the Transnational Context' *Law and Method* 1.

Jayasurya, K (2001) 'The Exception Becomes the Norm: Law and Regimes of Exception in East Asia' 2(1) *Asian-Pacific Law & Policy Journal* 108.

Ju-Sung, L and Nerghes, A (2018) 'Refugee or Migrant Crisis? Labels, Perceived Agency, and Sentiment Popularity in Online Discussions' 4(3) *Social Media + Society* 1.

Kalland Aarstad, Å (2015) 'The Duty to Assist and Its Disincentives: The Shipping Industry and the Mediterranean Migration Crisis' 20 *Mediterranean Politics* 413.

Kassoti, E and Idriz, N (2022) 'The Informalisation of the EU's External Action in the Field of Migration and Asylum' in E Kassoti and N Idriz (eds), *The Informalisation of the EU's External Action in the Field of Migration and Asylum* (The Hague, TMC Asser Press) 1–14.

Kilpatrick, RL (October 2017) 'The "Refugee Clause": Why Contractual Allocation of Rescue Costs is Critical during Periods of Mass Migration at Sea' (NUS Centre for Maritime Law Working Paper 17/09 National University of Singapore).

—— (2019–20) 'Why Evolving European SAR Policies Threaten Merchant Shipping' 7 *Maritime Safety and Security Law Journal*, Special Issue on the EU and Maritime Security 31.

Kilpatrick, RL and Smith, A (2016) 'The International Legal Obligation to Rescue During Mass Migration at Sea: Navigating the Sovereign and Commercial Dimensions of a Mediterranean Crisis' 28(2) *University of San Francisco School of Law Maritime Law Journal* 141.

—— (2020) 'Balancing the SAR Responsibilities of States and Shipmasters' in V Mitsilegas, V Moreno-Lax and N Vavoula (eds), *Securitising Asylum Flows: Deflection, Criminalisation and Challenges for Human Rights* (Leiden, Brill/Nijhoff) 81–101.

Kim, S (2017) 'Non-Refoulement and Extraterritorial Jurisdiction: State Sovereignty and Migration Controls at Sea in the European Context' 30 *Leiden Journal of International Law* 49.

Klabbers, J (2021) 'The Accountability of International Organizations in Refugee and Migration Law' in C Costello, M Foster and J McAdam (eds), *The Oxford Handbook of International Refugee Law* (Oxford, OUP) 1157–73.

Klein, N (2014) 'A Case for Harmonizing Laws on Maritime Interceptions of Irregular Migrants' 63 *International & Comparative Law Quarterly* 787.

Kleinfeld, R (2006) 'Competing Definitions of the Rule of Law' in T Carothers (ed), *Promoting the Rule of Law Abroad: In Search of Knowledge* (Washington, DC, Carnegie Endowment for International Peace) 31–74.

Klepp, S (2011) 'A Double Bind: Malta and the Rescue of Unwanted Migrants at Sea, a Legal Anthropological Perspective on the Humanitarian Law of the Sea' 23 *International Journal of Refugee Law* 538.

—— (2014) 'Malta and the Rescue of Unwanted Migrants at Sea: Negotiating the Humanitarian Law of the Sea and the Contested Redesigning Borders' in H Schwenken and S Ruß-Sattar (eds), *New Border and Citizenship Politics* (London, Palgrave Macmillan) 30–43.

Kneebone, S (2009) *Refugees, Asylum Seekers and the Rule of Law: Comparative Perspectives* (Cambridge, CUP).

—— (2009) 'Conclusions on the Rule of Law' in S Kneebone (ed), *Refugees, Asylum Seekers and the Rule of Law: Comparative Perspectives* (New York, Cambridge University Press) 281–309.

Koka, E (2018) 'Irregular Migration by Sea: A Critical Analysis of EU and EU Member State Extraterritorial Practice in Light of International Law' (PhD Thesis, University of Kent).

Koka, E and Veshi, D (2019) 'Irregular Migration by Sea: Interception and Rescue Interventions in Light of International Law and the EU Sea Borders Regulation' 21 *European Journal of Migration and Law* 26.

Komp, LM (2017) 'The Duty to Assist Persons in Distress: An Alternative Source of Protection against the Return of Migrants and Asylum Seekers to the High Seas?' in V Moreno-Lax and E Papastavridis (eds), *'Boat Refugees' and Migrants at Sea: A Comprehensive Approach* (Leiden, Brill) 222–47.

Korkea-aho, E and Leino, P (2019) 'Interviewing Lawyers: A Critical Self-Reflection on Expert Interviews as a Method of EU Legal Research' 12 *European Journal of Legal Studies* 17.

Kymlicka, W (1986) *Liberalism, Community, and Culture* (Oxford, OUP).

Lautenbach, G (2013) *The Concept of the Rule of Law and the European Court of Human Rights* (Oxford, OUP).

Leanza, U and Caffio, F (2015) 'Il SAR Mediterraneo. La Ricerca e Soccorso nel Diritto Marittimo: l'Applicazione della Convenzione di Amburgo del 1979' 12 *Rivista Marittima* 10.

Lippolis, V (1989) *La Costituzione Italiana e la Formazione dei Trattati Internazionali* (Rimini, Maggioli Editore).

Lister, MJ (2018) 'Can the Rule of Law Apply at the Border? A Commentary on Paul Gowder's the Rule of Law in the Real World' 62 *Saint Louis University Law Journal* 323.

Little, D (2014) 'The Justification of Human Rights' 3 *Brigham Young University Law Review* 585.

Lloyd-Damnjanovic, I (9 October 2020) 'Criminalization of Search-and-Rescue Operations in the Mediterranean Has Been Accompanied by Rising Migrant Death Rate' (Report, Migration Policy Institute).

Loxa, A (2023) 'Complementary Pathways: Pledging Protection at the Edges of EU Law' 25 *European Journal of Migration and Law* 226.

Magen, A (2016) 'Crack in the Foundations: Understanding the Great Rule of Law Debate in the EU' 54 *Journal of Common Market Studies* 1050.

Magen, A and Morlino, L (2008) *International Actors, Democratization, and the Rule of Law: Anchoring Democracy?* (Abingdon, Routledge).

Magri, M (2019) 'Obbligo di Soccorso in Mare, Funzioni della Guardia Costiera e Respingimenti "Delegati": sui Poteri del Ministro dell'Interno' 1 *Istituzioni del Federalismo* 149.

Mainwaring, C and DeBono, D (2021) 'Criminalizing Solidarity: Search and Rescue in a Neo-Colonial Sea' 39 *Environment and Planning C: Politics and Space* 1030.

Mann, I (2018) 'Maritime Black Holes: Migration and Rightlessness in International Law' 29 *European Journal of International Law* 347.

Manners, I (2002) 'Normative Power Europe: A Contradiction in Terms?' 40 *Journal of Common Market Studies* 235.

Marchesi, A (2021) *La Protezione Internazionale dei Diritti Umani* (Torino, Giappichelli).

Marchiafava, G (2020) 'The Impact of the New Italian Security Regulation on the Search and Rescue of Migrants at Sea' 174 *Comparative Maritime Law* 133.

Marochkin, S (2019) 'National and International Rule of Law: Proclaimed Adherence and Real-Life Policies' 44 *Review of Central and East European Law*, Special Issue 305.

Martin, M (June 2014) 'Prioritising Border Control over Human Lives: Violations of the Rights of Migrants and Refugees at Sea' (Policy Brief, *Euro-Mediterranean Human Rights Network*).

Martin, SF, Weerasinghe, S and Taylor A (eds) (2014) *Humanitarian Crises and Migration: Causes, Consequences and Responses* (London, Routledge).

Masera, L, 'L'incriminazione dei Soccorsi in Mare: Dobbiamo Rassegnarci al Disumano?' (2018) 2 *Questione Giustizia* 225.

—— (2021) 'Il Contrasto Amministrativo alle ONG che Operano Soccorsi in Mare, dal Codice di Condotta di Minniti, al Decreto Salvini bis e alla Riforma Lamorgese: le Forme Mutevoli di una Politica Costante' *Questione Giustizia* 1.

Mauri, F (2020) 'Un Nuovo Approccio Alla Rule of Law: la Checklist della Commissione di Venezia' 2 *Associazione Italiana dei Constituzionalisti* 37.

McCorquodale, R (21 July 2010) 'The Rule of Law and Migration: Some General Themes' (Conference, Asilah, Morocco).

—— (2016) 'Defining the International Rule of Law: Defining Gravity?' 65 *International & Comparative Law Quarterly* 277.

Miltner, B (2010) 'Human Security and Protection from *Refoulement* in the Maritime Context' in E and C Ferstman (eds), *Human Security and Non-Citizens: Law, Policy and International Affairs* (Cambridge, CUP) 195–224.

Minetti, M (2020) 'The Facilitators Package, Penal Populism and the Rule of Law: Lessons from Italy' 11 *New Journal of European Criminal Law* 335.

Mitrotti, A (2020) 'L'Atto Politico: Riflessioni Intorno ad Un Istituto in Perenne "Tensione" Tra Scienza Costituzionale ed Amministrativa' 1 *Nomos. Le Attualità nel Diritto* 1.

Mitsilegas, V, 'Extraterritorial Immigration Control in the 21st Century: The Individual and the State Transformed' in B Ryan and V Mitsilegas (eds), *Extraterritorial Immigration Control: Legal Challenges* (Leiden, Martinus Nijhoff Publishers, 2010) 39–68.

—— (2019) 'Extraterritorial Immigration Control, Preventive Justice and the Rule of Law in Turbulent Times: Lessons from the Anti-Smuggling Crusade' in S Carrera, JS Vara and T Strik (eds), *Constitutionalising the External Dimensions of EU Migration Policies in Times of Crises: Legality, Rule of Law and Fundamental Rights Reconsidered* (Cheltenham, Edward Elgar Publishing) 290–308.

Molinari, C (2022) 'EU Readmission Deals and Constitutional Allocation of Powers: Parallel Paths that Need to Cross?' in E Kassoti and N Idriz (eds), *The Informalisation of the EU's External Action in the Field of Migration and Asylum* (The Hague, TMC Asser Press) 15–37.

Moreno-Lax, V (2011) 'Seeking Asylum in the Mediterranean: Against a Fragmentary Reading of EU Member States' Obligations Accruing at Sea' 23 *International Journal of Refugee Law* 174.

—— (2017) *Accessing Asylum in Europe: Extraterritorial Border Controls and Refugee Rights Under EU Law* (Oxford, OUP).

—— (2020) 'The Architecture of Functional Jurisdiction: Unpacking Contactless Control on Public Powers, S.S. and Others v Italy, and the "Operational Model"' 21 *German Law Journal* 385.

Moreno-Lax, V et al (eds) (June 2021) 'The EU Approach on Migration in the Mediterranean' (Study, Policy Department for Citizens' Rights and Constitutional Affairs, European Parliament).

Moreno-Lax, V, Ghezelbash, D and Klein, N (2019) 'Between Life, Security and Rights: Framing the Interdiction of "Boat Migrants" in the Central Mediterranean and Australia' 32 *Leiden Journal of International Law* 715.

Müller, P and Slominski, P (2021) 'Breaking the Legal Link but Not the Law? The Externalization of EU Migration Control through Orchestration in the Central Mediterranean' 28 *Journal of European Public Policy* 801.

—— (2022) 'Shrinking the Space for Civil Society: (De)Politicizing the Obstruction of Humanitarian NGOs in EU Border Management' 48 *Journal of Ethnic and Migration Studies* 4774.

Mungianu, R (2017) *Frontex and Non-Refoulement: The International Responsibility of the EU* (Cambridge, CUP).

Napolitano, G (2020) 'The Rule of Law' in P Cane et al (eds), *The Oxford Handbook of Comparative Administrative Law* (Oxford, OUP) 421–42.

Natter, K (2022) 'Tunisia's Migration Politics throughout the 2011 Revolution: Revisiting the Democratisation–Migrant Rights Nexus' 43 *Third World Quarterly* 1551.

Neri, K (2021) 'The Challenges Faced by Private Ships in Large-scale Rescue Operations at Sea' in G Bevilacqua (ed), *Sicurezza Umana negli Spazi Navigabili: Sfide Comuni e Nuove Tendenze – Human Security in Navigable Spaces: Common Challenges and New Trends* (Napoli, Editoriale Scientifica) 95–108.

Nicolaidis, K and Kleinfeld, R (2012) 'Rethinking Europe's "Rule of Law" and Enlargement Agenda: The Fundamental Dilemma' (SIGMA Papers no 49, OECD).

Odello, M (2021) *Il Diritto dei Rifugiati: Elementi di Diritto Internazionale, Europeo e Italiano* (Milano, FrancoAngeli).

Office of the High Commissioner for Human Rights (OHCHR) (2019) 'Joint Communication from Special Procedures' (OHCHR, 15 May 2019).
—— (2020) *The Case for a Human Rights Approach to the Rule of Law in European Union* (OHCHR).
—— (May 2021) 'Lethal Disregard: Search and Rescue and the Protection of Migrants in the Central Mediterranean Sea' (OHCHR).
—— (13 April 2023) 'Türk Sounds Alarm at Escalating Migrant Crisis in Central Mediterranean' (Press Release, OHCHR).
Organisation for Economic Co-operation and Development (OECD) (2005) 'Equal Access to Justice and the Rule of Law Report' (OECD).
Olivito, E (2018) 'Il Cul-de-Sac Costituzionale degli Accordi in Forma Semplificata: Iniziativa Legislativa Parlamentare ed Esternalizzazione delle Politiche Migratorie' 24 *Diritto Pubblico* 435.
Orav, A (2022) 'Search and Rescue Efforts for Mediterranean Migrants' (Briefing, European Parliamentary Research Service).
O'Reilly, K (2005) *Ethnographic Methods* (Abingdon, Routledge).
Osamudiamen Eruaga, O (2018) 'Irregular Migration in the Mediterranean and the Challenges of Observing the Duty to Render Assistance at Sea' 17 *Loyola Maritime Law Journal* 33.
Pacella, F (2018) 'Cooperazione Italia–Libia: Profili di Responsabilità per Crimini di Diritto Internazionale' 4 *Diritto Penale Contemporaneo* 5.
Palmer Thompson, E (1977) *Whigs and Hunters: The Origin of the Black Act* (Harmondsworth, Penguin).
Palombella, G (2019) 'Two Threats to the Rule of Law: Legal and Epistemic (Between Technocracy and Populism)' 11 *Hague Journal on the Rule of Law* 383.
—— (2021) 'The Rule of Law and its Conception between "National" and "International"' in B Faedda (ed), *Rule of Law: Cases, Strategies and Interpretations* (Vicenza, Ronzani Edizioni Scientifiche) 72–80.
Palombino, FM (2018) 'Sui Pretesi Limiti Costituzionali al Potere del Governo di Stipulare Accordi in Forma Semplificata' 3 *Rivista di Diritto Internazionale* 870.
Panattoni, G (2020) 'La Controversa Figura dell'Atto Politico, alla Luce dei Casi "Diciotti" e "Gregoretti"' 8 *Federalismi.it*.
Papanicolopulu, I (2014) 'Human Rights and the Law of the Sea' in D Joseph Attard et al (eds), *The IMLI Manual on International Maritime Law Volume I: The Law of the Sea* (Oxford, OUP) 509–32.
—— (2016) 'The Duty to Rescue at Sea, in Peacetime and in War: A General Overview' 98 *International Review of the Red Cross* 491.
—— (2017) 'Immigrazione Irregolare, Via Mare, Tutela della Vita Umana e Organizzazioni non Governative' 3 *Diritto, Immigrazione e Cittadinanza* 1.
—— (2019) 'Le Operazioni di Search and Rescue: Problemi e Lacune del Diritto Internazionale' 2 *Rivista Trimestrale di Diritto Pubblico* 507.
—— (2020) 'Duty to Rescue and Entry into Port: The *Carola Rackete* Decision' 30 *International Yearbook of International Law* 453.
—— (2022) 'Informal Lawmaking in Maritime Migration' in N Klein (ed), *Unconventional Lawmaking in the Law of the Sea* (Oxford, OUP) 62–75.
Papanicolopulu, I and Losi, G (2023) 'La Sea Watch Davanti alla Corte di Giustizia dell'Unione European: Rapporti tra Fonti, Rapporti tra Stati e Regolazione (Indiretta) delle Attivita' di Soccorso in Mare' 1 *Diritto, Immigrazione e Cittadinanza* 235.
Papastavridis, E (2014) 'Is There a Right to be Rescued at Sea? A Skeptical View' 4 *Questions of International Law* 17.
Pasquero, A (2020) 'La comunicazione alla Corte Penale Internazionale sule Responsabilità dei Leader Europei per Crimini contro l'Umanità Commessi nel Mediterraneo e in Libia. Una Lettura Critica' 1 *Diritto, Immigrazione e Cittadinanza* 50.
Patane, F et al (2020) 'Asylum-Seekers Prosecuted for Human Smuggling: A Case Study of Scafisti in Italy' 39 *Refugee Survey Quarterly* 123.

Pech, L, 'A Union Founded on the Rule of Law: Meaning and Reality of the Rule of Law as a Constitutional Principle of EU Law' (2010) 6 *European Constitutional Law Review* 359.
—— (2011) 'Rule of Law as a Guiding Principle of the European Union's External Action' (CLEER Working Papers 2012/3, Centre for the Law of EU External Relations, TMC Asser Institute).
—— 'The Rule of Law as a Well-Established and Well-Defined Principle of EU Law' (2022) 14 *Hague Journal on the Rule of Law* 107.
Pech, L and Kochenov, D (September 2021) 'Respect for the Rule of Law in the Case Law of the European Court of Justice: A Casebook Overview of Key Judgements since the Portuguese Judges Cases' (Report no 3, Swedish Institute for European Policy Studies).
Peerenboom R, (2002) 'Let One Hundred Flowers Bloom, One Hundred Schools Contend: Debating Rule of Law in China' 23 *Michigan Journal of International Law* 471.
—— (2004) 'Varieties of Rule of Law' (Research Paper no 03–16, UCLA School of Law).
—— (10 January 2005) 'Human Rights and the Rule of Law: What's the Relationship?' (UCLA Public Law & Legal Theory Series, Los Angeles).
Pelliconi, AM and Goldoni, M (2020) 'La Banalità dei Porti Chiusi per Decreto. Osservazioni Sui Profili di Legittimità del Decreto Interministeriale 150/2020' 2 *Diritto, Immigrazione e Cittadinanza* 219.
Pepe, G (2017) 'Il Principio di Effettività della Tutela Giurisdizionale tra Atti Politici, Atti di Alta Amministrazione e Leggi-Provvedimento' 22 *Federalismi.it*.
Pijnenburg, A (2018) 'From Italian Pushbacks to Libyan Pullbacks: Is *Hirsi 2.0* in the Making in Strasbourg?' 20 *European Journal of Migration and Law* 396.
Pijnenburg, A and Pas, K van der (2022) 'Strategic Litigation against European Control Policies: The Legal Battleground of the Central Mediterranean Migration Route' 24 *European Journal of Migration and Law* 401.
Pisillo Mazzeschi, R (2020) *Diritto Internazionale dei Diritti Umani: Teoria e Prassi* (Torino, Giappichelli).
—— (2021) *International Human Rights Law: Theory and Practice* (Cham, Springer).
Pistone, M, Gallaher, A and Zammit, D (2007) 'The Subject of Rights Immersed in a "Sea of Troubles"' 11 *Mediterranean Journal of Human Rights* 9.
Pitino, A (2021) 'Controllo delle frontiere italiane e immigrazione nell'emergenza sanitaria Covid-19: tra *soft law* dell'Unione europea e misure nazionali' 1 *Corti Supreme e Salute* 1.
Pupo, V (2019) 'Le Istanze di Accesso Civico come Strumento di Trasparenza Democratica in Tema di Accordi Internazionli in Forma Semplificata' 2 *Diritto, Immigrazione e Cittadinanza* 211.
Pusterla, F (2021) 'Legal Perspectives on Solidarity Crime in Italy' 59(3) *International Migration* 79.
Quintavalla, A and Heine, K, 'Priorities and Human Rights' (2019) 23 *International Journal of Human Rights* 679.
Radjenovic, A (January 2021) 'Search and Rescue in the Mediterranean' (Briefing, European Parliament Research Service).
Raffiotta, E (2009) 'Potere Estero del Governo e Accordi Internazionali in Forma Semplificata: una Ricerca sulla Prassi' *Forum di Quaderni Costitutionali* 1.
Raz, J (1979) *The Authority of Law: Essays on Law and Morality* (Hong Kong, OUP).
Ricci, CM (2020) 'Criminalising Solidarity? Smugglers, Migrants and Rescuers in the Reform of the "Facilitators' Package"' in V Mitsilegas, V Moreno-Lax and N Vavoula (eds), *Securitising Asylum Flows: Deflection, Criminalisation and Challenges for Human Rights* (Leiden, Brill/Nijhoff) 39–68.
Richardson, HS (1999) 'Administrative Policy-making: Rule of Law or Bureaucracy?' in D Dyzenhaus (ed), *Recrafting the Rule of Law: The Limits of the Legal Order* (Oxford, Hart Publishing) 309–30.
Rigo, E (2020) 'Arbitrary Law Making and Unorderable Subjectivities in Legal Theoretical Approaches to Migration' 14(2) *Nordic Journal of Applied Ethics* 71.
Rokiciński, K (2020) 'The Possibilities of Saving Illegal Immigrants, by Ships Owned by the Non-Governmental Organizations on the Mediterranean Sea' XIV *Rocznik Bezpieczeństwa Morskiego* 169.

Romano, S (2021) 'L'(Ab)uso del Diritto Penale Contro le Azioni di Soccorso delle ONG' XXI *Diritto e Questioni Pubbliche*, Special Issue 41.
Ronzitti, N (2019) *Diritto Internazionale*, 6th edn (Torino, Giappichelli).
Rossi, P (2019) 'Politica dei "Porti Chiusi" e Diritto Internazionale: il Caso della Sea Watch 3' 6 *Osservatorio Costituzionale* 48.
—— (2019) 'The Role of National Courts for the International Rule of Law: Insights from the Field of Migration' 12 *European Journal of Legal Studies* 195.
Salau, C (2014) 'The Extra-Territorial Application of the Principle of Non-Refoulement in the Context of Sea Borders' (Bachelor's Thesis, University of Twente).
Salmons, J (2015) 'Designing and Conducting Research with Online Interviews' in J Salmons (ed), *Cases in Online Interview Research* (Thousand Oaks, CA, Sage Publications Ltd) 1–30.
Sánchez Legido, A (2019) 'The Walls of Fortress Europe: Externalization of Migration Control and the Rule of Law' 23 *Spanish Yearbook of International Law* 345.
Santer, K (2019) 'Governing the Central Mediterranean through Indirect Rule: Tracing the Effects of the Recognition of the Joint Rescue Coordination Centre Tripoli' 21 *European Journal of Migration and Law* 141.
Savino, M (2016) 'The Refugee Crisis as a Challenge for Public Law: The Italian Case' 17 *German Law Journal* 981.
Schotel, B (2021) 'EU Operational Powers and Legal Protection: A Legal Theory Perspective on the Operational Powers of the European Border and Coast Guard' 22 *German Law Journal* 625.
Sciurba, A (2021) 'Introduzione. Quel che Accade nel Mediterraneo Centrale come Emblema del Lato Oscuro del Diritto' in A Sciurba and M Starita (eds), 'Il Lato Oscuro della Criminalizzazione' XXI *Diritto e Questioni Pubbliche*, Special Issue 7.
Sevel, M (2023) 'Maritime Rule of Law: Some Preliminaries' 15 *Hague Journal on the Rule of Law* 385.
Siccardi, C (2021) *I Diritti Costituzionali dei Migranti in Viaggio: Sulle Rotte del Mediterraneo* (Napoli, Editoriale Scientifica).
Silvestri, G (2011) 'Lo Stato di Diritto nel XXI Secolo' 2 *Associazione Italiana dei Constituzionalisti* 1.
Smith, A (2017) 'Uncertainty, Alert and Distress: The Precarious Position of NGO Search and Rescue Operations in the Central Mediterranean' 5 *Paix et Securité Internationales* 29.
Sossin, L (2010) 'The Unjustified Project of Roncarelli v Duplessis: Justiciability, Discretion, and the Limits of the Rule of Law' 55 *McGill Law Journal* 661.
Spagnolo, A (2019) 'The Conclusion of Bilateral Agreements and Technical Arrangements for the Management of Migration Flows: An Overview of the Italian Practice' 28(1) *Italian Yearbook of International Law Online* 209.
Spielmann, D (2021) 'The Rule of Law Principle in the Jurisprudence of the Court of Justice of the European Union' in M Elósegui, A Miron and I Motoc (eds), *The Rule of Law in Europe: Recent Challenges and Judicial Responses* (Berlin, Springer International Publishing) 3–20.
Spijkerboer, T (2013) 'Moving Migrants, States and Rights: Human Rights and Border Deaths' 7 *Law & Ethics of Human Rights* 213.
—— (2017) 'Wasted Lives: Borders and the Right to Life of People Crossing Them' 86 *Nordic Journal of International Law* 1.
Starita, M (2021) 'Conclusioni: I Lati Oscuri del Diritto Internazionale sul Soccorso in Mare' *XXI Diritto e Questioni Pubbliche*, Special Issue 133.
Stierl, M (2021) 'The Mediterranean as a *Carceral Seascape*' 88 *Political Geography*.
Stierl, M and Dadusc, D (2022) 'The "Covid Excuse": European Border Violence in the Mediterranean Sea' 45 *Ethnic and Racial Studies* 1453.
Tamanaha, B (2002) 'The Rule of Law for Everyone?' 55 *Current Legal Problems* 97.
—— (2004) *On the Rule of Law: History, Politics, Theory* (Cambridge, CUP).
—— [2012] 'The History and Elements of the Rule of Law' *Singapore Journal of Legal Studies* 232.
Tamburini, F (2021) 'The State of Emergency and Exception in Algeria, Morocco and Tunisia: The "License to Kill" the Rule of Law' 56(6) *Journal of Asian and African Studies* 1286.

Timmermans, F (31 August 2015) 'The European Union and the Rule of Law' (Keynote Speech at Conference on the Rule of Law, Tilburg University).
Thompson, D (2010) *Restoring Responsibility* (Cambridge, CUP).
Tonolo, S and Pascale, G (2020) *La Dichiarazione Universale dei Diritti Umani nel Diritto Internazionale Contemporaneo* (Torino, Giappichelli).
Treves, T (2005) *Diritto Internazionale: Problemi Fondamentali* (Milano, Giuffrè).
—— (2007) 'Fragmentation of International Law. The Judicial Perspective' 23 *Comunicazioni e Studi* 821.
—— (2010) 'Human Rights and the Law of the Sea' 28 *Berkeley Journal of International Law* 1.
Trevisanut S, 'The Principle of Non-refoulement at Sea and the Effectiveness of Asylum Protection' (2008) 12 *Max Planck Yearbook of United Nations Law* 205.
—— (2010) 'Search and Rescue Operations in the Mediterranean: Factor of Cooperation or Conflict?' 25 *International Journal of Marine and Coastal Law* 523.
—— (2014) 'Is there a Right to be Rescued at Sea? A Constructive View' 4 *Questions of International Law* 3.
—— (2014) 'The Principle of Non-Refoulement and the De-Territorialization of Border Control at Sea' 27 *Leiden Journal of International Law* 661.
Tsourdi, E (2021) 'Asylum in the EU: One of the Many Faces of Rule of Law Backsliding?' 17 *European Constitutional Law Review* 471.
Türk, V and Dowd, R (2014) 'Protection Gaps' in E Fiddian-Qasmiyeh et al (eds), *The Oxford Handbook of Refugee and Forced Migration Studies* (Oxford, OUP) 1–14.
UNHCR, (November 2017) 'General Legal Considerations: Search-and-rescue Operations Involving Refugees and Migrants at Sea' (UNHCR).
—— (Operational Update, 2018) 'Tunisia – Operational Update' (UNHCR).
—— (6 April 2019) 'Independent Expert on Human Rights and International Solidarity, 'Human Rights and International Solidarity' (UNHCR).
—— (September 2020) 'UNHCR Position on the Designations of Libya as a Safe Third Country and as a Place of Safety for the Purpose of Disembarkation Following Rescue at Sea' (Policy Brief, UNHCR).
—— (30 December 2021) 'Libya: Last Evacuation Flight of the Year Brings 177 Vulnerable Asylum-seekers to Safety in Niger' (Press Release, UNHCR).
—— (21 April 2022) 'Arrivals in Europe from Libya – 2021 in Review' (Regional Bureau for Europe, UNHCR).
—— (21 May 2023) 'Mediterranean Situation' (Refugee Operational Data Portal, UNHCR).
—— 'Demography of Mediterranean Sea Arrivals from January 2022' (Refugees Operational Data Portal, UNHCR).
—— (July 2022) 'Italy Sea Arrivals Dashboard' (UNHCR).
United Nations Support Mission in Libya and Office of the High Commissioner for Human Rights (18 December 2018) 'Desperate and Dangerous: Report on the Human Rights Situation of Migrants and Refugees in Libya' (UNSMIL and OHCHR).
Van Liempt, I and Bilger, V (2018) 'Methodological and Ethical Dilemmas in Research among Smuggled Migrants' in R Zapata-Barrero and E Yalaz (eds), *Qualitative Research Methods in European Migration* (IMISCOE Research Series, Spring Open) 269–85.
Vari, E (2020) 'Italy–Libya Memorandum of Understanding: Italy's International Obligations' 43 *Hastings International and Comparative Law Review* 105.
Vassallo Paleologo, F (2021) 'Il Nuovo Piano Nazionale SAR 2020 ed i Soccorsi in Alto Mare, tra Prassi Operative e Diritto Internazionale' 3 *Diritto, Immigrazione e Cittadinanza* 316.
—— (2021) 'La Finzione della Zona SAR "Libica": Quale Giurisdizione sulle Acque Internazionali?' in G Bevilacqua (ed), *Sicurezza Umana negli Spazi Navigabili: Sfide Comuni e Nuove Tendenze – Human Security in Navigable Spaces: Common Challenges and New Trends* (Napoli, Editoriale Scientifica) 119–36.
Venn Dicey, A (1939) *Introduction to the Study of the Law of the Constitution*, 9th edn (London, Macmillan).

Versteeg, M and Ginsburg, T (2017) 'Measuring the Rule of Law: A Comparison of Indicators' 42 *Law & Social Inquiry* 100.

Virkkunen, J and Piiponen, M (2021) 'Informal Practices and the Rule of Law: Russia, Migration and the "Arctic Route"' in R Turaeva and R Urinboyev (eds), *Labour, Mobility and Informal Practices in Russia, Central Asia and Eastern Europe: Power, Institutions and Mobile Actors in Transnational Space* (London, Routledge) 192–221.

Waldron, J (2001) 'Is the Rule of Law an Essentially Contested Concept (in Florida)?' 21 *Law and Philosophy* 137.

Walzer, M (1996) *Spheres of Justice: A Defense of Pluralism and Equality* (New York, Columbia University Press).

Watts, A (1993) 'The International Rule of Law' 36 *German Yearbook of International Law* 15.

Webley, L (2010) 'Qualitative Approaches to Empirical Legal Research' in P Cane and H Kritzer (eds), *Oxford Handbook of Empirical Legal Research* (Oxford, OUP) 926–50.

Wouters, K and Heijer, M Den (2010) 'The Marine I Case: A Comment' 22 *International Journal of Refugee Law* 1.

Zammit, D (25 March 2022) 'The "Hermeneutics" of Suspicion: Linking Maltese Border Management and Migrant (Dis)integration Practices' ('Migration and Border Management. Challenges and Perspectives for Reform' Conference, University of Malta).

Zirulia, S (2020) 'Is that a Smuggler? The Blurring Line between Facilitating Illegal Immigration and Providing Humanitarian Assistance at the European Borders' in GL Gatta, V Mitsilegas and S Zirulia (eds), *Controlling Immigration through Criminal Law: European and Comparative Perspectives on 'Crimmigration'* (Oxford, Hart Publishing) 235–66.

Zirulia, S and Martinico, G (2022) 'Criminalising Migrants and Securitising Borders: The Italian "No Way" Model in the Age of Populism' in V Stoyanova and S Smet (eds), *Migrants' Rights, Populism and Legal Resilience in Europe* (Cambridge, CUP) 259–79.

WEB RESOURCES

Agenzia Giornalistica Italia, 'Il Braccio di Ferro tra Salvini e il PM di Agrigento sulla Sea-Watch 3' (AGI, 19 May 2019).

Agenzia Italia, 'Da Dove Vengono le 9 ONG Impegnate nei Soccorsi ai Migranti' (Agenzia Italia, 2 July 2017).

Agius, M, 'All Possible Witnesses in El Hiblu 1 Case Have Testified, Court Told' *Malta Today* (12 April 2022).

—— 'Malta is in Breach of its Obligations under International Law – Amnesty International' (*Newsbook*, 12 August 2018).

Al Jazeera Staff, 'What is the Arab Spring, and How Did it Start?' (*Al Jazeera Media Network*, 17 December 2020).

—— 'Five Dead after Boat Carrying Refugees Sinks off Tunisia's Coast' (*Al Jazeera Media Network*, 7 January 2023).

—— '"Deadliest Quarter" for Migrants in the Central Med Since 2017' (*Al Jazeera Media Network*, 12 April 2023).

Alarm Phone, 'Chain of Pushbacks from Tunisian Ports to the Libyan Desert!' (*Alarm Phone*, 3 October 2021).

—— 'Central Mediterranean Regional Analysis' (*Alarm Phone*, 5 January 2020).

—— 'Migrant Resistance against Yet Another New Level of Brutality' (*Alarm Phone*, 2 March 2022).

—— 'FAQ' (*Alarm Phone*, May 2022).

Ammirati, AP, 'Le "Navi Quarantena": l' Emergenza si fa Norma?' (*Melting Pot Europa*, 23 April 2022).

Amnesty International, 'EU–Africa Summit in Valletta Must Not Dress Up Border Control as "Co-Operation"' (Amnesty International, 10 November 2015).

—— '"Caso Osman": Tutte le Tappe che Hanno Portato alla Condanna del Governo Italiano' (Amnesty International, 31 August 2020).

—— 'Memorandum d'Intesa Italia-Libia: Quattro Anni di Complicità in Crimini di Diritto Internazionale' (Amnesty International, 1 February 2021).

—— 'EU: New Migration Agreement "Dangerous and Disproportionate"' (Amnesty International, 4 October 2023).

—— 'EU: Frontex's Lack of Transparency on Libyan Cooperation to Be Heard in Court' (Amnesty International, 10 October 2023).

ANSA, 'Mare Jonio Ship Seized' (*ANSA*, 3 September 2019).

Arci Porco Rosso and Alarm Phone, 'Dal Mare al Carcere. La Criminalizzazione dei Cosiddetti Scafisti' (*Dal Mare al Carcere*, 15 October 2021).

Associazione per gli Studi Giuridici sull'Immigrazione (ASGI), 'Mancata Ratifica Parlamentare del Memorandum Italia-Libia: al Via il Ricorso alla Corte Costituzionale' (ASGI, 28 February 2018).

—— 'Storica Vittoria del Diritto di Asilo: un Visto d'Ingresso in Italia per Richiedere Protezione' (ASGI, 30 August 2020).

—— 'ASGI Asks the Italian Court of Auditors for an Investigation into the Use of Public Funds in Detention Centres in Libya' (ASGI, 27 January 2021).

—— 'Memorandum Ue-Tunisia: L' Ue Sottoscrive Rastrellamenti, Deportazioni Illegali e Violenze Contro i Migranti' (ASGI, 20 July 2023).

—— 'Diritti in Rotta. L'Esperimento delle Navi Quarantena e i Principali Profili di Criticità' (ASGI, 23 April 2021).

—— 'Naufragio del 22 Aprile 2021: Presentato l'Esposto per Accertarne la Responsibilita' (ASGI, 29 July 2021).

—— 'Rimpatrio di Migranti Sub-Sahariani all Frontiera Libica della Tunisia' (ASGI, 2 October 2021).

—— 'Condanna di Asso 28: un Precedente Che Può Scardinare la Prassi dei Respingimenti in Libia' (ASGI, 19 October 2021).

—— 'Press Conference: Italy and Libya Brought before the UN CEDAW Committee by Two Women Victims of Trafficking' (ASGI, 3 December 2021).

—— 'Trasparenza e Accordi di Riammissione, il Consiglio di Stato al Governo: Va Chiarita la Natura dell'Accordo Italia–Gambia' (ASGI, 4 July 2022).

—— 'Strage di Bambini dell'11 Ottobre 2013: le Responsabilità e la Cronaca della Tragedia nella Sentenza sul Naufragio' (ASGI, 5 January 2023).

Asylum Information Database (AIDA) and European Council on Refugees and Exiles (ECRE), 'Country Report: Access to the Territory and Push Backs' (AIDA, 20 May 2022).

Attard, FG and Kilpatrick, RL, 'Reflections on the Maersk Etienne Standoff and its Ramifications for the Duty to Render Assistance at Sea' (*European Journal of International Law: TALK!*, 12 October 2020).

BBC, 'Italy Boat Sinking: Hundreds feared Dead off Lampedusa' *BBC News* (3 October 2013).

—— 'Migrants Allowed Off Maersk Tanker after 30 Days at Sea' *BBC News* (13 September 2020).

Baerwaldt N, 'The European Refugee Crisis: Crisis for Whom?' (*Border Criminologies*, University of Oxford, 20 March 2018).

Bagnoli L and Scavo N, 'Libyagate. Il Giallo della Nave "Italiana" che ha Respinto Migranti agli Ordini di Bija' *Avvenire* (1 February 2022).

Barretta, P, 'Da Eroi a Trafficanti: le Accuse ai Protagonisti delle Operazioni di Ricerca e Soccorso in Mare' (*Questione Giustizia*, 4 July 2017).

Bathke, B, 'Frontex Says It Used More Airplanes for Border Control in 2020' (*InfoMigrants*, 27 March 2021).

—— 'Migrants in Distress Returned to Libya – On Malta's Request' (*InfoMigrants*, 29 June 2021).

Berraggino, F, 'Migranti, Tribunale Impone L'Ingresso di un Sudanese Respinto in Libia: "Rischia Torture". Ma il Governo non Rispetta l'Ordinanza' *Il Fatto Quotidiano* (29 June 2023).

Border Forensics, 'Chain of Events' (*Alarm Phone*, July 2021).
Borg, T, 'Where Does One Draw the Line?' *Times of Malta* (19 July 2018).
Caffio, F, 'La "Direttiva Salvini" sulle Frontiere Marittime' *Analisi Difesa* (19 March 2019).
Camilli, A, 'L'Inchiesta Anomala della Procura di Trapani sulle ONG' *Internazionale* (9 April 2021).
Centro di Ateneo per i Diritti Umani Antonio Papisca, Università di Padova, 'Il Diritto d'Asilo: i Sistemi di Protezione dei Richiedenti Asilo e dei Rifugiati' (Center for Human Rights 'Antonio Papisca' University, 24 November 2015).
Citroni, G, 'No More Elusion of Responsibility for Rescue Operations at Sea: The Human Rights Committee's Views on the Case of A.S., D.I., O.I., and G.D. v Italy and Malta' (*OpinioJuris*, 9 March 2021).
Cociglio, M, Figoni, L and Mattirolo, M, 'Le Conseguenze Concrete degli Accordi Fantasma: Italia e Tunisia fra Rimpatri e Opacità' (ASGI, 20 December 2020).
Commissioner for Human Rights, 'Lives Saved. Rights Protected. Bridging the Protection Gaps for Refugees and Migrants in the Mediterranean' (Commissioner for Human Rights, Council of Europe, June 2019).
CONCORD, 'CONCORD Position Towards the Valletta Summit on Migration' (CONCORD, 5 November 2015).
Council of Europe, Organization for Security and Cooperation and United Nations (18 February 2005) 'Multilateral Organizations Rule of Law Pledge' (Press Release, OSCE Secretariat).
—— 'European States Migration Co-operation with Tunisia Should Be Subject to Clear Human Rights Safeguards' (Statement, 17 July 2023).
Cuddy, A, 'La Libia Crea la sua Zona SAR e Notifica l'IMO (con il sostegno UE)' *Euronews* (9 July 2018).
—— 'Prompted by EU, Libya Quietly Claims Right to Order Rescuers to Return Fleeing Migrants' *Euronews* (7 August 2018).
De Leo, A, 'S.S. and Others v Italy: Sharing Responsibility for Migrants Abuse in Libya' (*PILPG*, 6 January 2020).
Delia M, 'Photos Show AFM Illegally Forced Migrants out of Maltese Waters and Sent Them to Sicily' (*Truth Be Told*, 20 May 2020).
—— 'Maersk Tankers Warns Supplies Running out for Migrants, Crew on Board' *Times of Malta* (2 September 2020).
Di Valvasone, I, 'Sull'Attuale Illegalità delle Navi Quarantena' (*Melting Pot Europa*, 23 May 2022).
ECRE, 'Med: 150 Stranded at Sea as Malta and Italy Declare Ports "Unsafe"' (ECRE, 10 April 2020).
EU/Horn of Africa Migration Route Initiative, 'The Karthoum Process' (nd).
Euronews, 'La Libia Crea la sua Zona SAR e Notifica l'IMO (con il Sostegno UE)' *Euronews* (9 July 2018).
—— 'Ocean Viking: Migrant Rescue Ship Allowed to Dock in France after Italy's Refusal' *Euronews* (11 November 2022).
European Border and Coast Guard Agency, 'Migratory Routes: Eastern Borders Routes' (Frontex, nd).
European Commission, 'Memorandum of Understanding on a Strategic and Global Partnership between the European Union and Tunisia' (nd).
—— 'New Pact on Migration and Asylum' (nd).
—— 'Upholding the Rule of Law' (nd).
—— 'The European Union and Tunisia: Political Agreement on a Comprehensive Partnership Package' (16 July 2023).
European Community Shipowner's Association, 'Merchant Ships' Involvement in Migrants' Search and Rescue Operations Growing Again' (ECSA, 24 May 2017).
European Council and Council of the European Union (Consilium), 'Saving Lives at Sea and Fighting Migrant Smuggling' (19 October 2021).
—— 'Migration Flows in the Central Mediterranean Route' (23 January 2023).
—— 'Infographic – Migration Flows: Eastern, Central and Western Mediterranean Routes' (data up to April 2023).

—— 'Migration Policy: Council Agrees Mandate on EU Law Dealing with Crisis Situations' (4 October 2023)

European Council on Refugees and Exiles (ECRE), 'Central Med: Civil Fleet Continue to Save Lives as Italian Authorities Drop Charges, Italy Urged to End MoU with Libya Where List of Crimes against Migrants Grows' (ECRE, 4 February 2022).

—— 'Central Med: Despite Civilian Rescues Death Toll Continues to Rise, Interceptions and Returns to Libya, Cyprus' Only Registration Centre Overcrowded and in Deplorable Conditions' (ECRE, 29 April 2022).

EuroMed Rights (April 2021) 'The Policy of Forced Returns between Italy and Tunisia' in *Return Mania: Mapping Policies and Practices in the EuroMed Region* (*EuroMed Rights*).

—— (February 2022) 'Input for the Special Rapporteur's Report on Human Rights Violations at International Borders: Trends, Prevention and Accountability' (*EuroMed Rights*).

European Union Agency for Fundamental Rights (FRA), 'Fundamental Rights Considerations: NGO Ships Involved in Search and Rescue in the Mediterranean and Criminal Investigations – 2018' (Report, FRA, 1 October 2018).

—— 'Table 1: NGOs Involved in SAR Activities in the Mediterranean and Vessels/Aircrafts Deployed by Them (2015–2018)' (FRA, 1 October 2018).

—— 'December 2021 Update – Search and Rescue (SAR) Operations in the Mediterranean and Fundamental Rights' (FRA, 17 December 2021).

—— 'Table 1 – NGO Ships Involved in SAR Operations in the Mediterranean Sea Between 2012 and 15 June 2022' (FRA, 15 June 2022).

—— 'June 2022 Update – Search and Rescue (SAR) Operations in the Mediterranean and Fundamental Rights' (FRA, 20 June 2022).

—— 'Table 2: Legal Proceedings by EU Member States against Private Entities Involved in SAR Operations in the Mediterranean Sea' (FRA, June 2022).

—— 'June 2023 Update – Search and Rescue Operations in the Mediterranean and Fundamental Rights' (FRA, 11 October 2023).

European Union External Action Service (EEAS), 'Operation SOPHIA: Package 2 of the Libyan Navy Coast Guard and Libyan Navy Training Launched Today' (EEAS, 3 January 2017).

—— 'EUNAVFOR MED IRINI: European Union Naval Force Irini – Military Operation' (EEAS, 30 November 2020).

—— 'Working Document of the European External Action Service: EUBAM Libya Strategic Review 2021' (Integrated Approach for Security and Peace Directorate, EEAS, 19 February 2021).

Facchini, D, 'Accordo Italia–Libia per Fermare i Migranti: se la Revisione è una Farsa' (*Altreconomia*, 13 November 2019).

Forensic Oceanography, 'Privatised Push-Back of the Nivin' (nd).

Forin, R and Frouws, B, 'What's New? Analysing the Latest Trends on the Central Mediterranean Mixed Migration Route to Italy' (*Mixed Migration Centre*, 9 February 2022).

Frasca, E and Gatta, FL, 'The Malta Declaration on Search & Rescue, Disembarkation and Relocation: Much Ado about Nothing' (EU Immigration and Asylum Law and Policy, 3 March 2020).

Frontex, 'Migratory Routes: Central Mediterranean Route' (Frontex, nd).

—— 'Types of Operations' (Frontex, nd).

—— 'Profiting from Misery – How Smugglers Bring People to Europe' (Frontex, 18 February 2016).

FQ, 'Elenonore, Sbarcati i 104 naufraghi a Bordo. La Nave Aveva Violato il Divieto d' Ingresso: Sequestrata dalla Guardia di Finanza' *Il Fatto Quotidiano* (2 September 2019).

—— 'Migranti, Indagati il Capitano e Capo Missione della Nave Eleonore: "Favoreggiamento dell'Immigrazione Clandestina"' *Il Fatto Quotidiano* (3 September 2019).

—— 'Matteo Salvini, il Giorno della Prima Udienza a Catania: Perché il Caso Gregoretti è Diverso da Quello della Nave Diciotti e Della Open Arms' *Il Fatto Quotidiano* (3 October 2020).

Gaetano De Amicis, 'Stato di Diritto, Garanzie Europee di Indipendenza della Magistratura e Cooperazione Giudiziaria Penale: Quadri di un'Esposizione in Fieri' (*Sistema Penale*, 13 December 2021).

Gaita, L, '"Marina Iitaliana Ha Coordinato Respingimento Illegale di Migranti in Libia": Cinque Eritrei Citano in Fiudizio Governo e un'Azienda Privata' *Il Fatto Quotidiano* (12 February 2021).

Gamberini, A, 'Migrazione: Dichiarazioni alla Stampa dall'Avvocato Gamberini, Legale della Comandante della Sea Watch 3, Carola Rackete' *Radio Radicale* (Video Recorded Interview, 1 July 2019).

Gentilucci, P, 'Il Nuovo Decreto Immigrazione e il Ruolo delle ONG' (*Diritto*, 5 January 2023).

Giancristofaro Alberti, D, 'Alexander Maersk a Pozzallo/Migranti, Salvini "Apre" il Porto: Guardia Costiera, "Risponderemo Sempre a Sos"' (*ilsussidiario.net*, 2 June 2018).

Giuffrida, A, 'Sea Rescue Charities Rebel against Italian Anti-immigration Rules' *Guardian* (30 December 2022).

Global Legal Action Network, 'Legal Action Against Italy over its Coordination of Libyan Coast Guard Pullbacks Resulting in Migrant Deaths and Abuse' (*Global Legal Action Network*, 8 May 2018).

—— 'Privatised Migrant Abuse by Italy and Libya' (*Global Legal Action Network*, 18 December 2019).

GlobalProject, 'Tunisia – Blocco del Porto di Zarzis in Protesta contro la Guardia Costiera Libica' (*GlobalProject*, 13 September 2021).

Haq, SN, Magee C and Latza Nadeau, B, 'Europe's Migration Policies in Chaos as Arrivals Surge' *CNN* (16 April 2023).

Horowitz, J, 'Salvini's Standoff at Sea Highlights Italy's War on Rescue Ships' *New York Times* (16 August 2019).

Il Giornale di Sicilia, 'Migranti, in 40 Soccorsi da un Mercantile al Largo di Malta. Salvini: "Rimanga Dov'è"' *Il Giornale di Sicilia* (16 October 2018).

InfoMigrants, 'Italy: 40 NGOs, Unions Ask Government to Revoke Libya Memorandum' (*InfoMigrants*, 26 October 2022).

Il Post, 'Il caso della Asso 28, spiegato' *Il Post* (1 August 2018).

—— 'Cos'è Successo con la Sea-Watch' *Il Post* (20 May 2019).

Il sole24ore, 'Caso Gregoretti, Salvini prosciolto "Non luogo a procedere, il fatto non sussiste"' *Il sole24ore* (14 May 2021).

Indelicato, M, 'L'Ultimo Regalo dei Giallorossi: le Toghe Liberano le ONG' *Il Giornale* (18 June 2021).

InfoMigrants, 'Five Migrants Drown in Shipwreck Off Tunisia' (*InfoMigrants*, 9 January 2023).

—— 'Ocean Viking: Italy to Transfer Migrants to Quarantine Ship after Suicide Attempts' (*InfoMigrants*, 6 July 2020).

International Organization for Migration (IOM), 'IOM Definition of "Migrant"' (IOM, nd).

—— 'Protection of Migrants at Sea' (IOM, 17 September 2018).

—— 'About IOM' (IOM, 2019).

—— 'Migrant Deaths on Maritime Routes to Europe in 2021' (IOM GMDAC, 14 July 2021).

—— 'Deadliest Quarter for Migrants in the Central Mediterranean' (IOM, 12 April 2023).

—— Global Migration Data Analysis Centre, IOM, 'Arrivals' (IOM, 12 November 2023).

International Transport Workers' Federation (ITF), 'Boat Crisis "a Result of Inequality and Lack of Regulation"' (ITF, 26 May 2015).

Internazionale, 'Tutto Quello che C'e' da Sapere su Salvini e il Caso Open Arms' *Internazionale* (30 July 2020).

Iuventa Crew, Post (*Twitter*, 17 June 2019).

—— 'Whether in Ports or Courtrooms, Italy Disregards Basic Rights' (*Iuventa Crew*, 12 November 2022).

—— 'European Court of Justice to Examine Legality of the Offence of Facilitating Unauthorised Migration' (*Iuventa Crew*, 25 July 2023).

Jensen, PF and Eikeland, B, 'The Maersk Etienne Rescue Highlights the Difficulties in Disembarking Migrants Rescued at Sea' (*Gard Insight*, 8 October 2020).

Kingsley, P, 'Privatized Pushbacks: How the EU and Libya Use Merchant Ships to Block Migrant Boats' (*Migrants at Sea*, 23 March 2020).

—— 'Privatized Pushbacks: How Merchant Ships Guard Europe' *New York Times* (20 March 2020).
Knipp, K and Guizani, T, 'EU–Tunisia Migration Deal: Encouraging the People Smugglers?' *Deutsche Welle* (21 July 2023).
La Repubblica, 'Il Caso Diciotti alla Corte Europea dei Diritti dell'Uomo' *La Repubblica* (13 February 2019).
—— 'Diciotti, il Senato Vota No all'Autorizzazione a Procedere Contro Salvini. Che in Aula Ringrazia il M5s: "Le Cose Si Fanno in Due"' *La Repubblica* (20 March 2019).
Lambruschi, P, 'Migranti. Cinque Anni di Indagini e Menzogne: Cadono tutte le Accuse per Don Zerai' *Avvenire* (27 May 2022).
Lamparter, F, 'Challanging Restrictions on NGO Search and Rescue Operations in Italy: MSF's Complaint to the European Commission' (*humanrightscenter*, 14 September 2023).
Laux, M, 'The Evolution of the EU's Naval Operations in the Central Mediterranean: A Gradual Shift Away from Search and Rescue' (Heinrich Böll Foundation, 16 April 2021).
Libya Observer, '177 Asylum-Seekers Evacuated from Libya to Niger' *Libya Observer* (1 January 2022).
Lo Verde, L, 'Le "Navi Quarantena": una Misura Temporanea o un Nuovo Approccio Oltre l'Emergenza?' (*Border Criminologies Blog*, 9 June 2021).
Lohmüller, D, 'EU: Frontex Complicit in Abuse in Libya' (Human Rights Watch, 12 December 2022).
Malta Independent, 'Malta Stands Firm as Italy Insists on SAR Zone Reduction' *Malta Independent* (26 August 2009).
Maritime Executive, 'Last NGO-Run Rescue Vessel in Med Finds New Flag State' (Maritime Executive, 6 November 2018).
Martin, I, 'Exposed: Malta's Secret Migrant Deal with Libya' *Times of Malta* (10 November 2019).
Martine, C and Arnaud, D, 'Studio sulle Condizioni di Soggiorno e Sui Percorsi dei Migranti Tunisini Rimpatriati dall'Italia' (ASGI, March 2022).
Masera, L, 'La Cassazione sul Caso Rackete: la Strategia die Porti Chiusi è Contraria alla Disciplina dei Soccorsi in Mare' (*Questione Giustizia*, 26 February 2020).
—— 'La Legittima Difesa dei Migranti e l'Illegittimità dei Respingimenti verso la Libia (Caso Vos Thalassa)' (*Diritto Penale Contemporaneo*, 24 June 2019).
—— 'Il D.L. Piantedosi sulle Operazioni di Soccorso in Mare: L' Ennesimo Tentativo di Impedire Cio' che il Diritto Internazionale Impone e il Problema della Depenalizzazione come Fuga dalla Giurisdizione' (*Sistema Penale*, 13 February 2023).
Massini, A and Agresta, D, 'Italia–Tunisia e Accordo Fantasma' (*Nigrizia*, 7 December 2020).
Médecins Sans Frontières, 'Vessels at Sea' (Médecins Sans Frontières, nd).
—— 'Italy–Libya Agreement: Five Years of EU-Sponsored Abuse in Libya and the Central Mediterranean' (Médecins Sans Frontières, 2 February 2002).
—— 'MSF Committed to Saving Lives on Mediterranean but Will Not Sign the Italian "Code of Conduct"' (Press Release, Médecins Sans Frontières, 31 July 2017).
Mediterranea Saving Humans, 'New Judiciary Acquittal Coming for the "Mare Jonio" Ship' (Mediterranea Saving Humans, 20 October 2021).
Melting Pot Europa, '65 Naufraghi Soccorsi dalla Sea-Watch Lasciati in Alto Mare per Quattro Giorni Senza un Porto Sicuro' (*Melting Pot Europa*, 17 May 2019).
—— 'Open Arms, Terza Udienza del Processo Salvini' (*Melting Pot Europa*, 15 May 2022).
—— 'Tunisia Is Not a Safe Country for Us' (*Melting Pot Europa*, 21 June 2022).
Middle East Monitor, 'NGOs: Italy's New Decree "Obstructs" Migrant Rescue Operations' (*Middle East Monitor*, 6 January 2023).
Migreurop, 'Politique de Signature des Accords de Réadmission Italiens' (Migreurop, 2009).
Ministero dell'Interno, 'Sbarchi e Accoglienza dei Migranti: Tutti i Dati. Cruscotto Statistico del 31 Dicembre 2022' (Ministero dell'Interno, 31 December 2022).
—— 'Sbarchi e Accoglienza dei Migranti: Tutti i Dati. Cruscotto Statistico del 2 Novembre 2023' (Ministero dell'Interno, 2 November 2023).
Misculin, L, 'La Nave. Giorno 5 – Osservare l' Orizzonte' (Podcast, *Il Post*, 20 March 2023).

Noviello, J, 'Accordi Italia–Libia: tra Istituzionalità e Legalità. Il Doppio Volto del Fenomeno Migratorio nel Mediterraneo: Oggetto di Accordi Istituzionali e Fonte di Reddito per il Crimine Organizzato Transazionale' (Filodiritto.com, 19 July 2021).

O'Carroll, L, 'Italian MP Warns Migration an Issue for All of Europe on Lampedusa Visit' *Guardian* (17 September 2017).

—— 'What is the Controversy over the EU Migration Deal with Tunisia?' *Guardian* (18 September 2023).

—— 'Historic EU Deal Reached on How to Manage Sudden Rise in Asylum Seekers' *Guardian* (4 October 2023).

Open Migration, 'Rimpatri Forzati a Tutti i Costi' (Open Migration, 16 June 2017).

Pagella, C, 'Caso Asso 28: La Corte d' Appello di Napoli Conferma la Condanna per Sbarco Arbitrario e Abbandono di Minori o Incapaci sulle Coste Libiche' (*Sistema Penale*, 8 May 2023).

Paoletti, E, 'Migration Agreements Between Italy and North Africa: Domestic Imperatives Versus International Norms' (Middle East Institute, 20 December 2012).

Papastavridis, E, 'Sea Watch Cases before the EU Court of Justice: An Analysis of International Law of the Sea' (*Odysseus Network*, 12 December 2022).

Paris MoU, 'History: A Short History of the Paris MoU on PSC' (*Paris MoU*, February 2023).

Partipilo, FR, 'The Role of NGOs within Search and Rescue Activities at Sea' (*News*, Lebanese American University, 6 April 2022).

Perrone, M, 'Migranti, 16 Navi e 5 Aerei per Pattugliare il Mediterraneo: Ecco la Flotta delle ONG' *Il Sole 24 Ore* (14 November 2022).

Pijnenburg, A, 'What's Wrong with the EU-Tunisia Migration Agreement?' (*Verfassungsblog on Matters of Constitutional Law*, 21 August 2023).

Pitea, C, 'The Applicability of Human Rights Treaties to Search and Rescue Operations in the High Seas: A Landmark Decision of the Human Rights Committee' (*Criminal Justice Network*, 4 March 2021).

Pizzuti, A and Moran, CF, 'The Memorandum of Understanding between Italy and Libya: Does it Create Human Rights Obligations on the Part of Italy?' (*OpinioJuris*, 5 August 2021).

Porco Rosso, A and Alarm Phone, 'Dal Mare al Carcere. La Criminalizzazione dei Cosiddetti Scafisti' (*Dal Mare Al Carcere*, 15 October 2021).

Pressenza International Press Agency, 'Il TAR di Palermo Sospende il Fermo delle Navi di Sea-Watch' *Pressenza International Press Agency* (2 March 2021).

Pro Asyl and Alarmphone, 'Landmark Court Ruling on 2013 Shipwreck: Italian Coast Guard and Navy Responsible for Deaths of 268 Refugees' (*Alarm Phone*, 19 January 2023).

Redattore Sociale, '"Il Memorandum Italia–Libia ha Calpestato la Costituzione": Ricorso di Leu e Asgi' *Redattore Sociale* (Roma, 27 February 2018).

—— 'Migranti, Scoppia il Caso Asso 28. "Fatto grave, è respingimento"' *Redattore Sociale* (Roma, 31 July 2018).

—— 'Migranti, Rete legale: "Così abbiamo aiutato le persone della Diciotti"' *Redattore Sociale* (Roma, 22 February 2019).

Registrar of the European Court of Justice, 'The Court Decides Not to Indicate an Interim Measure Requiring that the Applicants Be Authorised to Disembark in Italy from the Ship Sea-Watch 3' (Press Release, Press Unit, 25 June 2019).

Reuters, 'Italy Criticises Germany for Funding Migrant Charity Groups' *Reuters* (22 September 2023).

Riccardi, A, 'Esternalizzazione delle frontiere italiane in Libia e Niger: una Prospettiva di Diritto Internazionale' (*Questione Giustizia*, 2020).

Rice-Oxley, M and Mahmood, M, 'Migrants' Tales: "I Feel for Those Who Were with Me. They Got Asylum in the Sea"' *Guardian* (20 October 2014).

Rolfi, E, 'Il Tribunale di Roma, Nove Anni Dopo, sul "Naufragio dei Bambini": un Problematico Caso di Prescrizione dei Reati e di "Responsabilita'"delle Autorita' Italiane' (*Sistema Penale*, 21 April 2023).

Rondi, L, 'Respingimenti in Libia: Governo Italiano e Società Private a Processo' (*Altreconomia*, 13 February 2021).
Rijtano, R, 'Respingimenti in Libia, Asso Ventinove a Processo' (*Lavialibera*, 15 February 2021).
Russo, R, 'Respingimenti Illeciti e Diritto d'Asilo: è Sufficiente il Risarcimento in Denaro? Nota a Trib. Roma, 28.11.2019 no 22917' (*Giustizia Insieme*, 5 February 2020).
Ruta, G and Ziniti, A, 'Migranti, la Mare Jonio Entra nel Porto di Lampedusa, la Gdf la Sequestra e Convoca il Comandante' *La Repubblica* (19 March 2019).
Sambataro, G, 'The Protection of Journalist Sources in Italian Criminal Proceedings: The Iuventa Case' (*Global Freedom of Expression, Columbia University*, 8 July 2022).
Sansone, K, 'Malta Should Give Up its Large Search and Rescue Area, Italian Minister Says' *Malta Today* (13 June 2018).
Savio, G, 'Favoreggiamento dell'Immigrazione Irregolare: Alcuni Dubbi di Costituzionalità. Nota a Margine dell'Ordinanza del Tribunale di Bologna 1.12.2020' (ASGI, 23 February 2021).
Sea-Eye, 'The Alan Kurdi' (Sea Eye, nd).
—— 'Seefuchs. The Second Rescue Ship' (Sea Eye, nd).
—— 'The Sea-Eye' (Sea Eye, nd).
'Sea-Eye Criticizes Italy's New Code of Conduct for Sea Rescue NGOs' (Sea Eye, 30 December 2022).
—— 'Sea-Eye Sues Italy for Unlawful Detention of Sea-Eye 4' (Sea Eye, 3 July 2023).
Sea Watch, 'What We Do' (Sea Watch, nd).
—— 'Sea-Watch 3 – Italy Ignores ECJ Ruling' (Sea Watch, 23 September 2022).
—— 'Sea-Watch Comes to an Agreement Concerning the Code of Conduct' (Sea Watch, 18 October 2017).
Servedio, A, 'Gli Accordi in Forma Semplificata e i Soggetti di Diritto Internazionale' (*Ministro della Difesa, Carabinieri*, nd).
Shaam, Q, 'I Enjoyed Being Commander of Such an Heroic Crew during the Rescue Operation' (*Maersk Tankers*, 7 December 2020).
SOS Humanity, 'Our Mission' (SOS Humanity, nd).
Spano, R, 'Rule of Law: la Lodestar della Convenzione Europea dei Diritti dell'Uomo. La Corte di Strasburgo e l' Indipendenza della Magistratura' (*Giustizia Insieme*, 10 March 2021).
Statewatch.org, 'Italy: UN Special Rapporteurs Call for Withdrawal of Salvini Decree Criminalizing Search and Rescue Activities' (*Statewatch*, 22 May 2019).
—— 'Urgent Warning: More Deaths at Sea, NGO Ships Blocked' (*Statewatch*, 30 August 2023).
Times of Malta, 'Updated: Malta's SAR Zone Too Huge for Country to Manage – Frattini' *Times of Malta* (22 August 2009).
Tondo, L, 'Rescue Ship Captain Arrested for Breaking Italian Blockade' *Guardian* (29 June 2019).
—— '"We Give You 30 Minutes": Malta Turns Migrant Boat Away with Directions to Italy' *Guardian* (20 May 2020).
—— 'Italy Considers Charges over Malta's "Shocking" Refusal to Rescue Migrants' *Guardian* (29 May 2020).
Trevisanut, S, 'Law of the Sea Symposium: Search and Rescue Operations at Sea – Who is in Charge? Who is Responsible?' (*Opinio Juris*, 28 May 2013).
Trilling, D, 'A commercial ship saved 27 migrants, but now the EU has abandoned them at sea' *Guardian* (4 September 2020).
Tumminello, F, 'Il Soccorso in Mare: i Concetti di "Porto Sicuro" e "Porto Vicino" nel Diritto Internazionale' (*Ius In Itinere*, 9 August 2020).
Vassallo Paleologo, F, 'Accordi di Riammissione – Maroni in Tunisia' (*Melting Pot*, 26 January 2009).
—— 'Respingimenti Collettivi Vietati, Tunisia e Libia non Sono "Paesi Terzi Sicuri"' (Associazione Diritti e Frontiere, 31 July 2018).
—— 'Soccorsi Clandestini e Respingimenti in Libia. Italia e Malta Violano gli Obblighi di Coordinamento SAR' (Associazione Diritti e Frontiere, 17 October 2018).
—— 'Obblighi di Ricerca e Soccorso in Mare Imposti dal Diritto Internazionale e Accordi con gli Stati di Transito' (Associazione Diritti e Frontiere, 8 November 2019).

—— 'Il Governo Inasprisce il Decreto Sicurezza Bis di Salvini e Criminalizza il Soccorso Umanitario' (Associazione Diritti e Frontiere, 8 April 2020).
—— 'Un Nuovo Decreto Ministeriale Disciplina il Salvataggio: Mai Più Abbandoni in Mare' (Associazione Diritti e Frontiere, 8 February 2021).
—— 'Ancora un Fermo Amministrativo per Bloccare i Soccorsi Umanitari nel Mediterraneo Centrale' (Associazione Diritti e Frontiere, 6 June 2021).
—— 'Il Tribunale di Napoli Condanna i Respingimenti in Libia. Ma Occorre Ancora Fare Giustizia' (Associazione Diritti e Frontiere, 14 October 2021).
—— 'Maggioranze di Governo e Processi Penali' (Associazione Diritti e Frontiere, 30 October 2021).
—— 'Come si Trasformano i Soccorsi delle ONG in "Eventi Migratori"' (Associazione Diritti e Frontiere, 11 November 2021).
—— 'ONG a Giudizio, il Caso IUVENTA Non è Chiuso' (Associazione Diritti e Frontiere, 21 February 2022).
—— 'Guerre Ibride e Sistemi di Accoglienza' (Associazione Diritti e Frontiere, 17 April 2022).
—— 'Salvini-Open Arms: un Processo Capovolto' (*Associazione Diritti e Frontiere*, 14 May 2022).
—— 'Caso Iuventa, Anomalie di un'Inchiesta Politico-giudiziaria' (*Associazione Diritti e Frontiere*, 19 May 2022).
—— 'Archiviata una parte dell'indagine Iuventa. Quali Prove Contro MSF e Save The Children?' (Associazione Diritti e Frontiere, 27 May 2022).
—— 'Indagini sul Caso Iuventa (con Save the Children e MSF): a Trapani un Ritorno alla Giurisdizione?' (Associazione Diritti e Frontiere, 23 May 2022).
—— 'Dalle Navi Quarantena alla Detenzione Amministrativa Informale' (Associazione Diritti e Frontiere, 2 June 2022).
—— 'Al Viminale Stato di Guerra all' Informazione' (Associazione Diritti e Frontiere, 25 July 2022).
—— 'Il Parlamento Ratifica le Missioni Military in Libia e Conferisce Pieni Poteri al Ministro dell'Interno' (Associazione Diritti e Frontiere, 28 July 2022).
—— 'La Corte Giustizia EU Pone Limiti alla Prassi dei Fermi Amministrativi' (*Melting Pot Europa*, 2 August 2022).
Vella, M, 'Malta "Not for Sale", Borg Replies to Frattini' *Malta Today* (23 August 2009).
—— 'Not Piracy, but Self-defence against EU's Deadly Abdication – NGOs on El Hiblu Rescue' *Malta Today* (28 March 2019).
Vita, 'Ecco Come 130 Persone Sono State Lasciate Annegare al Largo della Libia' (*VITA*, 23 April 2021).
Wallis, E, 'Can the Law of the Sea Regulate the Stormy Standoffs between Private Rescue Ships and EU Governments?' (*InfoMigrants*, 9 July 2019).
Wu, M, 'The EC's Guidance on the Facilitation Directive: Ending the Criminalisation of NGO-led SAR Operations?' (*Opinio Juris*, 30 October 2020).
Zagrebelsky, V, 'L'Unione Europea e lo Stato di Diritto. Fondamento, Problemi, Crisi' (*Giustizia Insieme*, 28 May 2021).
Ziniti, A, 'Migranti, le Foto Shock dell'Ultima Strage: "Noi Soccorritori in Mezzo ad un mare di Cadaveri". L'Italia Sapeva della Richiesta di Aiuto' *La Repubblica* (23 April 2021).
—— 'Caso Gregoretti, Perché è Diverso da Quello Open Arms' *La Repubblica* (14 May 2021).
—— 'Intervista al Ministro dell'Interno. Piantedosi: "I Soccorsi in Mare Garantiti dallo Stato. Le ONG Fanno la Spola Solo con la Tripolitania. Come Mai?"' *La Repubblica* (31 December 2022).
—— Un' Altra Sentenza "Contro" il Decreto Cutro: la Tunisia non É un Paese Sicuro, la Farnesina Riveda la Lista del Luoghi Che Non Rispettano I Diritti Umani' *La Repubblica* (5 October 2023).
Zirulia, S, 'Decreto Sicurezza-bis: Novità e Profili critici. Decreto legge 14 giugno 2019, n 53, recante Disposizioni urgenti in materia di ordine e sicurezza pubblica (G.U. n 138 del 14 Giugno 2019)' (*Diritto Penale Contemporaneo*, 18 giugno 2019).
—— 'Caso Sea Watch (Carola Rackete): Archiviate le Accuse di Favoreggiamento dell'Immigrazione Irregolare e Rifiuto di Obbedienza a Nave da Guerra' (*Sistema Penale*, 17 January 2022).

—— 'La Corte Costituzionale sul Favoreggiamento dell'Immigrazione Irregolare: Illegittima l'Aggravante che Parifica il Trattamento Sanzionatorio dei Trafficanti a Quello di Coloro che Prestano un Aiuto per Finalità Solidaristiche' (*Sistema Penale*, 23 March 2022).
Zirulia, S and Cancellaro, F, 'Caso Diciotti: il Tribunale dei Ministri Qualifica le Condotte del Ministro Salvini come Sequestro di Persona Aggravato e Trasmette al Senato la Domanda di Autorizzazione a Procedere' (*Dirito Penale Contemporaneo*, 28 January 2019).
Zirulia, S and De Vittor, F, 'Il Caso della Nave Alan Kurdi: Profili di Diritto Penale e Internazionale in Punto di Omessa Assegnazione di un Porto Sicuro' (*Sistema Penale*, 5 December 2019).
Zribi, N, 'Externalizing Borders or Externalizing Repression? Tunisia at the Center of a Failed Asylum Architecture' (The Thahir Institute for Middle East Policy, 21 August 2023).

LIST OF NATIONAL INFORMANTS

Interviews Conducted by the Author

Federico Alagna, Adjunct Professor of Political Science, Department of Political and Social Sciences, Università di Bologna (online, 11 May 2023).
Marco Borraccetti, Associate Professor of European Union Law, Università di Bologna (online, 2 May 2023).
Estelle Brentall, Head of Maritime, European Transport Workers' Federation, Brussels (online, 12 November 2020).
Constitutional Law Professor (online, 25 May 2023).
Giulia Crescini, Immigration lawyer, Rome (online, 8 May 2023).
Martin Dorsman, Secretary General of European Community Shipowners' Associations, Brussels (online, 6 November 2020).
Eugenio Cusumano, Lecturer in International and European Studies, University of Leiden (telephone, 14 June 2023).
Former ship captain of a unit participating in Mare Nostrum (email, 15 February 2023).
Italian Coast Guard Official (email, 28 June 2023).
Immigration lawyer no 5, Rome (online, 3 April 2023).
Lawyer no 4, Milan (online, 25 October 2023).
Lawyer no 3, Milan (online, 27 October 2023).
Giulia Losi, PhD Candidate, Università Milano-Bicocca (online, 2 May 2023).
Morten Glamsø, Head of Security, Danish Shipping, Copenhagen (online, 25 November 2020).
Luca Masera, Professor of Criminal Law, Università degli Studi di Brescia (online, 2 February 2023).
Marta Minetti, PhD Candidate, Queen Mary University, London (online, 9 February 2023).
Irini Papanicolopulu, Professor of International Law, SOLAS University of London (online, 10 May 2023).
Pierfrancesco Rossi, Adjunct Professor of International Law, Università degli Studi della Calabria (online, 15 June 2023).
SAR NGO Operator (online, 10 March 2023).
Luciano Scalettavi, President of NGO ResQ People (online, 6 February 2023).
John Stawpert, Manager of Environment and Trade, International Chamber of Shipping, London (online, 10 November 2020).
Stefano Zirulia, Associate Professor of Criminal Law, Università degli Studi di Milano (online 4 April 2023).

Interviews Conducted by Krista Bonello Rutter Giappone

Giovanni Bonello, former ECtHR Judge (emails, 19–20 April 2022).
Paul Borg Olivier, Lawyer with Repubblika, Malta (online, 10 December 2021).
Jean-Pierre Gauci, Senior Research Fellow, British Institute of International and Comprative Law, London (online, 8 July 2023).
Lawyer, Malta (online, 18 March 2022).
Officer of Armed Forces of Malta (online, 28 January 2022).
Ibtisam Sadegh, Lecturer and Lawyer, University of Malta (online, 18 February 2022).
UNHCR Malta (email, 21 February 2022).

Personal Communications

Email from Lawyer no 1 to author (28 September 2023).
Email from Lawyer no 2 to author (29 September 2023).

Index

www.ingramcontent.com/pod-product-compliance
Ingram Content Group UK Ltd.
Pitfield, Milton Keynes, MK11 3LW, UK
UKHW020804290926
15470UKWH00003B/945

9 781509 978489